COLLABORATIVE WRITING IN THE LONG NINETEENTH CENTURY

Bringing the collaborative process to life through an array of examples, Heather Bozant Witcher shows that sympathetic co-creation is far more than the mere act of writing together. While foregrounding the material aspects of collaboration – hands uniting on the page, blank space left for fellow contributors, the writing and exchanging of drafts – this study also illuminates its social aspects and reliance on Victorian liberalism: dialogue, the circulation of correspondence, the lived experience of collaboration, and, on a less material plane, transhistorical collaborations with figures of the past. Witcher takes a broad approach to these partnerships and, in doing so, challenges traditional expectations surrounding the nature of authorship itself, not least its typical classification as a solitary activity. Within this new framework, collaboration enables the titles of "coauthor," "influencer," "editor," "critic," and "inspiration" to coexist. This book celebrates the plurality of collaboration and underscores the truly social nature of nineteenth-century writing.

HEATHER BOZANT WITCHER is an assistant professor at Auburn University at Montgomery. Her research focuses on nineteenth-century poetics, collaboration, and sociability, as well as archival theory and digital humanities. She is the co-editor of *Defining Pre-Raphaelite Poetics* (2020) and was the 2016 Amy P. Goldman Fellow in Pre-Raphaelite Studies.

CAMBRIDGE STUDIES IN NINETEENTH-CENTURY
LITERATURE AND CULTURE

Founding Editors
Gillian Beer, *University of Cambridge*
Catherine Gallagher, *University of California, Berkeley*

General Editors
Kate Flint, *University of Southern California*
Clare Pettitt, *King's College London*

Editorial Board
Isobel Armstrong, *Birkbeck, University of London*
Ali Behdad, *University of California, Los Angeles*
Alison Chapman, *University of Victoria*
Hilary Fraser, *Birkbeck, University of London*
Josephine McDonagh, *University of Chicago*
Elizabeth Miller, *University of California, Davis*
Hillis Miller, *University of California, Irvine*
Cannon Schmitt, *University of Toronto*
Sujit Sivasundaram, *University of Cambridge*
Herbert Tucker, *University of Virginia*
Mark Turner, *King's College London*

Nineteenth-century literature and culture have proved a rich field for interdisciplinary studies. Since 1994, books in this series have tracked the intersections and tensions between Victorian literature and the visual arts, politics, gender and sexuality, race, social organisation, economic life, technical innovations, scientific thought – in short, culture in its broadest sense. Many of our books are now classics in a field which since the series' inception has seen powerful engagements with Marxism, feminism, visual studies, post-colonialism, critical race studies, new historicism, new formalism, transnationalism, queer studies, human rights and liberalism, disability studies, and global studies. Theoretical challenges and historiographical shifts continue to unsettle scholarship on the nineteenth century in productive ways. New work on the body and the senses, the environment and climate, race and the decolonisation of literary studies, biopolitics and materiality, the animal and the human, the local and the global, politics and form, queerness and gender identities, and intersectional theory is re-animating the field. This series aims to accommodate and promote the most interesting work being undertaken on the frontiers of nineteenth-century literary studies, connecting the field with the urgent critical questions that are being asked today. We seek to publish work from a diverse range of authors and stand for anti-racism, anti-colonialism, and against discrimination in all forms.

A complete list of titles published will be found at the end of the book.

COLLABORATIVE WRITING IN THE LONG NINETEENTH CENTURY

Sympathetic Partnerships and Artistic Creation

HEATHER BOZANT WITCHER

Auburn University at Montgomery

Shaftesbury Road, Cambridge CB2 8EA, United Kingdom

One Liberty Plaza, 20th Floor, New York, NY 10006, USA

477 Williamstown Road, Port Melbourne, VIC 3207, Australia

314–321, 3rd Floor, Plot 3, Splendor Forum, Jasola District Centre, New Delhi – 110025, India

103 Penang Road, #05–06/07, Visioncrest Commercial, Singapore 238467

Cambridge University Press is part of Cambridge University Press & Assessment, a department of the University of Cambridge.

We share the University's mission to contribute to society through the pursuit of education, learning and research at the highest international levels of excellence.

www.cambridge.org
Information on this title: www.cambridge.org/9781009073929

DOI: 10.1017/9781009072731

© Heather Bozant Witcher 2022

This publication is in copyright. Subject to statutory exception and to the provisions of relevant collective licensing agreements, no reproduction of any part may take place without the written permission of Cambridge University Press & Assessment.

First published 2022
First paperback edition 2025

A catalogue record for this publication is available from the British Library

Library of Congress Cataloging-in-Publication data
NAMES: Witcher, Heather Bozant, 1988– author.
TITLE: Collaborative writing in the long nineteenth century : Sympathetic Partnerships and Artistic Creation / Heather Bozant Witcher.
DESCRIPTION: Cambridge, United Kingdom ; New York : Cambridge University Press, 2022. | Includes bibliographical references and index.
IDENTIFIERS: LCCN 2021058583 | ISBN 9781316513491 (hardback) | ISBN 9781009072731 (ebook)
SUBJECTS: LCSH: English literature – 19th century – History and criticism. | Authorship – Collaboration – History – 19th century. | Influence (Literary, artistic, etc.) – History – 19th century. | BISAC: LITERARY CRITICISM / European / English, Irish, Scottish, Welsh
CLASSIFICATION: LCC PR461 .W58 2022 | DDC 820.9/355–dc23/eng/20211216
LC record available at https://lccn.loc.gov/2021058583

ISBN 978-1-316-51349-1 Hardback
ISBN 978-1-009-07392-9 Paperback

Cambridge University Press & Assessment has no responsibility for the persistence or accuracy of URLs for external or third-party internet websites referred to in this publication and does not guarantee that any content on such websites is, or will remain, accurate or appropriate.

*To my husband, my lifetime collaborator,
and Lottie, my ever-faithful, furry muse*

Contents

List of Figures	*page* viii
Acknowledgments	x
Introduction	1
1 Adam Smith's Liberal Sympathy	13
2 "O You Pretty Pecksie!": The Collaborative Process of Mary Shelley and Percy Bysshe Shelley	31
3 Written–Visual Aesthetics: The Rossettis and the Pre-Raphaelites	64
4 Typographical Adventures: William Morris, Community, and the Kelmscott Press	95
5 Sim and Puss: The Sympathetic Mirroring of Michael Field	144
6 Towards Empathy: Vernon Lee's Psychological Aesthetics	181
Conclusion	206
Notes	210
Bibliography	237
Index	250

Figures

3.1 *Lady Lilith*, 1866–1868 (altered 1872–1873), Rossetti, Dante Gabriel (British, 1828–1882). Oil on canvas, 39 × 34 inches, frame: 53¼ × 48 inches. Delaware Art Museum, Samuel and Mary R. Bancroft Memorial, 1935. *page* 94

4.1 1050.15, *The Clerk's Tale: The Dressing of Grisilde*. Burne-Jones, Edward (British, 1833–1898). Graphite within drawn graphite border on paper, height, drawn area, 129 mm, width, drawn area, 171 mm. For page 129 of the Kelmscott Chaucer. © The Fitzwilliam Museum, Cambridge. 120

4.2 Burne-Jones, Edward (British, 1833–1898). Illustrations for the Kelmscott Chaucer, Plate 15: verso. 1894–1895. PML 76853. Gift of John A. Saks, 1977. The Morgan Library & Museum/Art Resource, NY. 124

4.3 Burne-Jones, Edward (British, 1833–1898). Illustrations for the Kelmscott Chaucer, Plate 15: recto. 1894–1895. PML 76853. Gift of John A. Saks, 1977. The Morgan Library & Museum/Art Resource, NY. 125

4.4 1079.31, Top, preliminary study for *The Tale of the Clerk of Oxford: the arrival of the servant charged with the removal of the child*; bottom, three figure studies: *Grisilde cradling the baby, the servant waiting, a variation of the waiting servant*. Burne-Jones, Edward (British, 1833–1898). Graphite on laid paper, the uppermost sketch within drawn, rectangular, graphite borders, height, support, 323 mm, width, support, 200 mm. For page 132 of the Kelmscott Chaucer. © The Fitzwilliam Museum, Cambridge. 127

4.5 1050.16, *The Clerk's Tale: The Servant Arrives to Take the Child from Grisilde*. Burne-Jones, Edward (British, 1833–1898). Graphite within drawn graphite border on paper, height, drawn area, 129 mm, width, drawn area, 171 mm. For page 132 of the Kelmscott Chaucer. © The Fitzwilliam Museum, Cambridge. 128

4.6 Burne-Jones, Edward (British, 1833–1898). Illustrations for the Kelmscott Chaucer, Plate 16. 1894–1895. PML 76853. Gift of John A. Saks, 1977. The Morgan Library & Museum/Art Resource, NY. 129

Acknowledgments

This book began life as a dissertation project and was subsequently revised over five years. I am grateful for the generosity and support of my colleagues at Saint Louis University during my time as a PhD student and subsequent position as Visiting Assistant Professor. In particular, I am grateful for the generative conversations with Phyllis Weliver, Toby Benis, Ellen Crowell, Rachel Greenwald Smith, Anne Stiles, and Nathaniel Rivers.

Indeed, I am indebted to a number of people who have contributed to make this book what it is. I would like to thank Angie Blumberg for her friendship and support throughout the process of writing and revision. Florence Boos, Marion Thain, Jill Ehnenn, Mark Samuels Lasner, Margaretta Frederick, and Ewan Jones were also instrumental in their guidance and support of this project. I am grateful, also, for the thoughtful and detailed feedback provided by my readers at Cambridge University Press and to Bethany Thomas for her invaluable assistance as Commissioning Editor of the Cambridge Studies in Nineteenth-Century Literature and Culture series. Finally, and most importantly, this book would be impossible without the unconditional support and assistance of my family.

This project was funded by research support received from Auburn University at Montgomery, the University of Delaware Library and the Delaware Art Museum's joint Fellowship in Pre-Raphaelite Studies, and the William Morris Society of the United States. Additionally, I express my gratitude to the staff at all of the archives where I researched: the British Library, Fitzwilliam Museum, Bodleian Libraries, Mark Samuels Lasner Collection (University of Delaware), Bancroft Collection (Delaware Arts Museum), and Pierpont Morgan Library.

Earlier versions of material in this book have appeared in *Forum for Modern Language Studies* (52.2, April 2016) and *Victorian Poetry* (55.4, Winter 2017).

Introduction

> Our reliance on one another, whether on this plane or another, is what can never be explained. There have been many empty moments, long spaces of silence, both grappling with the same intangible idea. Sometimes the compelling creative urge would come on both, and we would try to reconcile the two impulses, searching for a form into which best to cast them—one releasing it, perhaps as a cloudy suggestion, to be caught up by the other, and given form and colour, then to float away in a flash of certainty, a completed sentence—as two dancers will yield to the same impulse, given by the same strain of music, and know the joy of shared success.[1]

Edith Œnone Somerville's account of her writing process with Martin Ross (Violet Florence Martin), written after Ross's death in 1915, uses metaphors of catch and release and partnered dancing to suggest that collaboration is an ongoing and continual process that cannot exist without "our reliance on one another" – the shared participation of both women. In the first sentence, Somerville goes so far as to refer to a participation that continues beyond the grave: she believed that Ross continued to collaborate with her, even after death, via automatic writing; therefore, she continued to publish all subsequent texts under their collaborative pseudonym: Somerville and Ross. Writing is also described as an elusive experience: the "intangible idea" is difficult to explain, but when "caught up" by the other, it is granted "form." Coming together in the creative process, the "cloudy suggestion" becomes clearly resolute through a shared communal experience, demonstrated by this metaphor of a game of catch, and elaborated in the image of dancers yielding to "the joy of shared success." Also of importance is the notion of shared exercise: forms of labor that depend upon the other for its completion. As Jill R. Ehnenn notes in *Women's Literary Collaboration, Queerness, and Late-Victorian Culture* (2008), "women represent collaborative labor as linked [to] a view of partnership-as-self that favors self-in-process and self-in-connection to others."[2] Female collaboration is therefore a reaction against commentaries on masculine collaboration: rhetoric that seeks textual control and preserves division in labor.[3] Ehnenn notes that her study is not as interested in the process of joint writing, but rather in the representations of this labor; thus, she reads descriptions of late nineteenth-century female literary partnerships as performances that work with and against prevailing understandings of authorship and creative labor. However, focusing on this unexplainable and fleeting collaborative process – while daunting and sometimes complicated – reveals important insights into the coming together of individuals in creative cooperation and the reasoning behind such a practice. It is, therefore, this elusive process of coming together that *Collaborative Writing in the Long Nineteenth Century* explores in its wide-ranging studies of collaboration across the long nineteenth century.

In the following pages, I examine the process of collaboration – drawing from manuscript marginalia, notes, journal/diary entries, and correspondence – and the influences of that process on poetry, drama, and fiction. By understanding the collaborative process as a means of identifying with the other at the same time as we identify with ourselves – "thinking of me thinking of you," as coined by Rae Greiner – we can come to a closer understanding of selfhood as a construction of a blend of dialogic voices, embodied not only in the act of collaboration but within the very texts constructed out of that collaboration.[4] Such a model is what I have termed "sympathetic collaboration." Guided by the current trend of literary studies around sympathy, emotion, and affect, this project demonstrates the long reach that eighteenth-century moral philosophy has on later literature and artistic thought by investigating the writing and creative processes to understand the ways in which communal relationships are inscribed within the literary product. In so doing, I suggest that collaboration is necessarily rooted in the ideals of Victorian liberalism: it is derived from a representation of sympathetic identification and emphasizes human sociability. In a broader sense, this book provides a fresh understanding of literary collaboration necessarily informed by the mechanics of the writing process and illustrated in the formal elements of literature, as well as textual or marginal traces within the manuscripts. My project offers a new theory of collaboration, whereby sympathy becomes a model framework for the collaborative process. Nineteenth-century artistic creation is rooted in sympathetic identification. This philosophical approach to life (seen in the lived attempts at community for each of my case studies) has larger implications for literary history: these sympathetic communities are mutually implicated in formal experimentation and innovation.

(Re)Defining Collaboration

What does it mean to collaborate? The Oxford English Dictionary definition fails to illuminate its meaning: "united labour; co-operation; *esp.* in literary, artistic, or scientific work" ("collaboration, n."). What, precisely, is meant by this method of cooperation? More to the point, would collaborators be any different than editors or other influences? Within the field of both common knowledge and criticism, relatively broad and narrow definitions of collaboration are evident. Many people today would agree on the narrower sense of collaboration as two or more individuals composing or creating something together. Broadening out, however, literary critics have suggested the inclusion of various factors and influences: James P. Bednarz includes "theft" from contemporary rivals or literary precursors; Jewel Spears Brooker includes the "capacity for assimilation" of other's works and proposes the relationship between writer and reader as a form of collaboration, a relationship also considered by Jack Stillinger.[5] Even broader, M. Thomas Inge believes that "[a]nytime another hand enters into an effort, a kind of collaboration occurs."[6] On the other hand, Thomas Hines prefers a simpler but comprehensive definition: "work artists do together to produce a joint creation."[7] It is this definition of collaboration that I, like Marjorie Stone and Judith Thompson in their *Literary Couplings* (2006), adopt for this study. The actual writing practices of creators are included in this relatively broad definition of "work," which takes a variety of written and spoken forms. By understanding collaboration as work – as a verb, rather than a noun – we can access more fully the processes that underlie collaborative efforts. In doing so, we capture not only the "joint creation," or the literary/artistic text, but also the associations and networks that go into artistic creation. In other words, we can capture the process inherent in the coming together of individuals – a coming together that takes place not only on the written page but also in social interactions and correspondences. These compositional practices and processes form the focus of rhetoricians Lisa Ede and Andrea Lunsford's *Singular Texts/Plural Authors* (1990), where they define collaborative writing as "any of the activities that lead to a completed written document," including "written and spoken brainstorming, outlining, note-taking, organizational planning, drafting, revising and editing."[8] Ede's and Lunsford's focus on the "spoken," implied also in Hines's definition, is of particular importance to my understanding of nineteenth-century collaboration: a focus on dialogue, a coming together on the written page that is informed by the social, by the community. Moreover, Hines's definition is inclusive of "artists" working upon a "joint creation" and therefore extends beyond literary authors to cross disciplinary boundaries.[9]

Conversation is vital to the collaborative process. In (re)defining collaboration as "work," I argue for its description as a verb – emphasizing action, or an act of being. In doing so, I follow the lead of philosopher Bruno Latour, whose scholarship emphasizes descriptive properties rather than definitions, and a return to original meaning in order to trace "associations between heterogenous elements."[10] In his introduction to *Reassembling the Social* (2005), Latour reconsiders the notion of the social by returning to its original meaning in order to trace a "trail of associations" or "a type of connection between things that are not themselves social."[11] By focusing on descriptive properties, rather than strict definitions, Latour provides an understanding of "social" as something that is not visible, but rather only visible "by the *traces* it leaves (under trials) when a *new* association is being produced between elements."[12] Thus, I take a Latourian approach to collaboration by tracing the ways in which we see collaboration as work in order to underscore the process of coming together through sympathetic identification. Verbs, unlike nouns, cannot be treated as an already known product; collaboration, in this study, is not given as an explanatory mechanism, but as an exploratory and necessarily social interaction. The conversations, associations, and networks that comprise the nineteenth-century collaborative process are traced in the chapters that follow to argue that sympathy enables collaboration.[13]

Fundamentally, studies of collaboration question the privileged conception of a singular and unitary author, despite the efforts of poststructuralist theorists and their attempts to deconstruct authorship. Michel Foucault's "What is an Author?" provides the foundation for considerations of authorship as a modern construct, leading to the belief that texts are not the products of individual creators. Rather, as Foucault argues, the writer's individuality is canceled out of the text because the concept of the "author" is a function of language itself. In declaring the death of the author, borrowed from Roland Barthes' "Death of the Author," Foucault deconstructs the idea of the author as the creator of something original and asserts that the "author" is the product – or function of writing – of the text. In other words, authorship does more than signify a specific, historical individual: authorship encompasses the ideas with which the author is attributed, his/her mode of thinking and methodology, and the writings – or works – associated with his/her name. As such, authorship serves as a means of identification, accompanying certain texts to the exclusion of others. Such is the problem with scholarship and canon formation, which continue to maintain an image of the author as a solitary figure of creative genius. Ede and Lunsford cleverly refer to the traditional rejection of collaboration in favor of this solitary, individual act of authorial creation as the "purloined letter effect" of the collaborative text: the pervasive denial that something – or some*one* – is "hidden in plain view" in the writing.[14]

In the field of literary studies, Jack Stillinger, in his pioneering and still unchallenged *Multiple Authorship and the Myth of Solitary Genius* (1991), turned attention to the increasing identification of the solitary author as a myth attributed to Romantic ideologies of the inspired creator. In the wake of poststructuralist theories, new models and technologies for editing and textual production, feminist and queer reframings of literary histories, and proliferations of collaborative digital projects, there remains renewed interest in the skepticism concerning the figure of the "solitary genius." Stillinger's exploration of "multiple authorships," figures who had a role in the literary production along with the "nominal author," include "a friend, a spouse, a ghost, an agent, an editor, a translator, a publisher, a censor, a transcriber, a printer."[15] This emphasis on the multiplicity of figures underscores that texts are not the products of individual creators; texts are produced under a number of influences. While Stillinger focuses on interactions with collaborative sources and influences, here, collaboration is an intentional action resulting in a shared creation, rather than that of inspiration. Further, Stillinger does not reflect on the social structures that shape the production of literary texts. Such a reflection arises in Jerome McGann's *The Textual Condition* (1991), which conceives of literary texts as "collaborative events."[16] Rather than an "autonomous and self-reflexive activity," McGann argues that textual production is "a social and institutional event."[17] Writing – art – cannot escape the influences that produce it, and tracing the associations of collaboration makes visible those social interactions or events. McGann's supposition aligns with my attention to the connections between the processes of collaborative writing; the multiple media used and envisioned by the writers; and the finalized products themselves. This approach helps scholarship to better understand the collaborative ideal and its ties to the social, an aspect that has been fundamentally neglected in recent literary discussions of collaboration.[18]

Of the current monographs on literary collaboration, there are none with the broader focus of the long nineteenth century. Approaches to male literary collaboration proliferated in the late 1980s and 1990s: Wayne Koestenbaum's *Double Talk: The Erotics of Male Literary Collaboration* (1989), a groundbreaking text arguing that the "double signature" of collaboration alters perceptions of authorship; Stillinger, as aforementioned; and Jeffrey Masten's *Textual Intercourse: Collaboration, Authorship, and Sexualities in Renaissance Drama* (1997), which analyzes the "corporate" authorship of early modern drama. These works emphasize the widespread nature of literary collaboration among men in specific literary periods, shedding light on the myth of the popular perception of solitary authorship as masculine, yet neglect the possibilities of female or familial collaboration.

Feminist criticism has been particularly productive in its research on collaboration, initially producing panels and special issues on the subject of female coauthors. At the Modern Language Association Conference in 1991, the Women's Caucus concentrated on female collaboration. In addition, *Tulsa Studies in Women's Literature* (1994 and 1995) contained a two-part "Forum on Collaborations," and *PMLA* published a series of articles on collaboration under its section of "Theories and Methodologies" (2001). Monographs have also been prevalent. Responding to the dominantly masculine discussion of coauthorship, Bette London's *Writing Double: Women's Literary Partnerships* (1999) examines nineteenth- and twentieth-century women collaborators and warns that the focus on the female writer's "dark double" – from Sandra Gilbert and Susan Gubar – has marginalized and rendered invisible female collaborations. By focusing on processes like mediumship and automatic writing, London asserts that female collaboration is an important means of alternative writing practice that challenges traditional perspectives on authorship. Holly Laird's *Women Coauthors* (2000) focuses on psychosocial interactions to "read coauthored texts as the realization of relationships."[19] Her dominant concern is on the self-representation of her collaborators, arguing that collaboration itself is thematized and reproduced in writing. Following closely on Laird's publication, Lorraine York's *Rethinking Women's Collaborative Writing: Power, Difference, Property* (2002) focuses on the power dynamics and "ideological polyvalences" of, primarily, contemporary female collaborations. York discusses some nineteenth-century examples of collaboration as predecessors for her focus on twentieth-century female partnerships, but is primarily concerned with the ways in which contemporary collaboration is informed by poststructuralism. Bringing female collaboration into a narrower focus in the *fin de siècle*, Ehnenn's *Women's Literary Collaboration, Queerness, and Late-Victorian Culture* (2008) examines four pairs of female collaborators. Her study examines how collaboration provides both a sexed and gendered perspective from which to assess the concept of authorship and a specific social and historical perspective of a particular time and place.

These studies are significant because they rediscover collaborative writing and emphasize collaboration as a project of recovery and expansion of the literary canon. In addition, these pioneering texts attempt to classify and situate collaborative writing within a variety of contexts: historical, feminist, and queer. At the same time, however, most of these texts participate in and perpetuate a gendered separation, while attempting to provide a "holistic" perspective of collaboration. This is one criticism that Marjorie Stone and Judith Thompson attempt to redress in *Literary Couplings* (2006). Acknowledging that attention is traditionally focused on the "*lives* of literary couples, not their texts," Stone and Thompson attest that work produced collaboratively by partners still remains organized into "separate oeuvres."[20] They seek to eliminate this separation in their study exploring literary couplings ranging from the Renaissance to the present. Stone and Thompson describe "coupling" as "a compositional activity, a publishing strategy and/or interpretive practice, as well as (in many contexts) a sexual or familial connection."[21] Their research remains important because of its breadth of collaborative discussion, its integrated methodology, and its refusal to maintain separations between the varied forms of collaboration.

While maintaining a varied breadth of approximately 100 years (1814–1912), this book is focused on case studies of partnerships from the major movements within the period: Romanticism, Pre-Raphaelitism, Aestheticism, and Modernism. While my exploration cannot be exhaustive, such an approach provides a rich exemplar of the trajectory of sympathetic collaboration in each movement. At its core, this study demonstrates the fluidity of canonical boundaries by tracing the associations of eighteenth-century moral philosophy as an undercurrent of nineteenth-century collaboration which ultimately informs nineteenth-century liberalism. While not focused on collaborative writing, Rae Greiner's *Sympathetic Realism* (2012) addresses sympathy as an integral aspect to the form of nineteenth-century realist fiction; thus, here, I have opted not to focus on the collaborative aspects of nineteenth-century realism, such as the work of George Eliot and George Henry Lewes. At the same time, I incorporate some of the same influences as current research in collaborative studies through my examination of gender and the power dynamics at work within the partnerships that I study: Mary and Percy Bysshe Shelley, Christina and Dante Gabriel Rossetti, Katharine Bradley and

Edith Cooper (together known under the pseudonym "Michael Field"); within the aesthetic press movement (William Morris's Kelmscott Press); and between Vernon Lee and her partners, A. Mary F. Robinson and Clementina "Kit" Anstruther-Thomson. In choosing these varied partnerships, I have attempted to balance recovered women writers alongside reconsiderations of more traditional/canonical literary collaborators, while providing a range of relationships (romantic, familial, and business). In this study, therefore, aesthetic, moral, and social judgments are interrelated, providing a cohesive focus for the collaborative partnerships analyzed. Such a focus follows Benjamin Morgan's materialist aesthetics in *The Outward Mind* (2017), exploring a reading of "Victorian aesthetic thought as participating in a tradition of philosophical aesthetics despite the fact that its practitioners often avoided philosophical idioms."[22] More to the point, I have chosen these partnerships for the insight into collaborative traces within their respective archives, and the undercurrent of eighteenth- and nineteenth-century sympathetic sociability made visible through such tracing.

Like Stone and Thompson's integrated "heterogeneity of coupled authorship," the approach taken here to collaboration is three-pronged.[23] This book integrates: (1) an archival-based analysis of collaborative writing processes with an exploration of formal experimentation and narrative structure; (2) a biographically and philosophically grounded investigation of partnerships with interdisciplinary and theoretical work on creative production and textuality; and (3) an inclusion of a variety of relationships that have been overlooked in a privileging of the erotics of sexuality, including heterosexual, familial, friendships and business partnerships, and same-sex relationships. Furthermore, by favoring the actual processes of collaboration with its attention to archival-based literary analysis, *Collaborative Writing in the Long Nineteenth Century* questions interpretations of the collaborative product – is collaboration a mode of writing, a question of editing and revising, or a question of influence? – to posit that sympathetic collaboration blurs the boundaries of all three relations. "Sympathetic collaboration" questions how and why cross-disciplinary artists come together in artistic creation and inscribe their relationships upon the works produced. This coming together is rooted in an understanding of sympathetic identification influenced by Adam Smith's theories of sympathy, explored more fully in the first chapter. Thus "sympathetic collaboration" is not only a model of the collaborative writing process but also a framework for the establishment of a moral and liberal community, underscoring the social nature of nineteenth-century literary production.

Chapter 1 continues to define and summarize the three interlinking areas of this study: collaboration, sympathy, and liberalism. This first chapter rehearses theoretical models of eighteenth-century sympathy, focusing primarily on Adam Smith. Such an overview lays the foundation for the latter half of the chapter: understanding "sympathetic collaboration" and its connections to Victorian liberalism, which is defined as a communal fraternity of sympathetic experience that uses art as a means of expression and experimentation.

In order to craft observations of sympathetic collaboration across the nineteenth century, subsequent chapters are framed as individual case studies that detail the collaborative processes between specific individuals in order to attenuate the production of an ideally liberal community, inflected by elements of Smithean sympathy, between the artists and formally constructed within the works produced. Throughout, chapters emphasize the collective nature of nineteenth-century literary production and its reliance upon lived experience as a means of constructing shared expression through formal experimentation. Tracing this process in archival materials verifies the influences of this coming together – the formation of a "unified" voice in a coauthored text – upon the poetry, drama, and fiction explored in each chapter. Demonstrating the extent to which Smithean sympathy influenced the Victorian establishment of a liberal community, my model of collaboration illuminates an innovative argument about the nineteenth century: namely, that sympathetic communities are implicated in formal experimentation. *Collaborative Writing in the Long Nineteenth Century* lends a fresh framework for viewing art and personal expression with an eye toward community building and solidarity. In choosing five collaborators, I have constructed a narrative of sympathetic collaboration that not only establishes a sense of Victorian collaboration, – its focus on individuation as a means of modulating toward a liberal community – but also one that anticipates the networks inherent in recent conceptions of Decadence and Modernism.[24] This monograph participates in Victorian scholarship devoted to understanding the inherently social nature of literary production and seeks to establish a model framework for the coming together of individuals in order to create both social and personal meaningfulness. This approach focuses, therefore, on both the production of art and the production of community in order to illuminate the interconnections between the public, literature, and formal experimentation.

Chapter 2 explores the 1814 collaboration between Mary and Percy Bysshe Shelley and extends scholarly attention to their travel journals, before moving onto *Frankenstein* (1818). Using the couple's shared journal as a way of marking their convergence and redefinition of themselves from a singular identity to a shared pluralism, the journal's entries witness a shared understanding – a sympathetic concord – between the couple. This understanding is rooted in the period's reassessment and identification of relationships in terms of shared sympathetic understanding and political solidarity and forms the basis of their collaboration. This close examination of the collaborative process indicates a willingness to assimilate and accommodate the other's sentiments and formal constructs and offers an analysis of conversation detected upon the manuscript pages. While the narratives of these entries show the completion of each other's thoughts and a reliance upon readerly circulation, the entries' form also gestures to their defined plural identity through a vocal blending. In a sense, analysis of the couple's life-writing, in combination with its attention to novelistic form, aligns with Ross Wilson's *Shelley and the Apprehension of Life* (2013), which analyzes Percy Bysshe Shelley's beliefs about life and the significance of poetry. Wilson demonstrates that Shelley views poetry as a "living melody," which is offered in contrast to the world in which life does not live.[25] While Wilson characterizes the poetic form as encapsulating the imaginative and humanizing lived experience, this chapter asserts a larger trajectory traced back to the couple's shared experience, initially formulated in their life-writing and prose, and later extends into Shelley's poetic form. Moreover, with its sustained focus on the sympathetic communities developed by the couple and the increased literary production as a result of this lived communal experience, the Shelley collaboration ultimately shapes the narrative form of *Frankenstein*. The novel's layered narrative of sympathetic texts makes possible a view of the collaborative compilation of the novel as a means of social reform: a view of society that relies upon the affective bonds of sympathy with a community of people, whether imaginative or genuine.

Continuing to explore the processes of sympathetic assimilation, Chapter 3 extends attention to Christina and Dante Gabriel Rossetti: a familial collaboration and a maintenance of difference in service to a harmonious whole – art and poetry. Whereas the second chapter draws attention to the assimilation and accommodation that occurs between individuals coming together, this chapter extends the focus of sympathetic collaboration to a broader interpretation of social community that suffuses the Rossetti collaboration and reclaims female agency in the affirmation of Christina's poetic experimental form. While the Pre-Raphaelites are generally known for their integration of art and literature, this chapter analyzes D.G. Rossetti's illustrations alongside a formal analysis of

Christina Rossetti's *Goblin Market* (1862) to draw further attention to the creative and communal processes associated with intertextual collaborative production. Reading this familial collaboration through the lens of sympathetic collaboration allows for an understanding of fellow-feeling dependent upon the articulation of both individual and communal viewpoints – acknowledging difference – and the means of self-assimilation to form community. Closely reading *Goblin Market* as a collaborative lyric establishes how the poem constructs a reproduction of the Rossetti collaboration and underscores the interrelationships between word and image and community development. Placing the poem alongside the reformative work Christina Rossetti completed at Highgate Penitentiary, this chapter provides a direct contextual link to sympathetic concord and its inflection of moral reform. Reading Christina's and D.G. Rossetti's contemporaneous literary productions as sympathetic collaborations that inform one another reveals, more broadly, the interlacings of shared experiences and literary and artistic productions within the Pre-Raphaelite movement.

Expanding the focus on the collaboration between art and image, Chapter 4 considers the late nineteenth-century aesthetic press as an embodiment of the collaborative process. Drawing from manuscript culture and William Morris's lectures, this chapter illuminates two integral processes: individuals coming together to form a liberal community and the mechanization of the Kelmscott Press as a joining of art and writing. By positioning the Press within a larger trajectory of Victorian liberal sentiment, this chapter foregrounds that fraternal communitarian conceptions of liberalism can be understood as the same as Morris's practical socialism. During the 1880s, liberalism and socialism were closely related; in fact, socialism, as Stefan Collini asserts via his reclamation of L.T. Hobhouse, – leading Liberal political theorist and founding father of British sociology – was initially seen as a continuation of early liberalism.[26] Further, by emphasizing Morris's belief that the production of art brings relief from the vulgarization of society, this chapter asserts that such reform occurs in the communal endeavor of the press as a business partnership, witnessed in the collaborative productions of Edward Burne-Jones and Robert Catterson-Smith, and William Morris and Charles Gere. Morris's ideal book serves as an exemplar of lived sociality in the embodiment of the Kelmscott Press: a site that combines work with social pleasure.

Returning to the first chapter's extended attention to life-writing and diary form, Chapter 5 explores the lived experience of communal relations and the importance of joining art to literature by examining the poetry and verse dramas of Michael Field. This chapter looks specifically at the ways in which the couple reclassify and revitalize female tragic history by experimenting with the boundaries of literary form. As a case study that aligns with the late Victorian transition into Modernism, Chapter 5 locates a shift in conceptions of liberal community development as Michael Field complicate critical dichotomies between Victorian and Decadent; Decadent and Modern. Michael Field carry traces of the liberal sympathetic experience witnessed in their life-writing into their amalgamation of specifically decadent characteristics in their poetry and verse drama. The shift toward Decadence that Michael Field mark in this project allows for a seamless move into Modernism.

Chapter 6, "Towards Empathy," focuses on the introduction of empathy into the English language in 1909, and the blurring of the Victorian notion of sympathy as a social process and Vernon Lee's conception of empathy as an aesthetic experience. As such, I read Lee as a figure of Modernism, finding within her work traces of a modernist aesthetic.[27] The chapter includes case studies of Lee's partnership with poet A. Mary F. Robinson and Scottish artist Clementina "Kit" Anstruther-Thomson; rather than a wholly sympathetic collaboration, the model here is not necessarily reliant upon individuals coming together in concord, but is founded on the privatization of the aesthetic experience and the discord that arises due to the individualist qualities advanced by the aesthetic imperative.

Sympathetic collaboration is not merely the act of writing together. Instead, by looking at collaboration as a verb – as a form of work – these case studies demonstrate a wide array of ways in which individuals come together. In the examples of collaborative processes detailed in this project, we witness material aspects of collaboration: hands uniting on the page, leaving space for the other to complete the production, and the writing and exchange of drafts. We also witness the social aspect of collaboration: the dialogue occurring in conversations, the circulation of correspondence, the lived experience of collaboration, and, on a less material plane, the transhistorical collaborations that occur with figures of the past. This study takes a broad approach to collaboration and, in doing so, questions traditional expectations of authorship – not only as solitary activity, but the very nature of authorship. Collaboration enables the titles of "coauthor," "influencer," "editor," "critic," and "inspiration" to coexist. This plurality underscores the social act of nineteenth-century writing.

CHAPTER I

Adam Smith's Liberal Sympathy

In a narrative of self, what is the place of people, of others, of community? Quite plainly, this question poses the paradox of the lyric poet. The lyric is well known for its meditation, its rumination upon the self, for its nostalgia. Yet, as Marion Thain argues in *The Lyric Poem and Aestheticism: Forms of Modernity*, in some respects, this definition of the lyric – and the lyric poet – is outmoded. The lyric, Thain argues, offers a richly reflective response to the rapid change and isolation common to the modern experience. Theorization of the lyric has received renewed scholarly interest, tracing its history and transformation across time.[1] Yopie Prins and Virginia Jackson posit that the general sense agreed upon in critical circles is that the "lyric is personal in expression"[2] and that the invention of the lyric is attributed to Romanticism, the same Romantic ideology that coined the myth of the author as a solitary genius.[3]

The lyric became, for Hegel, the purest representation of subjectivity. The poet becomes "'the centre which holds the whole lyric work of art together', and in order to do so he must achieve a 'specific mood' and 'must identify *himself* with this particularization of himself as with himself, so that in it he feels and envisages *himself*'."[4] Hegel's language certainly resonates with the Romantic circulation of feeling and sentiment. It also bears striking similarities to Smithean sympathy and the impartial spectator (a term defined at length in the following sections), paying close attention to the Hegelian aspect of self-division. For Hegel, the lyric would move society forward with the poet's perfection of self-expression. In the nineteenth century, the lyric became defined as "utterance overheard," based upon John Stuart Mill's argument that "eloquence is *heard*, poetry is *overheard*."[5] In "What is Poetry?," Mill declared that "Poetry is feeling confessing itself to itself, in moments of solitude"; however, as Prins and Jackson point out, this solitude is something that we – as readers – witness: It is "a solitude exhibited in public."[6] Implicitly, then, the lyric for Mill is innately social: it is something experienced by the reader.

I would like to consider the Victorian lyric as that which is social in origin but personal in expression. Such a definition aligns with Thain's study of the lyric as a genre "most commonly circulated primarily in print, and read, whether silently or aloud, from the page."[7] By focusing on the circulation of feelings and ideas associated with the coming together of individuals, this book also provides a way of understanding shifting conceptions of lyric as tied to cultural circulation and sociability. It attempts to recover the Victorian influence of the lyric as connected to formal experimentation: the Victorian lyric asserts relationality and sympathetic connection. Thain locates the "intentionality of consciousness" as a Decadent lyric possibility (Swinburne, Wilde, Symons).[8] However, this potential of the lyric stretches back to understandings of eighteenth- and nineteenth-century theories of moral philosophy. Certainly, Decadent poetry uses the language of intimate physical connection, relying on sensate techniques: smell, touch, and taste. The Decadent lyric, therefore, adapts the Victorian emphasis on cognitive processes of socialization into its focus on the materiality of language.

I have been focusing on the possibilities of the lyric – and specifically the Victorian lyric – as a form that is particularly suited to the production of community and sympathetic experience as a way of presenting the paradox of the solitary lyric poet and the sympathetic liberal impulses of the lyric poet. It is for this reason that poetry is, primarily, the genre chosen by the collaborators explored in these pages. Christina Rossetti's *Goblin Market* (1862), which is animated by a surprising lyrical mode, demonstrates this production in its formation of sisterly community: "For there is no friend like a sister / In calm or stormy weather; / To cheer one on the tedious way, / To fetch one if one goes astray."[9] These closing lines of *Goblin Market* are lyrical in expression: an intimation of personal experience – the love and sympathy between sisters – that is socially articulated to Lizzie and Laura's children, but also to the public reader. Throughout *Collaborative Writing in the Long Nineteenth Century*, the usage of sympathy is that of a theoretical framework underpinning the conception of collaboration. When we ask how individuals come together, the answer is sympathy, with the creative product best viewed as the reflection from the Smithean social mirror. To establish this argument, each of the following chapters not only focus on a specific literary case study but also on a certain aspect of sympathy. In what follows, I provide a brief overview of Smith's theory, while the chapters themselves expand upon moral adjudication (sympathetic accommodation and assimilation) in Chapters 2 and 3, the impartial spectator in Chapter 4, and imaginative transport in Chapter 5. Sympathetic collaboration illuminates sympathy's liberal processes and establishes the foundation of nineteenth-century collaboration within sociability, self-reflection, and self-modulation. By analyzing the writing process as sympathetic collaboration, I trace these sympathetic influences upon the literary product with my attention to form and style, thus underscoring a longer trajectory of eighteenth-century views of moral philosophy.

"Enter[ing] into" Smithean Sympathy

Initially defined by Adam Smith as "fellow-feeling," sympathy "denotes our fellow-feeling with any passion whatever"; later in *The Theory of Moral Sentiments* (1759), he writes that sympathy "in its most proper and primitive signification, denotes our fellow-feeling with the sufferings, not with the enjoyments of others."[10] This apparent contradiction has resulted in confusion, with some scholars claiming that sympathy only occurs with suffering. However, Smith is implicitly acknowledging the normative usage of the term and accepts that the majority of his examples are drawn from this area. This is not to say that Smith precludes the ability to sympathize with enjoyment. In particular, Smith concerns himself with understanding human behavior and the relations between individuals. Sympathy is not, as it is for David Hume, a spontaneous emotional connection; it is a practice by which individuals learn to become "social," to adjust their individual passions to a "pitch" equivalent to those living in society with them.[11] Fellow-feeling, in other words, is, necessarily, other-oriented.

Understanding this other-oriented aspect of sympathy is foundational to sympathetic collaboration, and, indeed, the social aspects of emotion are an integral part of the British eighteenth and nineteenth centuries. The eighteenth century is commonly conceived as the age of reason; however, as sociopolitical theorist Michael Frazer points out, there are two streams of moral and political reflection: rationalist and sentimentalist. In *The Enlightenment of Sympathy*, Frazer reclaims the sentimentalist account of reflection, asserting that sentimentalists begin where rationalists leave off: "with the empirical investigation of what actually leads real-world human beings to follow the norms that they do."[12] The sentimentalist stream "suggests an age not of reason alone, but also of reflectively refined feelings shared among individuals via the all-important faculty of sympathy."[13] Smith's "fellow-feeling" – sympathy – is central to the circulation of shared feeling within a community: it is "the bridge between the social and the psychological, the faculty by which inner mental states are shared among individuals."[14]

Sympathy, therefore, goes beyond mere feeling; the sympathetic concord extends a similarity of feeling, but it also extends judgment upon one's conduct.[15] For example, when one sympathizes with another's feelings, that individual approves of the other's feelings, as Smith attests: "To approve of the passions of another, therefore, as suitable to their objects, is the same thing as to observe that we sympathize with them."[16] Central to Smith's thought is this gap – the similarity of feeling – between individuals. A complete "unison" of sentiment between different people is entirely impossible:

> That imaginary change of situation, upon which their sympathy is founded, is but momentary. [...] What they feel, will, indeed, always be, in some respects, different from what he feels, and compassion can never be exactly the same with original sorrow; because the secret consciousness that the change of situations, from which the sympathetic sentiment arises, is but imaginary, not only lowers it in some degree, but, in some measure varies it in kind, and gives it a quite different modification.[17]

In other words, sympathy is – importantly – imperfect and fleeting because it is imaginary and dependent upon difference. In this cognitive account of sympathy, Smith famously makes special claims for the imaginative work of projective simulation, a transfusion of feeling: "[P]assions, upon some occasions, may seem to be transfused from one man to another, instantaneously and antecedent to any knowledge of what excited them."[18] How does Smith resolve this seeming contradiction? Using the rack as an example, Smith describes an imaginative transportation of one's self into another's situation:

> Though our brother is upon the rack, as long as we ourselves are at our ease, our senses will never inform us of what he suffers. They never did, and never can, carry us beyond our own person, and it is by the imagination only that we can form any conception of what are his sensations. [...] It is the impressions of our own senses only, not those of his, which our imaginations copy. By the imagination we place ourselves in his situation, we conceive ourselves enduring all the same torments, we enter as it were into his body, and become in some measure the same person with him, and thence form some idea of his sensations, and even feel something which, though weaker in degree, is not altogether unlike them.[19]

Sympathy is affective. It does not simply join individuals together; using the imagination, it places a person inside others' experiences. Through sympathy, individuals can "become in some measure the same person" as another and can achieve concord. But to what purpose? We cognitively work out "what *to* feel," as Stephen Darwall explains, "as though we were they."[20] In a similar vein, philosopher Charles L. Griswold, Jr. notes that sympathy has two meanings for Smith: "In its narrow sense, sympathy is an emotion (that of compassion); in its broader Smithean sense, it is also the means through which emotions are conveyed and understood."[21] Smith was not advocating a complete unison, but a "concord" of sentiment supported by the nature of human sociality. This concord is sufficient for social order: "These two sentiments [...] have such a correspondence with one another, as is sufficient for the harmony of society. Though they will never be unisons, they may be concords."[22]

By entering into a sympathetic concord, individuals come to know not only others, but they come to know also themselves. Smith performs a thought experiment to demonstrate this epistemology, using the metaphor of the mirror: suppose "a human creature could grow to manhood in some solitary place, without any communication with his own species."[23] If this were the case, the creature "could no more think of his own character, of the propriety or demerit of his own sentiments and conduct" because he has no social mirror:

> Bring him into society, and he is immediately provided with a mirror which he wanted before. It is placed in the countenance and behavior of those he lives with, which always mark when they enter into, and when they disapprove of his sentiments; and it is here that he first views the propriety and impropriety of his own passions, the beauty and deformity of his own mind.[24]

In this context, individuals come to know themselves and the world around them by coordinating a balance between the self and the public through an immersion into society and the corresponding development of Smith's social mirror. This process of epistemological understanding is another way of defining sympathy and is further explored in the next chapter. It resonates with Mary Shelley's *Frankenstein* and the ways in which Victor's creature (who does "learn" in solitude) immerses himself into society, longing for companionship. Sympathy is, for Smith, a social process by which individuals learn to "accommodate and assimilate, as much as we can, our own sentiments, principles, and feelings, to those which we see fixed and rooted in the persons whom we are obliged to live and converse a great deal with."[25] The sympathetic concord, then, occurs when people encounter one another in shared spaces, with the capability of coordinating together to produce a moral community.

In both the eighteenth and nineteenth centuries, sympathy is understood to address the moral problems associated with political conflicts and social dislocations. In an overview of sympathy, Ryan Patrick Hanley asserts that it emerged as a way of holding a society of strangers together: "the eighteenth century (especially but not only in Britain and France) witnessed a shift from traditional and more intimate forms of community to new forms of social organization; now societies of strangers emerged alongside more traditional and familiar communities of intimates."[26] Eighteenth-century philosophies of sympathy are a useful framework for analyzing the coming together of individuals; indeed, while I am not concerned here with the larger project of eighteenth- and nineteenth-century cosmopolitanism or urbanization, my focus on collaborative processes analyzes both intimate communities of individuals alongside public communities relating to publishing and acts of reading. In particular, by retaining a sustained focus on Smith's conception of sympathy, we come to a greater understanding of moral community, emphasizing relationality – the connections between individuals and the application of basic mores to social norms – rather than a religious understanding of morality.

To put it plainly, in the nineteenth century, Smithean sympathy has two different but interrelated effects: the creation of meaningful collaborations (i.e., fellow-feeling in collaboration) and the formation of communities (i.e., community-feel). In the following chapters, I pay special attention to the act of coming together upon the page and within the community – to the conversations between individuals – to heighten the social bonds between collaborators and emphasize the importance of lived communal experience. Social order is the product of the sympathetic process. As philosopher Jack Russell Weinstein notes in *Adam Smith's Pluralism*, "moral adjudication and self-identification are impossible in isolation."[27] The goal of sympathy is to align oneself with the shared values of the community, while maintaining a certain distance to be able to reconstruct and interpret community judgment. Hence the development of Smith's "impartial spectator": "the aggregate of a person's experience balanced with what he or she knows of the moderating power of community."[28] In the aforementioned example of witnessing another upon the rack, Smith's account of the imagination takes place within a shared space, a sort of theatrical stage.[29] By "changing places in fancy," the spectator sees the spectacle of suffering and imagines what the sufferer endures.[30] As cultural aesthetician John Jervis elucidates in his overview of sympathy theory in *Sympathetic Sentiments*, it "is the indirectness of the imagination that is important here, coupled with the emphasis on situation: it is not the other so much as the *place* of the other, the other *in relation to* context."³¹ By focusing on the situation rather than emotions or feelings, this imaginative projection entails identification with a different point of view (and thus makes Smith a favorite of literary scholars).

At the same time, Smith's model of sympathy remains effective for producing impartial judgment because the spectator is both involved and detached. Again, sympathy is not an emotional transference; it is an interpretation, a judgment made by an observer. Griswold puts it succinctly: "'Sympathy' articulates the fundamental fact of our already being, at least to some degree, 'in' each others' world," while "[o]ur fundamental separateness [...] is not obliterated through the imagination."³² This introduction of difference and the distance of observation (in contrast to participation) is crucial to Smithean sympathy and creates a momentous shift in emphasis from Hume and other Scottish Enlightenment thinkers because of its focus on reflexive awareness. Smith's impartial spectator reveals an understanding of sympathy as a social process of interaction: "Just as the spectator tries to meet the feelings of the potential recipient of sympathy, in an expansive move of self towards others, so too the latter modulates his feelings so as to meet the spectator halfway."³³

The impartial spectator's reflexive dimension, with its implications of self-division, showcases the active involvement of imagination and its dependence upon emotional response and judgment:

> When I endeavour to examine my own conduct, when I endeavour to pass sentence upon it, and either to approve or condemn it, it is evident that, in all such cases, I divide myself, as it were, into two persons; and that I, the examiner and judge, represent a different character from that other I, the person whose conduct is examined into and judged of. The first is the spectator, whose sentiments with regard to my own conduct I endeavour to enter into, by placing myself in his situation, and by considering how it would appear to me, when seen from that particular point of view. The second is the agent, the person whom I properly call myself, and of whose conduct, under the character of a spectator, I was endeavouring to form some opinion. The first is the judge; the second the person judged of. [...]
>
> It is from him only that we learn the real littleness of ourselves, and of whatever relates to ourselves, and the natural misrepresentations of self-love can be corrected only by the eye of this impartial spectator.³⁴

The process of sympathy appears to happen in a somewhat linear fashion. We respond, through feeling, to the joys or sufferings of others. Such responses – the situations we respond to and how we respond – have been shaped by our previous experiences, which allows for an element of reflection, thereby serving as a foundation for nineteenth-century liberal thinking. Here, we encounter the impartial spectator – "the personification of the public"[35] – and are enjoined to admire as praiseworthy or condemn as blameworthy the actions we have encountered. Such a division between spectator and actor allows for, according to Smith, the knowledge of one's own sentiments and, consequently, the ability to understand, deduce, and reconstruct others' sentiments.

Moral philosophers and political scientists continue to debate the essential aspects of Smith's *Theory of Moral Sentiments,* with some, like Weinstein, emphasizing the aspects of moral perfection, while others, like political scientist Fonna Forman-Barzilai, interpret the text with an eye to the "basic, minimal requirements of social coordination."[36] Likewise, I maintain a focus on sympathy's social processes. The social order appears as Smith's primary concern: "the immense fabric of human society [...] seems to have been the peculiar and darling care of Nature."[37] Indeed, earlier, Smith asserts in a footnote that the "welfare and preservation of society" is "the favorite ends of nature."[38] Entering into the experiences of others bridges difference and creates community; for Smith, moral judgment and community are the products of interaction, of relationships. Understanding sympathy as a cognitive and social process reliant upon the separateness of the impartial spectator illuminates the sociability inherent in Smith's conception. Such a view has important implications for the role of sympathy in socialization, nineteenth-century collaboration, and the creation and perpetuation of a liberal community.

Tracing Sympathy in the Long Nineteenth Century

Arguing that nineteenth-century communal development and liberal thought are founded upon sympathetic identification destabilizes the long-standing binaries of the Romantic and Victorian eras. Taking account of the role of sociability in the nineteenth century means understanding the long reach of eighteenth-century moral philosophy as it underpins conventions of conversation and networks typically associated as Romantic. As we will see in later chapters, however, these conventions resonate throughout the nineteenth century. Nineteenth-century sociability is currently under reconsideration by literary scholars evaluating networks and salon culture, complemented by a renewed focus on the lived experience of social groups and interactions.[39] By adding sympathetic identification to this scholarly reconsideration, we gain a new way of thinking about sociability and community in the long nineteenth century by foregrounding the interrelationships of aesthetic, moral, and social judgments.

In the early nineteenth century, Scottish Enlightenment philosophy – particularly the influences of Smith and his contemporaries – resonated with an international reading public.[40] In the eighteenth century, as we have seen, sympathy was discussed as action-motivated; its purpose was to establish social bonds between individuals. The same concerns occupied the Victorians, though Hume's influence, rather than that of Smith, has dominated in literary criticism.[41] *The Theory of Moral Sentiments* had a prominent effect on the Victorians, particularly in the sciences. Darwin, for instance, directly mentions Smith's philosophical treatise in *The Descent of Man* (1871), comparing the work to Alexander Bain's *Mental and Moral Science* (1868). Indeed, when *The Theory of Moral Sentiments* was published in April 1759 with a print run of 1,000 copies, initial sales "were brisk." By 1790, the sixth edition had expanded to two volumes, with the same print run, indicating a renewal of interest in Smith's philosophy. Though it remained in print throughout the nineteenth century, its popularity fluctuated due, in part, to the widespread impact of *The Wealth of Nations* (1776) on political economic thought.[42] And yet, literary evidence throughout the nineteenth century demonstrates the lasting influence of Smithian sympathy: his name, language, and metaphors used in *The Theory of Moral Sentiments* appear regularly throughout the period.[43]

Advocating self-control and social order, Smith's moral philosophy aligns with the qualities espoused by the Victorians, for whom understanding what to feel and how much to feel for others was of prime importance and is connected to the liberal practice of critical self-reflection. Toward the end of the nineteenth century, emotional maintenance was the subject of several issues of *Mind*, a British philosophical journal initially published in 1876. Concerns surrounding emotion and regulation can be traced back to Smith, who, in 1759, asserted sympathy as a formulation for not only thinking about others but also regulating one's emotions through cognition. We need look no further than the circulation of conduct books throughout the eighteenth and nineteenth centuries for evidence of the concerns of emotional regulation, though their proliferation at the end of the century reveals, as Lucy Morrison argues, that while women recognize traditional duties and regulations, the publication of conduct books subverted traditional constricting roles by providing opportunities – such as writing and authorship – beyond the restricting confines of the domestic sphere.[44] These domestic texts were not the only means of addressing concerns about emotional maintenance and control: it was a common concern, also, in the century's medical discourse as social conflict, theories of deviance, and criminality turn to regulation of feelings.[45] As Greiner notes in her overview of Victorian sympathy, "the value of emotion and emotional sharing was a disputed topic at the end of the nineteenth century and had long been a concern for moral philosophy, especially during the Scottish Enlightenment."[46] By 1882, however, Leslie Stephen considers sympathy "the condition for the possibility of thinking about others in any fashion at all,"[47] thereby removing the element of social preservation and welfare at the heart of Smith's doctrine. In some ways, we see that Smith's theory of sympathy remains consistent with nineteenth-century discussions of emotion and regulation; at the same time, however, we notice a changing trajectory as sympathy takes on different meanings by the end of the century.

The discussions surrounding sympathy across the nineteenth century are not static, and the sympathetic collaboration espoused by Mary and Percy Bysshe Shelley is not the same as that practiced by Michael Field or Vernon Lee at the end of the century. In a very simplistic view, we see a transition from discussions of the metaphysical aspects of sympathy to a more materialist understanding of sympathy – or empathy at the turn of the century – that evolves, today, into phenomenological cognitive science and the study of mirror neurons. By tracking the evolution of sympathy across the nineteenth century, we note the ways in which the collaborative process is underpinned by sympathetic identification and continuously shaped by shifts in conceptions of liberal community as the century progresses. As Rachel Ablow points out in *The Marriage of Minds*, the popularity of eighteenth-century sentimental notions of sympathy waned in the nineteenth century, particularly as the Victorians turned to institutional resolutions for social problems, often relegating sympathy to the private sphere. However, "even as sympathy's significance as a way to consolidate communities diminished, its function as a structure through which the subject is constituted in relation to others did not."[48] Ablow's overview of the trajectory of sympathy emphasizes, in fact, the significance of sympathy as a social process – a relation between individuals. As the following chapters indicate, however, Victorian England is very much concerned with sociability and the creative production inspired by community-feel. Certainly, however, this community-feel is less emphatic as the century progresses, giving way to new definitions of individualism and community at the *fin de siècle*. As Potolsky identifies, networks of affinity form the foundation of decadent style: nineteenth-century paradigms of nation, of moral community, of a bringing together of people engaging "the most pressing issues of nineteenth-century political and social theory"[49] give way to a community forged through a sense of shared aesthetic taste and the circulation of a "paradoxically apolitical politics that characterizes decadent writing."[50]

After Adam Smith, the study of sympathy develops in three branches. The Scottish Enlightenment developed "Common Sense philosophy, which was the cornerstone of nineteenth-century Anglo-American political, moral, and aesthetic philosophy," while the French notion of sympathy – inspired by Rousseau's *pitie* – develops a purely instinctual form of feeling, turning human beings into "unreflective feelers."[51] The final branch, and the branch most integral to this study, is the German tradition, which evolved into the aesthetics of Theodor Lipps, Associationist psychology, and the phenomenological sciences. As Adela Pinch notes, we traditionally associate Victorian Britain with science and scientific advancement, but it was "also a realm of metaphysical speculation."[52] Understanding sympathy within this vein of Victorian culture, we can read nineteenth-century philosophy alongside nineteenth-century psychology to understand the evolution of sympathy in the Victorian era. In the mid-nineteenth century, a growing body of discourses in "'mental physiology'—an understanding that psychological and philosophical issues need to be grounded in materialist approaches to the body—emerged in the works of Alexander Bain, George Henry Lewes, Herbert Spencer, William Carpenter, and others."[53] Linking the Associationist school of psychology with its interdependent qualities of the mind and body – describing both the mind and the soul of an individual as material entities – to the evolution of sympathy during the nineteenth century reveals a movement away from the metaphysical toward the corporeal; a shift, indeed, mirrored in the somatic tendencies of *fin de siècle* literature. Around the same time that psychologists entertain a dualism between the mind and body, German physicist Hermann von Helmholtz conducts acoustical research that connects sound to the body via sympathetic vibrations, later extending his theories to consider the vibratory responsiveness of the human body.[54]

This turn toward the body, indeed, becomes a crucial component of the materiality of intellect espoused by Vernon Lee's aesthetics of empathy. Abandoning the metaphysical tenor of the psychologists before him, Lipps suggests the possibility for *Einfühlung* – empathy – for both persons and objects, orienting his understanding away from emotional feeling toward visual perception. As Benjamin Morgan summarizes: "The question about how the mind interacts with embodied visual faculties then became central to his descriptions of *Einfühlung*." Whereas Associationists had developed a physiological aesthetics, Lipps develops a mechanical aesthetics, mechanizing "the human body in order to show the resonances between its structure and the physics of the architectural column."⁵⁵ It is at this central point, in the 1890s, that Lee began developing her version of an embodied aesthetics. With "Kit" Anstruther-Thomson, Lee published *Beauty and Ugliness* (1912), a collection of essays at the forefront of physiological empathy in Anglo-American aesthetics.⁵⁶ These diverse disciplinary frameworks provided the Victorians with innovative methods for imagining the link between aesthetic and embodied experiences, and demonstrate the dynamism of sympathy in the nineteenth century.

Sympathetic Collaboration and Smithean Liberalism

I have explored Smithean sympathy with an eye to its formation of community and concord as a means of forming the "harmony of society."⁵⁷ Nineteenth-century collaboration is deeply invested in not just a coming together of individuals, but the bridging of differences in order to form a cohesive identity that remains separate – unified, but at the same time, individualized. With its primary focus on life-writing and poetry, *Collaborative Writing in the Long Nineteenth Century* illuminates formal experimentation as tied to sympathy's socialization. While this book discusses fictional and nonfictional writing, attention remains on tracing the connections and associations between the process of collaborative writing and the multiple media used. I aim to understand how the collaborative productions of poetry and art are tied to community and to the conversations exchanged during the collaborative process. Such a focus comes from attention to life-writing and manuscript culture, and their influences upon the formal innovation of the creative product and its ties to lived communal experience. The chapters that follow present discussions of this complex process revealed in the life-writing and corresponding formal experimentation, to complicate current understandings of collaboration by illuminating the necessity of sociability and moral adjudication, which is derived from Smithean sympathy. This is an innovative way of thinking about nineteenth-century collaboration that situates sympathetic collaboration, with its formation of moral community, within discussions of Victorian liberalism. Smithean sympathy is liberal: it maintains separateness and reform to one's sense of selfhood in order to form a moral community. By emphasizing its liberal qualities, we can more fully understand the complexity of the collaborative experience – the how and why individuals come together to "produce a joint creation" (recalling Hines's definition of collaboration).

I am not the first to draw comparisons to Smith's ideas of sympathy and liberal thought; philosophers and political scientists have begun making these connections when they interpret Smith's pluralism. Of particular prominence in this field have been Weinstein, Darwall, and Frazer.[58] Weinstein, for instance, states that his *Adam Smith's Pluralism*

> is the first of what I expect to be a multivolume discourse concerning proposed 'Smithian shifts' for twenty-first century liberalism. The second book will examine what liberalism might look like if we used Smith instead of Kant to ground political theory; the third will investigate the nature of political participation in a Smithian liberalism.[59]

Of course, these many volumes are works in progress – at the time of writing, there remains only the first book, presenting an account of pluralism that prefigures modern discourses of diversity.[60] It is important to note that Weinstein focuses on the twentieth-century liberalism, while I am only concerned with the nineteenth century. While Smith's theory contains aspects that might, in modern parlance, be called communitarian – its advocacy for humanity as social, morality as the product of social processes, etc. – he also offers large liberal arguments, as Weinstein succinctly demonstrates when he looks forward to his upcoming volumes:

> he calls for a significant range of both political and economic freedoms, regards individuals as ultimately responsible for their choices, sees justice as largely a matter of refraining from harm, claims the government is responsible for protecting individuals' private pursuits, and hints at a proceduralist conception of justice distinguishing the rules regarding moral and religious interaction from the content of specific belief systems.[61]

This understanding focuses primarily on the political aspects of liberalism, an arena that, while largely important, is not my concern here. Instead, I am interested in how eighteenth-century views of moral philosophy, with its other-oriented and interactive means of reflection, influence later liberal thought. I conceive of liberalism in a necessarily broader sense: as a communal fraternity of sympathetic experience that uses art as a means of expression and experimentation. In doing so, I follow the philosophy of John Stuart Mill, for whom liberalism is tied to the potential afforded by community. Unlike John Locke, who "understands interest in terms of individual identity and individual property and attempts to separate questions of interest from the just operations of the mind and the state, Mill conceives of interest as potentially communal: a tie that binds individuals together, rather than, or as well as, a potential cause of social conflict."[62] Published in 1859, *On Liberty* asserts shared interest as the foundation for a progressive liberal society, contending that dialogue provides the means of achieving balance between individuals, as required for the formation of a liberal state. Indeed, while Anna Barton locates Mill's liberal methodology, "the steady habit of correcting and completing his own opinion by collating it with those of others,"[63] as modeled on a Platonic dialogic, Mill's liberalism, in fact, borrows from Smith's contention of sympathy as a means of self-regulation and critical self-reflection in order to produce social formation.

Liberalism, then, is a complex term. While historians and literary scholars once approached Victorian liberalism by divergent routes, recent interdisciplinary studies have blurred the boundaries between the Liberal party, the political ideology of liberalism, and the liberal discourse of social action.[64] We must acknowledge the emergent character of liberalism in the nineteenth century; just as sympathy evolves across the century, so too do conceptions of liberalism.[65] This approach to liberalism, therefore, aligns with intersectional approaches advocated by Elaine Hadley, Phyllis Weliver, Barton, and, to some extent, Peter Clark's "moral regenerationist" view.[66] At the same time, my approach pointedly differs from a more politically philosophical strain of liberalism in literary studies: Amanda Anderson's *Bleak Liberalism*. Anderson defines liberalism as "a philosophical and political project conceived in an acute awareness of the challenges and often bleak prospects confronting it."[67] Liberalism, in this sense, is born of crisis. With such a view in mind, Anderson notes the ironies of liberalism's negative connotation by the "Republican Right" and the "academic Left." In the case of the latter, she posits that liberal becomes an adjective for political formation:

> In this usage, the term is understood not only to denote the core elements of liberal philosophy (free-market principles and a conception of the subject as free-standing and autonomous) but also to signal a view of the world that systematically disavows the structural inequities of the capitalist system, the conditions of power animating the social field, and the ways in which individuals are always embedded in a myriad of social relations and interdependences.[68]

This passage resonates with Weinstein's focus on twentieth-century liberalism, certainly; but a deeper concern is Anderson's focus on "structural inequities" and "conditions of power" that "embed" individuals within social structures, which leads Anderson into critiques of Foucault and Giorgio Agamben. Anderson argues that liberalism is defined by a tension between a perspective of humanity emphasizing the bleakest traits of human populations and an emphasis on the situated actor, stressing the subject as a moral agent capable of self-examination. Anderson's examination of realist nineteenth- and early twentieth-century fiction focuses on the former tension: "Missing from such visions are the intractable energies of those moods of doubt, despair, and difficulty that frequently accompany the commitment to liberal democratic principles."⁶⁹ Such a view of liberalism, with its focus on political philosophy and commitments to the state and its institutions, contrasts with understandings of the collective nature of the nineteenth century, which relies upon sympathetic circulation and identification: a coming together, rather than such a bleak view of "embedded [...] interdependency."⁷⁰ Possibly, this contrast arises because of Anderson's focus on realist fiction, while my approach eschews realism in favor of tracing the collaborative process in a decidedly more materialist–aesthetic poetics, grounded in eighteenth-century moral philosophy. I remain unconvinced that liberalism is as bleak as Anderson supposes – or, at least, that it is not bleak of necessity. Rather, perhaps a liberalism born of crisis suggests a necessary recognition of the individual and one's need to act within the moral and social arena established by societal standards – standards which are not always reconcilable to the other. The challenge of liberalism lies in the articulation of one's actions in a way that is amenable to the social order. Liberalism is an opportunity to rethink the nineteenth century's desire for social bonds, an opportunity that opens up a consideration of the masses as communities, as collectives of individuals.

Sympathy is a socially cognitive process that relies upon both self-reflection and social circulation. Renewed emphasis on sympathy's social processes – as unfolded in the following pages – allows greater insight into the Victorian period's emphasis on social networks and practiced liberal values of progress or reform and individuality. As Weliver points out in *Mary Gladstone and the Victorian Salon: Music, Literature, Liberalism*: "Liberalism was more than self-reflexive thought and private study, and it was found beyond Parliament and the political platform."⁷¹ Considering a lived sense of liberalism, informed by "aesthetic socializing" in music and literary performance, Weliver capitalizes on the universal attributes of beauty – experienced and shared by all – and how this viewpoint is dependent upon social reform.⁷² Challenging traditional assumptions of liberalism (Anderson's attention to the "academic Left"), Weliver posits it to be both rational and relational:

> As well as a political party, it was a creed or principle governing a way of life. In the sense of liberalism as aligned with the creation of a feeling, democratic community [...] even leaders of the Conservative party practiced liberal values, which further highlights how lived practices that prioritize the humanist subject make more nuanced the political landscape of this period.⁷³

Such a humanist view of lived experience aligns with the impact of sympathetic community and circulation common to both the eighteenth and nineteenth centuries. Weliver's focus remains on an aesthetic experience of socialization and the "social usefulness of beauty," as enacted by the lived experiences of the daughter of the great Liberal Prime Minister, Mary Gladstone. I depart from Weliver by emphasizing the Romantic revolutionary keyword of fraternity – a challenging of the singular nature of political (and, for my purposes, textual) authority – and the prominence of sympathetic collaboration in the long nineteenth century. Art is implicated in the liberal experience, witnessed in attention to formal experimentation as a direct outcome of sympathetic collaboration.

By emphasizing sympathy's social process of interaction – much more than simply feeling and self-reflection – we can understand liberalism's focus on individuality and progress as influenced by Smith's impartial spectator and means of moral adjudication not only for one's self but also for the morality of society. Furthermore, viewing collaboration as a circular representation of sympathetic identification emphasizing human sociability – "sympathetic collaboration" – underscores that discourse is dialogically constructed from lived experience, rooted in a plurality of voices.

Liberal Impulses of a Sympathetic Poet

I began this chapter with a question underscoring the paradox of the lyric poet, and, in what follows, I attempt a resolution of that paradox, highlighting the sympathetic and liberal impulses of poetry in the nineteenth century, a genre foregrounded in this study. Beginning in the late 1990s, scholarship on Victorian literature has witnessed a shift from studies of the novel to considering the prominence of poetry throughout the nineteenth century. This is not to say that studies of the novel have died away, but only that there is a growing importance placed on the study of poetry. Joseph Bristow's historical overview of Victorian poetry clearly explicates poetry as a vehicle for reform, aligning the centrality of poetry to expressions of the social. In "Reforming Victorian Poetry," Bristow examines

> how early and mid-Victorian intellectuals explored the competing demands made upon the poet either to participate in or retire from the turbulence of modern society. Was the time ripe for poetry to embrace politics in the name of social change? Or should poetry repudiate social discontent and fix its attention instead on spiritual ideals? Whatever answers to such questions

were forthcoming, one thing was for sure: The language of poetics remained inextricable from reform—a word that certainly dramatized the uneasy relations between the poet and the people.[74]

Such a focus on the reformative qualities of poetry proves useful since it relies upon the connections between the poet – a singular, solitary poet in line with canonical representations of single authors – and the public. In other words, poetry's inextricable connection to reform becomes a means of connection between art and the experience of the public.[75] As seen in the Chartist poetry in the 1830s, critics and poets began to challenge the meaning of poetry – traditionally associated with the quintessential Romantic attributes of philosophical introspection – to incorporate, within its form and content, the lived experience (and dialect) of the people.

Indeed, when Elizabeth Barrett Browning began writing *Aurora Leigh* in 1844, she desired to compose a new poetic form, "one that would adapt established styles to contemporary needs, and particularly one that would combine narrative and speculative commentary with the requirements of aesthetic unity."[76] In so doing, Barrett Browning led the poetic playfulness that transgressed the boundaries defined by the Greeks: epic (narrative), drama, and lyric. Victorian poetry, therefore, is typified by its experimental nature and its focus on adaptation to the public – to "contemporary needs."[77] Scholarship in the field of Victorian poetry has already established the importance of situating art within society.[78] Carrying forward Romantic conceptions of radical poets, like Percy Bysshe Shelley, Victorian poetry links the public to poetry not only in terms of a poetic response but also in the construction of English culture. Poetry, therefore, "mediates, constructs and debates life, from the realistic depiction of current sociopolitical realities and intellectual debates to the imaginative realms of mythical worlds, which might still speak to contemporary issues."[79] As a result of the Romantic blurring of generic bounds and adaptations, the Victorian poetic impulse shifts toward emphasis on human agency – "on the psychology and politics of individuation"[80] – and on contemporary experience. E. Warwick Slinn points out the unsurprising nature of poetic experimentalism: "in an age of growing challenges to established knowledge, [...] it is hardly surprising that poetic forms emphasize the experiencing, thinking and feeling, human subject."[81] Such is the influence of moral philosophy and the cultural circulation of sympathy upon Victorian poetry: its focus on the sympathetic experience and imaginative transportation that was perceived to lead to the formation of community.

The formal elements of Victorian poetry contribute to this experiential focus and communal development. Through lived experience – that which is recoverable within life-writing and manuscript culture – a specifically Victorian poetic form comes into fruition and becomes, undoubtedly, social. What attribute of poetry during this time makes it Victorian, then? It is this emphasis on the interior cognitive processes that, through the imagination, connect with the larger public community in order to create, ideally, cultural and personal meaningfulness. Thus, we witness uncertainty in poetic structure and a reliance on the affective reading experience, as Chapters 3 and 5 explore in their close readings of poetic forms. Victorian poems contain movements and rhythms toward an end, but shroud that end in uncertainty or ambiguity, leaving it to the reader to enact a similarly sympathetic response to the poem in order to bring both public and poem to their fulfillment.

CHAPTER 2

"O You Pretty Pecksie!"
The Collaborative Process of Mary Shelley and Percy Bysshe Shelley

On the first anniversary of Mary Wollstonecraft Shelley's death, her son Percy Florence and his wife Jane opened the box desk that remained near her bed. Upon opening it, they found her journals, and – most unsettling – Percy Bysshe Shelley's heart wrapped in the pages of *Adonais*.[1] Drowned at sea, Shelley's body was found with his face and hands eaten away; he was identifiable only by his clothes and a book of John Keats' poems, found in his pocket. Buried in the sand, according to customary Italian quarantine regulations, his body was exhumed on August 16, 1822, and burned on a pyre in the presence of Lord Byron, Edward Trelawney, and Leigh Hunt. Shelley's heart, however, refused to burn. Fished from the ashes, Trelawney gave it to Hunt, who eventually surrendered it to Mary Wollstonecraft Shelley.[2] Or so the legend goes.

The haunting image of these findings has its iteration in the return of Wollstonecraft Shelley's beloved box desk. Having been left in Marlow, Buckinghamshire, in 1818, the desk was returned on October 7, 1822.[3] It held precious memories for Wollstonecraft Shelley, and its return sparked recollections of voices and memories from her past, as she writes in her journal:

> What a scene to recur to! My William, Clara, Allegra are all talked of—They lived then—They breathed this air & their voices struck on my sense, their feet trod the earth beside me—& their hands were warm with blood & life when clasped in mine. Where are they all? This is too great an agony to be written about.[4]

The forms of life, writing, and vocal expression that the desk symbolizes and contains (the material heart, journal, and *Adonais*) remain essential to Wollstonecraft Shelley in her attempts at deciphering what the heart, those writings, and writing itself intends. This entry emphasizes the materiality of the box's return at the same time as it outlines intangible voices and presence – her children, William and Clara; Allegra, Jane

"Claire" Clairmont's illegitimate child with Lord Byron; her past life and the agony of her immense loss. Such associations stand for something beyond language: the affective, transcendent, sympathetic bond between Wollstonecraft Shelley and her circle of companions – living or dead. This bond began in 1814 with the commencement of Mary Wollstonecraft Godwin and Percy Bysshe Shelley's collaboration.

In July 1814, Wollstonecraft Godwin and Shelley initiated one of the most famous romantic partnerships in British literary history when they evaded William Godwin's watchful eye and eloped to the continent. In the second entry of the couple's shared elopement journal, dated July 29, 1814, Wollstonecraft Godwin makes her first contribution (indicated throughout this chapter in passages containing both hands by plain text; Shelley's hand is indicated by italics): *"Mary was there. S.helley was also with me."*[5] Here, Wollstonecraft Godwin asserts her own presence, in her own hand, in the concluding words: "with me." Inserting herself into the lines of the travel journal, Wollstonecraft Godwin makes the journal collaborative by making space for her voice, her words. In the shared journals, a sympathetic collaboration takes place during the couple's early elopement, life together, and travels.[6] This chapter examines entries in the initially shared "Shelley and Mary's Journal Book" and shows the burgeoning collaboration between them, to suggest the ways in which formal elements of these journal entries illuminate the interlocked system of collaborative connection and interpersonal identification engaged by the couple.[7] Using the lens of sympathetic accommodation and assimilation, I trace these entries for evidence of convergence and collaboration. This examination underscores new insights into Wollstonecraft Shelley's voice and development as a writer and establishes Shelley's assimilation of her narrative tone and form. By investigating these entries in both the transcribed and manuscript forms, I posit that a multiplicity of collaborative processes takes hold: finishing each other's sentences, leaving textual space for the other, and creating dialogue or speaking directly to the other upon the written page. Tracing the entries as a way of marking the couple's convergence and examining the ways in which the Shelleys attempt to redefine themselves from singular individualism to a radical pluralism, we see the beginnings of a sympathetic collaboration taking place within these shared pages, a collaboration that ultimately lends itself to narrative form in Wollstonecraft Shelley's *Frankenstein* (1818 and 1831).

Joint authorship and collaboration were issues of conscious investment in the late eighteenth and nineteenth centuries. Recent literary readings of eighteenth- and nineteenth-century familial and friendly affection contribute to, in Christopher Flint's words, "widespread cultural reassessment of kinship and affective behavior."[8] These reassessments took on particular importance in the 1790s as relationships in the Romantic period became understood in terms of shared sympathy and understanding, as well as political solidarity. Indeed, recent scholarship on the Joseph Johnson Circle has discussed the importance of such circles and networks in the events of the Romantic period, revealing insights gleaned from studying collective communities and groups.[9] As Marilyn Butler rightly notes, questions of proprietorship, ownership, and property were central during the period: "Of the three revolutionary keywords, Liberty, Equality, Fraternity, we sometimes neglect the active political meaning of the second and third." While "Equality" becomes synonymous in Britain with an attack on a property in the counter-revolutionary period of the early nineteenth century, "Fraternity scatters into sociability, communitarianism, co-operatives, and combinations."[10] Fraternity is, first and foremost, a relational bond that compels individuals to live as equals – with equal rights and duties. In *Political Fraternity*, Angel Pujol clarifies that fraternity, as it derives from the French Revolutionary ideals, "tells us that *all of us, all people* have the right to be assured all the means necessary for us to be as socially and politically free as any other member of the community."[11] Fraternity offers this sense of equality because all are "equally necessary for the formation and representation of community."[12] Drawing from this 1790s circle, which included Mary Wollstonecraft and William Godwin, as a precursor to the Mary Shelley–Percy Shelley collaboration, I want to consider the Shelley collaboration as a form of "Fraternity" – indebted to the affiliations and beliefs of writers like Mary Wollstonecraft Shelley's parents in the late eighteenth century.

The Johnson Circle – and similar circles or networks – has become a key site in Romanticism as scholarship has come to appreciate the importance of circles and coteries of writers and intellectuals.[13] Johnson's reputation among Romanticists rests on understandings of the word "liberal": "In his case,' Marilyn Gaull writes, "it meant generous, ranging, inclusive eclectic, committed, inquisitive, non-judgmental, liberal as in liberal education."[14] As a publisher and bookseller, Johnson's network was expansive and intricate; his circle generated more circles, groups united around shared progressive political ideals and shared dinners. These networks are interesting because "such complex, communal sites of cultural production reveal the creative process in different ways."[15] Shelley, too, like Samuel Taylor Coleridge before him, was keen to establish such a communal site of productivity: on September 30, 1814, he writes in the shared journal of a discussion involving the *"possibility of converting & liberating two heiresses—Arrange a plan on this subject."*[16] In this entry, Shelley refers to his sisters, Elizabeth and Hellen, and details plans arranged with Wollstonecraft Godwin and Claire Clairmont (Wollstonecraft Godwin's stepsister who accompanied the couple during their elopement and lived with them until October 1820) to form a social group of their own. Such a group would include Thomas Hookham, Thomas Love Peacock, and Thomas Jefferson Hogg. Referred to by Clairmont in her journal as "an Association of philosophical people,"[17] the group planned to escape to the west of Ireland and set up an "ideal society of liberalized individuals."[18] As Kenneth Neill Cameron points out in *Shelley and His Circle*, although the plans for the social group fell through, "it is very important in proving conclusively that Shelley was still dreaming of illustrating by example that a group of liberalized people could live ideally."[19] The Johnson circle, envisioned as contiguous, and featuring intellectual exchange and cross-fertilization among those gathered, serves as a precedent for both the liberalized group initiated in 1814 and the ongoing intellectual exchange between Wollstonecraft Shelley and Shelley throughout their lives, an exchange initially witnessed in the couple's shared elopement journal. Tracing the lineage of Romantic literary circles and the participation of Mary Wollstonecraft and William Godwin – figures of importance to both Wollstonecraft Shelley and Shelley – in these circles indicates not only a precedent but an illustration of the kind of liberal community – "Fraternity" – imagined within the shared written pages of Wollstonecraft Godwin and Shelley's collaborative journal. In other words, this chapter reads these collaborative productions as a revised radical Fraternity that allows the couple to attempt shared vocal expression; indeed, examining the form of these journals shows a sympathetic concord, a moral community, happening in the very process of the couple's collaboration through conversations that occur upon the written page, conversations that surely inspired lively debate.

Circulating Feeling in Travels and Shared Life-Writing

Mary did not know our danger. She was resting on ↑between↓ my knees that were unable to support her. She did not speak or look. But I felt that she was there. I had time in that moment to reflect & even to reason upon death. It was rather a thing of discomfort & of disappointment than [?terror] to me. We could never be separated, but in death we might not know & feel our union as now. [...][20]

This first entry in "Shelley and Mary's journal book," dated July 28, 1814, and written by Shelley, dramatically details the couple's danger and his retrospective emotional reaction to Wollstonecraft Godwin's presence as they embark on this scandalous journey. In the above lines, he uses their situation to shift pronominally from the individuated *"I"* to *"we,"* marking the couple's convergence. Moreover, Shelley provides a glimpse into their physical union – he feels Wollstonecraft Godwin's bodily presence, her weight pressing upon his knees, and notes that he is physically *"unable to support her."* He also alludes to their affective and sympathetic union with his emphasis on nonphysical feeling: Wollstonecraft Godwin does not *"speak or look. But I felt that she was there."* It is with this almost ghost-like sense of her presence that Shelley shifts tonally to discomfort as he reasons that their union is physically bound: *"in death we might not know & feel our union as now."* Marking these pronominal and tonal shifts – and noting the importance of feeling in all forms – is likewise integral to understanding the second citation, dated July 29, as the couple enter France.

The couple shared their notebooks, reading and commenting upon each other's work. As Charles Robinson notes in his introduction to *The Frankenstein Notebooks*, "There are times in the [*Frankenstein*] manuscript when you can actually 'see' MWS and PBS at work on the Notebooks at the same time, possibly sitting side by side and using the same pen and ink to draft the novel and at the same time to enter corrections."[21] The manuscript of their first shared journal, then, represents the genesis of this joint writing process, beginning on July 29, with Wollstonecraft Godwin's initial entrance:

> *France Tuesday Friday. 29*
> *I said—Mary look. the sun rises over France. We walked over the sands to the Inn. We were shewn into an apartment that answered the purpose both of a sitting & sleeping room. Mary was there. S.helley was also w*ith me.[22]

In this shared circulation, perhaps Wollstonecraft Godwin's added "[w]ith me" continues Shelley's thought – noticeably without punctuation, as though trailing off into the margins – at the same time as her addition asserts her vocal presence and authority. Indeed, the manuscript reveals that Wollstonecraft Godwin's entrance – like their converged union at this early date – is, in fact, seamless: Shelley's hand begins the w, with Wollstonecraft Godwin completing the rest of the phrase, evidenced in what visually appears to be a switch in pen and marked by her squared characters. In other words, the couple completes each other's sentences, a characteristic that remains constant in the later entries of 1814. Also consistent in the 1814 entries is this back and forth shift in pronouns, occurring even after Wollstonecraft Godwin has installed herself as the subject of entries, a mixture of self-reference and second person plural.

The collaborative journal supports, in a broader sense, a new understanding of literary collaboration that is necessarily informed by the mechanics of the writing process, illustrated in the formal elements of the prose as well as textual or marginal traces within the manuscripts.[23] The couple's journals and letters point to the extensive collaborative nature of their intellectual and literary work, which eventually included editing each other's work, translations and transcribing, encouraging the other's work, and contributing to the same projects. Indeed, by focusing throughout this study on collaboration as a verb and foregrounding the process of coming together, we are afforded a vision of the networks involved in the collaborative process. The couple's life-writing promotes the plurality of ways in which they come together: encouragement, contribution, transcription, and editing. Throughout their relationship and the trials they endured, the Shelleys relied upon their collaboration to promote their shared sympathy, and to develop and articulate their individual artistic voices. Using the couple's initially shared journal, then, allows for a fuller understanding of the development of their collaborative process, which influences both Wollstonecraft Godwin and Shelley's literary productions.[24]

During the summer of 1814, while in Paris, Wollstonecraft Godwin and Shelley purchased the green notebook that was to become "Shelley and Mary's Journal Book." On July 28, 1814, the couple left London and eloped to France, bringing Jane – later changed to the more alliterative "Claire" or "Clara" – Clairmont with them. From July to August, the threesome journeyed through France to Switzerland, returning, when Shelley realized the depletion of his funds without the promise of future money, down the Rhine to Rotterdam. On September 13, the journal documents their return to London, where Shelley remained in danger of arrest for debt from October to November. At this point, Shelley's entries in the journal decrease as he constantly travels for two reasons: (1) his first wife, Harriet Shelley, was pregnant with his child, Charles; and (2) Shelley had hopes for securing his debts. Wollstonecraft Godwin returned from their tour pregnant, giving birth to a premature daughter on February 22, 1815 (who subsequently died on March 6). As Shelley became absorbed in his own personal and literary concerns, keeping the journal current falls upon Wollstonecraft Godwin; the journals, as a whole, provide "a reflection of

[her] development over the years which is seen nowhere else in her letters or her published works."²⁵

Shelley's initial entry on July 28, 1814 suggests that the journal was specifically begun as a documentation of their union, and further, as an account of their elopement travels. While elopement was not unusual for Shelley, since he eloped with both Harriet Shelley and Wollstonecraft Godwin, the collaborative journal remains unique to the Mary Wollstonecraft Shelley–Percy Bysshe Shelley relationship. It is possible that the shared journal was Wollstonecraft Godwin's idea, as she sought to establish her own literary credentials. In Shelley's entry on August 2, he references a box that Wollstonecraft Godwin brought with her, containing her juvenile writings and letters. When they traveled on to Switzerland, the box was left behind, making it impossible to establish her credentials as her mother, Wollstonecraft, had done. Therefore, it is plausible that Wollstonecraft Godwin may have begun this shared journal with similar intent. The shared journal also functions as a creation of a private world, experienced by the couple, to the exclusion of others and particular personal events: the initial exclusion of Clairmont, Harriet Shelley's pregnancy, and the birth of Charles Shelley. Although present throughout the elopement tour, there are multiple entries – significantly the aforementioned July 28 and 29 entries – that make no mention of Clairmont. Like Mary Jean Corbett, I read this exclusion as representative of their "conjugal privacy": "As the textual space they share, the journal constitutes a realm of conjugal privacy secure from what was construed, in the early part of their relationship, as Claire's intrusion."²⁶ Moreover, this exclusion from the couple's sympathetic concord is textually evident in the distancing created by dashes within entries.²⁷ Another prominent exclusion from the 1814 portion is Harriet Shelley's pregnancy and the birth of Charles on November 30, an event that explains a portion of Shelley's frequent travels during October and November. These exclusions, formally constructed through dashes and blatant omissions, create a private construction of a pseudo-honeymoon experience rather than an accurate reflection of the trip itself.

Corbett emphasizes the importance of "intersubjective connection" in Wollstonecraft Godwin's journals: "the pleasure and power of journal-writing both proceed from and depend upon the participation of another reader and writer."²⁸ Wollstonecraft Godwin structures her life in the journal upon intersubjectivity with Shelley, which is why it is important to distinguish her initial phrase in the 1814 shared journal's second entry: "*with me.*" Ending this entry with both voices showcases the couple's reliance upon each other, the necessarily communitarian understanding of their collaboration. The private circulation of feeling and sympathy shown within the individual entries mimics the physical circulation of texts and ideas between Wollstonecraft Godwin and Shelley. Through exclusion, the journal locates the importance of collaboration, not only in their shared process, but in their participation as readers and their response in future entries. In this way, we can read the shared journal as a revised form of radical Fraternity, founded upon conversation (reader response). More than simply a record of romantic flight, the 1814 journal initiates a circulation of feeling between the travelers and a growing sympathetic concord between Wollstonecraft Godwin and Shelley as they embark on a personal life together and on a shared literary life. As a mark of their union — because of its illicit nature — the couple asserts their identity in the form of written collaboration, traced in their continued attempt to formulate a vocal blending that defines themselves as a united "we."

The initial entries in the first journal locate the couple's attempts at convergence, witnessing the initial hesitancy or discomfort experienced by both Wollstonecraft Godwin and Shelley as they begin their collaborative endeavor. Such an attempt illustrates the implausibility of sympathetic unison and locates the problems inherent in conceiving the gap between individuals — two individuals cannot converge into the same person, as Adam Smith noted in *Theory of Moral Sentiments*. Yet, through assimilation, two individuals become participants in a concord: through a shared circulation of feeling, Wollstonecraft Godwin and Shelley, in Smith's terms, "become in some measure the same person." Shelley, in fact, references this cognitive circulation of sympathetic feeling upon the couple's arrival in Paris:

> Tuesday 2 August
> We arrived at Paris. We engaged lodgings [a]t the Hotel de Vienne.—Mary looked over with me the papers contained in her box They consisted of her own writings, letters from her father & her friends, & my letters. She shewed me one letter from Harriet which recommended her to write such that would to me which should calm me, & enable me to subdue my love for her. —She promised that I should be permitted to read & study those productions of her mind that preceded our intercourse. I shall claim this promise at Uri. In the evening we walked to the Gardens of the Thuilleries.[29]

If sympathy is, for Smith, "the faculty by which inner mental states are shared among individuals," Shelley is particularly interested in bridging the gap between himself and Wollstonecraft Godwin by "*read*[ing] *and study*[ing] *those productions of her mind.*" Indeed, Shelley's "*claim*" of Wollstonecraft Godwin's "*promise*" highlights the male privilege that feminist scholarship finds problematic when considering the extent of Shelley's exertion of control over his lover/wife.[30] And yet, in these early life-writings, Shelley's insufficiency and inadequacy are on full display, indicating emasculation. Indeed, this August 2 entry identifies pronoun shifts, distinguishing the united "*we*" from individual actions. The use of the initial dash separates the united image of self from Wollstonecraft Godwin's independent action of showing her box. Within the dash, Shelley's pronoun references remain somewhat unclear: Wollstonecraft Godwin shows a letter from Harriet recommending "*her*" to write and calm Shelley's love for "*her*." The "*her*" in question appears to be Wollstonecraft Godwin; and the reference to Harriet remains distanced from Shelley's shared intimacy with Wollstonecraft Godwin, an intimacy echoed here in Shelley's restatement of Wollstonecraft Godwin's initial "*with me*." In contrast to the sympathy between Wollstonecraft Godwin and Shelley, Harriet's presence in this entry remains distant: eloping with Wollstonecraft Godwin, Shelley has neglected his first wife and children. This first Shelleyan concord had failed.

When Wollstonecraft Godwin, at sixteen years old, returned to London from an extended stay in Dundee and met the poet who had impressed her father in March 1814, she represented to Shelley his philosophical ideal. In a letter to Hogg, dated April 10, 1814, an enraptured Shelley writes of his initial feelings:

> I speak thus of Mary now—& so intimately are our natures now united, that I feel whilst I describe her excellencies as if I were an egoist expatiating upon his own perfections—Then, how deeply did I not feel my inferiority, how willingly confess myself far surpassed in originality, in genuine elevation & magnificence of the intellectual nature until she consented to share her capabilities with me.[31]

In this letter, Shelley expresses his intimate awareness of their union and shared personage, before drawing attention to his inadequacy: Wollstonecraft Godwin's knowledge and originality far surpass his own. Shelley's insufficiency seems to be a recurring motif. Recalling his initial journal entry on his elopement with Wollstonecraft Godwin, Shelley noted that he was physically unable to support her. Here, in this early letter, Shelley is mentally insufficient. Humbled by her presence, Shelley is drawn to Wollstonecraft Godwin primarily because of her intellect and the radical union she represents – the daughter of his idols, Godwin and Wollstonecraft. In contrast to the obligation Shelley felt to marry Harriet Westbrook, he describes his love for Wollstonecraft Godwin, "the noblest and most excellent of human beings," in a letter to Harriet, dated September 14, 1814.³² His attachment to Wollstonecraft Godwin, Shelley writes, "neither could nor ought to have been overcome: our spirits & [*blank space*] are united. We met with passion, she has resigned all for me."³³ The blank space in the letter visualizes a union that is beyond language, that is a cognitive process prior to a bodily (or sexual) one – "she has resigned all for me." This prioritization of their intellectual union, expressed in Shelley's letters, becomes realized also in the couple's journal. The August 2 entry, then, establishes the height of the sympathetic collaboration at work in the coauthored journal. Shelley emphasizes his desire to, utilizing the Smithian metaphor, "enter into" the sentiments and principles of Wollstonecraft Godwin's mind, an engagement that she "*promises.*" This sympathetic contract – to be claimed at Uri – verbalizes the affective circulation of shared understanding and feeling.

Once the couple establishes regularity in their traveling plans, the journal's travel entries take on an alternating pattern by their authors, documenting their shared and individual daily activities. In this way, the journal circumnavigates a private articulation of shared thought, which, as Mary Jean Corbett notes, is complimentary to Shelley's "empathic ideal of heterosexual love as unreserved communion between like souls."³⁴ Eschewing the documentation of individual introspection, Corbett argues that the journals record their representation of daily life by "marking time." "'This joint method of 'marking time,'" she states, "underwrites the household and helps to constitute it as a site of value; the journal gives shape and form to the experience of a shared daily life as much by what it excludes—the interior or psychological realm, for example—as by what it reports."³⁵ Complicating Corbett's argument, however, is an approach that foregrounds interiority by exploring the places of convergence and dialogue. Examining the text in places where writing converges, where the indication of shared circulation occurs, offers remarkable insight into the couple's collaborative process. The sympathetic exchange of ideas happens not only within the written lines, but formally, visibly documenting the couple's growing assimilation and concord.

The entries covering the elopement tour predominately follow a similar formula: an account of the travel departure and arrival, a walk, some reading, and discussion by Wollstonecraft Godwin and Shelley concerning plans. For example, on August 23, Wollstonecraft Godwin begins the entry (in plain text, below) describing their arrival to Lucerne; however, it is Shelley who closes it (in italics) and completes the record for the following day:

> Teusday [sic] 23ᵈ
> We leave Sursee at 4 o clock and arrive at Lucerne about 10—after breakfast we hire a boat to take us down the lake—Shelley & Mary go out & buy several needful things—and we then embark—It is a most divine day—the fa↑r↓ther we advance the more magnificent are the shores of the lake—rock and pine forests cloacking ↑covering↓ the feet of the immense mountains—we read part of l'Abbé Barruels historie de Jacobinism—we land at Bessen—go to the wrong inn where a most comical scene ensues. *We sleep at Brunen. Before we sleep however, we look out of the window.*³⁶

The dashes in this entry seem to serve as breaks in actions and visualize a division that establishes intimacy by separating actions completed by Wollstonecraft Godwin and Shelley alone. This intimacy is reinforced through their self-identification by proper name: "Shelley & Mary." However, concerning the couple's growing concord, this entry is differentiated in its attempt to describe the magnificence and immensity of their natural surroundings. Very rarely does Wollstonecraft Godwin attempt such a description; it is usually Shelley who elaborates on such scenes. Comparing her entry with Shelley's earlier one from August 18 illustrates sympathy's social process of assimilation among those within one's circle:

> Thursday 18
> *We leave Maurt at 4. After some hours of tedious traveling thro' a most beautiful country, we arrive at Noé. From the summit of one of the hills, we see the whole expanse of the valley, filled with a white undulating mist over which the piny hills p[i]erced like islands. The sun had just risen, & a ray of red light lay on the waves of this fluctuating vapour. To the west opposite the sun, it seemed driven by the light against the rocks in immense masses of foaming cloud; until it became lost in the distance mixing its tints with the fleecy sky. –At Noé, whilst our postilion waited, we walked into the forest of pines. It was a scene of enchantment where every sound & sight contributed to charm. [...]*³⁷

Here, Shelley characteristically describes the poetic beauty of his surroundings, using periphrasis. In Shelley's entry, he likens the "piny hills" to islands and describes the sunlight breaking through the clouds to form a "fleecy sky." Using "piny" and "fleecy," Shelley embellishes his language to raise the register and promote grander poetic effect. The comparison of Shelley's depiction of the "piny hills p[i]erced like islands" and "rocks in immense masses of foaming cloud" with Wollstonecraft Godwin's later description of her "divine day" shows similarities, and striking differences, in their language. Like Shelley, Wollstonecraft Godwin focuses on the "rock and pine forests cloacking ↑covering↓ the feet of the immense mountains," descriptive phrases that are oddly inconsistent with Wollstonecraft Godwin's earlier voice. While Shelley's entry chooses

Latinate-based adjectives – such as "undulating" and "fluctuating" – and a nonce word – "piny" – to elevate his language to poetic diction, Wollstonecraft Godwin's choice of adjectives remains prosaic and factual, despite increased descriptors. Whereas Shelley's elevated diction and periphrasis allow for an imaginative transportation – to use the language of Smithean sympathy – into the scene at Noé, Wollstonecraft Godwin's prosaic description keeps its readers on the written page. Looking at the transcription, little else remains to be mentioned. However, the manuscript has uneven spacing, beginning with her description of "the magnificent [...] shores of the lake." These lines creep closer to the lines above, visually documenting Wollstonecraft Godwin's attempt at poetic prose as noticeably different from the rest of her entry. Further, the strikethrough of the verb and replacement of "covering" for "cloacking" begins her visible accommodation of Shelley's descriptive entries. In other words, this entry seems to be an exercise in stylistic diction, with Shelley in the role of educator and Wollstonecraft Godwin as a willing pupil. Such an exercise is reminiscent of the couple's bouts-rimés in their early relationship. In these poetic games, one player compiles a list of words that rhyme and gives the list to another player, whose role is to compose a poem fitting the rhymed ends in the order placed upon the list.[38] Reading the difference in Wollstonecraft Godwin's poetic prose as a stylistic exercise modeled on a poetic game enjoyed by the couple locates the pleasure inherent in the assimilation of language. Finally, another stylistic aspect of the manuscript not included in the transcribed *Journals* is a double strikethrough of an unintelligible character before Wollstonecraft Godwin's choice of the word "feet." Shortly after this brief description, she abandons Shelley's style and resumes her regular entry formula, referring to the couple's reading of Baurruel's *Mémoires pour servir à l'histoire du Jacobinisme* and their landing at "Bessen."

These shifts indicate a growing awareness of difference in narrative entries, a difference that becomes normalized from this point forward in the remainder of the 1814 travel entries as Shelley adopts Wollstonecraft Godwin's narrative style of journal entries. Forgoing his poetic descriptions by assimilating to statements of nondescriptive fact, Shelley completes Wollstonecraft Godwin's entry on August 23. In these closing lines, which bear resemblance to the Creature appearing outside of the window during Victor Frankenstein's honeymoon in Wollstonecraft Shelley's novel, Shelley's sympathetic assimilation occurs in the last sentence: *"Before we sleep however, we look out of the window."* What appears outside of the window? Shelley's usual poetic description is missing. This sentence is repeated at the close of the next entry on August 24: "*We come home look out of the window & go to bed.*"³⁹ These entries perform a shared understanding – a sympathetic concord – between the couple: they are literally coming home (in each other), looking out the window together, and going to bed (presumably sexually and literally). Ideologically, this understanding pinpoints their attempt at outward pluralism, and a willingness to accommodate the other's sentiments and formal expressions. While the entries' narratives show the completion of each other's thoughts and a reliance upon readership, the entries' form also gestures to their defined plural identity through a vocal blending. If anything, examining the process by which these authors create their narratives demonstrates the fleetingness of imaginative sympathy and the importance of sympathetic concord between the collaborators.

Such emphasis on the readerly response and conversation within the couple's entries locates the affective circulation – or, in Smithean terms, transportation – of feeling in the form chosen by the couple to begin their shared literary life: travel writing, a physical transportation. This affective sympathetic bond is clearest in those entries in which the couple creates a dialogue between themselves. Knowing that the journal is circulated privately, these instances reveal the pleasure that they take in their shared exchange and make tangible a form of the "imaginary" exchange of places, the ways in which Wollstonecraft Godwin and Shelley enter into one another's minds, hearts, and written language. While we cannot reconstruct the communication between the partners, their life-writing allows us to consider the importance of conversation to the collaborative process – there is a natural give-and-take, a natural responsiveness that arises in sympathetic collaboration, foregrounding collaboration as an evolving process composed of multiple parts. Linked in the bonds of fellow-feeling, they become confidants within the written page, as seen by Wollstonecraft Godwin's entry on November 9, when she directly addresses Shelley: "—[Jane] is very sullen with Shelley—Well never mind. my love we are happy—."⁴⁰ Beyond this direct address, evidence of their literary collaboration is revealed through their encouragement of one another's literary endeavors. As Wollstonecraft Shelley herself acknowledged, Shelley encouraged her ambition to write and "obtain literary reputation, which even on my own part I cared for then, though since I have become indifferent to it." Although she writes of Shelley's encouragement in reference to *Frankenstein* in her 1831 preface, the shared journal demonstrates that Shelley had already "judge[d] how far I possess the promise of better things hereafter."⁴¹ On September 10, 1814,

Shelley describes a story written by Wollstonecraft Godwin which is, unfortunately, no longer extant: "*Mary begins Hate. & gives S. the greater pleasure. S. writes part of his Romance.*"[42] Shelley receives "*the greater pleasure*" certainly due to Wollstonecraft Godwin literary production, but also from reading her work. Knowing that the journal would be read by Wollstonecraft Godwin, Shelley emphasizes the esteem that he holds for her achievements – even at this early date, prior to drafting *Frankenstein* – while he emphasizes his reaction to and encouragement of her writing. Wollstonecraft Godwin, too, corroborates the pleasure taken by Shelley in this circulation, as the entry on the following day reveals her continued writing.

Reunifying Circles: Free Love and Ideal Sympathetic Communities

By reading these entries as a constructed narrative placed contextually in a readerly exchange and response – in other words, as communal – Wollstonecraft Godwin and Shelley's collaborative process within the shared journal indicates the sympathetic exchange between minds united in concord. Embracing the 1790s radicalism and deriving inspiration from the Godwin–Wollstonecraft relationship, the couple, as Scott Krawczyk argues, "at once resuscitated and reunified [this earlier] collaborative consciousness in a marriage of creative and physical intimacy."[43] Living the philosophy espoused by William Godwin in *Political Justice* (1793), Shelley left his first wife, whom he no longer loved, to be with Wollstonecraft Godwin:

> Friendship, if by friendship we understand that affection for an individual which is measured singly by what we know of its worth, is one of the most exquisite gratifications, perhaps one of the most improving exercises of a rational mind. Friendship therefore may be expected to come in aid of the sexual intercourse, to refine its grossness and increase its delight. A friendship of this sort has no necessary connection with the cowardice which so notoriously characterizes the present system of marriage, where each party desires to find in the other that flattering indulgence that overlooks every frailty, and carefully removes the occasions of fortitude.[44]

For Godwin, friendship – and all personal relationships – arises from the demand that justice informs all human actions. Godwinian justice involves a disinterested benevolence and subordination of the self to society.[45] Friendship is a rational principle, arising from reflection, with the greater interest of society in mind. In the late eighteenth century, the concept of friendship was under debate. While some philosophies focus on the psychological conceptions of friendship, others articulate a moral component underlying the concept. For instance, in 1793, Charles Atkinson notes in *The Mind's Monitor*:

> A real Friend is the agreeable Moderator in all our Actions and inward Sensations. His Genius we carefully consult in all that concerns our Amusement and Interest. It is his principles which actuate our Motives. [...] The more learned our Friend, the greater his Value. By his superior Knowledge we are instructed to adhere to such Principles as will not only obtain for us a lasting Pleasure, but also render us of more Benefit to ourselves and to others.[46]

In this view, the language of friendship is influenced by the framework of moral philosophy, structured around theories of sympathy and personal identity as it configures sociability and community. The "real Friend" becomes that person who provides a social mirror, to return to Smith's metaphor, that conforms to societal principles in order to provide an individual with "more Benefit to ourselves and to others" – in other words, to form a community that provides "lasting Pleasure."

Friendship denotes not only sympathy, but political solidarity based upon egalitarianism and Fraternity – recalling the Romantic keywords of liberty, equality, and Fraternity. As Gurion Taussig notes: "Within the highly charged political landscape of the 1790s, the term 'friend' loses its ideological innocence as it is appropriated by revolutionary and counter-revolutionary ideologies alike."[47] Indeed, friendship took on a larger role within the discourse of patriotism, beginning in the 1760s and continuing throughout the late eighteenth century: "Friendship came to be seen as an essential aspect of British liberty. Conversation was interpreted as an unequivocal symptom of 'social freedom,' and betrayal of friendship was equated with betrayal of country."[48] By engaging with the circulating ideas surrounding friendship as it configures community, we see Shelley's commitment to radical reform and what he, later, refers to as a freedom granted by "burst[ing] and rend[ing]" the "mortal chain / Of Custom."[49]

By the end of the summer of 1814, Shelley "genuinely believed that in shaking off the bonds of matrimony when a relationship had faltered he was living his life in accordance with a set of principles that would reform the world."[50] In Wollstonecraft Godwin, Shelley found his ideal, and in their living situation, he found the model environment to begin sharing his reformist ideas. He began with free love, introducing Thomas Jefferson Hogg into their community, and encouraging Hogg and Wollstonecraft Godwin to have an affair, an idea which she, initially, found agreeable.

The radical nature of free love and its ties to Godwinian understandings of friendship – in that friendship "aid[s...] sexual intercourse, to refine its grossness and increase its delight"[51] – normalizes, in a sense, the sexual openness of the threesome through its liberal impulses. By January 1815, Hogg spent much time with the couple, and the three discussed spirit worlds and the aforementioned "Association of philosophical people." In this communal circle, Shelley believed he had found the perfect group of people who understood the importance of an intellectual community. However, we would be remiss not to consider Shelley's exertion of privilege by questioning the consensual nature of this union. In many ways, while Wollstonecraft Godwin acquiesces to Shelley's formation of a *ménage a trois* with Hogg, her loyalty remains to the poet. Wollstonecraft Godwin's letters to Hogg reveal her fluctuating feelings. As expressed clearly in one such letter dated January 24, 1815, Shelley forms the center of the threesome:

> you [Hogg] are to teach me Italian you know & how many books we will read together but our still greater happiness will be in Shelley—I who love him so tenderly & entirely whose life hangs on the beam of his eye and whose whole soul is entirely wrapt up in him—you who have so sincere a friendship for him to make him happy[52]

This letter perfectly captures Wollstonecraft Godwin's youthful voice – at only seventeen, her writing to Hogg is different in both style and tone to the voice in her shared journal with Shelley. Indeed, the majority of Wollstonecraft Godwin's letters to Hogg reveal a relationship predicated on learning and friendship, with her "greater happiness" and tenderness reserved for Shelley. Formally illustrating this demarcation between the two men, she again employs the dash, distancing her poetic and ethereal description of her love for Shelley from her practical friendship with Hogg. It is in fact, telling, that – in the same letter – we witness a brief instance of Wollstonecraft Godwin attempting to illuminate the meaning of the *menage*: "When I think of all that we three in ea--------."[53] Significantly, she cuts herself off, leaving only a line instead of a true utterance. Apologizing to Hogg for losing her train of thought, she blames the interruption upon the entrance of Shelley and Clairmont, "which is not a very good accompaniment when one is writing a letter to one, one loves."[54] Of course, the interruption could be a form of self-censorship, calling into question the consensual queerness of this community's sexual openness, highlighting the awkwardness that she feels despite her philosophical inclination toward free love.

Wollstonecraft Godwin's ambivalence toward the principles of free love during this strange wooing period by Hogg is well documented and, combined with the premature birth and subsequent death of Wollstonecraft Godwin and Shelley's first unnamed daughter along with her continued annoyance at Clairmont's presence, form the basis for the downfall of this initial philosophical community. "The business is finished," Wollstonecraft Godwin wrote at the end of the first volume of the 1814–1815 journal. Drawing a line, she initiates a separation from the "business" – Clairmont, Hogg, financial affairs – that occupied the couple's initial years together and focuses again on establishing a sense of radical pluralism with an emphasis on "our": "I begin a new journal with our regeneration—."55

The regeneration that Wollstonecraft Godwin hoped for in the closing pages of her first journal emerged in the couple's shared domestic and literary lives, with the birth of William on January 24, 1816, and their individual literary productions. In a letter written to Leigh Hunt on March 2, 1817, Wollstonecraft Shelley describes their home in England as "very political as well as poetical"; indeed, in such an atmosphere of mutual support and admiration, the couple spent their time reading and writing.56 The extensive book lists in Wollstonecraft Shelley's journals attest to the development of a learned atmosphere, indicating both individual and shared reading experiences. Putting aside their earlier experimentation with free love, the couple concentrated instead on establishing a liberal community of intellectuals in which ideas could be freely exchanged. Wollstonecraft Godwin and Shelley created an environment of productivity by inviting Thomas Peacock into their circle in 1815. When Shelley wrote *Alastor* in the autumn of 1815, he narrated a dilemma which preoccupied him for the remainder of his life: whether a poet needed companionship or isolation to produce a work of genius. In some ways, this poem's composition has its roots in the influences of collaboration; the title was suggested by Peacock, and Shelley discussed with Wollstonecraft Godwin the failures of William Wordsworth, evidenced in her derisive reading note on his *Excursion* on September 14, 1814: "Shelley [...] brings home Wordsworths Excursion of which we read a part—much disappointed—He is a slave."57 For the first time since the couple's elopement, Shelley was poetically productive, as he gathered a sympathetic community around himself: "less avowedly political than the ideal communities of his imagination," the Bishopsgate community with Peacock "provided him with an opportunity to think seriously about how poetry might provide a more subtle and philosophically ambitious vehicle for reforming the world."58 Understanding the influences of the sympathetic community upon literary production illuminates, also, nineteenth-century liberalism's concentration on individuation, embodied in lived experience and intellectual discussion, and expressed in literary experimentation.

Following *Alastor*, Shelley continued his productive streak by writing *Laon and Cythna* (later heavily censored and published as *The Revolt of Islam*) in 1817. Beginning his longest poem with a dedication "To Mary ---- ----," Shelley attributes his writing, in the first stanza, to the companionship and sympathy espoused by "mine own heart's home"[59] and considers Wollstonecraft Godwin – and his fame – in light of the generative powers of their collaborative union: "[…] that ere my fame become / A star among the stars of mortal night, / If it indeed may cleave its natal gloom, / Its doubtful promise this I would unite / With thy beloved name, thou Child of love and light."[60] The poem's form enacts the poet's view of his coupling with Wollstonecraft Godwin: Shelley unites himself with Wollstonecraft Godwin in the formal symmetry of the Spenserian stanza, which lends itself to rhyme because of the emphasis on "unite" and "light." With this union, Shelley intends to make his fame. Indeed, Shelley's awareness of his union with the collaborative and radical legacy instilled in his partner is made explicit by his reference to her parentage: "thou Child of love and light" born of "glorious parents."[61] In stanza eight, he writes that he is "no more companionless" and recalls, much like his earlier letter to Hogg, Wollstonecraft Godwin's ability to share in his intellectual endeavors:

> Thou Friend, whose presence on my wintry heart
> Fell, like bright Spring upon some herbless plain;
> How beautiful and calm and free thou wert
> In thy young wisdom, when the mortal chain
> Of Custom thou didst burst and rend in twain,
> And walked as free as light the clouds among,
> Which many envious slave then breathed in vain
> From his dim dungeon, and my spirit sprung
> To meet thee from the woes which had begirt it long.[62]

Written as a Spenserian stanza, following the overall meter of *Laon and Cyntha*, the first line of stanza eight could be read as a line of iambic pentameter with a spondee on "Thou Friend." In this direct address to Wollstonecraft Godwin, the double stress of the spondee is further emphasized by Shelley's capitalization to reflect his admiration of Wollstonecraft Godwin's companionship. The specific placement of the break in the fourth line – "mortal chain / Of Custom" – indicates the break in a chain of custom, even before "burst[ing]" occurs. These enjambed lines comprise the stanza's center and esteem Wollstonecraft Godwin's ability to "burst and rend" the "mortal chain / Of Custom" by eloping with him and beginning a collaborative union. Indeed, the lines themselves, like Wollstonecraft Godwin, are "free."[63] Wollstonecraft Godwin walks freely, just as the poem is freed by enjambment, a freedom to which Shelley responds as his spirit is "sprung" across the enjambed line to meet her.[64] Shelley uses this enjambment as a way of formally embracing his partner's liberalness, at the same time as he sentimentalizes their union by uniting the lines rather than using periods. Using the Spenserian stanza offers Shelley the possibility of capturing a detailed narrative due to the form's sheer capacity.[65] By recalling the early days of their elopement, Shelley brings to mind his anxieties (evidenced in the desert-like and solitary imagery evoked throughout the eighth stanza), which he narrated in the first entry of their shared journal, when Wollstonecraft Godwin's bodily presence – "like bright Spring" – assured him of their safety. In this poetic retelling of Shelley's initial journal entry dated July 28, 1814, there are parallels to his feeling of anguish and expression of his affective union with Wollstonecraft Godwin. In the journal, Shelley notes that "*Mary did not know our danger.* [...] *She did not speak or look. But I felt that she was there*" before reflecting upon the "*discomfort & disappointment*" of death. Wollstonecraft Godwin's physical presence provides a means of assurance before the discomfort of his ruminations. Here, in this poetic stanza, he provides further insight into Wollstonecraft Godwin's role during this dangerous period of their union: "Thou Friend, whose presence on my wintry heart / Fell, like bright Spring upon some herbless plain." The emphatic double stress of Wollstonecraft Shelley as Friend further solidifies the couple's engagement with Godwinian friendship and fraternal community, providing a focus on the intellectual aspects of both their collaborative and personal relationship. Poetry, therefore, enables an expression of social and communal reform. Whereas, in the journal, Shelley is aware of his inability to support Wollstonecraft Godwin and of the "herbless plain" as a result of his morbid rumination, in poetry, the lyrical form draws attention to her ability to overturn Custom and embrace the liberal values they espouse. The social order is reformed in favor of a liberal collaboration. In this way, Shelley's literary productiveness during the period of 1816–1817 can be attributed to the influence of the shared life-writing that the couple used to initiate their life together; an influence that lends itself to the very stanza form Shelley chose to compose his poem, as the hexameter of the last line also gestures toward freedom from the octet's iambic pentameter.

During this same period, Wollstonecraft Shelley, too, recalled their elopement tour by piecing together a narrative of the couple's 1814 and

1816 travels into *History of a Six Weeks' Tour* (1817), a volume incorporating a multiplicity of forms (journal entries, letter writing, and poetry). Using the shared journal for its formal construct and narrative material in this collaborative publication, the sympathetic exchange witnessed in their shared life-writing remains instrumental to the collaboration at work formally occurring throughout the couple's corpus. By uniting Shelley's poetry with the couple's life-writing through the elopement journal, letters, and Wollstonecraft Shelley's published *History of a Six Weeks' Tour*, these generative moments in their relationship offer fresh insight into their collaboration and the ways in which this sympathetic process, accentuating Fraternity, lends itself to narrative form. Moreover, while preparing her collaborative publication with Shelley, Wollstonecraft Shelley remained devoted to writing and revising *Frankenstein* (1818), a manuscript written during the famed summer of 1816 and well-known to indicate the couple's collaboration.

Constructing *Frankenstein*: Animating Sympathetic Narratives

Recalling the significance of their 1814 journey narrated in their elopement journal, Wollstonecraft Godwin eagerly left England in the summer of 1816 when Shelley proposed they accompany Claire Clairmont to Switzerland in pursuit of Lord Byron. Bringing their child William with them, the couple landed with Clairmont at the chalet Chappuis (or Mont Alègre) on the banks of Lake Geneva near Byron and his physician, Dr. William Polidori. Wollstonecraft Godwin's terrifying, yet inspiring, nightmare and the narrative of the ghost story competition as the germination of *Frankenstein* is a myth almost as well-known as the novel itself. In the companionable atmosphere of the Villa Diodati, Wollstonecraft Godwin began to knit together ideas which she had been cultivating for years. Synthesizing the narratives and visions of her parents with Shelley's philosophies of the origins of life, and combining images and ideas collected and stored over a period of time, *Frankenstein* – like Shelley's *Alastor* – critiques isolated and selfish creativity.[66] In contrast to the third canto of *Childe Harold* written by Byron during this productive summer, Wollstonecraft Shelley's novel upholds and celebrates the idealized community of individuals that she and Shelley attempted to assemble in January 1814 and successfully gathered in the autumn of 1815 and summer of 1816. Concluding her 1831 account, in the oft-quoted "hideous progeny" passage, Wollstonecraft Shelley speaks directly of this communal process:

> And now, once again, I bid my hideous progeny go forth and prosper. I have an affection for it, for it was the offspring of happy days, when death and grief were but words, which found no true echo in my heart. Its several pages speak of many a walk, many a drive, and many a conversation, when I was not alone; and my companion was one whom, in this world, I shall never see more.[67]

Wollstonecraft Shelley's process here details a method in which ideas achieve fruition through "many a walk, many a drive, and many a conversation," a method absent from Victor Frankenstein's creative process, but represented in the sympathetic construction of the frame narratives of the novel. By centering on the act of writing within the novel as a celebration of the communal atmosphere in which Wollstonecraft Shelley and Shelley found themselves in the congenial Genevan summer, a clearer understanding of the collaborative influence of the couple's relationship on this generative moment in their lives comes into focus.

The Abinger Collection at Oxford's Bodleian Library houses the two surviving manuscripts of *Frankenstein*, both of which remain incomplete. One draft, written in Wollstonecraft Shelley's hand with linear and marginal additions by both she and Shelley, lacks Walton's initial letters; the other is a fair copy of the last portion (estimated by Johanna M. Smith to be 12–15 percent) of the draft, written by Wollstonecraft Shelley, excepting the narrative of Frankenstein's death, which is written by Shelley.[68] In addition to the incompleteness of the manuscripts, further textual issues arise when considering that there are multiple print versions of the novel: the anonymous 1818 edition comprising three volumes; a copy of the 1818 edition given to Wollstonecraft Shelley's friend Mrs. Thomas (known as the 1818 Thomas, housed in the Pierpont Morgan Library), containing Wollstonecraft Shelley's annotations and corrections; an 1823 edition supervised and corrected by William Godwin; and, finally, Wollstonecraft Shelley's 1831 one-volume revision of the 1818 text, published in the Standard Novel series.[69] The textual questions raised by the instability of these variations abound, including James Rieger's questioning of whether there can, in fact, be one definitive text of *Frankenstein* or whether, since scholars generally follow two significantly different textual versions (1818 and 1831), there are two competing sources of final authority.[70] Moreover, the feminist issue of interpretative instability arises from the "conditions of women's authorship"[71] posed by the lack of proof pages for the 1818 text and Wollstonecraft Shelley's instructions in a letter to Shelley giving "carte blanche to make what alterations you please" to at least one set of those proofs.[72] As Smith and Mary Poovey argue, feminist analysis of the Shelley collaboration could be read as a condition of female authorship: "is Percy to be seen as a meddler or as a collaborator?"[73]

Shelley played a pivotal role in the development of *Frankenstein*. His hand is interlinked with Wollstonecraft Shelley's in the pages of the manuscript, transforming it into a powerful representation of cooperative creativity and sympathetic identification. A central issue in the *Frankenstein* notebooks is the evidence they provide for the degree of collaboration in the composition of the novel. Indeed, the nature of the poet's involvement has been the subject of much critical debate, often misinforming or misleading scholarship by subordinating Wollstonecraft Shelley to the more famous poet, as is the case with Rieger's edition of *Frankenstein*, and even changing Shelley from collaborator to coauthor, as Marie-Helene Huet argues in *Monstrous Imagination*.[74] Romanticists today know of a number of examples in which friends, siblings, lovers, husbands, and wives enacted the role of editor or transcriber of the manuscripts of their partner. And, as Robinson attests in his reflections on the *Frankenstein* Notebooks, Shelley's contributions "were no more than what most publishers' editors have provided new (or old) authors or, in fact, what colleagues have provided to each other after reading each other's works in progress."[75]

And yet, despite this knowledge, the scholarly debate over the authorship of *Frankenstein* persists. Such a debate recalls the canonical desire for the "solitary author," despite evidence that "social authorship" was common in the eighteenth and nineteenth centuries. It is not my intention to engage in this debate centering on the extent of Shelley's involvement, besides merely drawing notice to the accurate fact that Shelley made changes to and suggested advice for *Frankenstein*.[76] Instead, I argue that this collaboration is influenced by the assimilated collaborative identity the couple initiated when they began their life together. My interest lies in the sympathetic nature of Shelley's involvement and its evolution up to *Frankenstein*. Acting as her confidant and editor, as well as agent in securing a publisher, Shelley expanded his role in this fictional creation from that of his shared role in the jointly written travel journal. Moreover, Wollstonecraft Shelley credits him with the development of the tale from a short ghost story into a novel:

> At first I thought but of a few pages—of a short tale; but Shelley urged me to develop the idea at greater length. I certainly did not owe the suggestion of one incident, nor scarcely one train of feeling, to my husband, and yet but for his incitement, it would never have taken the form in which it was presented to the world.[77]

Here, Wollstonecraft Shelley alludes to the encouragement Shelley provides and the circular representation of readerly exchange and response – previously evident, as I have shown, in their 1814 writings. In this description of their creative process, Wollstonecraft Shelley's word choice of "urged" and "incitement" foregrounds the significance of conversation, demonstrating that this enlargement of her project took place after the draft was read and discussed between themselves. Just as the shared journal created a written space for an individual to record and respond to the other, the *Frankenstein* manuscript becomes a similarly shared space. The manuscript certainly reveals, as Hays eloquently verifies, "cooperative Romantic sociability at its best: equitable, constructive, sympathetic, and incisive. It is a testament to the characters of both Mary and Shelley—and to the strength of their relationship—that they worked so well together."[78] Through the artistic production of a manuscript bearing both hands, Wollstonecraft Shelley and Shelley established an alternative to the creation modeled by Frankenstein himself and demonstrated, in this meta-narrative on authorial reproduction, the possibility of interweaving their lived communal experience into their collaborative creative process.

Rather than an imagined reconstruction of the other's situation, the *Frankenstein* manuscripts reveal a conversation taking place during the process of composition, evidencing Adam Smith's sympathetic identification – "becom[ing] in some measure the same person" – and recalling the dialogues present in the 1814 shared journals. In Draft Notebook A, Wollstonecraft Shelley's misspelling of "igmmatic" was canceled by Shelley in pencil, following a personal address to Wollstonecraft Shelley: "o you pretty Pecksie!"[79] Similarly, in Draft Notebook B, Shelley again uses his pet name for Wollstonecraft Shelley to address a correction on naming the discoverer of gunpowder. She had initially attributed the discovery to "Lord Chancellor Bacon," later canceling the title to replace it with "Frier." Shelley writes in the margin: "no sweet Pecksie—'twas friar Bacon the discoverer of gunpowder."[80] These comments have become infamous in Shelleyan scholarship. E. B. Murray claims that the marginalia is endearing, while Mellor disagrees: The comments "demonstrate that [Shelley] did not regard his wife altogether seriously as an author [...] her deference to his superior mind was intrinsic to the dynamics of their marriage, a marriage in which the husband played the dominant role."[81] Given the playfulness of these comments – "o you pretty Pecksie!" and "no sweet Pecksie" – and the aforementioned dialogues that take place upon the shared page in 1814, Shelley's personal addresses to Wollstonecraft Shelley can be seen in a sympathetic light. In the last pages of the first two journals, the couple uses the space for reading lists and doodles, sometimes accompanied with translations and transcriptions of poetry and prose usually written upside down to clearly delineate a separation from the privacy of the shared text. In particular, these final pages of the shared first journal show a visual depiction of the journal's entries via doodles and inscriptions and include the couple's nicknames written in Shelley's hand: "The Pecksie Doormouse" and underneath "The Maie & her Elfin Knight."[82] The first mention combines two of Wollstonecraft Shelley's pet names – Pecksie and Dormouse – while the second combines the affectionate name – Maie – used by Shelley in the journal to describe Wollstonecraft Shelley during childbirth and pregnancy with a pseudonym Shelley used on several occasions for himself – Elfin Knight. These names were, first and foremost, mutual signs of affection and endearment for one another, initially used in the shared journal and letters – in the private realm of their dialogue. Second, if we consider the tenor of the Shelleys' relationship as one of the Smithean sympathies, and Shelley's involvement in the *Frankenstein* manuscripts as that of an editor, these affectionate notes witness a certain form of education at the root of each message: correcting misspellings. Such a view, in fact, recalls the collaborators' sympathetic assimilation and accommodation from their August 1814 elopement journals. As Robinson notes, "If Mary submitted chapters to Percy as she completed them, then it follows that she would have learned from his editorial changes and advice as she continued to draft her novel."[83] Rather than infantilizing his partner, these infamous marginalia can be seen in a Fraternal light: as a continuation of the privacy envisioned in the shared journal through Shelley's use of the affectionate nickname, at the same time as he performs his new role as editor.

In the written messages to one another and subsequent alterations, the manuscript displays the circular sharing or exchange of ideas as the foundation of the couple's collaborative process. For instance, in Draft Notebook B, Victor's father proposes that Victor accompany Clerval to England. In the margin, however, Shelley writes: "I think the journey to England ought to be <u>Victor's</u> proposal. –that he ought to go for the purpose of collecting knowledge, for the formation of a female. He ought to lead his father to this in the conversations—the conversation <u>commences</u> right enough."[84] In response to the poet's suggestion, on what appears to be the back of an envelope, Wollstonecraft Shelley complies, canceling two pages of the original draft to include the following passage:

> I found also that I was unable to compose a female without fresh again devoting several months to study & laborious disquisition. I had heard also of some discoveries having been made by an e English philosopher the knowledge of which was material to w my work success and I thought of writing some times thought of obtainting my fathers consent to visit England for this purpose but I clung to this [cancelled out by PBS] *every* pretence of delay & could not resolve to interrupt my returning tran q uility.[85]

Importantly, Shelley's marginalia is simply a suggestion. He makes no attempt to change the prose; rather, Wollstonecraft Shelley's hand accommodates Shelley's editorial note in her revisions. Just as in the shared journal when Shelley assimilated to Wollstonecraft Shelley's form, here, she, in effect, assimilates Shelley's narrative proposals. Murray attests in his article on Shelley's contribution that "during the period of *Frankenstein*'s composition, through to its publication, Mary and Shelley were effectively two bodies with but one soul."[86] Rather than spiritualizing the soul, perhaps we can instead formulate a Smithian sympathetic concord. Sympathy is not, as John Durham Peters writes, "a matching of emotions, a heart-to-heart transfer from one person to another, but a judgment made by an observer, an interpretation."[87] In witnessing the circular representation of sympathy described by Audrey Jaffe – as Wollstonecraft Shelley identifies with Shelley, so too does she identify with herself – we also see Smith's depiction of the importance of the social mirror as a process of sympathy. Assimilating with Shelley, Wollstonecraft Shelley is

> immediately provided with a mirror which [s]he wanted before. It is placed in the countenance and behavior of those [s]he lives with, which always mark when they enter into, and when they disapprove of [her] sentiments; and it is here that [s]he first views the propriety and impropriety of [her] own passions, the beauty and deformity of [her] own mind.[88]

The manuscript shows the social mirror by which the sympathetic process is made visible. While we will never know for certain why Wollstonecraft Shelley followed Shelley's suggestions, one way of parsing these interpretive judgments is as a fulfillment of the concord of sentiment achieved through the sympathetic dynamic of Wollstonecraft Shelley and Shelley.

The exact process behind the couple's exchange of the notebooks comprising the *Frankenstein* manuscript will remain a mystery. Robinson points to the "ample pen and ink evidence to show that PBS read sections of the text at least twice [...] He most likely read each chapter (or groups thereof) as MWS wrote them, and then appears to have read all of Notebooks A and B at one final sitting, probably when MWS was correcting them."[89] By drawing attention to the shared circulation of the *Frankenstein* notebooks as influenced by the couple's communal process, this mutual exchange of ideas clearly reinforces the sympathetic collaboration that gives shape and form to *Frankenstein*. Robinson emphasizes the authorial and editorial metaphor for the novel as text – with Shelley's hand in the novel likened to Walton and Frankenstein as editors of each other's narratives – and concludes that "*Frankenstein* is a series of texts in search of an editor, one who will ultimately give form and shape to the novel."[90] The pluralism of the text and authors afforded by the novel's framing structure remains a noted complexity in scholarship; Robinson's argument adds to this complexity by including the fictional editors as echoes of Wollstonecraft Shelley's writing process when she expanded her "ur-text" – the no longer extant story drafted during the summer of 1816 – into a novel developed throughout 1816–1831. Robinson's reflections on his own editorial labors in compiling *The* Frankenstein *Notebooks*, moreover, directs scholarship to consider "more precise and accurate explorations of the novel, especially with regard to the collaboration between the two Shelleys."[91] Building on Robinson's scholarship, I argue that Wollstonecraft Shelley and Shelley's collaborative process highlights the ways in which the couple's voices embrace and disguise one another in the first edition of 1818, illustrating the social and circular effect of sympathetic identification that defines their collaborative process. The blend of voices in this process easily lends itself to a study of the narrative frames – narrating for another – that construct *Frankenstein*'s composition. Some attention has been paid to the narrative structure of the novel, focusing on questions of authority. Jeanne M. Britton, however, focuses on *Frankenstein*'s reformulation of sympathy as a "narrative phenomenon that implicates engaged listening and textual production."[92] I would extend Britton's excellent argument to include a consideration of the manuscript evidence and the importance of a vocal pluralism, initially attempted in the shared journal, in the fictional narrative frames, and in the manuscript as a means of understanding how and why Wollstonecraft Shelley animates her text with multiple layers of narration.

In a novel associated with the failure of establishing fellow-feeling, the characters and readers are left to seek alternative forms of sympathy. This failed sympathy is noted by many scholars, including James C. Hatch and Britton. Hatch identifies the failure of Smithean sympathy due to the Creature's ugliness – the disgust and shame inspired by the face of a creation composed of both human and animal parts undermine fellow-feeling due to a lack of self-identification.[93] However, as Britton points out, "when feeling for another becomes impossible, narrating for another, in speech or text, becomes the novel's most reliable substitution."[94] These moments of narration are, nonetheless, continually marked by experiences of sympathy – notably, failed sympathy. Opening and closing with Walton's letters to his sister Margaret, the epistolary form envelopes the novelistic form, which contains the narrations of Victor Frankenstein and his Creature. Each of these frames begins with an invocation of sympathy and closes with the failure of sympathy, creating an alternative form of sympathy within the collaboration of the texts themselves.[95] In the first frame, Walton's letters persistently point to his desire for fellow-feeling: "I desire the company of a man who could sympathize with me,"[96] and end with his expression to Frankenstein of his "desire […] of finding a friend who might sympathize with me, and direct me by his counsel."[97] After much deliberation, Frankenstein responds to Walton's desire for friendship by agreeing to tell his tale in order to prove that his fate is sealed: "nothing can alter my destiny: listen to my history, and you will perceive how irrevocably it is determined."[98] However, this demand to "listen" does not end the epistolary frame; rather, the last lines of letter IV – written by Walton – recall the aforementioned journal entry from September 10, 1814, describing the pleasure Percy Bysshe Shelley derives from reading Wollstonecraft Godwin's *Hate*: "This manuscript will doubtless afford you the greatest pleasure: but to me, who know him and who hear it from his own lips—with what interest and sympathy shall I read it in some future day!"[99] Walton's final letter, like the pleasure Shelley derives from the circulated exchange of feeling with Wollstonecraft Godwin, points to the imagined sympathy that Frankenstein's tale will provide to himself and his readers (both Margaret and the audience of *Frankenstein*). Walton's epistolary frame thus opens with a call for sympathy and imagines the finding of that sympathetic partner in Frankenstein, before introducing Frankenstein's narrative.

The second frame that invokes sympathy occurs when, upon finding the Creature in the Alps, the Creature implores Frankenstein to "listen to me and grant me your compassion. […] Hear my tale."[100] Echoing the words that Frankenstein himself utters to Walton in the opening epistolary frame, the Creature repeatedly commands his creator to listen – to hear him:

> Listen to my tale! when you have heard that, deny or commiserate with me as you shall judge that I deserve. But hear me. The guilty are allowed by human laws, bloody as they may be, to speak in their own defence before they are condemned. Listen to me, Frankenstein. You accuse me of murder, and yet you would with a satisfied conscience destroy thine own creature. Oh, praise the eternal justice of man! Yet I ask you not to spare me; listen and then, if you can and if you will, destroy the work of your hands.[101]

Thrice repeated, the act of listening serves as the means by which the Creature evokes sympathy. Sympathy cannot occur through the spectatorial act of looking – as Hatch explores in his examination of the failure of Smithean sympathy – because looking at the Creature evokes disgust and horror, but it can occur in the realm of the oracular, the language of books, of storytelling. Frankenstein follows, "partly urged by curiosity, and compassion confirmed me."[102] Confirmed by Frankenstein's diction of compassion, the Creature assimilates his creator's language to appeal to Frankenstein's sympathy and feel for his "fellow creatures."[103] Following the Creature into the hut, Frankenstein extends fellow-feeling and listens to his creation and the third, final, and most sympathetic narrative frame commences: that of the Creature.

Moreover, each frame concludes with a form of sympathetic failure. The Creature's narrative ends with his request for a female companion, a call for fellow-feeling – "one as deformed and horrible as myself would not deny herself to me."[104] This request, as we know, remains unfulfilled as Frankenstein destroys his female creation in front of the Creature's eyes, and sympathy is replaced instead by revenge and the promise to upend the so-called "natural" – that is, heteronormative – order of creation through the Creature's vow to "be with you [Frankenstein] on your wedding night."[105] Frankenstein's tale, too, closes with his appeal to the sympathy of Walton: "The task of [the Creature's] destruction was mine, but I have failed. Once when actuated by selfish and vicious motives, I asked you to undertake my unfinished work; and I renew this request now, when I am only induced to make it by reason and virtue."[106] Although tempered by "virtue" in this early version, Frankenstein renews his appeal by manipulating Walton's expression for friendship and urges him to destroy the Creature as an act of necessity. Contrasting selfishness with virtue, Frankenstein seeks to make his "unfinished work" a work of ethics, a work grounded in the fellow-feeling that Frankenstein imagines he shares with Walton.

Walton, however, fails in this task of destruction, demonstrating, in fact, that Frankenstein had not "entered into" – to borrow Smith's language – a moral concord with his "friend" and savior. Upon finding the Creature standing over the lifeless body of Frankenstein and exclaiming his grief, Walton's initial reaction is not destruction, but overture: "I shut my eyes involuntarily while I called on him to stay."[107] Despite the involuntary disgust he feels, Walton calls out to the Creature, who looks upon Walton "in wonder and then again turn[s] towards the lifeless form of his creator, [and] seemed to forget my presence."[108] Locked in emotional turmoil, the Creature rejects the sympathetic ear that Walton offers: He "wonder[s]" at Walton's desire for him to remain, but is ultimately overcome with grief over his loss. Walton too has a momentary loss of memory – forgetting Frankenstein's dying wish: "my first impulse, which had been to obey the dying request of my friend in destroying his enemy, now was overwhelmed in a mixture of curiosity and pity."[109] Like Frankenstein before him, Walton is moved by compassion as he listens to the Creature standing before him. This final frame closes with the Creature informing Walton that he "do[es] not seek for a fellow-feeling in my misery—I feel it deeply and truly—and for sympathy that I may never find."[110] The Creature's grief, therefore, is not only over the loss of Frankenstein, but for that which is inaccessible to him: a moral community inspired by "fellow-feeling." Like the selfish motives of Frankenstein, the Creature too was motivated by self-interestedness and revenge, ultimately denying the possibility of sympathetic experience.

Finally, the very end of the novel – Walton's letter to Margaret – concludes with an erasure. The final letter closes without a signature, leaving behind no trace of the Creature: "He was carried away by the waves, and I soon lost sight of him in the darkness and distance."[111] The novel ends ambiguously, begging the question of whether the Creature survives as Walton loses sight of him. As I have illustrated, the narrative frames open simultaneously with an experience of sympathy. Conversely, as each frame closes, the impossibility of sympathetic experience silences each character's voice. The failure of sympathy here is due, primarily, to the inability of individuals to enact a sympathetic experience: it is a failure of social relations that results in the erasure of individual voice. In refusing to create a blended society open to difference, the characters demonstrate the impossibility of feeling for another while providing an alternative to this failure in the material act of textual construction.

Frankenstein includes a transcription that takes place centrally in the text itself, a transcription recalling the authorial collaborative process and the need for Fraternity. Walton remains the ultimate source of Frankenstein's words – which are the source of the Creature's initial narrative – as he tells Margaret: "I have resolved every night [...] to record, as nearly as possible in [Frankenstein's] own words, what he has related during the day."[112] However, at the end of the novel, we also realize, when Walton again picks up the epistolary form, that Frankenstein has become interested in editing the tale: "Frankenstein discovered that I detailed or made notes concerning his history; he asked to see them, and himself corrected and augmented them in many places; but principally in giving the life and spirit to the conversations he held with his enemy."[113] Here, then, the narrative demonstrates a fictional collaboration at work in the composition of a tale composed of multiple parts, inflected by the collaboration between its author and Shelley. Like Frankenstein, Shelley "corrected and augmented" Wollstonecraft Shelley's tale, preserving both of their voices in the final narrative and within manuscript evidence of the drafts. So too do we see the same practice at work in the dialogic voices collaborating and embracing each other in the multiple narrative frames in *Frankenstein*.

Just as Wollstonecraft Shelley and Shelley's collaboration produces evidence of their circular sympathetic process in the manuscripts, the individual narrative frames enact a social mirror, reflecting the circularity and community integral to Smithean sympathy. As the prefaces dictate, *Frankenstein* is a novel pieced together and expanded in multiple parts throughout multiple periods, a piecing together illustrated in the textual make-up of the novel's narrative frames. Moreover, each of these frames illustrates the construction of a moral community, or sympathetic concord, composed of independent parts. Recalling, in the 1831 edition, Walton's imagined vision of Frankenstein's "full-toned voice," and "his thin hand raised in animation, while the lineaments of his face are irradiated by the soul within,"[114] Britton points toward sympathy's central role in textual reanimation. She argues that "textual reanimation may be a formal parallel to the novel's plot of corpse reanimation, but sympathy's role here suggests that its novelistic function extends beyond that of structure mirroring plot: the novel reproduces, in its acts of transcription, experiences of sympathy."[115] Further, I contend that understanding the individual frames as constructions of sympathetic collaboration foregrounds the circular identification reflected in the textual reenactment of a social mirror.

My reading of *Frankenstein* proposes that each embedded act of narration is framed as one individual asking to enter into another sympathetic confidence, so that the sections – both separately and together – replicate the process of sympathetic collaboration that this chapter has traced throughout Wollstonecraft Godwin and Shelley's early lives together. Building upon one another, each of the narrative frames is not only interconnected in the act of transcription, but they reflect each other, with each character's narration identifying "the beauty and deformity of his own mind."[116] As the frames come into contact with one another, they enact a circular sympathetic identification as they open and close upon the possibility and impossibility of sympathetic experience. Moreover, it is through the understanding of the frames as a whole, as an understanding of the sympathetic collaboration between Frankenstein and Walton, that we, as readers, are given to understand the "hideous progeny" of Wollstonecraft Shelley's creation. In other words, as each of the frames converges with one another, they not only reflect the impossibility of sympathy in the narrated tales, but observe – and preserve – the possibility of an imagined concord of sentiments in the act of collaboration – both fictional and authorial – that binds the novel together.

Exploring the idea of sympathetic texts in the narrative levels that comprise *Frankenstein* foregrounds the collaborative compilation of the novel, evidenced in the *Frankenstein* Notebooks and the collaboration between the narrative frames, as a model of Smithean sympathy. But what are the implications of this framework? For Smith, sympathy was a social process. By understanding *Frankenstein* as a novel that incorporates the blend of voices comprising the personal collaboration between Wollstonecraft Shelley and Shelley into the very narrative form of the novel, we are able to imagine the fleeting possibility of a concord of sentiment or moral community. Importantly, Smith's idea of a momentary concord that develops between individuals is one way of understanding the emphasis that Wollstonecraft Shelley places upon the failures of sympathy within her novel. Sympathy fails not in textual construction, but when individuals (the Creature, Frankenstein, Walton) fail to enact a sympathetic experience. *Frankenstein*, therefore, might be seen as an allegory for sympathy. The novel demonstrates what is required for sympathy to work – illustrated in the collaborative production of the text by the narrator and the Creature – and the effects of sympathetic failure: creation in isolation as the product of a male mind; violence and distrust as the product of a world created without sympathy. And what, then, might this mean for the materiality of collaboration? By focusing on the paratextual elements of the novel – the narrative frames influenced by the collaboration between the Shelleys – we can read *Frankenstein* as a novel that examines the materiality of collaboration to question whether body parts can work together to become a whole.[117]

Frankenstein enacts a theory of collaboration that is rooted in human sociality. As Frankenstein ends his tale and awaits his death, Wollstonecraft Shelley emphasizes the importance of the affective bonds of sympathy with a community of people – imaginative or genuine. Draft Notebook B foregrounds this very community constructed by the fictional text through the plurality of voices upon the written page:

	My thoughts & every feeling of my soul
	&̶ ̶h̶a̶ ↑*have*↓ been drunk up by the interrest
Which this	I̶ ̶f̶e̶l̶t̶ in ↑*for*↓ my guest ⁁ I wish̶e̶d̶ to soothe him
x tale, & his	yet c̶o̶u̶l̶d̶ ↑*can*↓ I t̶e̶l̶l̶ ↑*counsel one*↓ so infinitely miserable.
own elevated	W̶h̶o̶s̶e̶ ̶m̶i̶n̶d̶ ̶c̶o̶n̶t̶i̶n̶u̶a̶l̶l̶y̶ ̶d̶w̶e̶l̶t̶ ̶o̶n̶ ̶h̶o̶r̶r̶o̶r̶s̶
& gentle man	so destitute of every hope of consolation to
-ners have	live? Oh no—the only joy he c̶o̶u̶l̶d̶ ̶f̶e̶e̶l̶ ↑*can now feel know*↓
created	w̶a̶s̶ ↑*will be*↓ i̶n̶ ↑*when he*↓ composes̶g̶ his shattered m̶i̶n̶d̶ ↑*feelings*↓ to
	peace & death—Yet o̶n̶e̶ ̶f̶e̶e̶l̶i̶n̶g̶ he enjoys,
	one comfort, the s̶o̶u̶r̶s̶e̶ ↑*offspring*↓ of solitude
	& delirium—he t̶h̶o̶ believed that when
& derives from	in dreams he s̶a̶w̶ ↑*holds converse with*↓ his friends, w̶h̶o̶ ̶c̶o̶n̶s̶o̶l̶e̶d̶
that communion	his miseries or i̶n̶s̶t̶i̶g̶a̶t̶e̶d̶ ↑*excited*↓ h̶i̶m̶ to ↑*his*↓ vengeance
consolation for	
	that they w̶e̶r̶e̶ ↑*are*↓ not the creations of his
	fancy but the real beings t̶h̶a̶t̶ ̶h̶e̶ ̶s̶a̶w̶
who visit	b̶e̶h̶e̶l̶d̶ ̶a̶n̶d̶ ̶c̶o̶n̶v̶e̶r̶s̶e̶d̶ ̶w̶i̶t̶h̶ –This ↑*faith*↓ gives a solemni
him from	ty to his reveries that m̶a̶d̶e̶ ↑*rendered*↓ them p̶e̶c̶u̶l̶i̶a̶r̶l̶y̶
the regions	i̶n̶t̶e̶r̶e̶s̶t̶i̶n̶g̶.̶ to me, almost as imposing & inte-
of a remoter world	resting as truth.[118]

Only by embracing the collaborative text, revealed by the manuscript, does the relevance of Wollstonecraft Shelley and Shelley's words in the denouement of the novel emerge. Indeed, the manuscript underscores the central purpose of *Frankenstein*: the necessity of a lived community of individuals and the destruction of self that occurs without such a community. This passage reveals not only the grammatical and stylistic changes made by Shelley, but showcases the shared fellowship and thought between the couple in the expansion (revealed by Shelley's marginal annotations) and continuation of the other's thought, demonstrated in the passage's closing lines. By understanding collaboration as a means of identifying with the other at the same time as one identifies with one's self – "thinking of me thinking of you" – I contend that the Shelleys' relationship and writing process allow for a closer understanding of selfhood as a construction of a blend of dialogic voices, embodied not only in the act of collaboration but within the very texts constructed out of that collaboration.

When, in 1814, Wollstonecraft Godwin and Shelley embarked on a shared life together, they demonstrated their new identity in the form of sympathetic collaboration. In doing so, the couple espoused writing as a means of celebrating their lived community. Despite their troubled relationship, with Shelley's polyamorous tendencies and Wollstonecraft Shelley's distancing of herself from her husband during her grief over the loss of their children, writing becomes a process of sympathetic and harmonious reconciliation for the couple. In their many collaborations, the Shelleys reenact their coming home to one another, so eloquently written in the shared journal of 1814. Bennett reads Mary's *Mathilda* as a continuation of the couple's *The Cenci* collaboration and, likewise, suggests that "these writings may also have served as a gesture of personal reconciliation between the couple rather than, as some critics have suggested, a subjective expression of Mary Shelley's anger at P.B. Shelley or Godwin."[119] As a whole, their collaborative writings emphasize the shared sympathy that characterizes their personal and literary lives and bears witness to their lived communal experience.

It is, therefore, no surprise that Wollstonecraft Shelley confides her deepest anxiety with the loss of her partner and collaborator within the now solitary pages of her journal. In the months immediately following Shelley's death, her "Journal of Sorrow" became her regular companion. Begun on October 2, 1822, she intimates:

> I have now no friend. For eight years my soul I commun↑i↓cated with unlimited freedom ↑with one↓ whose genius, far transcending mine, awakened & guided my thoughts; I conversed with him; rectified my errors of judgement, obtained new lights from him, & my mind was satisfied. Now I am alone! Oh, how alone! The stars may behold my tears, & the winds drink my sighs—but my thoughts are a sealed treasure which I can confide to none. White paper—wilt thou be my confidant? I will trust thee fully, for none shall see what I write.[120]

In this entry, Wollstonecraft Shelley memorializes the transcendent and "unlimited freedom" espoused by the collaboration between herself and her husband. Moreover, she emphasizes her solitary state and her desire – like that of the characters she previously created in *Frankenstein* – for a friend. In the absence of physical fellowship and the circles that she had once helped to create, she devotes herself to paper: asking her journal to be her confidant, for the paper to sympathize with her. In her "Journal of Sorrow," Wollstonecraft Shelley continued to communicate the sympathetic collaboration between not only persons, but between persons and text.

CHAPTER 3

Written–Visual Aesthetics
The Rossettis and the Pre-Raphaelites

In the mid-1850s, Christina Rossetti recorded a dream that bears a striking resemblance to the themes in contemporary Pre-Raphaelite paintings by William Holman Hunt and Dante Gabriel Rossetti. In 1854, experiencing a crisis of faith, Holman Hunt traveled to Jerusalem with the intent of depicting biblical narratives in their actual location and found himself on the shores of the Red Sea painting *The Scapegoat* (1854–1856), a depiction from the Book of Leviticus. In contrast to religious fervor, during the same year, D.G. Rossetti confronted the contemporary subject of prostitution in his famously unfinished oil painting *Found* (1854–1855; 1859). In terms of aesthetics and moral themes, then, Christina's dream contains traces of the Pre-Raphaelite visual imagination during the 1850s:

> Night, but clear with grey light. Part of church in the background with the clock-side towards the spectator. In the church-yard many sheep with good innocent expressions; one especially heavenly. Amid them with full face a Satan-like goat lying, with a kingly look and horns. Three white longish-haired dogs in front, confused with the sheep though somewhat smaller than they: one with a flattering face, a second with head almost entirely turned away, but what one sees of the face sensual and abominable.[1]

Following the entry, she added – as late as the 1880s – the following note: "This *real* dream left me with an impression it was my duty to paint the above subject as a picture—contingent duty, perhaps. Of course I never became competent."[2] What this account reveals is twofold: the detail apparent in the description of her dream exposes Christina's visual imagination and her desire – nay, "duty" – to join the visual culture of the Pre-Raphaelite Brotherhood, revealed in the thematic comparisons with her contemporaneous social circle; as well as her acute awareness of her inability, years later, in the self-deprecating final sentence: "Of course I never became competent."[3]

Christina's promise as an artist, it seems, was also noted by D.G. Rossetti: "had she chosen to study and take pains, [... she could] have done something as an artist."[4] Her brother, however, fails to note his privileged status. From an early age, he was selected by his family for his artistic virtuoso; as the eldest son, his career as a painter was thought to bring renown to the Rossetti name. Beyond his immediate family, too, D.G. Rossetti – as a male artist – enjoyed free entrance to the Royal Academy School of Arts. Christina, on the other hand, had more of an uphill battle: she had no access to the Royal Academy; private art schools for women artists were established separately and charged tuition.[5] Even so, she persevered in her desire to study art, taking pains to develop her drawing and painting skills: she joined the female-segregated classes led by Charles Lucy and Ford Madox Brown at the North London School of Drawing and Modeling, where "tuition fees were 1s 6d per month."[6] Such formal instruction, however, was short-lived. From 1851 to April 1853, she and her mother departed London for Frome to assume responsibility for a small school. During this time, to offset the teaching that she found unpleasant, she turned more fully to art, taking an especial interest in portraiture, sketching the likenesses of her mother and their servants. By late summer 1853, however, Christina's lack of confidence in her abilities exerts itself in a letter to her friend Amelia Heimann: "I have not much faith in my own achieving greatness and fame in the Art."[7] This pessimism surrounding her artistic talent led directly to her focused ambition for fame as a poetess. Poetry, rather than art, would become her means of acclaim.

Redirecting her visual imagination from the artistic realm, Christina instead turned to poetic form as a means of experimenting with word-painting, and engaged wholeheartedly in another visual aspect central to the Pre-Raphaelite movement: illustration.[8] While the Pre-Raphaelite focus on the interrelationship between art and literature has been generally explored by scholarship, there remains only one full-fledged account of Christina's visual imagination and materialist aesthetic as a means of poetic production. Lorraine Janzen Kooistra's *Christina Rossetti and Illustration* provides a pioneering account of Christina's life and work as intimately connected with illustration: "Combining pictures and words in printed form may therefore be seen as an important element in the production of the commodity known as Christina Rossetti in the international marketplace."[9] Kooistra provides an in-depth analysis of the complexities surrounding Christina's production of illustrated poetry, mapping the "genealogy of her publications" during her lifetime and ongoing reproduction after her death. I extend Kooistra's analysis of Christina's illustrations alongside her poetry by analyzing the image and poetical composition in terms of Smith's sympathetic assimilation to focus attention on the processes associated with intertextual collaborative production.

More specifically, this chapter reveals the collaboration between art and poetry by unveiling the process behind Christina's *Goblin Market, and Other Poems* (composed 1859; published 1862), in contrast to the later collaborative production on her second volume, *The Prince's Progress, and Other Poems* (1866). Fundamentally, this chapter is concerned with the collaboration between Christina and D.G. Rossetti and suggests a consideration of the influences of D.G. Rossetti's illustrative process with Christina upon his own "double works," produced contemporaneously. To demonstrate how sympathy underlies the siblings' collaborative ideal, and D.G. Rossetti's collaborative process in his double works, this chapter begins with an overview of the "Golden Age" of illustration as it intersects with Pre-Raphaelitism. Situating Christina's productions within this moment of publishing history, the chapter provides an epistolary glimpse into the siblings' collaborative process, revealed in letters pertaining to the production of *The Prince's Progress, and Other Poems*. These letters complicate and address the power relationship at play in their collaboration, and provide a means of understanding sympathetic collaboration and its foundation upon separation and difference through its continuing exploration, from the previous chapter, of the Smithean concept of sympathetic assimilation. Following this explication of the siblings' collaboration, closely reading *Goblin Market* establishes the poem's reproduction of the Rossettis' collaborative process through its attention to experimental form, structured around the creation of a moral community. Finally, the chapter offers, in the form of a coda, a reconsideration of D.G. Rossetti's revisionary process in his "double works" to showcase his indebtedness to the collaboration with his sister. Analyzing the canonical works of Christina and D.G. Rossetti reveals an understanding of how a lived experience of communal relations underlies their sympathetic collaboration and becomes a cornerstone of Pre-Raphaelitism.

The Golden Age of Illustration: Books as Social Processes

Seeking to combine text and image to enhance, of course, the desirability and marketability of her books, Christina was primarily interested in the illustrative capability to extend the meaning of her verse by introduction of a nonlinguistic form. Her interest, as Kooistra points out, coincided with England's "Golden Age" of illustration in the 1860s. In their first editions, four of Christina's five published volumes were illustrated: *Goblin Market, and Other Poems* (1862), *The Prince's Progress, and Other Poems* (1866), *Sing-Song* (1872), and *Speaking Likenesses* (1874). Rather than simply viewing illustrated books as *objets de art*, or commodified products, Kooistra extends Jerome J. McGann's understanding of the book as a compilation of social processes: "involving a complex network of relationships in historically specific situations that change over time."[10] Books, she asserts, are "always collaborative acts" – a collaboration traced in William Morris's Kelmscott Press in the next chapter. Here, however, I am interested in understanding the process involved in illustrating poetic verse and how those processes are bound up in the social relationship between the Rossettis.

During the 1860s, illustrated volumes of poetry became an important literary commodity. Kooistra articulates the relevance of such gift books to literary culture and its social importance: "middlebrow art form," she argues, belongs alongside considerations of nineteenth-century illustrated books because of its aesthetic and ideological representations of the "middle-class home itself, and its most cherished values, while also marking boundaries of inside and outside, public and private, female and male, individual and community, nation and world."[11] More broadly, Kooistra calls for a reevaluation of how visual images shaped the impact and reception of the texts they accompanied, and her monograph does so through discussions of publishing history and readership, and commodity theory. Studying the sympathetic collaboration at work in the intertextual and interpersonal relationships of the Rossettis supplements Kooistra's reevaluation by reassigning value to the individual and community, illuminating the collaborative process as reinforcing understandings of a lived communal experience. Reading the Rossetti collaborations as grounded in Smith's liberal sympathy allows for an understanding of fellow-feeling that is dependent upon articulating individual and communal viewpoints, acknowledging the differences between individuals, and the means of self-assimilation to form a harmonious community. Recalling from the first chapter: the gap between individuals is central to Smith's conception of sympathy. Sympathy is – importantly – imperfect and fleeting because it is imaginary and dependent upon difference. The Rossetti collaboration provides a case study in the centrality of difference within sympathetic collaboration, at the same time underscoring the associations between difference and liberalism.

Epistolary Evidence in *The Prince's Progress* (1866)

Although *The Prince's Progress, and Other Poems* (1866) forms the siblings' second published collaboration, I begin with this endeavor because of the archival evidence explicating their process. Unfortunately, letters regarding the compilation and process of *Goblin Market, and Other Poems* are no longer extant – though Rebecca Crump's variorum edition of Christina's poetry evinces the revisions made by D.G. Rossetti to the poem. However, the letters for *The Prince's Progress* provide significant insight into their familial collaboration, noting a sympathy founded on difference, displayed through disagreements. The letters exchanged between the Rossettis for *The Prince's Progress* reveal a starkly different creative process than that which will be discussed in the section on *Goblin Market*; however, the epistolary evidence reveals insight into Christina's development of her own voice by way of sympathetic assimilation, similar to that which was previously seen between the Shelleys. In her discussion of the illustrations for *The Prince's Progress*, Kooistra reveals that, based on the extant sketches and studies for this second collaboration, D.G. Rossetti "seems to have begun work on preliminary studies for the illustrations before the poem itself was finished [. ... The] process of composing pictures and poems occurred in tandem."[12] In addition, Jan Marsh devotes an entire chapter in her *Christina Rossetti: A Literary Biography* to the production of this second volume, providing a full account of D.G. Rossetti's interventions. Mary Arseneau, too, presents an extensive analysis of *The Prince's Progress*, noting the deliberation (at times, almost painful) documented in the extensive correspondence with D.G. Rossetti during the spring of 1865. In other words, literary scholarship continually encounters the question of D.G. Rossetti's intervention and influence upon Christina's poetry, a question that remains in vogue when discussing the Rossetti circle, as the same questions surface when examining William Michael Rossetti's editions and annotations to his siblings' works. Here, I will first provide an overview of the collaborative process as it unfolds within the familial exchange, drawing particular attention to the degree of agency that Christina asserts in the early letters regarding the title-poem, and what seems to be a later surrendering to the acceptance of D.G. Rossetti's "revising hand," before providing an analysis of the process in terms of sympathy to reveal how the sympathetic underpinning of the Rossetti collaboration maintains a difference in service to a harmonious whole: art and poetry.[13]

Despite the tandem creation of poem and illustration, evidence for *The Prince's Progress* reveals significant disagreements between the siblings. At first glance, it would appear to be more like discord than sympathetic concord. On January 30, 1865, Christina wrote to D.G. Rossetti, acknowledging her haste in creating her second volume of poetry for fear of something "dreadful" happening to their Mother:[14]

> One motive for haste with me is a fear lest by indefinite delay I should miss the pleasure of thus giving pleasure to our Mother, to whom of course I shall dedicate: suppose—but I won't suppose anything so dreadful: only knowing her intense enjoyment of our performances, I am keenly desirous to give her the pleasure *when possible*."[15]

Acknowledging the pleasure that their family – particularly their mother – receives from their collaborative performance, Christina underscores the communal process as a lived experience. This sense of lived communal experience becomes, of course, one of the cornerstones of the Pre-Raphaelite Brotherhood, but has significant traces in the Rossetti household. Frances Mary Lavinia Rossetti's passion for poetry and literature certainly shaped the imaginations of her children, and, while employed as a governess, Mama Rossetti kept a Commonplace Book into which she entered edifying and noteworthy passages.[16] As her children grew, they, too, were encouraged to contribute to the notebook, preserving stanzas by Byron, Southey, Shelley, and Keats, among others, alongside original stanzas and poems by her husband and children.[17] Literary imagination, for the Rossettis, is ignited by familial experience and collaboration. In her letter to D.G. Rossetti on January 30, Christina moves from familial affection to an acknowledgment that her second volume must be filled with the inclusion of some poems "not skimmed by you as cream, but I have a predilection for some of these; and I have by me one or two new little things which *may* help."[18] Here, we witness Christina's assertion of her own will regarding the compilation of what would become *The Prince's Progress, and Other Poems*. Although her notebooks indicate D.G. Rossetti's suggestions and revisions, Christina declares her poetic authority by granting them a "predilection" despite her brother's displeasure. Knowing that her choice of remaining poems could provoke his ire, she situates her suggestion in terms of favoritism, only after referring to the pleasure she knows their Mother would experience. Further evidence of her willingness to assert her agency occurs in a letter written a few days later, on February 10, 1865, in response to D.G. Rossetti's suggestion of adding a tournament to *The Prince's Progress*:

> How shall I express my sentiments about the terrible tournament? Not a phrase to be relied on, not a correct knowledge on the subject, not the faintest impulse of inspiration, incites me to the tilt: and looming before me in horrible bugbeardom stand 2 tournaments in Tennyson's *Idylls*. Moreover the Alchemist according to original convention took the place of lists: remember this in my favour, please. You see, were you next to propose my writing a classic epic in quantitative hexameters or in the hendecasyllables which might almost trip up Tennyson, what could I do? Only what I feel inclined to do in the present instance, plead good will but inability. Also (but this you may

> scorn as the blind partiality of a parent) my actual *Prince* at present seems to me invested with a certain artistic congruity of construction not lightly to be despised: 1st a prelude and outset; 2nd an alluring milkmaid; 3rd a trial of barren boredom; 4th the social element again; 5th barren boredom in a severer more uncompromising form; 6th a wind up and conclusion. See how subtle elements balance each other and fuse into a noble conglom![19]

Although Christina claims "good will but inability" in her declination of D.G. Rossetti's suggestion of adding a tournament, her phrasing suggests a tone of near-animosity. Good naturedly (as belied by "terrible"), she begins this passage with a question. In response to the question, she repeats negation ("not") in a lyrical manner, reminiscent of sing-song rhythm with its repetitive clauses. Her response also includes an accusatory list of reasons – including a lack of inspiration, implying the dullness of the tournament motif in narrative poetry – on why the tournament is a "terrible" idea. To continue her rejection, Christina's tone becomes insistent: "remember this in my favour, please." Pleading for writing according to her own form and construction, she appears to set herself against the formal dexterity of Tennyson's classic epic, while insisting upon her chosen symbolic structure and provided outline, "not lightly to be despised."

The letters between the Rossettis regarding the creative and revisionary process of *The Pilgrim's Progress* are particularly noteworthy for their revelation of Christina's agency and unwillingness to bend her poetic principles, despite D.G. Rossetti's suggestions, with an especial focus on the title-poem.[20] Indeed, these letters also foreground what we would today consider "female" speech patterns: Christina employs questions, qualifications, hesitancies, and tags as a rhetorical strategy for manipulating the situation to achieve her desired outcome.[21] Yet, this passive-aggressive ploy still demonstrates her agency in regard to her poetic style. In artistic matters, perhaps, she was likely to give way and allow her illustrators a degree of flexibility, arising from her belief that illustration should provide insight into the poetic verse. Throughout March 1865, Christina's correspondence with D.G. Rossetti includes responses to his critiques and defenses of her poetic choices. On March 3, she provides reasons for rejecting elements of D.G. Rossetti's critique:

> I think the plot now is obvious to mean capacities without further development or addition.—*Aftermath* is left for various reasons: the most patent I need scarcely give; but also I think it gives a subtle hint (by symbol) that the any more delays may swamp the Prince's last chance. In the same way, the obnoxious *pipe* having been immolated on the altar of sisterly deference, *Now the moon's at full* seems to me happily suggestive of the Prince's character. Of course I don't expect the general public to catch these refined clues; but there they are for such minds as mine.[22]

Noting her sacrifice of "sisterly deference" in accepting certain suggestions made by D.G. Rossetti, Christina staunchly defends her *Prince's Progress* as suggestive of her own methods of composition and sense of formal structure. Such a defense is mounted through heavy modality. When referring to the overall plot and structure, Christina expresses surety: "I need" and "I don't expect." On the other hand, hesitancy arises – "I think" and "it seems to me" – when looking at specific words or phrases that her brother has highlighted for revision. Noting these modal markers accentuates Christina's attentive cognizance to the composition's overall structure, while specific diction remains somewhat ambiguous in the drafting stage. Ultimately, however, the obviousness of her plot is foregrounded in this epistolary defense of the poem's structure, while her note of being aware that her public may not "catch these refined clues" underscores her belief that while she writes her volume for profit and reputation, her underlying desire is for the pleasure of self – the creation of her own mind – and, as her earlier letter mentioned, family, specifically her mother.

As her previous letter noted, Christina is not aiming for the stylistic complexity of Tennyson, preferring sympathetically minded readers, able to pick up on her symbolic structure and experimental form.[23] Mary Arseneau rightly considers Christina's two audiences as the general public, whom she attempts to guide along with the obviousness of her plot, as well as "like-minded readers who she believes capable of interpreting refined clues such as the symbolic and suggestive details that she lists above."[24] Further, Arseneau claims that Christina does not include D.G. Rossetti in her consideration of like-minded readers since she explains these clues to him, not as a condescension of his intellect, but because "for Christina, right reading is not simply a matter of intelligence, no matter how acute: it is a matter of faith."[25] Arseneau's evidence comes from tracing D.G. Rossetti's divergence from his religiously symbolic early work in the 1850s during involvement in the Pre-Raphaelite Brotherhood to his agnosticism in the middle and later phases of his artistic career.[26] However, Arseneau neglects to account for the presence of Frances, their mother, in the letter. It is Christina's desire to provide pleasure for her family – for the communal circle – that ultimately leads to her hesitant assimilation of D.G. Rossetti's revisions for *The Prince's Progress* in later letters. Writing, as mentioned previously, was a familial project for the Rossettis. I argue elsewhere that D.G. Rossetti relied upon the communal aspect of writing, drawing upon his friends and family to offer suggestions.[27] Four years after the drafting of *The Prince's Progress*, in a letter from D.G. Rossetti to W.M. Rossetti dated August 26, 1869, D.G. Rossetti explicitly asks for Christina's advice: "If Christina would read my things & give any hints that occur to her I would be thankful. Tell her this with my love."[28] Moments such as these, in which the Rossetti siblings rely upon each other as both readers and writers, demonstrate the pleasure found in community and the sympathetic assimilation that comes of concord.

Viewing the Rossetti collaboration as one founded upon Smithean sympathy focuses attention on the social circle and the necessity of sympathetic assimilation to feel with and for another in order to form a moral community. On March 6, Christina begins her response to D.G. Rossetti after receiving the sketches for his woodcuts with a reminder of familial amusement:

> You confer favours as if you were receiving them, and I am proportionately thankful: but what says the Poet?
> Feelings there are, &c.—
> so I need not aim at self-expression. I hope the peccant "word or two" may yet be tackled between us: meanwhile I readily grant that my *Prince* lacks the special felicity (!) of my *Goblins*; yet I am glad to believe that you consider with me that it is not unworthy of publication. What a most delightful pair of woodcuts; thank you with all my heart. [...] Of course you shall have back the charming sketches; only *via* home instead of direct from me, as I know the pleasure their sight will give our Mother to whom I take the liberty of lending them [...].[29]

In his *Rossetti Papers*, William Michael Rossetti notes that the quotation "refers to a distich which used to amuse all of us considerably – I don't remember in what 'poet' we found it – Feelings there are that warm the generous breast: / They may be known but cannot be expressed."[30] In her letter, Christina capitalizes upon this inexpressible quality of feeling identified in the distich since she does not express the end of the poetic line. She recalls the lived experience that they shared and highlights the integrity of their shared communal sympathy as a means of overcoming their disagreements over her volume. Christina's usage of "with me," which echoes the previous chapter's focus on Mary Wollstonecraft Godwin's insertion of the same phrase at the start of her collaborative union with Percy Bysshe Shelley, further emphasizes such integrity. Here, Christina's inclusion of herself and her ideas provide, like Wollstonecraft Godwin, a vocal insertion of authority. What initially begins as deferential acknowledgment of the "lack" of *Prince's Progress* when compared to *Goblin Market* becomes a statement of authorial intent and pride: D.G. Rossetti's assertion that the volume is "not unworthy of publication" is, in fact, a repetition of her own initial admission of her volume's worth. It is a view shared between the siblings, but Christina's "with me" indicates a certain ownership of the concept with her inclusion of "me." Returning to the letter's opening lines of shared experience, Christina reestablishes her joy over D.G. Rossetti's sketches and again recalls their familial bond – not withstanding her desire to have revisions made – by reminding her brother of the pleasure she knows (like the distich) their mother will enjoy.

These letters also witness similar conciliatory strategies as Christina attempts to retain creative control. Scholarship has been indebted to Kooistra's revelation of Christina's management of her publishers and her ability to negotiate business contracts for herself, alongside the help of her brothers.[31] Future letters, however, reveal continuing discussions between the siblings regarding emendations in which Christina accommodates her brother's requests, but affirms her own inclinations, with an allusion to *Aurora Leigh's* "I, writing thus," an intertextuality to which I will return. On March 11, she writes: "Please make your emendations, and I can cull them over the coals in the proofs: – only don't make vast changes as "I am I."[32] This back and forth epistolary exchange reveals similarities discussed in the previous chapter: sympathetic assimilation occurs among like-minded individuals. Here, however, Christina relies upon their collaboration and its roots within their familial bond as a means of overcoming differences and outright conflict. Rather than assimilating D.G. Rossetti's suggestions, we witness in this private exchange Christina's mounted defense of her poetic form and diction and her aversion to change that reflects any discontinuity with her formal or creative constructs. Grounded in the sociability of the Pre-Raphaelite circle, therefore, she finds familiarity in the sympathetic exchange of drafts, acceding to D.G. Rossetti's suggestions when necessary, yet remaining true to her individualism and agency, as revealed on March 13 with her repetition of "I am I": "The *Prince* shall keep your modification of stanza 2, as regards the main point: though 'I am I' is so strong within me that I again may modify details."[33]

By April, the Rossetti correspondence asks us to rethink understandings of collaboration between the siblings, as Christina appears increasingly to give way to D.G. Rossetti's suggestions. On April 4, the letters reveal a change in tone and style, as she tersely writes: "Thanks many. On almost all points I succumb with serenity: now for remarks."[34] Succumbing to D.G. Rossetti's "revising hand," this letter paints a complicated picture of their collaborative relationship.[35] Christina subsequently adopts many of his suggestions, while including proposals of her own with slight defenses. Rather than the strength of her earlier rejections for the volume's title poem, this letter's relinquishing of control over the other poems to be included in the volume portray Christina in a different, and less headstrong, light.

Instead of relying on the strength of her poetic accomplishments and sense of stylistic innovation, this letter points to the feelings that she reserves for certain poems and decisions. Responding to D.G. Rossetti's suggestion for changing the names of Meggan and Margaret in "Maiden-Song," Christina's defense of retaining the name is that they "sound pretty and pleasant." Similarly, she requests D.G. Rossetti to

> re-consider your verdict on *Come & See*? It is, to own the truth, a special favourite of mine; and seems to me unlike any other in the volume, or indeed in *G.M.* I have moreover altered what you call the *queer rhyme*. In short, I should like particularly to put this piece in, and it has already been printed by Mr Shipley. If however after all you cannot bear it, would you rather see *Easter Even* put back?[36]

Despite her request, D.G. Rossetti included neither poem in the volume. Again, this letter shows Christina's reliance on feelings: her "Come and See" is a particular favorite; moreover, it had already been revised at D.G. Rossetti's earlier request for its unconventional rhyme.

What does this change from willful assertion to docile submission suggest about the Rossetti collaboration? It is noteworthy that this seeming submission occurs during the selection of "other poems" to fill the volume, while her assertion of poetic authority remains intact for her title poem. Recalling Christina's repetition of "I am I" in regard to her writing style offers additional insight. As mentioned previously, this claim recalls Elizabeth Barrett Browning's opening monologue in *Aurora Leigh* (1856), a "novel-poem" about the growth of a female artist:[37]

> And I who have written much in prose and verse
> For others' uses, will write now for mine,–
> Will write my story for my better self,
> As when you paint your portrait for a friend,
> Who keeps it in a drawer and looks at it
> Long after he has ceased to love you, just
> To hold together what he was and is.
>
> I, writing thus, am still what men call young;[38]

The "novel-poem" begins with a retrospective first-person narrative, written by Aurora as an effort to make sense, or order, out of her life. Writing a "story" of her life, this opening is a recognizable form of the prominent first-person *Künstlerroman* during the Victorian period: Aurora promises a "portrait" of an ambiguous "better self" or "friend [... who] has ceased to love" her. This self is written as a means of "hold[ing] together" the narrative, as a sort of compositional glue. In other words, this self is the hoped-for result of *Aurora Leigh*'s composition. Complicating this narrative – and the form of *Künstlerroman* – readers are presented with a successful authoress: "I who have written much." Yopie Prins and Virginia Jackson also comment on the personification of the Poetess and the complex generic and subjective "crossings," positing that *Aurora Leigh* is both a reflection of and a reflection on generic conventions. Prins and Jackson assert that the verse novel be read as "a lyrical study of mid-nineteenth-century literary culture: it narrates the paradigmatic career of a poetess, in order to meditate on the production of that generically gendered figure."[39] Reading generically, then, readers discover autobiographical writing in the lines "I, writing thus." At the same time, twentieth-century feminist critics rediscover in Barrett Browning's work a gendering of the subject in their subscription of "a subjectivist reading":

> an assumption that 'I, writing thus' can be read as a woman. But the gendering of the subject is complicated in *Aurora Leigh* by its overt juxtaposition of literary genres, making 'I' the symptom of conflicting conventions rather than the expression of a coherent self.[40]

"I, writing thus" becomes a lyrical metaphor for a divided self: a narrative held together by conflicting genders and genres – a female narrator comparing herself to a male friend who no longer loves her – and competing histories, who the poet/friend "was and is."

Christina's "I am I" recalls Barrett Browning's "I, writing thus" in its complex gender play, gesturing to the differences in the literary marketplace and in public consumption for male and female writers. Her assertion of self and self-identified writing style also bears identification with Barrett Browning's formal experimentation – revising the masculine form of the *Künstlerroman* into a hybrid narrative of dual selves and "novel-poem." Indeed, "I am I" refers specifically to Christina's own writing process, which was in deep contrast to her brother D.G. Rossetti. While he was a compulsive and obsessive reviser because of the marketplace, continuing emendations through many proof changes in both his poetry and art, Christina regarded her works as finished productions.[41] William Michael Rossetti recalled in his memoir, attached to his *Poetical Works of Christina Georgina Rossetti* that her compositions were "entirely of the casual and spontaneous kind. [...] If something came into her head which she found suggestive of verse, she put it into verse."[42] Further, he asserts that, as far as he knew, writing came to his sister

> very easily, without her meditating a possible subject, and without her making any great difference in the first from the latest form of the verses which embodied it; but *some* difference, with a view to right and fine detail of execution, she did of course make when needful. [...] What she wrote was

pretty well known in the family as soon as her impeccably neat manuscript of it appeared in one of her little notebooks; but she did not show it about as an achievement, and still less had she, in the course of her work, invited any hint, counsel, or co-operation.[43]

Christina's notebooks in the British Library contribute to W.M. Rossetti's assertion of a "neat manuscript."[44] There are, of course, penciled revisions, strikethroughs, and annotations by her brothers. These revisions were made, presumably, over the course of D.G. Rossetti's assistance with her publications and with W.M. Rossetti's posthumous compilation of her works. For the most part, however, the notebooks prove this assertion of neatness and contribute to a sense of Christina's works as finished products. At the same time, the notebooks themselves also correct the last sentences of W.M. Rossetti's memoir: yes, the notebooks were circulated among family for reading, but they also display invitations of counseling and cooperation in the marginalia preserved and the aforementioned letters exchanged between Christina and Dante Gabriel. The notebooks preserve the foundational collaborative experience of artistic production, in opposition to W.M. Rossetti's constructed narrative of his sister. In his memoir of Christina, he seeks to preserve an image of her as a solitary poetess creating verse that springs to mind in full-fledged form. Such preservation recalls the Romantic myth of the solitary artist; however, as the evidence from *The Prince's Progress* demonstrates, art is a necessarily conversational and collaborative project, rooted in communal experience. "I am I," therefore, signals a move toward a reassertion of agency, but also a reclamation of Christina's writing process and affirmation of experimental form in the previous defenses of her title poem.

While scholarship tends to focus on D.G. Rossetti's "revising hand" – and on the traditionally masculine role of revision in female writing – less attention has been paid to Christina's revisions of her brother's works, revisions based upon their shared familial sympathy and the sympathy of the so-called "sister-arts." In turning to *Goblin Market*, we see the outcome of the Rossetti collaborative process, turning away from the interpersonal relationship in favor of the intertextual collaboration between art and verse. Analyzing image and language in terms of sympathy is a novel and revealing approach that illuminates, more broadly, the compositional process of the Pre-Raphaelites. The collaborative process is rooted in a lived communal experience. If the previous chapter focused on sympathetic concord as a communal bond between persons, here, we consider a broader interpretation of community that suffuses the Rossettis' collaborative process and inflects their understanding of the relationship between word and image. Dante Gabriel and Christina Rossetti maintained different visions of the world and how to live in it, and an investigation of their collaborative process reveals their shared aesthetic vision. In addition to their familial bonds, their concord is founded upon an agreement on what constitutes beauty and poetry. Closely reading *Goblin Market* with an eye to sympathetic collaboration exposes a strong sense of duty and regard for religious and artistic truth, a reading unveiled when considering Christina's poetry as revisionary of D.G. Rossetti's contemporaneous works.

Situating Christina Rossetti within the Brotherhood

Upon first reading *Goblin Market*, leading Victorian critic John Ruskin wrote to D.G. Rossetti that Christina's "irregular measure[s]" were the "calamity of modern poetry." Further, Ruskin instructed that she "should exercise herself in the severest commonplace of metre until she can write as the public like."[45] Although Ruskin was appalled by the poem's metrical irregularity, *Goblin Market*'s formal novelty and experimentation with word and image distinguished Christina's work and won her the praise of her contemporaries. Indeed, in the context of the Pre-Raphaelite Brotherhood, Algernon Swinburne associated Christina with the Brothers and praised her as "the Jael who led their host to victory." This "victory," of course, refers to the fact – and it cannot be understated – that *Goblin Market* is the first Pre-Raphaelite book of poems. In terms of Pre-Raphaelite poetics, it is Christina who leads the revolutionary charge. Swinburne's allusion to Jael, the wife of Heber the Kenite who killed the leader of King Jabin's army to deliver Israel from the Canaanites, portrays Christina as a Christian heroine and pays homage to her fidelity to her religious convictions, which influences the creation and formal style of *Goblin Market*. Of all the Pre-Raphaelite poets, it was only Christina who "produced her poetry in a physical form which conformed to the movement's commitment to visual/verbal and author/artist partnerships."[46] It is commonly known that, for the Pre-Raphaelites, image and text were intertwined. Examples of this interconnection abound in various forms: from the founding members of the Brotherhood's (failed) conception of *The Germ* (1850), a journal in which each of the four numbers began with an engraved illustration followed by an accompanying poem; to D.G. Rossetti's elephant pen and ink sketches accompanying his 1870s letters to "Fanny" Cornforth; to William Morris's conception of the ideal book with his Kelmscott Press (the subject of the next chapter), in which art and text are claustrophobically contained upon the page to constitute an aesthetic whole.

D.G. Rossetti found narrative poetry most conducive to his vision of an equal partnership between illustrator and poet in order to "allegorize one's own hook," as he puts it in a letter to Anglo-Irish poet and close associate of the Pre-Raphaelites, William Allingham.[47] Indeed, Laurence Housman chronicles in his 1896 monograph on British painter and illustrator Arthur Boyd Houghton, that D.G. Rossetti's illustrations embody a particular response from a reader: "The illustrations of the pre-Raphaelites [sic] were personal and intellectual readings of the poems to which they belonged, were not merely echoes in line of the words of the text."[48] This response is an enactment of the sympathetic process: translating poetry into art reveals an underlying sense of "fellow-feeling" in the sister-arts that is grounded in a sense of the social in life. The Pre-Raphaelites were intensely social: they shared studios, held nightly PRB meetings, and combined business and home. Publications, drawings, exhibitions, and decorative ventures were all influenced by a continued sharing of work and lived relations. It, therefore, comes as no surprise, that D.G. Rossetti, in an 1855 letter to Allingham laments the Dalziel Brothers' woodcutting of his "Maids of Elfen-Mere" and describes this social aspect of his illustrative process:

> On getting your letter I marked parts of the proof with white, and find something might probably be done [to improve the Dalziels' 'mangled treatment' of Rossetti's drawing]. But first I would like to show the whitened proof to one or two friends, and take their opinion as to whether, even if the changes were properly made, the thing could possibly be allowed to come out.[49]

D.G. Rossetti's emphasis on circulating the proof among friends as an integral part of his productive process demonstrates how deeply he felt the "fellow-feeling" among his Pre-Raphaelite companions.[50] Their opinion seems just as important as the whitened proof in dictating whether any satisfaction could be derived from the Dalziels' engravings. Similarly, Christina understood "that good illustrations embodied the symbolic response of an engaged reader."[51] Believing that illustration depicted individual and personal interpretation, the Rossettis were clearly influenced by William Blake. Blake believed his illustrations to be a personal interpretation of the Bible, providing visionary insight – rather than literal representation – into the stories.[52] Providing illustrations for Christina's works, then, D.G. Rossetti also delivers an element of inspiration, guiding audiences to greater insight into her verse.

Christina believed that her brother's illustrations and collaboration were critical to the success of *Goblin Market*, as she indicates in later correspondence: his woodcuts were "essential to my contentment" and helped her "face my small public."[53] Indeed, her refusal to go to print without them, even if it delayed publication by a year, shows her equal commitment to their collaboration. Certainly, advertisements for *Goblin Market* always featured her brother's name prominently on the publisher's title page: "With 2 illustrations by D.G. Rossetti." In the publishing process, therefore, we see an ideal interpersonal sympathetic collaboration: working closely together with shared sentiments, D.G. Rossetti sent Christina his preliminary sketches and proofs for her consultation and approval. This transmission of sketches and shared ideas, like the elopement journal of Chapter 2, enacts the circulation of feeling and sympathy detailed in the Rossetti correspondence and in the nature of their familial relationship. Together they ensured that *Goblin Market* met their rigorous standards, as demonstrated when, for the second edition of the volume (1865), D.G. Rossetti wished to recut the title-page vignette to correct the jawline. Despite its disruption of the production schedule, Christina wrote to her brother: "as to the delay to *G.M.* it is nothing" compared to the calamity of publishing an imperfect book.[54]

Concord between Illustration and Verse

In addition to the private familial relationship, the union of illustration with poetic verse is also applicable to the enactment of a sympathetic concord. As frontispiece and title page, the illustrations shape the reader's preliminary experience of the poetry. At the same time, the illustrations are displaced from the text, occurring pages before the first poem and out of context with the narrative sequence. D.G. Rossetti seems to have seen this displacement as problematic because he inserted hand-lettered captions taken directly from *Goblin Market*: "Buy from us with a golden curl" and "Golden head by golden head." The captions invite its public to read the pictures closely, as hooked to narrative moments, creating a relational experience between art and the poem that follows. As discussed in the conclusion of this chapter, D.G. Rossetti continued to use this illustrative framing technique in his contemporaneous "double works," in which the frames of his paintings bear inscriptions. Incorporating text *within* visual and text *alongside* visual, the Rossettis create an affective experience for their public: transfusing their understanding of visual–verbal aesthetic into their conception of the ideal book, the public is invited to personally and intertextually experience their art. Interestingly, because of the separation of illustration from its corresponding poetic lines, the public is somewhat unaware that they are thus guided, enacting a distancing representative of, and integral to, Smith's impartial spectator. These famous illustrations allow a personal interpretation of the poem through side-by-side accompaniments with diagonal lines within the image to foreground the poem's message of doubling.[55] Looking at both illustrations, if we draw a diagonal line from the top left corner to the bottom right corner, the image becomes divided, offering a doubled perspective of the sisters and goblins. In "Buy from us with a golden curl," the slope of the hill provides a dividing line, with the sisters on the left and the goblins on the right. This depiction showcases Laura's initial temptation, and the illustration corresponds with its clear division between the sisters and the goblins. On the other hand, "Golden head by golden head," occurs after Laura has succumbed to her temptation and, while the sisters and goblins are again triangulated, there are two ways to divide the image. First, the sloping hill again provides the diagonal: the heads of the sisters and the goblins are aligned on the right; second, if we divide the image between the sisters, Laura's temptation and division from her sister becomes apparent as Laura is aligned with the goblins on the left and Lizzie remains alone in her triangle on the right. Framing the illustrations with solid lines in "Buy from us with a golden curl" and roses on the title page further suggests personal experience as the public sees themselves looking in through the framed illustrations depicting two forms of community. If we understand these illustrations and their framing as enactments of a social mirror, then the personal experience comes from the viewer looking into the frame and judging what they view from their own experiences (enacting Smithean sympathy with both individuality and interaction) – as such, the public is both distanced from and participating in the materiality of the book.

If these illustrations were indispensable for Christina's conception of her ideal book, further evidence of the collaborative nature of verse and illustration can be found in her use of poetic rhythm. Initially, dedicated to Maria Rossetti, her "dear only sister," *Goblin Market*'s interplay between goblin brothers and sister protagonists depicts the centrality of community and doubling. There remains an insoluble connection between the lavish description of the goblins' fruits and their illusory promise of forging a community between the goblins and the sisters. The poem, in fact, opens with the double temptation of the vocal cry of the goblins and their wares:

> Morning and evening
> Maids heard the goblins cry:
> "Come buy our orchard fruits,
> Come buy, come buy:
> Apples and quinces, 5
> Lemons and oranges,
> Plump unpecked cherries,
> Melons and raspberries,
> Bloom-down-cheeked peaches,
> Swart-headed mulberries, 10
> Wild free-born cranberries,
> Crab-apples, dewberries,
> Pine-apples, blackberries,
> Apricots, strawberries;—[56]

The alternating dactyls and trochees (mostly) suggest the cry of vendors selling their wares in an open market.[57] Indeed, what could sound like a shopping list doesn't – because the passage increasingly repeats "berries," seeming almost incantational through a limited lexicon. Such verbal bewitching emphasizes the circulation of affects in its seductive sing-song rhythm, drawing not only the sisters into the sound, but the public as well. This sonorous incantation suggests that the words themselves are integral to the spell under which Laura will fall. Sound, then, is particularly important to Christina. Peeping at the goblin men, Laura describes their actions to her sister, Lizzie, who refuses to look. Lizzie, however, knows that the temptation lies primarily in sound, demonstrated by her actions: "'No,' said Lizzie: 'No, no, no; / Their offers should not charm us, / Their evil gifts would harm us.' / She thrust a dimpled finger / In each ear, shut eyes and ran:."[58]

It is, in fact, this image of Lizzie running up the hill that D.G. Rossetti chose to depict in his frontispiece. In the background, we see that Lizzie has begun her ascent but, contradicting Christina's verses, has turned to look back and gaze upon "Curious Laura" who has begun "wondering at each merchant man."[59] The frontispiece conflates lines 64–125 of the poem in its depiction of Laura's aural and visual temptation, for the price of her golden hair. It illustrates the struggle of the sensuous and the spiritual, while the verses depict the struggle of aurality. Plugging her ears first and then shutting her eyes, Lizzie suggests that it is the goblin cry – that which opens the poem – that is more dangerous than eating the exotic fruit, alluding, of course, to the story of Adam and Eve: the snake's words are perhaps the true danger, for they lead to the apple. In fact, the unison of the goblin voices features prominently in the poem:

after Laura's description of the goblin creatures, "she heard a voice like voice of doves / Cooing all together: / They sounded kind and full of loves / In the pleasant weather."[60] Observing that the unified voice of the goblins "sounded kind and full of loves," Christina echoes her earlier statement describing the fruits: "Sweet to tongue and sound to eye."[61] The homonymic "sound" is critical to understanding the poem's moral: sounding the same confuses difference. In the case of *Goblin Market*, there is a crucial difference between that which is trustworthy and that which is heard or seen as such. In line 79, sound becomes a modal marker, highlighting deception because the goblin voices are not truly "kind and full of loves." The seductive unified cry of the goblins mirrors the illusory promise of forging a community between themselves and the sisters, or more broadly, the female community in which the poem takes place.

In contrast to this illusive community is the genuine sisterly community at the end of the poem, a kinship that mirrors the sibling collaboration at work between poet and illustrator and recalls the domestic setting of the Rossetti home. Eliding time – "Days, weeks, months, years"[62] – the poem's final stanza reverses the goblins' vocal cry to the children's' recitation of Laura's moral. In the poem's opening lines, listing their wares, the goblins call out to the maidens: "Sweet to tongue and sound to eye; / Come buy, come buy."[63] Replacing the goblins' voices with the singular voice of a penitent and wiser Laura, the sweetness of the wicked fruit is revealed to emphasize their honeyed, yet poisonous, nature: "Their fruits like honey to the throat / But poison in the blood; / (Men sell not such in any town);."[64] The cry of the goblins, in other words, has become in this final stanza the tale of Laura's temptation and redemption. At this point in the verse narrative, Laura and Lizzie have become wives and mothers. At the end of the poem, the "Goblin Market" suddenly transitions into a nursery fairytale or fable, as Laura recounts to their children her temptation by supernatural creatures and paints Lizzie as a heroic savior, providing "the fiery antidote."[65] Redeeming her narrative, Laura shapes it into a moral that praises a different sort of community in the form of sisterhood, rather than the goblin brotherhood:

> "For there is no friend like a sister
> In calm or stormy weather;
> To cheer one on the tedious way,
> To fetch one if one goes astray,
> To lift one if one totters down,
> To strengthen whilst one stands."[66]

As the repetition of "one" suggests, sisterhood facilitates the achievement of a singular communal identity, the very identity that the goblins had falsely promised. But the infinitive "to" also repeats, which sounds like the number two. In recitation, apart from the context which makes the meaning clear, "to" can create an auditory confusion with the number two. Certainly, this repetition of the number two enacts the doubling throughout the poem. However, if paired with the achievement of a unified communal identity in the repetition of "one," this repetition of "two" implies, perhaps, a third: "Two cheer one on the tedious way, / Two fetch one if one goes astray." This third, to my way of thinking, suggests the children. Some scholars, such as Sharon Smulders, have read these lines as the children exclaiming the moral in unison; however, the line can also be read as Laura singularly exclaiming these lines to the children – and Christina's public – drawing the children together in verse to actively bind them.[67] It is, in fact, Laura's words reciting the moral that provide the antidote to the dangers depicted in the poem. Laura's words here, with their emphasis on singularity and plurality, in a sense also pay homage to the collaborative nature of her relationship with D.G. Rossetti.

In contrast to the poem's ending vignette of female happiness, D.G. Rossetti chose for the title page a depiction of the "Golden head by golden head" scene, in which Lizzie has remained resolute while Laura has succumbed to the goblins' temptations, pictorially indicated by a spherical dream above her sleeping head. This emphasis on the closeness of women is part of a larger visual iconography, as demonstrated by Julia Margaret Cameron's photography, which she began one year after the publication of *Goblin Market*. In perhaps a twist on D.G. Rossetti's use of photography to explore possibilities for his painting (indicated by the 1865 photographs of Jane Morris, which he used in combination with his studies and sketches for completed paintings), Cameron looked to painting and sculpture as inspiration for her photographic subjects, and was known to be influenced by the Pre-Raphaelites.[68] The commingling of the female forms, their faces turned toward each other, make the figures seem nearly identical. D.G. Rossetti's illustrated intimacy between the women – their physicality and similarity of form – visually enacts a sympathetic concord, mirroring the concord found in the sisterly community within the poetic verse. As Gail Lynn Goldberg describes, "Rossetti often uses a single outline to delineate twinlike forms: the heaving bosom of one suggests the curved neck of the other, and with one line hands and shoulders seem to merge."[69] Through art and linear precision, D.G. Rossetti seemingly achieves in art what Adam Smith deemed impossible in life:

sympathetic unison – the merger of individuals. Despite the suggestion of this unison in his artistic lines, the illustration still depicts two images. He creates an illusion of union, just as Christina illuminates the dangers of the unison through the unity of the goblin's cry. This emphasis on difference, in fact, aligns with an understanding of sympathetic collaboration, which also maintains a focus on separateness and individualism, – core liberal values for society. Sympathy does not dissolve the fundamental separateness of either party; there is an insistence on entering, through imaginative transport, into another person's *situation* (rather than emotions or sentiments).

Christina's "Inner Consciousness": Sympathy and Social Concern

The purpose of Adam Smith's sympathetic concord is to be able to form a moral community: exactly the lesson learned in *Goblin Market*. Using the imagination, individuals are able to judge their own actions not only to create analogous emotions but also to see their individual selves candidly and impartially in order to lead to better self-knowledge. Recognizing ourselves in our community, we form a sort of social mirror that reflects our actions and individuals respond accordingly. As a method of discovery, sympathy allows for a modulation in feeling and action, cultivating a moral community founded on concord. Reading connections to the formation of social community into the formal experimentation of Christina's verse, in fact, coincides with metrical theories during the Victorian period, as Anne Jamison points out in *Poetics en Passant*: "[s]ince metrical theory of the day strongly connected prosodic and other forms of social identity, it is tempting to see a claim about personal and social identity emerge from the recombinatory exuberance of [*Goblin Market*]."[70] Jamison points to period sources on nursery literature and Skeltonics meter to validate her claim of connecting meter to social identity, relying on James Halliwell and George Saintsbury. Halliwell commented that nursery rhyme was concerned with moral edification, while Saintsbury scanned "short, strongly accented two-and three-beat lines" as Skeltonics, the meter that dominates much of *Goblin Market*, and introduced a debate on the "moral, national, and prosodic identity and merit of the Skeltonic form."[71] Connecting Christina's sense of moral community with the formal construction of her poem makes further sense when considering that, as early as 1859, – the same year in which *Goblin Market* was composed – she undertook voluntary work at the St. Mary Magdalene

Penitentiary at Highgate (also referred to as Highgate Penitentiary), a ministry for young prostitutes wishing to relinquish a life of what was considered at the time to be a great social evil.[72]

Established in 1855, Highgate was a "House of Mercy," supervised by Sisters as part of a new effort of the Church of England to "recover some of her lost daughters, so that many who now walk the streets of this our Babylon as outcasts, may one day be found within the gates of the New Jerusalem."[73] Christina's work at Highgate is shrouded in mystery: although she worked as a volunteer and became an Associate, she did not advertise her ministry there. Marsh indicates that although the exact date of her joining as a voluntary worker is unknown, by summer 1859, her letters to Amelia Heimann indicate that she was spending long periods at Highgate. In fact, as Margaret Sawtell argues, this time frame occurs during the period of 1855–1861, an "uncharted time" when almost nothing precise is known of Christina's activities and creativity.[74] W.M. Rossetti mentioned his sister's association with Highgate only briefly to her biographer, and, when editing her letters, said simply, in reference to the institution, that "Christina stayed there from time to time, but not for lengthy periods together, taking part in the work."[75] What, then, would Christina have done during her time with the women? While details regarding her work at Highgate are currently unknown, it can be supposed that the work generally centered on domestic training and spiritual instruction.[76] Moreover, Marsh indicates that although there is no evidence that reading or storytelling formed part of spiritual instruction, it does seem probable that her composition of *Goblin Market* was conceived as a moral tale of instruction for the women she encountered at Highgate.[77] D.M.R. Bentley also suggests that due to the association of dating, the answer to whether *Goblin Market* was ever read to the inmates "can only be a grudging 'perhaps' or a more speculative 'possibly.'"[78] Jerome McGann, on the other hand, argues that her involvement at Highgate was directed toward the "spiritual improvement" of the fallen women; not "social work": "Rossetti would not have set out to 'reform' these women in order to transform them into productive and useful members of society. On the contrary, her object would have been to turn them away from a preoccupation with the world and the world's ways, to turn them toward their 'true life.'"[79] Margaret Lonsdale's biography *Sister Dora* provides a helpful starting point to the activities that would have taken place in such institutions. In 1864, Dorothy Wyndlow Pattison joined the Sisterhood of the Good Samaritans at Coatham, Middlesbrough, where she took the name Sister Dora, and was sent to work as a nurse at Walsall's hospital in 1865. The Sisterhood was established by Rev. John Postlethwaite and Teresa Newcomen in 1854, wishing to establish a community of women to nurse the sick and care for the poor. The community studied Scripture and sent its "Sisters" to perform charitable works – the women, however, did not take religious vows. While a lack of evidence precludes any direct assumptions about Christina's work at Highgate, it remains a logical possibility that when, on April 27, "A Peep at the Goblins" was entered into her notebook, her experiences with the women who had "fallen" from moral society guided her imagination.[80] In this way, we can conceive of the poem as an act of sympathetic transportation, guiding its audience into a greater sympathetic concord with the plight of women. As such, in addition to a reading of the poem's indebtedness to collaboration and the formation of a moral society, I argue – in opposition to McGann – that Christina's volunteer work *was* tied to "social work" and reform, providing a direct contextual link to sympathetic concord within the poem's formal experimentation.

Conceptualizing the Highgate period of Christina's life as a means of social reform has roots in the social theology espoused by T.H. Green in the third quarter of the nineteenth century, when he established the British Idealist school of philosophy. Arguing that ethics applies to the conditions of social life, Green believed that self-reflection reveals human responsibility and the evolution of a moral code.[81] An individual's sense of self and satisfaction, therefore, is derived from the achievement of mutual benefit to all society. Self-examination is rooted in the desire to act virtuously: "the physical and moral degradation of the lower class lay as a heavy burden on society as a whole. No member of society could achieve a truly moral existence while other members were prevented from doing so."[82] Thus, social reform for the impoverished and morally degraded individuals in society was essential for those of more privileged backgrounds to progress and realize their best self, as indicated by Phyllis Weliver's paraphrasing of Green's ideology.[83] Of course, this was not a self-serving satisfaction derived for the benefit of those in privilege. Rather, Green advocated for the achievement of mutual benevolence, derived from his sense of liberalism. In other words, Green's sense of liberal reform is entrenched in helping people help themselves. Indeed, D.G. Rossetti may have had contact with these ideas during his time at Oxford from 1857 to 1859, while executing the Oxford Union murals with William Morris and Edward Burne-Jones. Although Green was not made Whyte's Professor of Moral Philosophy at Oxford until 1878, he first went to Balliol College in 1855 and, as an undergraduate, was influenced by the idealism of Benjamin Jowett, one of the first to bring Hegel's writings to England.[84] Thus, during D.G. Rossetti's time in Oxford, the influences that led Green to his liberal sense of moral reform, were already circulating. Such a liberal philosophy applies also to Christina's charitable work and its impact upon her creative productions. Lyrical poetry, in addition to her deeds at Highgate, becomes a means of establishing a sense of sympathetic community through its content and formal experimentation.

Such attention to the moral and social component of *Goblin Market*'s composition also foregrounds what I read as Christina's revisions to – or reworking of – D.G. Rossetti's "Jenny," a poem that was drafted and emended over many years, but was first composed ca. 1847–1848 (though this initial copy is no longer extant).[85] The earliest existing copy of the revised poem is held in the Bancroft Collection at the Delaware Art Museum and is dated 1858–1860. In D.G. Rossetti's typical revisionary fashion, subsequent copies and emendations were made: an exhumed manuscript copy from Lizzie Siddall's grave; a typescript dated 1869; the version published in his *Poems* (1870); and a final revision in his *Poems, A New Edition* (1881). Thus, Christina would have been familiar with her brother's choice of poetic subject, as critics have suggested. The two poems contain echoes of one another, and should be read as revisions – or, at the very least, as sympathetic collaborations that inform one another. One obvious interrelationship between the poems is that the transaction demanded by Christina's goblin men – "Buy from us with a golden curl" – recalls the tension of golden hair/golden coin in "Jenny": [...] And there / I lay among your golden hair / Perhaps the subject of your dream, / These golden coins."[86] Perhaps these lines were also what prompted D.G. Rossetti's choice of illustration. When he chose to illustrate "Golden head by golden head" from *Goblin Market*, D.G. Rossetti chose a contemplative moment, and used his illustration as a means of displaying consciousness – or his own coinage of an "inner standing-point" – and revealing essential character: an insight into the sisters' different responses to temptation.[87] Though different – though "fallen" and pure – the sisters are still commingled, as earlier discussed, and are still bound to one another in sisterhood.

Moreover, the illustration "Golden head by golden head" alludes to lines added in a late copy of his own "Jenny," composed in the manuscript between 1869 and 1870:

> Of the same lump (as it is said)
> For honour and dishonor made,
> Two sister vessels. Here is one.

> It makes a goblin of the sun.
>
> So pure,--so fall'n! How dare to think
> Of the first common kindred link?[88]

In his poem, D.G. Rossetti posits that the "kindred link" between the "fall'n" and "pure" is severed: there can be no sympathy or imagined "inner standing-point" between a virtuous and "fallen" woman, though, problematically, the poem asserts that such a connection can happen between Jenny and the narrator, a male profligate. Christina, of course, depicts otherwise in *Goblin Market* – to which D.G. Rossetti alludes with visual emphasis in line 206 by being a singleton, standing alone between the surrounding stanzas: "It makes a goblin of the sun."[89] Through the interplays found in both early drafts of "Jenny," we witness the impact of sympathetic collaboration, as each sibling posits their own consideration of sympathetic concord between individuals conceived in terms of difference. Christina revises D.G. Rossetti's "Jenny" in a revision that becomes her own *Goblin Market*, while D.G. Rossetti continues to explore the question of difference within a sympathetic framework in his many revisions to his poem. In recasting her brother's viewpoint in her poem – and encouraging, as displayed by his choice of illustration, a reconsideration of his position – Christina foregrounds the possibility of concord and sympathy between the "two sister vessels." Indeed, on March 13, 1865, she would write a spirited defense to D.G. Rossetti on his objection to the topic of illegitimacy in one of her poems, showcasing her own experience of imaginative transport to feel for those less fortunate than herself: "whilst it may truly be argued that unless white could be black and Heaven Hell my experience (thank God) precludes me from hers, yet I don't see why 'the Poet mind' should be less able to construct her from its own inner consciousness than a hundred other unknown quantities." Drawing specific attention to the opportunities afforded by poetry, – "the Poet mind" – Christina highlights poetic expression as a vehicle for sympathetic reform. Understanding the lyrical mode as that which is social in origin but personal in expression allows for a reading of *Goblin Market* that adheres to this communal context avowing private expression or "inner consciousness." We witness in Christina's focus on the capabilities of poetry an indebtedness to lived experience and sympathetic circulation of ideas. Such interconnections between the siblings' work underscore their collaboration and communal endeavors: both, at this early period, are attempting an "inner standing-point" by, as Smith would say, "plac[ing themselves] in [another's] situation" to conceive their experiences.

I began this section acknowledging the moral lesson from *Goblin Market* as the formation of community, which is further illuminated by exploring the sympathetic collaboration of Christina and Dante Gabriel Rossetti. Foregrounding Christina's "inner consciousness," I turn now to a consideration of how the poetic form enables the sympathetic transportation required to feel with and for another in order to establish Smithean concord. During the years of her association with Highgate, Christina's poetical contributions to her notebooks and published ballads emphasize that her "Poet mind" could – and did – enter into the experiences that were commonly thought to lead young prostitutes on their way to social ruin. Recalling Smith's assertion that sympathy is situational, Christina's social work at Highgate enabled her to maintain a distinct separateness. Though not sharing their experience of "sin," she imaginatively feels with and for the young women surrounding her and innovatively interprets their narratives to form moral injunctions. Such inner consciousness was part of her moral and religious duty. "She had a very strong sense of duty and the most rigid regard for truth," wrote W.M. Rossetti in his *Memoir*, "With several people she was extremely friendly, and no one felt more strongly than she the Christian obligation of being at charity with all men."[90] Consistently, therefore, in opposition to D.G. Rossetti's beliefs, Christina relied upon her view of God as Christ the Redeemer: rescuing the strays and cleansing them with his suffering so that they could be reborn in innocence and purity. Hence, her "obligation" of charity: her poems, therefore, convey a powerful imagining of the sense of the outcast, but also feature means of redemptive salvation. Reading *Goblin Market* as a social mirror, and with an eye to the context of voluntary social work at Highgate, offers even greater meaning to the moral tale at the end: a reflection on one's own road to temptation and the possibility of redemption in the formation of community. In other words, the "fiery antidote" becomes an affective experience, traced back to D.G. Rossetti's "Golden head by golden head" illustration: just as the sisters enter into one another's situations as a means of redemption, – and illustrated with the metaphor of spherical dreams – Christina's public, too, is asked to join the imagined community by participating in the sympathetic reformative process.

Coda: Towards a "Totalized Art"

Paying attention to the social aspect of the poet-artists' process illuminates the sociability inherent in Christina's poetry and the illustrations that D.G. Rossetti completes for his sister, as well as his paintings finalized alongside his picture-sonnets of the 1850s and 1860s. In what follows, I offer a brief overview of how the Rossetti collaboration influenced the poetic and artistic work of D.G. Rossetti. Future scholarship on D.G. Rossetti could benefit from a fuller understanding of the collaborative, communal, and liberal influences of the nineteenth century upon his poetics. Indeed, in *Defining Pre-Raphaelite Poetics,* Amy Kahrmann Huseby and I put forward the initial groundwork towards defining what we might consider literary Pre-Raphaelitism and the impact of the social, aesthetic, and gendered forms of making that contribute to the movement's poetics. Here, I consider the implications of collaboration upon D.G. Rossetti's "double works" – an area of scholarship upon which future scholarship can, and should, build.

If we read the Rossettis' works as reworkings of the other, as collaborations that transcend the illustrated works of *Goblin Market* and *The Prince's Progress*, we can begin to trace the influences of D.G. Rossetti's illustrative process upon his contemporaneous paintings. To my knowledge, there has been little scholarship that has analyzed the overlapping influences of D.G. Rossetti's multimodal compositional process of these picture-sonnets with the collaborative process of the *Goblin Market* illustrations. Elizabeth Helsinger comes closest in her pioneering study, *Poetry and the Pre-Raphaelite Arts,* and yet she still separates by chapter divisions D.G. Rossetti's double-works from his illustrative work with C. Rossetti. When D.G. Rossetti composed poems for his paintings, he famously inscribed the sonnets on the picture's frames, or, as in *Proserpine* (1874), painted the sonnet onto the very canvas. These inscribed frames are suggestive not only for interlacing the theme of the painting with its literary counterpart, but also bear resemblance to his captioning of illustrations for *Goblin Market* and *The Prince's Progress*.

Like the inscribed frames, the captions for D.G. Rossetti's illustrations are derived from Christina's poems and literally frame the illustration, creating a similar visual effect to the gilded frames for the sonnet pictures. At the same time that he was invested in illustrating his sister's poems, D.G. Rossetti was experimenting with his vision for a "totalized approach to art," a concept that was influenced by James McNeill Whistler.[91] Whistler conducted every action of himself as an artist as though it were "intrinsically a work of art":

> Before the word *Gesamtkunstwerk,* Wagner's dream of a total work of art, entered French and English art discourse, Whistler conceived of the identity of the artist and all that he produced as just such a *Gesamtkunstwerk.* In the totality of Whistler's self-presentation, from the clothes he wore, to

his manner of speech, to the letters he wrote, to the paintings he exhibited, to how he exhibited them, to the catalogues and books that excoriated his critics, Whistler conducted every action of the artists as if it were intrinsically a work of art.[92]

From exposure to Whistler's art, D.G. Rossetti learned of the integral design of the entirety of art. As McGann points out, however, it was not Whistler – as he himself promoted – who invented the idea of integrating picture and frame. It was the invention of D.G. Rossetti and Ford Madox Brown. Whistler "learned this after he left Paris and began to live in London in the early 1860s. At that point, he saw the work that Madox Brown and especially Rossetti had been doing along these lines since about 1850."[93] The planarity and gold leaf of the frames became striking characteristics of D.G. Rossetti's framing technique; equally striking as the decorative elements invented by D.G. Rossetti for his frames – the symbolic devices (roundels or emblematic designs) and various textual materials related to the picture in various ways.[94] As McGann suggests, the frames are designed "to integrate with his pictures in two respects, pictorially and conceptually. They are in this way doubly integrated, replicating the dialectical structure of Rossetti's paintings and drawings themselves."[95] With this in mind, during the 1860s, D.G. Rossetti transferred his interest in totalized art to his illustrations and book design. For this reason, the style of his illustrations for Christina is strikingly different from his earlier illustrations for William Allingham's *The Music Master* (1855) – "The Maids of Elfen Mere" – or his four illustrations for the Moxon Tennyson (1857). It is also significant that after his collaboration with Christina on *The Prince's Progress*, his experiments in illustration ceased as he turned his full attention to his own literary and artistic works, and book design.[96]

Eventually, the series of "Sonnets for Pictures" was included in his *Poems* (1870). The poems expand on the sensory effect of the painting's visual images. For example, *Lady Lilith* (1864–1868) depicts Adam's first wife brushing her hair and gazing at herself in a mirror.[97] D.G. Rossetti's own account of the painting emphasizes Lilith's narcissism: "[this is] a Modern Lilith" he writes to his friend and English poet Thomas Gordon Hake in 1870, "gazing on herself in the glass with that self-absorption by whose strange fascination such natures draw others within their own circle."[98] Here, D.G. Rossetti discusses a mystical or enchanted form of sympathetic concord: "strange fascination" draws and binds individuals together.

The accompanying sonnet's octet, however, reimagines Lilith not as self-absorbed, but as a spectacle watched by men – an external perspective:

> Of Adam's first wife, Lilith, it is told
> (The witch he loved before the gift of Eve,)
> That, ere the snake's, her sweet tongue could deceive,
> And her enchanted hair was the first gold.
> And still she sits, young while the earth is old,
> And, subtly of herself contemplative,
> Draws men to watch the bright web she can weave,
> Till heart and body and life are in its hold.
> The rose and poppy are her flowers; for where
> Is he not found, O Lilith, whom shed scent
> And soft-shed kisses and soft sleep shall snare?
> Lo! As that youth's eyes burned at thine, so went
> Thy spell through him, and left his straight neck bent,
> And round his heart one strangling golden hair.[99]

The published sonnet is – like his illustrations – no "mere echo" of his own painting. In fact, the sonnet's inscription on the frame contains a slight variation on the beginning of the sestet, at line nine: "Rose, foxglove, poppy are her flowers." As has already been noted by Sarah Phelps Smith, this variant focuses attention on the painting's floral symbolism as tokens of love and death. In the sonnet, however, D.G. Rossetti, like Christina, uses sound to create an affective experience that draws his audience in and evokes a different symbol from the floral: that of the snake. Using exaggerated assonance, alliteration, and verbal repetition ("shed scent / And soft-shed kisses and soft sleep shall snare"), the lines affect a kind of hypnosis through the sibilant hiss of the snake: a vocal slowing down so as not to trip over the words. Rather than the "Modern Lilith" evoked in the painting, D.G. Rossetti's sonnet encourages a reading derived from Talmudic legend: Lilith as female demon, half-woman, and half-snake, casting a spell on humankind. Lurking in the sound of the poem, the snake appears as Lilith's other half and furthers D.G. Rossetti's claim that Lilith's deception is prior to Satan's deception in the Garden of Eden. Reading his poem-painting alongside *Goblin Market* reveals interesting interconnections, further suggesting links between D.G. Rossetti's illustrative process and his own artistic and poetic process. Like *Goblin Market*'s allusion to Adam and Eve, the painting of *Lady Lilith* can be seen as a monstrous garden of Eden (noting the profusion of white roses and the reflection of a garden in the standing mirror at the left corner), while the sonnet's aural component encourages a reading of hypnotizing enchantment – like the enchanting sounds of Christina's goblin cries. Indeed, the sonnet's closing lines, from D.G. Rossetti's translation of Goethe's discussion of Lilith, envision her strangling golden hair as serpent-like: twisting, tangling, and constricting the youth's heart.[100]

This hypnotizing effect of sound is not only heard, but felt in the sonnet's succession of tangled words, ultimately creating a sense of entrapment, alluding to the crowded space of the painted Lilith. At the same time, the sonnet invokes the painting's visual cues: asking the reader to embody and enact the masculine role of spectator. This combined auditory and embodied experience marks a key sympathetic moment with the use of apostrophe at line 12: "Lo!" In sympathy with the legend of Lilith, we read – and view – an account not only of the masculine spectator in the sonnet's closing lines, but of ourselves gazing upon the art object: eyes burning, and, perhaps, neck sympathetically bending and heart strangling. This sympathetic transportation, in fact, is furthered by the progressive present tense of the poem: the sonnet, unlike the painting, is not overtly modern; it could be set at any time. As the picture and sonnet come together, in other words, an affective sympathetic concord takes place due to the shared understanding and imaginative transport happening at three levels: between poem and painting, viewer and painting, and reader and poem.

Coming together on the page or within the final painted product, the visual–verbal aesthetic implicitly showcases the interconnected social construction of lived community. Despite the artwork's showcase of a single woman, the poem emphasizes Lilith's participation in a community of voyeurs, bringing together both the sonnet and viewers of the painting. Such collaboration and its indebtedness to the social, however, only become realized through an analysis of the creative process, witnessed in the origins of *Lady Lilith*. *Lady Lilith*'s modernity and sensory pleasure were fully captured by the voluptuousness of D.G. Rossetti's original model, Fanny Cornforth, in 1868 (see Figure 3.1). The painting was initially commissioned as part of an ensemble to be hung with other paintings assembled in Frederick Leyland's house; at Leyland's request, the picture was repainted at Kelmscott from 1872 to 1873, replacing Cornforth's sensuality with the distant expression of Alexa Wilding. Image and text, in the Pre-Raphaelite collaborations, were produced out of a common context, working together to affect a public understanding and interpretation of poetry.

Probing the overlapping area of the familial collaboration between D.G. Rossetti's illustrations and Christina's poetry alongside D.G. Rossetti's own intertextual collaborations in his poem paintings reveals innovative insights into the siblings' processes of composition and the interlacing of their communal experiences within the finalized product. Moreover,

Figure 3.1 *Lady Lilith*, 1866–1868 (altered 1872–1873), Rossetti, Dante Gabriel (British, 1828–1882). Oil on canvas, 39 × 34 inches, frame: 53¼ × 48 inches. Delaware Art Museum, Samuel and Mary R. Bancroft Memorial, 1935.

drawing attention to the creative process as founded upon sympathy will, in future, encourage a scholarly pursuit dependent on artistic construction and rooted in sociability and lived experience with a continual investigation into the Pre-Raphaelites' multimodal processes of creation.

CHAPTER 4

Typographical Adventures
William Morris, Community, and the Kelmscott Press

"One of my earliest recollections of William Morris is of the starting of the press," said William H. Bowden, who was initially hired as compositor and pressman before Morris promoted him to overseer of the Kelmscott Press. Bowden made his remarks in a lecture given on November 27, 1896 (less than two months after Morris's death) by Frank Colebrook, a printer and enthusiast of the Kelmscott Press, to students at the printing school at St. Bride Foundation Institute in London. "When the type came in from the founder, [Morris] was very anxious to help lay it in the cases"; Bowden continues:

> But not having served his time in the business, more often than not put the type in the wrong box. It was very amusing to hear him saying to himself, every now and then, 'There, bother it; in the wrong box again!' But he was perfectly good humoured, and presently ran off, and came back, bustling up the path—and in my mind's eye I can see him now—without a hat, and with a bottle of wine under each arm, with which to drink the health of the Kelmscott Press.[1]

The Kelmscott Press, as Bowden remembers it, was begun in a state of exuberance in the spring of 1891. Excited to begin his printing endeavor, Morris appears almost childlike in this pleasant image of the famed craftsman mistaking the types in the cases. Indeed, this anecdote illustrates an aspect often overlooked in Morris scholarship: Morris's initial ignorance of printing and his increasing appetite for knowledge. "Not having served his time" as printer, Morris, here, is depicted as inexperienced. Indeed, as William S. Peterson's pioneering history of the Kelmscott Press points out, Morris never set a line of type, but "asked questions constantly, peered over the shoulders of his printers, and familiarized himself with all the technical aspects of printing."[2] William Morris is known today as a so-called "jack of all trades": poet, artist, designer, visionary, socialist, rebel, revolutionary, genius, and the list continues.[3] It would be, however, a great disservice if scholarship failed to remember the zest and pleasure that he took with him into every project, and the interconnected webs of influence that each venture had upon each other, driven by Morris's insatiable thirst for knowledge and perfection. This chapter, therefore, probes this lived sense of pleasure and commitment in its attempt to explore sympathetic collaboration in William Morris's Kelmscott Press.

"It was the essence of my undertaking," wrote William Morris in *His Aims in Founding the Kelmscott Press* (1898), "to produce books which it would be a pleasure to look upon as pieces of printing and arrangement of type."[4] Morris's pleasure in his experiment, or, as he called it, "a typographical adventure," never diminished. As Peterson notes, the Kelmscott Press was intertwined with Morris's family life, and thus was both interpersonal and social: "snatches of conversation with [Emery] Walker and others in the library floated up the stairway into the drawing-room; proofs and trial pages lay scattered about Kelmscott House, and in time the books themselves drifted into the house in great piles."[5] This small example serves as a reminder that Morris inscribed the Pre-Raphaelite ideal of lived collaboration, discussed in Chapter 3, into the Kelmscott Press, and into his conception of the "ideal book." The Kelmscott Press, then, embodies an interpersonal and intertextual collaboration within its very operation, and exemplifies a lived experience of communal relations, drawing from the communities that Morris established throughout his life.[6] In the brief history of the Kelmscott Press (1891–1896), we witness sympathetic identification in the processes involved with printing and with the arrangement of type and ornament upon the page in order to imagine the possibility of a fleeting moment of concord, a fleeting moment of moral community. Although Morris was certainly, in some respects, influenced by a Ruskinian philosophy of sympathy,[7] there are clear differences between Morris's conception of sympathy as it relies upon the coming together of individuals. Whereas Ruskin's aesthetic principles, while morally grounded, remain on the sympathy between things or objects, Morris is fundamentally concerned with the possibility of art as a means of bridging the gap between individuals. This chapter, therefore, examines the printing process and its communal operations alongside the finalized product as a means of collaboration that enables sympathetic concord. Importantly, Morris's ideal books came to fruition in the last years of his life: the first volume, Morris's *The Story of the Glittering Plain*, was printed April 4, 1891 and issued May 8, 1891, only five and a half years before Morris's death. However, this chapter positions the Kelmscott Press—what may initially seem an impulsive interest in printing—within Morris's lifelong interest in sympathetic collaborations. The founding of the Kelmscott Press has a significantly long history that comes to its denouement on the night of November 5, 1888, when Emery Walker lectured on "Letterpress Printing and Illustration." This lecture aroused Morris's enthusiasm and set off a chain of events that led directly to the founding of the Kelmscott Press three years later. Because most people date the press as beginning in 1891, it has been thought of as, primarily, a socialist project. By acknowledging, however, this longer trajectory – stretching back to the 1860s – I contend that the Kelmscott Press be viewed as a liberal project: defining liberalism with its fraternal communitarian conceptions can be, when viewed via the lens of sympathetic collaboration, understood as the same as practical socialism.

When Morris developed the Kelmscott Press, he enlarged the conception of book production to incorporate aesthetic and social reform, in part, to redeem late-Victorian society from what he saw as its mechanical ugliness. Morris's creed of harmony in all aspects of the book – particularly between text and illustration – is one deeply influenced by Ruskinian thought and formulated only after Morris experienced much dissatisfaction with the world around him. Ruskin's *The Stones of Venice* (1853) greatly impacted the world of Victorian England, making direct connections between art, nature, and morality, as Ruskin argued that the decorative arts affected the men who produced them. If we read Ruskin as Linda Dowling does, in a liberal vein, we see that his creed also contains the core of sympathetic collaboration.[8] Morris's interest in the book as material object flickered throughout his life, guided by his interests in illustrated manuscripts. As the story goes, in the 1870s, Morris reportedly picked up a book printed around 1490 by Aldus Mantius, and, turning through its pages, remarked, "Ah! I wish I could get my books printed like that!"[9] It was this dawning desire that led to the eventual founding of the Kelmscott Press twenty years later. The Kelmscott Press embodies an ideal interpersonal and intertextual collaboration in both its operation and its establishment of community.

Although previous chapters followed a structure of introducing manuscript evidence to illustrate the collaboration between individuals before interweaving the traces of the life-writing within the literary product, this chapter departs slightly in its form. My argument here offers a different approach by considering the aesthetic press as an embodiment of the collaborative process. As such, this chapter illuminates two integral processes: (1) the mechanization of the Kelmscott Press as a joining of art and word, continuing the previous chapter's focus on the Rossettis' illustration and poetry, and (2) of the individuals coming together to form an aesthetically moral community. To fulfill this argument and position the Press within Morris's life-long interest in aesthetic reform activity and liberal sentiment, we begin with the William Morris Paradox, which focuses on the impact of Socialism and the seeming contradiction between Morris's theory and practice, before lending a possible solution in Smithean sympathy: the metaphor of the impartial spectator. Once this theoretic framework is established, the chapter unconventionally interweaves various moments of Morris's life outside of chronological context to showcase Morris's fundamental aim: the production of art as a means of relief from the vulgarization of Victorian society. I offer two case studies that trace the fundamental collaborative processes within the Kelmscott Press to demonstrate the practical application of sympathetic translation: Edward Burne-Jones and Robert Catterson-Smith's collaboration during the production of the Kelmscott *Chaucer*, and Morris and Charles Gere's collaboration on the frontispiece illustration for *News from Nowhere*. Finally, the chapter broadens out to consider how Kelmscott, as a place, exemplifies the lived experience of communal relations for which Morris strove throughout his life.

The William Morris Paradox

When, in 1883, Morris announced at Oxford that he was a Socialist and, afterward, devoted himself to socialist propaganda, his consequent actions were perceived by some of his contemporaries as a paradox. It is, furthermore, a well-known paradox, illustrated in dichotomies describing Morris as romantic or revolutionary, and is also what scholars have called the "decisive antagonism" of Morris's life and teaching: "His work, the revival of handicraft, is constructive; the essence of his teaching is destructive."[10] From such thinkers, Morris scholarship devolves into viewing Morris's activism as short-lived; once the riots began in London in 1887 (known as Bloody Sunday) and revolution – for a brief moment – seemed likely, Morris is seen as recoiling: gradually withdrawing back into "his world of poetry and beauty" – the world of the Kelmscott Press and book collection.[11] Such a paradox still remains in current scholarship, though many, notably Florence Boos and Elizabeth Carolyn Miller, are now invested in tracing a lineage of socialist thought throughout Morris's life. Morris continued his advocacy of socialism until his death. In other words, scholarship is now recognizing – as Morris himself stated – that there was no sudden transition to political activism in the latter part of his life; the socialist within Morris was already extant, embedded within his aesthetic philosophy and way of life.[12]

Although it is beyond the scope of this chapter to trace the paradox in detail, both the question of Morris's conversion to Socialism and the contradiction apparent in Morris's practices are impossible to ignore in conversations surrounding the Kelmscott Press. Indeed, all of Morris's creative endeavors – or, as I will term them in this chapter, social experiments – labored under the same contradiction.[13] While the Kelmscott Press pioneered "a new concept of a press as a community with a life and creative volition of its own," its workmen were dependent employees and its books were exclusive: initially, Morris aimed to distribute them only among friends; eventually, they were sold by subscription.[14] Morris's contemporary critics were profoundly aware of this problem, as discussed in a damning critique by capitalist critic Thorstein Veblen, who noted the Kelmscott Press as the epitome of the "conspicuous waste" characterizing modern consumption:

> These products, since they require hand labour, are more expensive; they are also less convenient for use [...] they therefore argue ability on the part of the purchaser to consume freely, as well as ability to waste time and effort [...] The Kelmscott Press reduced the matter to an absurdity [...] by issuing books for modern use, edited with obsolete spelling, printed in black-letter, and bound in limp vellum fitted with thongs.[15]

Ignoring the aesthetic aspect of reading, Veblen argues that despite Morris's desire for art to be of and for the people, his very productions were not available to all. As Anna Vaninskaya points out in *William Morris and the Idea of Community*, "The pleasure that Morris and his friends [...] could take in the communal labour of book creation, the same pleasure that earlier in the century he and his Pre-Raphaelite brethren had taken in the design of Red House, could not be shared with the rest of society."[16] Such understandings of Morris's work as elitist focus on the productions of the Kelmscott Press, but ignore Morris's issuing of his socialist designs and writings at low costs for public consumption.[17] Given this paradox, it may seem strange for Morris to advocate and align himself with Socialist philosophies. To understand this slippery slope, it may be helpful to rehearse Morris's own definition of Socialism.

In "How I Became a Socialist," published July 1894 in *Justice*, Morris clearly defines his understanding of Socialism as the realization of a commonwealth:

> I will say what I mean by being a Socialist, since I am told that the word no longer expresses definitely and with certainty what it did ten years ago. Well, what I mean by Socialism is a condition of society in which there should be neither rich nor poor, neither master nor master's man, neither

idle nor overworked, neither brainsick brain workers nor heart-sick hand workers, in a word, in which all men would be living in equality of condition, and would manage their affairs unwastefully, and with the full consciousness that harm to one would mean harm to all—the realization at last of the meaning of the word COMMONWEALTH.[18]

In this definition, Morris emphasizes two aspects: (1) equality for all and (2) the importance of community, both aspects that resonate with the liberal Fraternity described in Chapter 2. This definition, then, should come as no surprise to those aficionados who had followed Morris throughout the development of his Arts and Crafts Movement because it summarizes the aims of his entire life. As Morris continues, he identifies "*practical* Socialism" as the ideology that he espouses; and specifies that it was this "ideal" that "forced me to look for practical Socialism."[19] Here, then, is the common thread throughout Morris's endeavors: his ideal, which was founded upon the rebellion of Thomas Carlyle and John Ruskin. "It was through [Ruskin] that I learned to give form to my discontent, which I must say was not by any means vague. Apart from the desire to produce beautiful things, the leading passion of my life has been and is hatred of modern civilization."[20] Morris's enterprise, then, is art: this production of beautiful things comes foremost because it is his means of salvation, his means of reform. Morris's ideal was an art rooted in aesthetic reform. Furthermore, for Morris, practical socialism was also an ideal, and not the Socialism commonly associated with the late nineteenth century because, as Pevsner points out, "there is in it more of [Thomas] More than of Marx."[21] Morris's fundamental question requires him to look backward – to the forms of craft guilds and cathedral buildings as articulated by Ruskin – to question how society can recover a state in which work is "worth doing" and, at the same time, is "pleasant to do."[22] Morris's socialism is more like a communitarian utopia. Thus, to get around the William Morris Paradox, we must begin to recognize the threads of influence that make up Morris's aesthetic philosophies, the philosophies that guide his creative and essentially communal experiments. The starting point to doing so is recognizing the traces of liberalism that Morris carries with him, even in his espousal of Socialist political activism.

As clarified in the introduction, my understanding of liberalism does not focus on its political aspects, as Amanda Anderson's recent works have explored. Instead, I follow a similar trajectory to that of Elaine Hadley's conception of "lived liberalism," a liberalism with roots in the fraternal leanings of Romanticism and which can be understood best through the sympathetic lens of Adam Smith. As Vaninskaya aptly points out, nineteenth-century "socialists adapted both the Liberal narrative of democratic Teutonism and the anthropological emphasis on revival to their own dialectical theory of history, in which the principle of community and its notional opposite were represented by different agents at different stages in the evolutionary spiral."[23] The socialist emphasis on community – the ideal which resonated most with Morris – comes from the hallmarks of Victorian liberalism, as Phyllis Weliver argues: "The heart of the Liberal party message was enhancing quality of life and protecting liberties, including the creation of meaningful social relationships."[24] For Morris, in particular, such an emphasis also has roots in his veneration of medievalism. How is this liberal message different than the Socialist one espoused and defined by Morris from 1882 to 1896? Rather than assaying the seeming impasse between Liberalism and Socialism as we understand it today, I see the tension between both sides of the William Morris Paradox as that between the priority placed upon the individual – commonly believed to be a liberal sentiment – or the group – commonly believed to be a socialist sentiment. Viewing moral judgment and social unity through the lens of Adam Smith, however, offers a way of avoiding this stalled debate because Smith's theory does not require a choice between priorities. By identifying this longer history and tracing the influence of Smithean sympathy and concord in the collaborative process of the Kelmscott Press, the Press should be thought of in terms of its liberal (and Romantic) roots. Viewing the Kelmscott Press as rooted in the 1860s, we can complicate the identification of the press as a socialist project, and, in doing so, capitalize on the shared pleasure that arises from this project's conception of liberalism as fraternally communitarian. After all, as Stefan Collini argues, the lines between liberalism and socialism were not as firm as they are today.[25] Examining the Press by emphasizing the Smithean ideal of sympathetic concord illuminates the communal production process, a process which Morris had earlier used in his life-long collaborative endeavors, including his Oxford Brotherhood set. We can see, then, that lived liberalism can be traced back to the ideals of Enlightenment thinkers. In saying this, I do not mean to dissociate Morris's socialism from the project; in fact, I do not believe that to be possible. After all, it is Morris's liberalism that lead him to socialism: his dissatisfaction with Prime Minister William Ewart Gladstone's 1880 Liberal government led to Morris's 1883 avowal of Socialism.[26] But, by understanding liberalism's emphasis on lived community, we can begin to see past the contestation of the William Morris Paradox and view the Kelmscott Press and William Morris's communitarian experimentations as part of the long nineteenth century's focus on sociability and cohesion, as well as collective literary production.

Circles of Sympathy: Smith's Impartial Spectator and Liberal Community

Moral judgment, Adam Smith argues, is impossible without the social:

> Were it possible that a human creature could grow up to manhood in some solitary place, without any communication with his own species, he could no more think of his own character, of the propriety or demerit of his own sentiments and conduct, of the beauty or deformity of his own mind, than the beauty and deformity of his own face.[27]

No judgment, moral or aesthetic, is possible without the social structure surrounding sympathy: in society, individuals are provided a mirror, which "always mark[s] when they [society] enter into, and when they disapprove of his [the individual] sentiments; and it is here that he first views the propriety and impropriety of his own passions, the beauty and deformity of his own mind."[28] Here, Smith uses the same language of imaginative transport ("enter into") as when describing the social process of sympathy. Sympathy provides social unity. Using the metaphor of a mirror, Smith adopts the belief that an individual's self-awareness derives from a socially constructed self-reflection, a reflection inspired by the judgments of others.[29] The central point of the social foundation of sympathy is, as intellectual historian Knud Haakonssen attests, that "we only become aware of ourselves—gain self-consciousness—through our relationship to others."[30] Put another way, as philosopher Samuel Fleischacker notes, "the process of moral judgment is the means by which individuals most deeply build the views of their society into themselves."[31] Smith's concept of social unity within a community, therefore, places equal pressure on the individual and society – returning to the possibility of using a sympathetic lens as a way out of the William Morris Paradox, a choice between the individual and society is not required because the two are dependent upon one another.

Sympathy enables the formation of a moral community, of a bringing together of individual human beings and forming connections between them. As philosopher Jack Russell Weinstein summarizes, "Smith is an empiricist, coping with the fundamentally separate nature of human beings. Our physical separation requires a moral theory derived from sensations and events occurring to others."[32] How, then, does this occur? Smith's imagined impartial spectator, discussed in the introduction, plays a key role: when the spectator experiences a similar sentiment as an observed "actor," Smith's terminology for the observed member of society, then the spectator is said to sympathize with the actor. Sympathy, therefore, indicates approval of a sentiment, and, by extension, the moral position inherent in that sentiment. The impartial spectator is, of course, an ideal: through this metaphor, Smith is able to describe how individuals rationalize decisions regarding propriety and moral judgment, and thus illustrates the coming together of individuals in concord within a community. In other words, sympathy forms a moral community and the foundation of moral judgment by "devising criteria of acceptable action after repeated similar observations and after determination of community judgment. The impartial spectator is the aggregate of a person's experience balanced with what he or she knows is the moderating power of community."[33] Sympathy, then, is both contextual and perspectival: involving both the imaginative reconstruction and interpretation of an experience. Because of this, a necessary tension arises: Smith insists that the spectator judges from his or her own perspective; on the other hand, sympathy requires that the spectator determines appropriate sentiments and actions based on how *this* particular agent should act in *this* particular situation. To resolve this tension, Smith offers the example of another's grief over a loved one:

> When I condole with you for the loss of your only son, in order to enter into your grief I do not consider what I, a person of such a character and profession, should suffer, if I had a son, and if that son was unfortunately to die: but I consider what I should suffer if I was really you, and I not only change circumstances with you, but I change persons and characters. My grief, therefore, is entirely upon your own account, and not in the least upon my own.[34]

Sympathy is not self-interested due to the imagined, and momentary or fleeting, change of circumstances and persons: the spectator "consider[s] what I should suffer if I was really you." This process, then, involves a complex and constant balancing act between self-knowledge and knowledge of others. Based on the social mirror afforded by society and the creation of the imagined impartial spectator, sympathy can be viewed as a liberal cognitive process, inspiring self-reflection and self-modulation in order to form an ideal community.

Of course, distance and proximity are questions that necessarily arise when considering the ability of individuals to sympathize with another. Smith addresses this concern by asserting that both physical and psychological distances affect sympathy: we are intimately connected to ourselves; then to our families and those with whom we work; third, those within our neighborhood; and, finally, those within our "state or sovereignty."[35] Moral philosophers have discussed this progression in terms of "spheres of intimacy"[36] or "circles of sympathy."[37] Such a progression demonstrates that individuals sympathize most effectively with others with whom we share common lived experiences: family, coworkers, collaborators, or those in our social community. Smith believes that humanity is naturally benevolent, and that this benevolence varies based on familiarity, based on the progression within the circles of sympathy. This natural benevolence is rooted in the aforementioned processes of sympathetic assimilation and accommodation from our imagined spectator's observations of the social. The impartial spectator, as an imagined personification of an individual's moral sentiments, insists – via Kantian concern for the equal worth of all human beings – that we treat others as ends in themselves and never means:

> It is not the love of our neighbour, it is not the love of mankind, which upon many occasions prompts us to practice those divine virtues. It is a stronger love, a more powerful affection, which generally takes place upon such occasions; the love of what is honourable and noble, of the grandeur, and dignity, and superiority of our own characters.[38]

There is a conflict between an individual's desire to prioritize oneself over others, and the desire to prioritize one's needs over pleasing others. Weinstein argues that Smith resolves this conflict by positing that "the closer people are to one another, the more the natural tendency towards others can be combined with the natural tendency towards one's self."[39] Life is enhanced by proximity; humanity is naturally social. Thus, it makes sense that Smith defines affection as "habitual sympathy."[40] It is not biological elements that constitute family as an emotional unit; rather, it is their day-to-day lived experience. Shared experiences and shared standards allow others to come together, to compromise one's self-regarded tendencies with concern for others. Sympathy resolves the conflict to balance self-and-other-regarded interests, based on our capacity to assimilate, accommodate, and self-modulate or interpret, the social situation. Using Smith's sympathetic lens derived from his moral philosophy as a means of understanding communal development and collaboration allows us to envision community as an acknowledgment of social difference and diversity, bridged by sympathetic imagination that allows individuals to "enter as it were into [an actor's] body, and become in some measure the same person with him."[41]

Through Smith's process of sympathy, the individual self-regulates and modulates into "greater consistency": Smith's theory, unlike those of Hume or Shaftesbury, allows for a criticism of the existing social order, as Michael Frazer attests: "our proper and impartial sympathetic approval of the warranted resentment of those victimized by an unjust society leads us to demand social reform."[42] Victorians sought to identify with and advocate for particular methods of organization. Thomas Carlyle and John Ruskin, famous advocates for theories of community, were spurred on by their increasing disenchantment with modern society and promulgated their views in the aftermath of the Industrial Revolution. Connecting with an awareness of communal life, their ideas mourn, also, the inevitable passing away of traditional – specifically, medieval – ties; thus, Linda Dowling asserts links between these voices "associating art with liberal or utopian reform" and the voices of William Morris, Oscar Wilde, and Walter Pater, imagining that art within such degraded and vulgar "situation[s] might possess a grand power of social redemption."[43] Using Dowling's terminology of "aesthetic democracy," – drawn from the conclusion that Morris's aim has been "none other than the democratisation of beauty"[44] – here, I explore how sympathetic collaboration enables an understanding of the aesthetic community's facilitation of social reform through sympathy.

In "What Socialists Want," a lecture reportedly delivered in 1888 and unpublished in his lifetime, Morris recapitulates his desire for liberty for all as a means of living reasonably, and likens the society that he wishes to see in terms of sympathy and family:

> My own belief is that when we are once bound together by ties of honesty and mutual self-respect all this will tend to get simpler and simpler until our business becomes very easy to transact. For instance I have been speaking as if there would still be some social inequalities, as if one man would earn more money than another, though none would earn less than enough to keep him comfortably: but I do not think that this would last long: we should find that when we ceased to fight with each other for livelihood and to rob each other that all ordinary necessaries and comforts would be so abundant and so cheap that they would be free for everybody to take as he needed [...] let me give you an illustration: when a family that is comfortably-off sit down to leg of mutton how do they act? do they bring in a pair of scales and weigh out to each one his share of the victuals? No that is done in a prison, but not in a family. [...] and the reason for this is that enough has been provided, and that the members of the family trust one another. My friends it is for you to choose whether you will live in a prison or a family. [...][45]

In this lecture, given during Morris's activism in the Socialist League, he defines his future society in terms of Smithean sympathy, with its emphasis on a family "bound together by ties of honesty and mutual self-respect." Morris's communal vision, once afforded a mirror by which to gauge their actions, locates a society that has become self-regulated – that has adopted an impartial spectator. Society has modulated itself to such a key that it becomes founded on "ties of honesty and mutual self-respect" as paralleled by the ties of family.

This emphasis on communal family is certainly the driving force of Dowling's examination of Morris's aesthetic democracy. It is also the foundation for the sympathetic bonds that Morris created in his friendships with Edward Burne-Jones and many others, and attempted to generate in his creative circles, specifically in his overlapping communities at the Kelmscott Press, Socialist League, Society for the Preservation of Ancient Buildings, and Morris & Company.[46] It is worth pointing out, also, that such an ideal vision bears resonance with Jane Morris's affair with D. G. Rossetti, beginning after the death of Elizabeth Siddall in 1862 and continuing on and off until Rossetti's death in 1882. In Morris's personal life biographers have noted his doubly personal hurt: spouse and friend. In contrast to this unsympathetic circle, then, is the creation of his Kelmscott circle and relationship with Burne-Jones, recalling the radical communal circles created and envisioned by the Shelleys. Elements of "habitual sympathy" are at the core of each of Morris's social experiments, and such sympathy ultimately finds its fulfillment in the Kelmscott Press. When Morris set out his understanding of harmony within a book as material object, he identified the usage of ornament as purposeful, not as a means of decoration. Moreover, the book itself incorporates the metaphor of the impartial spectator in order to formulate an intertextual concord. With his own production of books, such a theoretical concept of "habitual sympathy" becomes practically fulfilled.

Social Experimentation and Typographical Adventure

Having traced how Smith's concept of the impartial spectator lends itself to a reading of liberal community, I will consider Morris's fascination with medieval communal ideologies and his return to the chivalric past as a means forward for his aesthetic and social reform in order to show Morris's creation and expansion of liberal fraternity as a life-long undercurrent leading to the Kelmscott Press. As an undergraduate at Exeter College, Oxford in 1853, Morris formed his closest friendship with Edward Burne-Jones, and began the first of many social experiments in his discovery of "the Set" (later known as "the Brotherhood"). As a second-generation Pre-Raphaelite Brotherhood, "the Set" was already in place when Morris arrived in Oxford. The group included William Fulford, Charles Faulkner, and Richard Watson Dixon. In this early period of his life, Morris read and idealized Kenelm Digby's *The Broadstone of Honour* (1822), a rambling overview of the history of chivalry.[47] With Digby's text as a guide, "the Set" read Tennyson: Morris reading aloud in his famed sing-song voice, laying emphatic stress on the rhymes to demonstrate Tennyson's inherent musicality. Tennyson's poetry – "The Lady of Shalott," "Sir Launcelot and Queen Guinevere," "Morte D'Arthur," and "Sir Galahad" – formed part of an Arthurian cult, inspired by Sir Walter Scott's rediscovery of Malory's *Morte D'Arthur* in the late eighteenth century.[48] MacCarthy establishes that, for Morris and Burne-Jones, Arthurianism "was not merely an intellectual exercise. They fell upon it as an extension of religion, adopting the chivalric as a rule of life. Embedded in their visions of the San Graal were the memories of the high emotions of those early weeks at Oxford, and their mutual recognition."[49] Arthurianism and chivalric fraternity formed the starting point for Morris's ideal community and shared experience; indeed, the Set's engagement with medievalism and the Arthurian stories was not an isolated experience, but of a whole with English culture in the 1850s: "By the time Morris and Burne-Jones arrived in Oxford, Victorian Arthurianism was approaching its grand climax. William Dyce had already started painting his cycle of Arthurian frescoes in the Queen's Robing Room in the Palace of Westminster."[50]

Throughout their lives, Morris and Burne-Jones would lay their own claims on the Arthurian myth. Morris's interpretation was, primarily, poetic, noticed in his early *The Defence of Guenevere* (1858), although he also produced Arthurian-inspired paintings during his collaborations with Rossetti and, famously, the collaborative atmosphere of Red House. Burne-Jones would remain consumed with the San Graal for the entirety of his life, dwelling on themes in paintings and tapestries, and completing the irises in *Avalon* just before his death.[51] The Kelmscott Press, too, is seen as a return to medievalism – not as nostalgia, but as a means of aesthetic reform. It is no coincidence that the Press was started with the intent of printing William Caxton's books, the first English printer, and that the Press's most famous achievement was its *Chaucer*.[52] Within this fascination with medievalism, Morris's yearning for solidarity within a community finds new ground. Understood in conjunction with his knowledge and desire for chivalric fraternity, Morris creates community as a means of social reform. This reform is rooted in emulation of chivalric ideals, not in a regressive way, but in an innovatively creative one, as will be further discussed at the end of the chapter. As depicted in Morris's romance *News From Nowhere* (1890), he envisioned that out of the past chivalric age, Victorian England could redeem itself. Throughout his life, in all of his communal endeavors and experimentation, Morris formulated and expanded his ideas for social reform: new societies based on equality of class, fraternal and liberal styles of community, and principles of shared labor and pleasure – like the haymaking and road construction in his Utopian romance.

The founding of the press, the works produced, and its influence on later printing endeavors have been documented, most notably by William S. Peterson.[53] What has been less considered, however, is the day-to-day life and process of the press. Morris imbues his aesthetic press with the qualities of his ideal society (grounded in the aforementioned values of medieval fraternity), the qualities of sympathetic collaboration. Morris emphasized the ornamentation of book production in *His Aims in Founding the Kelmscott Press,* which, upon first glance, appears as a statement about typography and printing:

> I began printing books with the hope of producing some which would have a definite claim to beauty, while at the same time they should be easy to read and should not dazzle the eye, or trouble the intellect of the reader by eccentricity of form in the letters. I have always been a great admirer of the calligraphy of the Middle Ages, & of the earlier printing which took its place. As to the fifteenth-century books, I had noticed that they were always beautiful by force of the mere typography, even without the added ornament, with which many of them are so lavishly supplied. And it was the essence of my undertaking to produce books which it would be a pleasure to look upon as pieces of printing and arrangement of type.[54]

Morris's mission, as he describes here in the final book produced by the Kelmscott Press, was dictated by delight in the book as an art object. Pleasure, beauty, and admiration form the foundation of this statement, tempered by his caution against lavishness for lavishness's sake: his books "should be easy to read and should not dazzle the eye, or trouble the intellect." Inserted within his dictum of experienced or embodied pleasure, Morris includes an idealization of medieval crafts. This veneration of medieval art becomes a thread carried throughout Morris's aesthetic philosophy, an approach which bled into his lived experience within the artistic and experimental communities he created. In this way, the sociability of Morris's philosophy comes to the fore, in contrast to Ruskin's objective sympathy of "felt immediacy."[55] Ruskin's extensive aesthetic philosophy demonstrates the shift in nineteenth-century conceptions of sympathy as it moves closer to empathy or *Einfühlung,* as will be discussed in the final chapter. For Spuybroek, Ruskin, in "Of the Turnerian Picturesque," offers a "more advanced sympathy" than that of the eighteenth-century moral philosophers – who rely on a humanist and ethical approach – because Ruskin's sympathy is "not exclusively human and distributes itself among all things, organic and nonorganic, since they are all equally saturated with life and force."[56]

Here, however, I draw attention to Morris's aestheticism of illuminated manuscripts, which shows not only the collaboration venerated by the Pre-Raphaelites, but also the transhistorical collaboration between his Press and the medieval past. In actuality, this statement on typography recalls the influences from his earlier conceptions of art and lived community. In this way, the opening lines of Morris's *Aims* also dictates how he believed society ought to live: production with "a definite claim to beauty" and "beautiful by force of the mere typography." A late Victorian society should look toward community that derives pleasure from labor, a beautiful society whose splendor originates from its formal construct, from its concord. The working model of the press simulates and achieves the collaboration of art and literature in the texts produced and its communal operations, emphasizing a collision of aesthetic modes and a culmination of historic moments. By focusing on the Kelmscott Press itself as a model of collaboration, rather than the specific products produced, we can see that sympathetic collaboration is built into its very mission. Therefore, it is first necessary to understand Morris's conception of the ideal book and the harmony – or concord – that resulted from joining ornament and story before demonstrating how this ideal becomes embodied in the operations and productions of the Kelmscott Press.

"Sympathetic Translation": Concord in the Ideal Book

William Morris, as MacCarthy's biography demonstrates, was interested in things, specifically the materiality and sensory experience of things. In this way, certain aspects of Morris's aesthetic philosophy are influenced by Ruskin's sympathy, which can be traced, argues Spuybroek, in the later philosophies of William James and Henri Bergson. For them, sympathy is an immediacy of feeling, as well as a specifically "mental, but not psychological, and a bodily though not sensual, reciprocity between us and things."[57] Whereas the moral philosophers of the Scottish Enlightenment provide an ethics-based framework of sympathy, mainly operative between people, by the mid-to-late nineteenth century, philosophers are more concerned with reinvestigating the relationship between things, or between people and things.[58] This increasing emphasis on the material world, it comes as no surprise, impacts Morris's conception of book production, compelling him to make his own paper, type, initials, borders, and ornaments for the Kelmscott Press. In a fragmentary essay entitled "Some Thoughts on the Ornamented Manuscripts of the Middle Ages" (c.1892), Morris presents the Victorian period's superabundance of books as a curse of the "utilitarian production of makeshifts, which [...] has swept away the book-producer in its current."[59] Eliminating the book producer, for Morris, was a fault of publishing; indeed, one of Morris's complaints about Victorian book production involved the elimination of the *craft* of book production in favor of mechanical reproduction.[60] In contrast with the Victorian printing process, bookmaking in the Middle Ages – with its focus on art as a collaborative process – is upheld by Morris: the book was "a palpable work of art, a comely body fit for the habitation of the dead man who was speaking to them: the craftsman, scribe, limner, printer, who had produced it had worked on it directly as an artist, not turned it out as the machine of a tradesman."[61] The book as a "palapable work of art," then, is palpable not only in its "comely body," or its physical attributes – its pages, type, illustrations, ornaments, and story – but also in its lineage of production, from craftsman through printer. It is here that Morris's philosophy diverges from Ruskinian sympathy. For Morris, art cannot be divorced from its social production; it is embedded within a lived experience of communal relations. The book of the Middle Ages speaks to the present from the dead; its process of production and, significantly, the individuals involved in that production unfold within its pages.

Contrasting the machinery of his present age with the direct physicality – the lived experience – of the Middle Ages, Morris calls attention to the importance of a sensate world, of the art object deriving its aesthetic beauty from its own materiality and the fellow-feeling inspired by its production. Such a somatic experience was one that Morris had realized at Oxford while reading Ruskin's "Nature of the Gothic." As Linda Dowling argues, this epiphanic moment at Oxford "represents the proximate moment when art became available to Victorians as a moral source, 'the love of which empowers us to do and be good.'"[62] Indeed, such an epiphany becomes realized in the Kelmscott productions themselves as art becomes a moral source within lived life experience. Importantly, Dowling seems to neglect the means by which art becomes a mode of morality and social reform in her focus on the inward experience and Morris's realization from Ruskin that "response to beauty was universal."[63] Jerome McGann and Jeffrey Skoblow, too, consider the Kelmscott Press's deliberate attention to materiality. McGann argues that the effect of the Kelmscott Press's *The Earthly Paradise* "foreground[s] textuality as such, turning words from means to ends-in-themselves. The text is [...] thick with its own materialities."⁶⁴ Such self-referentiality enacts a "rigourously materialist impulse," as Skoblow articulates, involving "the exploration of objectification, sensory alienation, commodification, and the negative dialectics of resistance."⁶⁵ These analyses are rooted in Marxist terminology, yet fail to acknowledge the processes of production at work and, in their failure, such scholarship enacts the complaint Morris voiced. The means of production – the materials and the artists at work upon those materials – should not be divorced from the product. Morris's belief in the inseparable nature of process and product forms the basis of his philosophy regarding ornament and content – the materiality within the book – and his aim in producing beautiful books: harmonious wholes that are dependent upon their parts. In other words, Morris's ideal involves an emphasis on art as an end in itself, as a form of "habitual sympathy" that is reliant upon its producers – the roles of the craftsmen and artisan – as demonstrated by the sociability and relationality of the Kelmscott Press.

Throughout his lectures, Morris argued that epic and ornament, or decoration, are one production. In "The Woodcuts of Gothic Books," his lecture for the sixth session of the Applied Art Section of the Society of Arts on January 26, 1892, Morris asserted the inseparability of ornament and story:

> You have not got to say, Now you have your story, how are you going to embellish it? Nor, Now you have made your beauty, what are you going to do with it? For here are the two are together, inseparably a part of each other.⁶⁶

The designs of Pre-Raphaelite illustrators – and the tradition of the aesthetic press that follows from the Pre-Raphaelites – materialize, as Lorraine Kooistra points out, "a bold poetics of reading, making a spectacle of the art interpretation and asserting the reader's right to make meaning."⁶⁷ Similarly, Morris's lectures and writing on his theory of the ideal book illustrate this "bold poetics" through the formation of concord between epic and ornament within the context of a complete work. Indeed, Morris's prescription of an ideal book incorporates what he terms "sympathetic translation":

> The illustrator [of an early printed book] has to share the success and the failure, not only of the wood-cutter, who has translated his drawing, but also of the printer and the mere ornamentalist, and the result is that you have a book which is a visible work of art. [...] If any real school of wood-engraving is to exist again, the wood-cutter must be an artist translating the designer's drawing [...] The executant [artist of a book], on his side, whether he be the original designer or someone else, must understand that his business is sympathetic translation, and not mechanical reproduction of the original drawing.⁶⁸

"Sympathetic translation" links the conception and meaning of the book to its production, and to its social function as a social act in the creation of a "real school of wood-engraving." It also emphasizes the shared feeling between the various workers: illustrator, printer, and executant. Taking, presumably, Morris's theorization of "sympathetic translation" to heart, Colebrook elaborates Morris' teachings on illustration:

> "no book can be [a true work of art] whose designs and illustrations do not comport themselves in harmony and in virtual submission to the printed page. That is the keynote with which everything else must harmonize. [...] There must be fellow-feeling in art. There must be unity. There must be simplicity—simplicity—always simplicity." These are not Morris's words, but my effort to express his teaching's essence.[69]

Enabled by a sympathetic concord, demonstrating an inheritance from Pre-Raphaelite conceptions of text and the visual (explored in Chapter 3), representations of community unfold within physical and textual spaces that visualize a lived experience of Pre-Raphaelitism.

Extending Pre-Raphaelite ideas to incorporate social change, Morris views art as a means of cooperation, as a collective concord. "A work of art is always a matter of co-operation," he asserted in October 1893 at the Arts and Crafts Exhibition in the New Gallery, just two years after the founding of the press. "After all, the [individual's] name is not the important matter," he continues. "If I had my way there should be no names given at all."[70] Morris does not here mean to denigrate the individuals working for him by reducing them to nameless individuals. In fact, he founded the Kelmscott Press with the aim of "overhauling book production to reinsert the role of the craftsman inside the covers, typography, and printing of the book."[71] Instead, he is focused on the work of a collective, of beautiful work done in concord, by placing the artisan/craftsman within the aesthetic object itself. Standing in front of his own great tapestry, a resurrection of the art of the fifteenth century, Morris, in 1893, describes the object of his Arts and Crafts as the work of medieval guilds, work done in collaboration. When asked about the process of making the tapestry – who made it, how long it took, and how much it cost – Morris describes the value of apprenticeship, of the collaborative process:

> It occupied three persons—as many as can comfortably sit across the warp—for two years. [...] The people who made it are boys—at least they're grown up by this time—entirely trained in our own shop. It is really freehand work, remember, not slavishly copying a pattern [...] and they came to us with no knowledge of drawing whatever, and have learnt every single thing they know under our training. And most beautifully they have done it! I don't think you could want a better example than this of the value of apprenticeship.[72]

Morris was a man who firmly valued the work of his craftsmen, witnessed here in his memory of the three boys trained in Morris' own shop. And yet, Morris not only remembers them as workers, but moves to a personal recollection in considering them as men who have created, like himself, beautiful work. Here, attention is drawn to collaboration, rather than paid labor. Thus, it is with pride and admiration that Morris exclaims, "And most beautifully they have done it!" Indeed, although he emphasizes that they "learnt every single thing they know under our training," he shifts toward his ending of personal fondness by stressing the pronoun "they" in "*they* have done it," rather than the "our" from the training, and points towards the importance of sympathetic collaboration. Elizabeth Carolyn Miller, too, underscores Morris's effort to unite Ruskinian ideals of art and labor with an anti-utilitarian form of socialism in his vision of a future society that "valued individual distinction among persons and in production."[73] The key to escaping the vulgarity and decay of industrialization is, therefore, a consideration of the craftsmen and their role within aesthetic production: the individual within the community. This is how sympathetic collaboration, for Morris provides a means of social reform. In other words, if consumers were forced to consider the artisans who created their artwork – such as tapestry, wallpaper, and books – then the objects themselves exceed commercial value by being raised into objects of art.

Although this anecdote involves a tapestry, his idea of "cooperative" or collaborative art crosses over to Morris's book illustration and printing, where he continued his mode of collaboration and his fellow-feeling for the master printers and workmen at the Kelmscott Press. All the workers became union members of the London Society of Compositors, and when Morris was initially approached by the union authorities, Peterson chronicles that Morris "was able to truthfully reply that his printers were well treated."[74] Frank Colebrook emphasizes such treatment when he eulogizes Morris's aims in setting up the Kelmscott Press:

> He sets up his press, not really to make money, whether out of the rich or out of the poor, but with the sole and simple aim to produce a book as beautiful as he can make it. When he has paid a high price for his paper [...] when he has used black ink [...] when he has designed his three types and had them cut; when he has paid fair wages to his workmen, from whom he does not require a longer week than 46 ½ hours, he is not able to sell the product of all this for a less sum. And what a service he renders to workmen everywhere in demonstrating that people will lavish money to buy books on which master printers and workmen have lavished care.[75]

Many have criticized Morris for the high prices of the books produced by the Kelmscott Press, but here, just two months after Morris' death,

Colebrook pays particular attention not just to the costliness of Morris's materials, but also to the fair wages and hours that he promises his workers. For Morris, the production of an ideal book was beautiful not only in its typography and ornamentation, but also in the care that had been taken in the collaborative endeavor of bookmaking. Production, then, is tied to fellow-feeling, to the care that "printer and workmen have lavished" on the book, but also on one another.

"Part of a Whole": Morris's Ideals versus Victorian Practice

Although it would be gratifying to know the exact methods and means by which Morris designed and produced his books at Kelmscott, there is surprisingly little documentation of the actual process and techniques themselves. Morris wrote and lectured at length about his broad principles of design and the ideal book, alongside his legacy of fifty-two Kelmscott Press editions. And yet, it would be difficult – and, as Peterson notes, dangerous – to offer broad generalizations about the production of the books: "The process by which Morris designed and printed the *Epistola*, for example, was very different from that followed in manufacturing *The Well at the World's End*, which was in production from 1892 to 1896."[76] Morris did not create precise drawings of the pages he envisioned, and this lack of documentary evidence says something about Morris's own belief in sympathetic translation. Providing detailed designs would inhibit the freedom of the craftsman to translate the design. "No doubt," Peterson philosophizes, Morris instructed "his compositors at the Kelmscott Press [...] orally, with Morris often at their elbow, and he never hesitated to demand that they produce one trial page after another until he was satisfied."[77] In order to probe more fully the tension between collaboration and paid labor, as identified in Morris's exacting nature, we turn to the voices of the workers, specifically the illustrators, to understand their perspective.

To combat the dearth of evidence collected, Peterson suggests a consideration of the day-to-day problems encountered during the production process, and he traces the publication of three books – Morris's *Poems by the Way* (1891), W. S. Blunt's *The Love-Lyrics & Songs of Proteus* (1892), William Caxton's *The Golden Legend* (1892) – before devoting an entire chapter to the *Chaucer* (1896). Although there is a lack of evidence regarding the actual typographical work done at the press, there is no shortage of archival material relating to the collaboration between Morris and

Burne-Jones, or any of his illustrators.[78] Tracing the manuscript evidence of the collaborative process alongside Morris's understanding of sympathetic translation within his ideal book, we not only see evidence of lived liberal experience and community, but also witness the transformation of the book itself into an archival artifact or object embodying Morris's vision for future societal reform.

Morris's belief in concord between all elements of his book brought him to an older method of print production: printing wood-engraved illustrations locked in the same frame as the type, as opposed to contemporary nineteenth-century printing techniques of separating the illustrations from the type for a speedier process. The same held true for illustrated books, in Morris's view: "The illustrations should not have a mere accidental connection with the other ornament and type, but an essential and artistic connection. They should be designed as a part of the whole, so that they would seem obviously imperfect without their surroundings."[79] The centrality of the engraved line and the artistic freedom of the craftsman is certainly Ruskinian and provides an attractive theory of illustrated production; the practice, however, was not always as simple.

Part of the problem was Morris's belief in sympathetic translation; prior to Morris, engravers were taught and trained to produce exact replicas, or facsimiles, of the design. Such was the case for William Harcourt Hooper, who engraved the majority of the Kelmscott designs. Based on Hooper's resume of engraving the drawings of artists such as John Millais, George du Maurier, John Tenniel, and others, for the *Illustrated London News* and *Punch*, Emery Walker suggested that Morris persuade the artist to return from his retirement.[80] Immediately, however, there was conflict between Morris and Hooper's aesthetic principles, revealed in two letters between Morris and Walker. Enclosing a block for *The Defence of Guenevere*, Morris asks Walker, on February 2, 1892, to copper the block for production; other blocks need retouching and "one I fear must be plugged; but I can't tell till I see my design. I fear Hooper must have been in a bad temper when he cut it, and was damning my eyes for hurrying him. A very slight touch or two will set the others right."[81] Presumably, based on the letter, Morris fears that one block would need to be completely redone, and blames Hooper's temper. Interestingly, Morris accuses more than temperament, and focuses the action as a purposeful blinding: "damning my eyes." In other words, Morris sees Hooper's actions as retaliation for hurrying Hooper's progress. At the end of the letter, Morris returns to blaming Hooper's temperament, warning Emery not to mention his "jokes" to Hooper because "he is sensitive & might cut up rough, & I don't want to quarrel with him, as he has been very obliging as well as skillful."[82] Two days later, on February 4, Morris's dissatisfaction resurfaces over Hooper's cuts:

> I think these not at all good: in fact I think them downright bad, and chiefly of use as illustrating every fault that a wood cut can have. Of course I know that [Hooper] can do better, and that he is doing this out of perversity. Anyhow, anybody can do them as well as this, as they are quite *unintelligent* in cutting; and Leverett may as well cut them at a lower price. But I daresay with a little talking to I can bring Hooper round and get him to do better: if not I must in future go to someone else.[83]

Morris's anger was usually short-lived, and Hooper – despite these threats – was not replaced. However, this letter showcases the fidelity with which Morris took his theories of illustrated production and transferred them into practice. In the first letter, Morris mentions joking, presumably in reference to Hooper's "damning my eyes"; however, this joke can also be read – and I think it more likely – as an allusion to Hooper's temperament. Morris's concern is not over an individual's personality; in fact, Morris was quite used to being teased within his circles for brief episodes of rage. Rather, I find that Morris uses displacement – "joking" – to evade his displeasure at the diminishment of his ideal. Once again, the tension between Morris's vision of collaboration and paid labor rises to the forefront.

In the second letter, this displacement moves into focus: in mentioning "every fault that a wood cut can have," Morris alludes to his aforementioned concern about Hooper's method of engraving as fidelity to the design, rather than sympathetic translation. This may read like a failed concord, with its lack of sympathetic assimilation and accommodation. Again, displacement occurs as Morris places blame on Hooper's perversity before returning to his theoretical model of unintelligent cutting. Here, Morris refers to his lecture "The Lesser Arts," in which he argues that the "art of unconscious intelligence" is dead, and that the future must hope to see the unintelligent art replaced by the art of "conscious intelligence." He defines the ancient art of unconscious intelligence as the "masterly scratchings on mammoth-bones" – the art of hieroglyphics, the art of communication prior to verbalized means. Such art, he argues, is dead – certainly among the industrialized regions, but lingers, perhaps, "among half-civilized nations, and is growing coarser, feebler, less intelligent."[84] In other words, the art of unconscious intelligence is the art that is found within nature and becomes a part of its surroundings. When Morris condemns Hooper's engravings as unintelligent, Morris focuses on the discord between his ideal of creative – or sympathetic – craftsmanship and Hooper's ideal of facsimile.[85] In this disagreement, Hooper becomes a symbol for all that Morris stands against; and yet, fifteen years later Morris maintains his hope – just as he did in 1877 – that conscious intelligent art will persevere. Indeed, Morris's optimism remains constant, for despite his differences with Hooper, he continually strives for sympathetic community.

Despite scholarship that dismisses the Kelmscott Press as Morris's lapsed hope for the future, here, in Morris's interactions within his aesthetic community, we witness the liberal sentiment that Morris carried with him throughout his life: a Ruskinian and Arnoldian sentiment that understands art and aesthetic reform as democratic, to be experienced by every individual. Morris tells Walker that he can persuade Hooper to do better; and it seems Morris was right: four months later, on May 2, Morris indicates to Walker that Hooper has assimilated to Morris's view of sympathetic translation. Examining a proof of *A Dream of John Ball*, Morris writes ironically: "Ah I see he has altered my drawing to its disanvantage [sic] in the 'Corner;' so his principle of exact copying has gone by the board, and I can chaff him."[86] Hooper remained with the Press until its closure, and would continue his work as engraver, translating designs for Charles March Gere and Charles Robert Ashbee for the Ashendene and Essex House Presses. But Hooper's imitative preferences were not the only obstacles that Morris encountered in his attainment of sympathetic translation. As Morris would soon discover, a more personal obstacle arose: Edward Burne-Jones.

Morris's "little job": Producing the Kelmscott *Chaucer*

"I want you to try a little job in connection with the designs for wood cuts which Burne-Jones is doing for me," wrote Morris to young artist Robert Catterson-Smith on January 8, 1894. Prior to meeting with Burne-Jones, Morris continues, "I should be glad if you would come over to me as a preliminary tomorrow Tuesday say at 9 p.m. & I can explain the matter more fully & give you a design to take to the Grange."[87] Morris's belief that Catterson-Smith would be engaged upon "a little job" makes sense given the date of 1894. Just two years prior, on October 22, 1892, the "Fine Art Gossip" section of the *Athenaeum* was the first periodical to feature and admire the collaborative project that would make the Press famous:

> Lovers of Chaucer on both sides of the Atlantic will rejoice to hear that [Edward Burne-Jones] has made very great progress with a series of designs, fifty or sixty in all, which are to be cut in wood under his own superintendence, and intended to illustrate the "Canterbury Tales" and the other poems of Chaucer. These designs promise to be charmingly graceful and

> beautiful in execution. [...] The text to which these designs are adapted will be collated with the best manuscripts and carefully edited by Mr. W. Morris and Mr. F.S. Ellis. The typography will be worthy of the occasion, and the volume a stately quarto.[88]

Peterson notes in his historical biography of the Kelmscott Press that Burne-Jones began work on the *Chaucer* illustrations "in late 1892 or very early 1893," initially conceiving – like Morris – the project to be a "little job." In a trial dummy of eleven leaves, Burne-Jones sketched preliminary plans, including the note, "There are 48 planned here but I may add to the Knights tale & the early part – there may be 60 in all."[89] In a later note, Burne-Jones calculated seventy-two illustrations, noting that Morris "won't have more."[90] It would appear, however, that Burne-Jones was persuasive. In total, what was planned as "a little job" morphed into the most ambitious and richly ornamented book produced by the Kelmscott Press, totaling eighty-seven Burne-Jones illustrations, in addition to the ornaments and frontispiece designed by Morris.

Because the *Chaucer* is the most famous of the Kelmscott productions, there is a tendency to erroneously assume that it is typical of all the productions. Instead, it should be emphasized that most of the Press editions were issued as octavos and the majority were unillustrated; though all contained Morris's decorative borders and initial blocks. For Morris, the book was, first and foremost, a beautiful object: "I lay it down [...] that a book quite un-ornamented can look actually and positively beautiful, and not merely un-ugly, if it be, so to say, architecturally good."[91]

Morris did not achieve his ideal book, with its insistence on sympathetic translation and concord between ornament and type, until the publication of his *Chaucer* in 1896. The *Chaucer*'s elaborate design required its own press – the third Albion press that Morris used was purchased for the sole purpose of printing the *Chaucer* – and Burne-Jones's illustrative process posed a dilemma. With Hooper at the helm of engraving, with his standards of fidelity to design, Morris found himself in a bind because of Burne-Jones's reluctance to provide finished drawings to scale.[92] This reluctance was a known problem, and publicly shared in an 1894 interview with Morris, who explained how Morris and Co. overcame the obstacle when producing textiles. This interview is worth quoting at length because it also provides insight into the role of photography, despite misleading claims that Morris opposed technological interventions:

> The original studies are not above 15 inches high. The figures are grouped and drawn from carefully prepared studies: for the rest there is but little minuteness of detail; and they are only slightly tinted. That is the form

in which they come into our hands. We have to have them enlarged by photography, in squares varying in size and number according to the full dimensions required. The enlarged sections are then fitted together, and the whole, now of the proper size, submitted, together with a small coloured study, to the artist for his revision and approval; and on these enlargements he does a great deal of work, especially the heads and hands. The ornamental accessories, the patterns of brocades in the draperies, the flowers and the foliage, are left to us. [...][93]

In a later interview, Vallance discusses again the "practice of co-operation" adopted by the Firm for stained glass: "there grew up the custom of Burne-Jones designing nothing but the figures. [...In a work dating to about 1870–1875,] The two figures of Adam and Eve at Frankby, Chesire were drawn by Burne-Jones simply nude, and the trees and lead-lines provided by other hands."[94] It was, therefore, this practiced custom of collaboration that Morris relied upon for the Kelmscott Press. In addition to Morris's admission of the central role that photography plays in his compositional process, these quotes identify what would become commonplace for Burne-Jones's process: revisions to the figures, particularly the heads and hands, while leaving the ornament to others. Here, we see the practical application of sympathetic translation – adapting the ornament when the designs focus on the figure. Moreover, wood-engravings can only render blacks and whites; "intermediate tones must be suggested by parallel lines (which Morris believed should be used sparingly) or cross-hatchings (which he thought should not be used at all)."[95] Burne-Jones's designs, however, were delicate sketches, filled with nuances of shading (see Figure 4.1). Obviously, quite a large portion of translation would need to occur before a wood-engraving could be produced.

Bookseller and collector Bernard Quaritch, in his letter accompanying the platinotypes of the *Chaucer* illustrations at The Morgan Library (New York), details the process needed in order to produce a satisfactory engraving for the woodcutting: "it is necessary to take a photograph of the design for transference to the block. As it is impossible to get a sufficiently clear photo from a pencil drawing the designs of Burne Jones had all to be copied in ink and then touched up and passed by him before they were photographed and transferred to wood."[96] Aside from Hooper's rigid loyalty to faithful representation, Peterson notes that there was no rapport between Hooper and Burne-Jones; the next candidate for translating Burne-Jones's designs was Charles Fairfax Murray, who had done similar tasks for D. G. Rossetti and Burne-Jones in the past (and who had translated photographic copies of Burne-Jones's illustrations for

Figure 4.1 1050.15, *The Clerk's Tale: The Dressing of Grisilde*. Burne-Jones, Edward (British, 1833–1898). Graphite within drawn graphite border on paper, height, drawn area, 129 mm, width, drawn area, 171 mm. For page 129 of the Kelmscott Chaucer. © The Fitzwilliam Museum, Cambridge.

The Golden Legend before Hooper engraved them). However, Murray's work was much delayed: Quaritch specifies that the first five woodcuts were prepared by Murray "but there was so much delay in his work, that Morris decided to dispense with him."[97] The seriousness of Morris's problem seemed to have no solution until Robert Catterson-Smith, a young artist who later became Headmaster of the Birmingham School of Art, redrew Burne-Jones's frontispiece from *A Dream of John Ball* (1892) on a larger scale for reproduction in the *Daily Chronicle*.[98] Here was Morris's solution to his impasse.

"Fingers, Eyes, and Sympathy": Robert Catterson-Smith and Edward Burne-Jones

Catterson-Smith's contributions to the Kelmscott *Chaucer* were not publicly acknowledged until controversy arose in 1898.[99] Even so, little scholarship has focused on Catterson-Smith's participation in the arduous process of the *Chaucer*. When an anonymous contributor to the *Daily Chronicle* suggested that Morris had dishonestly failed to acknowledge Catterson-Smith's role as collaborator of Burne-Jones in the *Chaucer*, Sydney Cockerell and Catterson-Smith both responded.[100] On November 25, 1898, Catterson-Smith defended Morris, noting "the statement is of the briefest, and you will notice that [Morris] has not mentioned his own share in designing and drawing the borders and capital letters—which was a pretty huge piece of work."[101] In response to his own collaboration with Burne-Jones, Catterson-Smith describes his view of their collaborative process in terms of Morris's ideal sympathetic translation:

> I only claim to have made myself as complete a tool for Burne-Jones as I could [...] Fingers, eyes, and sympathy I brought, but Sir Edward was responsible for every line and dot in the eighty "Chaucer" drawings which I did under his guidance. I worked at his very elbow for months, often spending whole days seeking out a simple and expressive treatment of a passage, and in many cases doing drawings over and over again, until he was satisfied that the treatment or convention (he used to call it his "shorthand") expressed *him*.[102]

Certainly, Catterson-Smith's awareness of being a "tool" in the artist's hands serves, to twenty-first century readers, as an uncomfortable awareness that Morris's ideological ideals of sympathetic translation and concord could be misrepresented in practice. This first statement underscores the practical undermining of the Kelmscott Press's ideology, and "illustrates once again the chasm that sometimes appeared between Morris's theories of bookmaking and what actually took place at the Press."[103] And yet, it is important to remember the context of Catterson-Smith's epistle: a defense of Morris, and, by extension Burne-Jones, as the illustrator responsible for the work of art. By referencing Burne-Jones's centrality, and focusing on the artist's "shorthand" – which Robinson describes as linear abbreviations for Burne-Jones's "pencil work, to provide marks the engraver could follow that were approved by the artist himself"[104] – Catterson-Smith removes attention from his own role, effectively giving up his agency in the public view of the *Daily Chronicle*. In doing so, this context emphasizes the myth – even held by someone so central to the Kelmscott *Chaucer*'s production – of solitary artistry: that there is only one person responsible for a work of art. As this book argues, however, the process of collaboration sheds important light on the method itself and the individuals involved, bringing forth names that have otherwise been marginalized in favor of those with whom scholarship and history are familiar. Within a more private light, evidenced in letters, lecture notes, and the manuscripts themselves, a sympathetic collaboration unfolds that, in practice, accords with Morris's ideological basis for his Press.

There is no doubt that the collaboration between Catterson-Smith and Burne-Jones for the Kelmscott *Chaucer* was a successful venture; one need only look at the illustrations surrounded by their ornamental borders, initialed blocks, and Chaucer type in their finalized form. To examine the process behind this production proves slightly complicated, as the materials are scattered internationally. Only recently, in December 2015, did Sotheby's auction a "Catterson-Smith Lot," further scattering letters and ephemera.[105] Furthermore, the illustrative materials are divided between New York and Cambridge: Burne-Jones's sketching and preliminary drawings are today found in the Fitzwilliam Museum, Cambridge, while the translations by Catterson-Smith for the process of wood-engraving are found in the Morgan Library, New York. And yet these materials are central to piecing together the collaborative process in order to understand how Catterson-Smith and Burne-Jones enacted Morris's ideal of sympathetic translation. Despite their transatlantic distribution among multiple public and private collections, it is crucial to see these materials in tandem. In his handwritten and unpublished lecture notes for his role in the production of the *Chaucer*, Catterson-Smith acknowledges that he translated the "romantic" drawings of Burne-Jones "from delicate pencil work into strong black ink drawings to be engraved on wood. That may appear a very simple matter—but it had to be done to the satisfaction of these two great craftsmen."[106] Indeed, what Catterson-Smith describes as appearing "simple" was quite labor-intensive. In his June 1, 1917 autographed manuscript, Catterson-Smith details the cutting of the *Chaucer* woodcuts and the "translation" involved:

> Emery Walker made a very pale print of a photograph (a platino) from Sir E.B-J's pencil drawing—the exact size of the drawing—I then stuck the print down on stout cardboard, and, in order to avoid the expansion of the paper I put the paste on the cardboard first and then applied the paper print very quickly, so quickly that it had no time to absorb moisture and so expand, then I immediately ran a hot smoothing iron over it when at once dried the paste. Next I gave the print a thin wash of Chinese white with a little size in it.[107] The result was to get rid of everything but the essential lines. Next I went over the pale lines with a very sharp pencil, copying and translating from the B-J drawing which was in front of me. The line of shading were put in pencil. These shadow lines were very difficult as they have to be translations of very gray pencil tones, and they often took a long time to fit into their spaces. When the pencil drawing was finished all trace

of the photograph had disappeared. Next came the inking over, which was done with a fine round sable brush and very black Chinese ink which I bought in bottles. By putting a little size in the Chinese white, as above mentioned, the ink was not absorbed by the white and so remained jet black—otherwise it would have become gray [...] When difficulties arose in the treatment of passages I consulted B-J [...] Some of the drawings were done over several times. [...] Finally E. Walker made a photograph on the wood block and Hooper cut it.[108]

His account illustrates an exacting process, and, upon first glance, can appear as though the "translation" is, perhaps, merely a tracing over of Burne-Jones's sketches, since the whiting over of the platino leaves behind "essential lines" to be copied and translated. In other words, this account alone might demonstrate the exact replication that Morris denounced in Hooper, and certainly provides evidence for the public account of Catterson-Smith as a tool in Burne-Jones's hands. However, looking at the sketches by Burne-Jones that Catterson-Smith refers to above, and the resulting reworked platinos, provides a different aspect.

Despite being damaged, the platinotype of Griselda from the second part of the Clerk's tale offers a visualization of Catterson-Smith's account (see Figure 4.2). Because Catterson-Smith worked directly from the platino, washing it in white and translating in black ink, Walker's photographic print is usually no longer extant. Fortunately, in damaged instances, Catterson-Smith appears to have struck through the unusable platino, and turned the cardboard over for sustainability and conservation: the damaged platino remains on the verso of the reworked reproduction for engraving by Hooper. This platino was made from Burne-Jones's sketch of the dressing of Grisilde in "The Clerk's Tale," for page 129 of the Kelmscott *Chaucer* (see Figure 4.1). Looking at Burne-Jones's sketch, we see the enormous challenge that Morris faced when turning these illustrations into engravings, and the reasoning for the detailed process recounted by Catterson-Smith. The platino reveals a considerably clearer view of the sketch, providing, of course, darker lines, while eliminating some of the delicate gray lines that Burne-Jones used to delineate shading in the drapery folds, as well as the dots in the wooded background, presumably to draw further attention to the branches in opposition to the thatched border and wall behind the female figures. If anything, the platino provides an exemplar of Morris's rejection of exact imitation, which makes sense given the nature of photographic reproduction. The interesting aspect arises when considering the sketch and platino alongside Catterson-Smith's reworking or translation. Here, we see the workings of sympathy within the collaborative process.

Figure 4.2 Burne-Jones, Edward (British, 1833–1898). Illustrations for the Kelmscott Chaucer, Plate 15: verso. 1894–1895. PML 76853. Gift of John A. Saks, 1977. The Morgan Library & Museum/Art Resource, NY.

As previously mentioned for the stained glass, Burne-Jones focuses his attention on figures, leaving the ornamental decoration to other hands. The same is true with his illustrations for the *Chaucer*. For the dressing of Grisilde, Catterson-Smith sympathetically translates Burne-Jones's sketch by staying faithful to the artist's foregrounding of the female figures, amending the sketch where it obscures the figure. In Burne-Jones's sketch, the female holding the chest on the left is hidden by an entwined tree; in the translation for engraving (see Figure 4.3), the tree is moved to the background, behind the thatched wall, thus foregrounding the figures. In addition, the largest change in terms of decorative ornament appears to be solely from Catterson-Smith's hand: "Fingers, eyes, and sympathy" he brought to fill the background space with foliage and flowers, a space previously filled with branches and faint dots. In other words, Catterson-Smith provided the tools – his hands and eyes – to translate the sketch into a suitable illustration that unifies Morris and Burne-Jones's visions.

"*Fingers, Eyes, and Sympathy*" 125

Figure 4.3 Burne-Jones, Edward (British, 1833–1898). Illustrations for the Kelmscott Chaucer, Plate 15: recto. 1894–1895. PML 76853. Gift of John A. Saks, 1977. The Morgan Library & Museum/Art Resource, NY.

Carrying the motif of natural imagery from Morris's decorative borders and initial, Catterson-Smith's translation achieves concord between the ornaments to bring unity to the entire page. In his lecture, he notes the harmony that underlies Morris's ideal book:

> Morris required the drawings to be such as to harmonise with the printed type, looking as if the pictures and type had been cut from the same block; and by the way, that requirement of his had a great influence on much of the work since done—even in the daily press; you will now see advertisements treated in that way—some very good. Sir EB-J of course was anxious that as much as possible of the fineness of his designs should be retained. I am very proud to say that the work I did gave entire satisfaction to these two men. (MSL Collection)

Like Morris, Catterson-Smith took pride in his work at the Kelmscott Press, and, in particular, the pleasure that he had in satisfying two men well-known for their high demands. Certainly, in Burne-Jones's sketch, the dots from the background and in the grass at bottom demonstrate the aforementioned shorthand; but as the manuscripts demonstrate, the sympathy between the collaborators allows for an adaptation and assimilation within the means of production. Of course, there may have been conversations about how to fill the spaces, but Burne-Jones does not dictate how to fill these spaces in his sketches; Catterson-Smith's artistic adaptation enables a concord that satisfies both Morris and Burne-Jones's demands: harmony and artistic finesse.

In another example from "The Clerk's Tale," we again see evidence of Burne-Jones's artistic attention to the figures, revealed in a preliminary study for what would become page 132 of the Kelmscott *Chaucer*. The study reveals a concentration of poses of the knight/servant, while Grisilde's attitude of cradling the infant remains the same (see Figure 4.4). In the upper portion, the knight holds his hands before his body; below, his arms are outstretched and, in the smaller study on the right, Burne-Jones drafts a variation on the waiting servant. Such a study reveals Burne-Jones's hesitation: is this a knight or a servant waiting to remove the child from Grisilde? Dependent upon the character, the pose and mannerism change in these drafted variations. Burne-Jones's sketch reveals, in terms of figure, a combination of servant and knight (see Figure 4.5). The male figure contains a helmet and chain-mailed feet, with his left hand on a sheathed sword. However, the most startling difference between Burne-Jones's study and sketch is the background. In the study, the background features a larger room with visible fireplace; the sketch reveals a smaller, more enclosed room – solid walls with small windows and narrowly arched doorways – creating a feeling of claustrophobic containment. Unlike the previous example of Catterson-Smith's translation, here, the translation is remarkably faithful to Burne-Jones's sketch (see Figure 4.6). What bears noting, however, is the marginalia surrounding the translation on the cardboard. Again, Burne-Jones remains fixated on the servant figure – all notation regards the figure on the right. Carrying over from his process with Morris's firm, Burne-Jones focuses on the figure's hands and provides detailed studies of the hands holding the hilt and of the sheathed sword itself. The notations at right provide a listing of revisions: "mail in left arm"; "sword hilt"; "alter proportion of soldier head"; "change hand on soldier hilt"; "increase size of child"; "Best for general work yet"; "perspective of stone stair wall not true."

Hidden among this list of revisions, Burne-Jones provides Catterson-Smith with a compliment: it is his "best [...] work yet." Once again, we see the centrality of conversation – of dialogue and response – to sympathetic

Figure 4.4 1079.31, Top, preliminary study for *The Tale of the Clerk of Oxford: the arrival of the servant charged with the removal of the child;* bottom, three figure studies: *Grisilde cradling the baby, the servant waiting, a variation of the waiting servant.* Burne-Jones, Edward (British, 1833–1898). Graphite on laid paper, the uppermost sketch within drawn, rectangular, graphite borders, height, support, 323 mm, width, support, 200 mm. For page 132 of the Kelmscott Chaucer. © The Fitzwilliam Museum, Cambridge.

Figure 4.5 1050.16, *The Clerk's Tale: The Servant Arrives to Take the Child from Grisilde*. Burne-Jones, Edward (British, 1833–1898). Graphite within drawn graphite border on paper, height, drawn area, 129 mm, width, drawn area, 171 mm. For page 132 of the Kelmscott Chaucer. © The Fitzwilliam Museum, Cambridge.

collaboration. If Burne-Jones's focus, as Catterson-Smith notes, was on retaining the "fineness of his designs," it makes sense that a faithful reproduction elicits praise. And yet, looking again at the sketch, the ornament on the sheath is absent. In the reworked platino, however, there is an ornate floral pattern. Catterson-Smith's small addition promotes a synthesis of Burne-Jones and Morris's ideologies. Incorporating the natural motifs for which Morris is famous, Catterson-Smith provides a harmonious concord upon the page. Catterson-Smith – in this triangulated collaboration – might be seen as the Smithean impartial spectator, observing and modulating his design based upon the components available to him from Burne-Jones's drawings and Morris's ornament. In the illustration, the sheath's ornament is the only element of nonlinear design, and thus, stands out among the engraved lines. Placed within Morris's elaborate frames, however, the sheath's ornament is normalized, and brings out the floral motif from its surroundings.

Figure 4.6   Burne-Jones, Edward (British, 1833–1898). Illustrations for the Kelmscott Chaucer, Plate 16. 1894–1895. PML 76853. Gift of John A. Saks, 1977. The Morgan Library & Museum/Art Resource, NY.

"A Thing Is Either All Right or Wrong"

Examining the collaboration of Burne-Jones and Catterson-Smith demonstrates how sympathetic translation can be put into practice. In contrast to this method of translation, Morris's own process of creating the Kelmscott borders and initials is striking for his belief in allowing the design to take a form of its own. The *Chaucer* contained fourteen border designs, in addition to the eighteen frames surrounding the illustrations, and twenty-six large initial words, and the woodcut title – all of which were designed solely by Morris. As Sparling notes, these ornaments were integral to the conception of the *Chaucer*, composed as "organically harmonious parts of a designed page."[109] Morris enriched his books with such ornamentation because "his mind and hand were irresistibly architectural in all things."[110] Indeed, Morris's notes from meetings and lecture drafts are covered in sketches of flowers or design elements. William Richard Lethaby, a renowned Arts and Crafts architect and theorist, described Morris's working method as almost unconscious:

> He would have two saucers, one of Indian ink, the other of Chinese white. Then, making the slightest indications of the main stems of the pattern he had in mind, with pencil, he would begin at once his finished final ornament by covering a length of ground with one brush and painting the pattern with the other. If a part did not satisfy him, the other brush covered it up again, and again he set to put in his finished work.[111]

In this description, we see Morris as a draughtsman whose hand had, by the time of the Kelmscott Press, woven an extraordinary number of graphic ornaments and designs. At this stage, Morris knew exactly what he wanted and would go about designing with both hands. Such a tactic demonstrates Morris's theory that "a harmonious piece of work needed to be the result of one flow of mind."[112] Perhaps, it is for this reason that Catterson-Smith found it startling that Morris had "little respect for sketches." Instead, Morris "only recognised completed, clear cut drawings as works of art. [...] He was by no means an impressionist. Sketches were for him only working drawings He did not care to trouble a thing right [sic]. He was very decisive."[113] To demonstrate such decisiveness, Catterson-Smith provides an anecdote about Morris throwing a design he had been at work on for a length of time straight into the fire. "I said 'surely some of it is right'?," writes Catterson-Smith, "He said 'No a thing is either all right or wrong.'"[114] Such an observation stands in contrast to the sympathy between Catterson-Smith and Burne-Jones; and yet, makes sense given that Morris was, in a sense, engaged not in interpersonal collaboration, but *intertextual* collaboration, and thus more aligned with the Ruskinian sympathy between things – objects on the page.[115] Morris's conception of the harmonic whole – the concord between all elements of a finished page – comes about in the finalized product, or, from "the result of one flow of mind."[116]

Aside from Burne-Jones, illustrators found Morris nearly impossible to please. Peterson points out that Burne-Jones is the only artist to have illustrated more than one Kelmscott book. Interestingly, Aubrey Beardsley and Charles Shannon were both snubbed by Morris, after offering a sampling of illustration and journal. Beardsley visited Morris at Kelmscott in 1892 with an illustration prepared for *Sidonia the Sorceress*, which Morris declined, perhaps because it was too decadent. The illustration is no longer extant, as Robert Ross notes in *Aubrey Beardsley*: "it is almost certain that the drawing was destroyed by the artist."[117] Based on this experience, Beardsley "nursed a grudge against Morris and sought revenge by creating a witty parody of the Kelmscott style in his ornament and illustrations for the Dent edition of Malory's *Le Morte D'Arthur* (1893–1894)."[118] Likewise, in the same year, upon receipt of Shannon's *The Dial*, Morris returned a reply of "mixed feelings": "I confess that I looked at the art portion of it with some what mixed feelings, as the talent & aberration of the talent seemed to me to be in about equal proportions."[119] Despite the later successes of these *fin de siècle* artists, Morris found almost all illustrators unsatisfactory. One could argue that Morris's deep-seated and long-term friendship with Burne-Jones enabled their concord, with Morris learning to sympathetically accommodate and assimilate Burne-Jones's style; however, when Morris approached fellow socialist and friend Walter Crane to illustrate *The Story of the Glittering Plain* (1894), Morris was unsatisfied, and even Crane doubted "if I was ever quite Gothic enough in feeling to suit his taste."[120] Friendship alone, it seems, was not the answer.

Morris and Charles Gere's Collaboration for *News from Nowhere*

Instead, Morris turned to Birmingham, where the Arts and Crafts movement flourished through the influence of the municipal School of Art.[121] In an interview with the *Daily Chronicle*, Morris is quoted praising its students in a qualified tone: "there is a great quantity of excellent art, but the only thing that is new, strictly speaking, is the rise of the Birmingham school of book decorators, [...] these young men of the Birmingham School of Art [...] have given a new start to the art of book decorating."[122] Two years later, however, in *Bookselling*, Morris remarks that these same book decorators "have ideas and originality. For the most part, however, they follow too slavishly the opposition to conventionality [...] but you must remember that the Birmingham people have not yet found their feet. They will do good work yet, I am sure."[123] Peterson suggests that Morris's attitude toward the Birmingham artists, specifically Arthur Gaskin and Charles Gere, was ambivalent, as expressed in these interviews. However, letters between Morris and Gere tell a slightly different story. Like Morris's collaboration with Hooper, these letters show Morris guiding Gere towards a sympathetic translation.

On November 5, 1892, Morris wrote to Gere, requesting him to stay at Kelmscott House in order to begin the famous illustration of the house for the Press edition of *News from Nowhere*. "What I want you to do is to make drawings (sketches) of the house from any points that you think would do for an *ornamental* drawing for a book of mine (News from Nowhere) now in press – to be cut in wood by the way. The sketches made we would then talk of what use is to be made of them."[124] Morris's emphasis on "ornamental" draws attention to his ideal of book design, and, importantly, focuses Gere's consideration to the purpose of the sketch as ornamental in this overture to the project. In "The Ideal Book," Morris provides his understanding of ornament as an architectural concord with the press's type:

> if we really feel impelled to ornament our books, no doubt we ought to try what we can do; but in this attempt we must remember one thing, that if we think the ornament is ornamentally a part of the book merely because it is printed with it, and bound up with it, we shall be much mistaken. The ornament must form as much a part of the page as the type itself, or it will miss its mark, and in order to succeed, and to be ornament, it must submit to certain limitations, and become *architectural*; a mere black and white picture, however interesting it may be as a picture, may be far from an ornament in a book; while on the other hand, a book ornamented with pictures that are suitable for that, and that only, may become a work of art second to none, save a fine building duly decorated, or a fine piece of literature.[125]

For Morris, type and ornament become, in a sense, one whole – they form a sympathetic concord upon the written page. In this way, Morris creates a divide between illustrations that are merely illustrative (recalling Morris's prior admonishment of Hooper, such illustrations would be an unintelligent form of art) and those that are, in his terms, ornamental. Morris further articulates his belief in form and quality, noting not only a balance between ornament and type, but a symmetry that occurs whereby the page becomes architectural. His conception that the ornamented text achieves an architectural form pinpoints the centrality of formal structure alongside the pleasure derived from ornament. Morris's emphasis on architecture, of course, has Ruskinian elements, but also becomes the foundation for his cathedral-like *Chaucer* collaboration with Burne-Jones. Morris's lectures lack pragmatic application: the audience is left questioning how the ideal book would become architectural.

The correspondence reveals Morris's reliance upon the Pre-Raphaelite turn to Nature as the means of providing concord and architectural wholeness. When Morris returned to Kelmscott and Gere's drawings, his next correspondence indicates this Ruskinian return to Nature. On November 14, the first paragraph of Morris's letter to Gere demonstrates the extent to which Morris was indebted to an experiential view of art: "I have your drawings of the house and think them very good & pretty; but I doubt if any of them will *quite* do for the foundation of our cut. In fact I hardly expected this from your first visit; I rather wanted you to go there to familiarize yourself with the house, than for anything else."[126] The first lesson, then, that Gere learns from Morris, is to draw from Nature: to sketch the house from his familiarity with it, presumably so as to create a translation of the house, rather than an exact replica. This notion, however, becomes complicated as Morris continues his discussion, deciding which of Gere's sketches would be most suitable for a wood-engraving: "the one of the entrance front of the house is the only one which is about the right shape for the cut, and I think that this must be the view taken only if something more could be got in of the tapestry block, and of the 2nd gable to the S. it would be better."127 Familiarity with the *News from Nowhere* illustration proves that this initial sketch was ultimately the drawing chosen for the frontispiece. Morris's concern with the faithfulness of the illustration to the house seems, initially, surprising, particularly in contrast to the correspondence illustrating Hooper's progress toward sympathetic translation earlier the same year.

Crafting a message around specific details of his home – including the tapestry room and the second gable – Morris implies a necessary realism for this particular illustration from Gere. Furthermore, one month later, Morris admonishes Gere's revisions in a detailed letter suggesting changes, while providing Morris's own sketch of the gables as a means of demonstration:

> I think some alterations are needed. The chimney-stack mixes up too much with the gable, & is much too small I should say.
>
> The markings of the stone work joints are too black and heavy, and would give the <drawin [sic]> block a sooty look. The copings of the gables are wrong I should say; I think some indication of their mouldings must be shown I think. [Morris includes a sketch of the copings alongside his text.]
>
> I think also that the stone path up to the porch might be drawn with more literality. Again the plants against the house wall are *vines* and should have some indication of the<ir> habit of vines.
>
> There is much good about your drawing, and the general effect is good: but I think if you could spare the time in the course of a month it would be better if you could see the house again and take this drawing with you I think I might be able to meet you there in that time. There is no very great hurry about getting the book out.128

With such minute specificity in this letter, Morris's ideal of sympathetic translation appears to have vanished. Morris's belief that the craftsman should not be merely a tool disappears from this epistle favoring illustration verbatim from the master. Gone is the sympathetic method of adaptation and modulation, intensifying the tension between collaboration and paid labor. This letter provides a list of inadequacies, despite Morris's ending belief that "there is much good" – if only the details could be gotten right. Familiarity with the house is no longer of primary importance for Morris; accuracy has become the ideal for this illustration. But for Morris, these two concerns are related.

Despite the detailed corrections Morris notes in the above letter, Gere accepted only a few of Morris's notes. Kelvin's collection of Morris's letters includes reproductions of preliminary drawings by Gere for the frontispiece.[129] The printed wood-engraved illustration shows that Gere lightened the stone-work joints, and improved the copings and stone paths; however, the vines do not appear to gain "the<ir> habit of vines" and appear, in the printed frontispiece, much the same as in the preliminary sketch, bearing more resemblance to trees. The chimney stack, too, remains almost indistinguishable from the gable. A larger revision – and one unmentioned by Morris – is Gere's removal of tree branches along the left of the frame. In the preliminary sketch, Gere creates a left border of foregrounded leafed branches, covering the house and its gable. In the published frontispiece, the situation is reversed: Kelmscott Manor is foregrounded and Gere's leafy border is removed, presumably in favor of Morris's own decorative border encasing Gere's illustration and the caption. Kelvin notes that "Morris was never quite satisfied with any version of Gere's drawing but used the one he did because in fact it was not possible to delay any longer."[130] However, there is no evidence in the correspondence to suggest Morris's displeasure; indeed, had Morris been wholly dissatisfied he would not have used the illustration, or simply would have replaced Gere with another illustrator. Such a replacement was not unusual for Morris: in 1893, Morris requested that Arthur Gaskin, another Birmingham artist, illustrate *The Well at the World's End*. Despite Morris's detailed criticisms and Gaskin's continual revisions, the illustrations remained unsatisfactory, and, in 1895, Morris could delay the publication no longer and wrote to Gaskin that the illustrations would remain unused. When *The Well at the World's End* was published in 1896, the edition was ornamented with four illustrations by Burne-Jones. In any case, Morris continued to work with Gere for *News from Nowhere* in 1892, providing instruction until the illustration met his approval, an approval that – as we have seen – was difficult to obtain.

Echoing Morris's own insistence on accuracy, the engraved illustration itself became a permanent fixture in the popular imagination of what Kelmscott Manor ought to look like. Peterson notes that custodians of the house in recent history "rearranged and in some cases replanted [the trees and bushes in front the house] so that they would appear exactly as they do in Gere's illustration."[131] Norman Kelvin, in *"News from Nowhere* and *The Spoils of Poynton*: Interiors and Exteriors" (1999), discusses in a brief postscript the possibility that Gere's illustration may have been autobiographical for Morris. *News from Nowhere* has been read as autobiographical – with William Guest as a substitute for William Morris and his dream for a collaborative and pleasurable postrevolutionary future. Noting the work's subtitle, an "Epoch of Rest," Kelvin surmises that "Kelmscott Manor was the only place in which Morris ever felt completely in repose," and, as such, suggests that "the desired image is a piece of autobiography for Morris, and in a very subtle way this representation of an exterior becomes a manifestation of interiority when we recall how intimate were Morris's feelings about Kelmscott Manor."[132] This reading sheds light on the change from Morris's ideal sympathetic translation to critical focus on detail and reality. One could argue that the element of autobiography lends structure to the romance, and, therefore, Gere's illustration was meant to serve an express purpose. Certainly, Morris's direct caption accompanying Gere's illustration explains his creative process in that the Kelmscott edition creates a sort of book end. Upon opening the book, the reader enters Morris's vision in an imaginative sympathetic transportation both through the image itself – readers fancy themselves walking up the path lined with trees into the welcoming gabled house – and within William Guest's dream of a utopic future. The novel repeats this image with its vision of Kelmscott Manor in the culminating scene of the novel. The Kelmscott edition, then, foregrounds this structural transport for the reader.

However, the 1893 Kelmscott *News from Nowhere* is not the only edition of Morris's novel. Initially, *News from Nowhere* was serialized in Morris's socialist newspaper the *Commonweal* in 1890, bearing an illustration by Walter Crane. Crane's illustration contains no trace of Kelmscott Manor; instead, the "Solidarity of Labour" cartoon that ran in the May 24, 1890 issue of the *Commonweal* depicts a decidedly liberal evocation of global harmony, with an angel brandishing a banner: "Fraternity," "Equality," and "Freedom," alongside banners bearing the names of continents. Elizabeth Carolyn Miller discusses the editions of *News from Nowhere* in her monograph *Slow Print*, emphasizing the continuities between the *Commonweal* and Kelmscott Press.[133] In so doing, Miller aims to "show how Morris exploited aspects of each print medium to critique the political effects of mass print culture" and argues that Morris's perception of a failed liberal notion of print as "an agent of progress" becomes reinvented as an ideal radical printing practice.[134] Unacknowledged by Miller, however, the banner's "Fraternity," "Equality," and "Freedom" holds similarities to the eighteenth-century revolutionary keywords of Liberty, Equality, and Fraternity, discussed in Chapter 2. The *Commonweal*'s assertion of Freedom over Liberty situates itself within the ideals of nineteenth-century liberalism, emphasizing freedom as the ultimate goal of a progressive and moral society. Indeed, as this book has demonstrated, liberalism values active individuals who are conscious (self-reflective) of their actions and free. As Lauren M. E. Goodlad asserts in her application of Foucault's later essays on governmentality as a framework for understanding the conceptions of nineteenth-century liberalism, "to be free is not – as in crude liberal thought – to escape to some autonomous realm outside of power, but, rather, to exercise one's own power to influence and be influenced by others."[135] Such influence is a result of the long reach of Smithean sympathy, specifically the social mirror and its implications of liberal self-help and self-reliance. Moreover, if, as I suggested in Chapter 2, Fraternity becomes a form of collaboration reliant upon sympathy and communal experience, how might reading the Kelmscott frontispiece alongside the *Commonweal* cartoon reveal Morris's creative process and sympathetic collaboration between himself and Gere – and, broadening out, the collaborative processes at work in the operations of the Kelmscott Press – within his vision of a cooperative society?

Like Morris, Crane also believed in a form of sympathetic translation. In similar terms, Crane describes his belief in art as a representation of an abstract idea, or, as he says, an "inner vision" rather than an outward expression. In 1898, Crane, like Morris before him, distinguished between an imitative art – "art which springs directly out of nature" – and art as "the record or re-creation of ideas, which selects or invents only such forms as may express a preconceived idea, as a poet uses words."[136] Rather than realist particulars, Crane's work focuses on abstract forms, which, as Miller argues, "constitutes a utopian language that refers to what could be rather than what is."[137] Crane's cartoon for *News from Nowhere* appears embedded within Chapter 17, "How the Change Came," not coincidentally the chapter that describes the socialist revolution. Whereas Morris's chapter depicts his vision of revolution as a reaction to governmental violence, Crane's inner vision demonstrates his view of change occurring through the power of idealism: hand in hand, the continental men encircle the globe, as wheat or corn frames the bottom of the globe, and the tools of labor (shovel, hoe, pickaxe) repeat, at the bottom of the frame, the outward stretch of the angel's arms. Such a politically idealistic cartoon makes sense, as Miller points out, because *News from Nowhere* was serialized alongside "articles on topics such as the labor struggle, the abuse of Russian political prisoners in Siberia, and the brutality of African colonization."[138] Crane's illustration, then, resonates with the newspaper's contents to "recreate" a vision that responds to the political context within which it is embedded, and also reaches back to liberalism's radical history. At the same time, Crane's usage of the eighteenth-century revolutionary keywords in the angelic banner recalls a historically liberal trajectory that is foregrounded by Crane's choice of title emphasizing solidarity and his depiction of fraternal men, hand-in-hand, who have, ostensibly, come together to celebrate the fruits of their labor. The illustration recalls the Romantic literary circle – groups united around shared progressive political ideals – and their capacity for communal sites of productivity. Thus, Crane's cartoon also reads as an ideal collaborative endeavor – the very collaboration that comes out of Nowhere's revolution – and provides a counterpart to the fraternal community within the walls of Kelmscott Manor, which seems to include both men and women.

Rather than using Crane's illustration for the frontispiece of the Kelmscott *Nowhere*, Morris opted for Gere's illustration of Kelmscott Manor. If Morris's correspondence with Gere reveals a desire for almost literal representation, in one respect it makes sense that Morris would choose not to use Crane's "inner vision" of the postrevolutionary world. At the same time, however, approaching the illustrations as liberal compositions promoting sympathetic collaboration reveals a larger initiative. Dedicating his illustration to the "workers of the world," Crane's cartoon records a collaborative endeavor that speaks both to Morris's *Nowhere* and the global political issues discussed within the *Commonweal*; the dedication here works as a means of embedding the illustration within both fiction and reality. The Kelmscott edition features Gere's illustration surrounded by Morris's decorative leafy border and uses, as Miller points out, a caption printed in clean, capital letters to insist on material presence, at the same time as it depicts a scene detached from historical reality. Miller argues that such material presence, derived from decorative frames and borders and sharp capital letters, is a feature of the "utopian form" of the Kelmscott editions: "They signify that the image is not continuous with phenomenal reality but exists in a separate space and chronology."[139] Certainly, the ornamental usage of Morris's border and designs creates, at once, an integration of the artwork into organic nature while also demarcating artificiality through its delineated division. However, the process behind Gere's illustration suggests something quite different: Morris's insistence that Gere get his sketch right by creating a more faithful representation of Kelmscott Manor places the image within a specific space and historic moment: that of Kelmscott, a site of collaborative production and lived fraternity. Like the cognitive process of sympathy – by which one enters into the feelings of another – here, at the opening of his novel, the Kelmscott illustration beckons its readers to enter into a specific place and space where communal production can be experienced. Morris's insistence upon detail to Gere portrays an extension of Crane's inner vision of liberal fraternity – of collaboration as a form of revolutionary community – an extension that foregrounds the site of collaborative production. In this way, the collaborative process between Gere and Morris extends an understanding of sympathy that demonstrates its imaginative transportation: through the literal insistence of the material presence of Kelmscott, Morris's readers are invited to imagine, within the house's walls, the kind of hand-in-hand solidarity previously captured by Crane, a solidarity experientially reflected in the interpersonal and intertextual collaborations within the Kelmscott Press.

Pleasure in the "Lesser Arts"

In this final section, I return to my previous claim concerning the larger trajectory of the Kelmscott Press and the impact that my focus on liberalism has upon Morris scholarship. Beyond Morris's ideal of creating beauty in his surroundings lies his belief that, as Linda Dowling argues, community can contest "the system which insists on individualism and forbids co-operation."[140] In 1883, however, Morris's idealistic search for "compensatory structures of human communality and solidarity set aside Shaftesburian 'benevolence,' 'refinement,' and 'taste.'"[141] In the fourth quarter of the nineteenth century, a "morality of anti-individualism" became viable, in the form of socialism, for those who resisted individualism and opposed the seeming chaos of modernity. Morris's liberal emphasis on lived community – demonstrated in this chapter by the interpersonal collaboration and conversation between workers – and moral-aesthetic sense remains the animating principle in Morris's *News from Nowhere* (issued March 24, 1893), which foregrounds Kelmscott House and is the 12th book printed by the Kelmscott Press. The romance features the people of Nowhere's instinctual goodness and fellowship, and, although there are occasional transgressions, William Guest – the narrator and stand-in for William Morris – identifies them as "the errors of friends, not the habitual actions of persons driven into enmity against society."[142] By looking at the message, which advocates an egalitarian community, within the books that Morris chose to be reprinted by the Kelmscott Press, we see traces of Morris's liberalism alongside his embrace of socialism at the end of his career. J.W. Mackail describes Morris's "innate socialism" as the guiding force behind the development of Morris's communities.[143] Dowling expands on Mackail's observation, noting Morris's "ability to merge himself into the social totality without suffering either anxiety or loss of identity. This seamless merging of the individual into the social whole"[144] is what forms Morris's conviction that he belongs to a communal body, working sympathetically for all – each member working alongside one another – to bring about real and pleasurable equality. Dowling – and, by extension, Mackail – argues that this underlying ability supplied the basis for Morris's later commitment to practical Socialism. However, Dowling's reliance on Shaftesburian Whiggery neglects the importance of Smith's impartial spectator and the capability of sympathetic imaginative transport. Morris's ability to "merge" within "the social totality" without a loss of individuality imitates the language of sympathy as a cognitive process. Imaginative projection allows Morris to assimilate, and self-modulate, within his communities. As such, we can see his progression of communal experimentation as an enactment of the role of the impartial spectator, which enables the harmonic whole of society. By positioning the Kelmscott Press within a liberal tradition, I posit that Morris's fraternity of aesthetic reform, rooted in Smithean sympathy, is an expression of Morris's socialist beliefs. Morris sought to emulate his ideal collaborative process as a means of creating an ideal, and liberal, community. This same practice of imaginative projection at work within the foundation of lived community becomes embedded in Morris's formal experimentation.

Morris famously associates himself with the so-called "lesser" arts as the means by which pleasure is achieved. In 1877, in a lecture entitled "The Lesser Arts," delivered before the Trades Guild of Learning, Morris argued that there should be no division between the "lesser arts," those "comprising the crafts of house-building, painting, joinery and carpentry, smiths' work, pottery and glass-making, weaving, and many others," and the "higher arts" of painting, architecture, and sculpture.[145] When severed, both arts suffer:

> the lesser ones become trivial, mechanical, unintelligent, incapable of resisting the changes pressed upon them by fashion or dishonesty; while the greater, however they may be practised for a while by men of great minds and wonder-working hands, unhelped by the lesser, unhelped by each other, are sure to lose their dignity [...] and become nothing but dull adjuncts to unmeaning pomp, or ingenious toys for a few rich and idle men.[146]

The great fault of the late Victorian period, in Morris's view, was the divorce of the arts: the higher arts of the intellect had separated from the everyday beauty of decoration. This separation led to the mechanized and "trivial" aspects of handiwork and craftsmanship that Morris famously deplored as the result of capitalism; by the same token, the great arts "lose their dignity" as they become inaccessible to the masses: turned out as "toys" by demand for the wealthy. Morris attributes classism to the divorce of the arts: creating social imbalance in the appreciation of beauty when the aim and purpose of art has been separated from its context. His democratic conception of the arts is in contrast to T. H. Green's mutually beneficial idealism, rehearsed in Chapter 3, by which the upper classes require the lower classes (and vice-versa) for self-fulfillment. For Morris, there should be no "I over classes" – all are equal. Furthermore, Morris's repetition of "unhelped" focuses attention to the necessity of influence. The greater arts require the "help" of the lesser, of the everyday, to form a sort of concord, to establish a reformed art that reflects the simple elements found in historical and natural influences.

Understanding Morris's theory as founded in Smithean sympathy pinpoints comparison with the metaphor of the impartial spectator, whereby the process of mutual emotional adjustment gives rise to virtue and pleasure through projective imagination. The greater and lesser arts, in Morris's view, must also enact a sort of impartial spectatorship to provide relief to an alienated Victorian public. The remedy for the Victorian separation of the arts comes through sympathetic assimilation:

> the handicraftsman, left behind by the artist when the arts sundered, must come up with him, must work side by side with him: apart from the difference between a great master and a scholar, apart from the differences of the natural bent of men's minds, which would make one man an imitative, and another an architectural or decorative artist, there should be no difference between those employed on strictly ornamental work; and the body of artists dealing with this should quicken with their art all makers of things into artists also, in proportion to the necessities and uses of the things they would make.[147]

Like Smith, Morris acknowledges that the complete merger of the arts would be impossible; instead, he allows for the differences between the minds of the handicraftsman and the artist. But exactly how would this occur? Morris's lectures are known for their idealism and limited concern with practical application. Reading Morris's remedy with a sympathetic lens, however, demonstrates how such a merger might take place, a union that comes to its fulfillment in Morris's communal artistic endeavors. In order for there to be no difference between the employment of those in the greater and lesser arts, the artists must work side-by-side – forming a mirror by which the work of one is reflected in the work of the other. This superimposition, of course, recalls Smith's social mirror and formulation of the impartial spectator; only, Morris's concern is that his artisans reflect the influences of Nature and History. By bringing the two influences alongside one another, or, in Smithean terms, into society with one another, Morris's greater and lesser arts form a sort of self-modulation, learning one from the other, how to best incorporate Nature and History: "if we do not study the ancient work directly and learn to understand it, we shall find ourselves influenced by the feeble work all round us, and shall be copying the better work through the copyists and *without* understanding it. [...] Let us therefore study it wisely, be taught by it, kindled by it; all the while determining not to imitate or repeat it."[148] Just as Smithean concord necessarily involves sociability, from which individuals derive pleasure through mutual sympathy, Morris's application of the lesser arts as a reflection of the greater arts in its interweaving of the past with the present provides the ultimate aim of art: to provide pleasure and rest.

In 1877, Morris believed that the office of decoration was twofold: "to give people pleasure in the things they must perforce *use*" and "to give people pleasure in the things they must perforce *make*."[149] By 1882, Morris extends this pleasure of the lesser arts to democratization in his lecture, "The Lesser Arts of Life," delivered before the Birmingham and Midlands Institute:

> I want the democracy of the arts established: I want every one to think for himself about them, and not to take things for granted from hearsay; every man to do what he thinks right, not in anarchical fashion, but feeling that he is responsible to his fellows for what he feels, thinks, and has determined.[150]

Morris's larger ambition for "the democracy of arts," as Dowling asserts, "impelled him to seek not simply a local set of decorative arrangements or artistic relations but the sociopolitical ideal I have been calling aesthetic democracy."[151] Dowling's understanding of aesthetic democracy involves a "social transformation by which the unanimous yet uncoerced bond between the citizens and their polity approximated the relation between aesthetic perceivers and the beautiful."[152] The pleasure that Morris describes in 1882, therefore, becomes a democratic pleasure – or aesthetic democracy – by which *all* are able to perceive art and think for themselves: "In these lesser arts everyone should say: I have such or such an ornamental matter, not because I am told to like it, but because I like it myself, and I will have nothing that I don't like, nothing; and I can give you my reasons for rejecting this, and accepting that."[153] Vitally, such dependence of thought springs from a knowledge that derives from sympathy, as Morris's acknowledgement of rejection and acceptance is similar to the role of the impartial spectator. Just as sympathy is a social process, so too is Morris's conception of art.

Morris's emphasis on a lived sociality, on a concord between individuals, comes to its fulfillment at Kelmscott, as a site that combines work with social pleasure. When Morris opened his Press, he named it after the Manor that was chosen as a summer home in 1871 and signed as a joint lease with Dante Gabriel Rossetti. Morris selected the house for its true craftsmanship, in harmony with its natural setting. Such sociability and communal pleasure are best illustrated, perhaps, with a final anecdote illustrating the coming together of Morris with his employees. William Morris and May Morris joined his printers on a yearly outing known as a "Wayzegoose." After dinner, the printers celebrated with a lengthy program of toasts, songs, and recitations. Peterson chronicles one such event in 1894 when they heard "Binning toast the Kelmscott Press, F. Collins sing 'At Trinity Church I Met My Doom,' and Binning (once more) recite 'Cassius instigating Brutus.' The bill, paid by Morris, came to a total of £ 9 15s. 4d. and included both luncheon and dinner for seventeen, many bottles of wine and port, and a good supply of cigars."[154]

While such images of concord between individuals maintain a brightened outlook, the Kelmscott Press remained a business, and Morris's relationship with his printers was not always peaceful. Morris's pursuit of perfection both impressed and horrified his workers and visitors. When Morris was unimpressed with the trial pages that came across his desk, he returned them to be redone for, perhaps, the sixth or seventh time. Peterson chronicles that when Morris "discovered an error on the first sheet off the press, he had the passage reset while the pressmen stood idly by."[155] Sparling, too, tells a story in his journal of the head of a commercial printing firm watching Morris's compositors in their careful setting and justifying, line after line. The individual "looked with a discontented eye at the pressmen heedfully pulling sheet after sheet, minutely examining each one to see whether it were up to the mark; and as he left, summed up his impression: 'We-e-ll? That's all very well for Mr. Morris, but there isn't a man here that would be worth a penny an hour to me after he'd been here for a week.'"[156] The tension between Morris's ideal and the growing mechanization of Victorian printing serves as a sad commentary on the incompatibility of Morris's ideal in the actual conditions of late nineteenth-century society. At the same time, this tension also reveals a core concept of Smithean sympathy: sympathetic identification with another, or within a community, allows us to imagine the possibility of a *fleeting* moment of concord.

By investigating the collaboration embodied in the Kelmscott Press, we are able to recognize the difficulty of its categorization. How do we classify a single project composed of disparate artistic endeavors? The answer lies in understanding Morris's conception of the ideal book and community fulfilled in the Kelmscott Press via Smith's theory of sympathy. With a sympathetic lens, we analyze not only a blending of aesthetic and historic modes, but the Kelmscott Press's mission of bringing together multiple professional classes of people (printers, engravers, editors, illustrators, and authors) in an interpersonal collaborative effort to feel with and for another person, and the product created. By looking at collaboration holistically, Morris's pursuit of Pre-Raphaelitism and sympathetic collaboration as a way of life becomes enshrined in the Kelmscott Press.

CHAPTER 5

Sim and Puss
The Sympathetic Mirroring of Michael Field

"The year will not be dull," wrote Edith Cooper confidently in the opening page of the 1911 *Works and Days*, a multivolume collaborative journal kept with her aunt and partner, Katharine Bradley. Proving these words true, in late January after her forty-ninth birthday, Cooper was diagnosed with terminal cancer. With great courage, the poets, who wrote together under the name "Michael Field," refused to be idle; they remained preoccupied with their work, each other, and Cooper's death. Originally written in 1912 for inclusion in *Mystic Trees*, but ultimately unpublished until 1930 in *Wattlefold*, a posthumous collection of Michael Field's previously unpublished poems, Bradley's poem "Lovers" describes the couple as entangled strings:

> Lovers, fresh plighting lovers in our age
> Lovers in Christ—so tender at the heart
> The pull about the strings as they engage—
> One thing is plain: —That we can never part.[1]

Bradley could not have known that these words were prophetical: in June 1913, she was diagnosed with breast cancer at the age of sixty-six. Cancer was a family illness, but perhaps the diagnosis could also be attributed to Bradley's determination "That we can never part," her refusal to be left behind in Cooper's absence. Despite a lifelong sharing of ideas and confidences, when Bradley needed Cooper's sympathies the most, she refused to cause her beloved further pain by sharing her own illness. Bradley's decision to keep her diagnosis a secret suggests her role as elder and protector – after all, Cooper was her niece and, initially, ward. There is no mention of Bradley's diagnosis in their diary; only John Gray – a decadent poet turned Catholic priest and member of the couple's wide Aesthetic circle – and her doctor knew Bradley's secret.

On December 13, 1913, Edith Cooper died, her last words indicating her endless appetite for life: "Not yet, not yet."[2] Bradley's first hemorrhage was brought on by her grief upon the occasion of Cooper's funeral, recorded in the joint diary, as Bradley continued her habit of personally addressing her lover: "Two days after thou wert gone, bleeding came."³ Bradley had only nine months after Cooper's death to live without her constant friend, companion, and coauthor. On September 26, 1914, Bradley wrote to illustrator and book designer Charles Ricketts upon waking; while being dressed for Mass, she fell into the arms of her nurse and died. In their last moments, Cooper and Bradley remain joined, yet separate. At the same time, however, such a narrative also points toward the inclination of romantic myth-making; my focus in this chapter teases out a more nuanced understanding of their collaboration, focusing on the separateness of their union, while demonstrating the shifting conceptions of sympathetic collaboration influenced by the change in community formation at the end of the long nineteenth century.⁴

The couple's twinned deaths and the corresponding strength that Katharine Bradley and Edith Cooper find in each other resonates with definitions of decadence. In 1893, Arthur Symons applied the adjective "decadent" to define "[t]he latest movement in modern literature."⁵ Symons acknowledged that decadent writing included qualities associated with the decline of great periods – highlighting the Greek and Latin – and named characteristics such as "an intense self-consciousness, a restless curiosity in research, an over-subtilizing refinement upon refinement."⁶ These decadent characteristics (self-reflection, research, refinement), and an extreme preoccupation (marked by the adjectives "intense," "restless," and "over-subtilizing") with finding strength and revitalization in death, or tragic history, were primary concerns in the lives and writing of Bradley and Cooper. However, Michael Field remained uneasy about the application of the term "decadent" to their writing, noted in their "abhorrence of the *Yellow Book* and its circle of contributors." Such a view toward this terminology is further complicated by the couple's widespread reading of French decadents.⁷ Michael Field carries traces of the liberal sympathetic experience, explored in previous chapters, into their literature's amalgamation of specifically decadent characteristics (reliance on research, self-reflexivity, tactility), while also looking inevitably toward a new conception of society that, for them, remained historically indeterminate. As such, this chapter notices a shift in communal development that marks the increasingly fractured understanding of the self that, in broad strokes, characterizes Modernism. Such a position aligns with Matthew Potolsky's innovative view of Decadence as characteristic of a "preoccup[ation] of communities."⁸

This chapter considers the changing constructions of community at the end of the century, and the shifting views of sympathy away from a metaphysical understanding toward a more materialist aesthetics. By tracing a view of sympathetic collaboration across the nineteenth century, I have demonstrated the influences of liberal community and sociability upon the collaborative form in both life-writing and poetic or narrative structures. This is a decidedly Victorian – and liberal – conception of the process of coming together as involving self-reflexivity, modulation, and assimilation in order to form a harmonious whole: a democratic society rooted in the reformative expressions of art. In culminating such a trajectory with a couple who finds themselves outside of time – experimenting with both Victorian literary constructions and developing innovative anticipations of Modernism – and with the turn toward empathy explored in the next chapter, I support Potolsky's claim that decadent writers "participated in [...] efforts to imagine new forms of affiliation and sociality."[9] Literary scholarship has associated decadence with an isolationist characteristic: "a turn away from the world and the public interest to the interiority of the private self."[10] Potolsky's original – and much needed – corrective to such "social atomization" is a view of the decadent community that "foster[s] a sense of attachment through the appreciation, repetition, and circulation of artists, texts, and tropes that signal an ever-expanding subculture of dissident taste."[11] This corrective is one that develops alongside a nineteenth-century liberal conception of sympathetic experience, but that differs from such a sensibility in its turn away from nineteenth-century affiliations with the creation of moral community for the sake of a greater good. The decadent "sense of community," Potolsky asserts, "could begin with the opening of a book, and end when the book is put aside."[12] It is, notably, a community with an ending; a transitory circulation that creates a so-called "dissident subculture." This "decadent republic of letters" contains traces of the liberal tradition that I have explored throughout this book, and it is specifically those traces that are the focus of this chapter: Michael Field's formation of communal experience within their oeuvre.

Too often the divide between the Victorian and Modern periods obscures the cross-pollination between individuals and the literary movements themselves.[13] Michael Field offers a unique opportunity to read across the late nineteenth and early twentieth centuries because the writers acknowledge their own atemporality and question their sense of belonging. Thus, in the midst of late nineteenth-century changes in understandings of sympathy and community, there is also a difference in the process of coming together. The Fields' archive visualizes the traces of their collaboration and its roots within sympathetic collaboration, even while asserting separateness. We witness, at the end of the century, a shift away from prior chapters' emphases on sympathetic assimilation and accommodation to underscore the distinct separateness in the couple's tone and formal construction, and the coming together of these individual parts to form a whole.[14]

During their lifetime, Michael Field was warned that they would be strangers to fame during their literary moment. Robert Browning, among others, cautioned that their fortune would be realized in the future: "Wait fifty years."[15] As Kate Thomas asserts in her article on the queer temporality of Michael Field, "Michael Field has always been—and perhaps always will be—'out of time.'"[16] Such ambiguous temporality foregrounds what Thomas perceives as "ricocheting between the ends of the nineteenth and twentieth centuries. It is an echo of the conceit that Michael Field awaits a new century, a new era in which to be discovered."[17] Of singular importance is the couple's own sense of inevitability. Rather than a warning or a delay, as in Browning's words, Michael Field recognizes that they will not achieve recognition in their time, but that they will one day, in some indeterminate future. "That glitch, that recognition that they are not and will not be famous in their lifetimes, is very important. It shows that they feel historical and that this feeling derives from their embrace of a specifically broken, interrupted teleology."[18] Thomas argues that this sense of indeterminate temporality provides a "dreamed-of immortality" as a "generative poetic stance" embracing the "unappreciative present" while "looking backward to past ages and imagining a future immortality."[19] While I am not overtly interested in making large claims about periodization here, it is important to recognize that Michael Field was very much aware of their historical moment and the feelings of disturbance and disruptiveness that marked the late nineteenth century.

At the same time, however, understanding Michael Field's awareness of not belonging to any particular historical moment pinpoints the influence of their shared life experiences upon their creative production. We can trace the influence of Victorian poetry's experimental nature and its adaptation to contemporary needs through the meditation, construction, and debate of life from the realistic depiction of shared experience – a point highlighted in Chapter 2. In paying special attention to Michael Field's own historical instability, I focus primarily on how these circulated feelings of indeterminacy become formalized in the couple's life-writing and poetic structures. Feeling outside of their time, Michael Field relates their own sense of themselves by experimenting with traditional poetic verse structures and genres, like the verse drama, that deliberately blur conventional boundaries. Indeed, just as the opening vignette uses narrative to enable readers to sympathize with Michael Field by offering a glimpse into their joint lives, the couple themselves use a combination of narrative and lyric forms in their life-writing and historical verse dramas to transport their readers into the couple's experiences of the world in which they lived. Remaining united in their literary productions, Michael Field is strengthened by a reliance on the historical past and the importance of rediscovering the historical moment in order to revitalize the present.

Examining the couple's collaborative process and the importance they place on their unified persona in the crafted autobiographical account of their life together in *Works and Days* reveals that Michael Field enacts a sympathetic mirroring within the diary's textured pages and extends this mirroring to their literary production. Indeed, while pseudonyms were not uncommon in the Victorian period, it is quite unusual for two writers to share one pseudonym. Their pseudonym, in fact, explicates a bipartite understanding of Michael Field's collaborative process: signifying an assumed name of two separate women, while appearing to signify a singular masculine identity, "Michael Field" – as a whole – represents the unity of Katharine Bradley and Edith Cooper in both literary (public) and personal arenas. In other words, their very signature illustrates their sympathetic concord. Since the couple's life-writing preserves a distinct separateness, which allows an experimental hybridity of voices to emerge, I maintain the plurality of Michael Field (or "the Fields" as their friends called them), asserting their distinctness as individuals who come together in a social construction of coauthorship. The hybridity found in their life-writing becomes inscribed in the formal experimentation of Michael Field's verse dramas, which incorporate prose, poetry, and song. As such, the form of these dramas blends perspectives and voices, and blurs genre conventions in an act of collaboration fashioned to mirror Michael Field's own collaborative process. In the last twenty years, scholarship has witnessed a resurgence in work on Michael Field, the majority of which has examined the couple's poetry, linking their verse to late-Victorian aesthetic theory, and analyzing the eroticism within their poetry with an eye toward feminist and queer theories.[20] More recently, attention has been given to situating the collaborators within their literary moment, both socially and textually: Michael Field was on the verge of transition between the Victorian and the Modern – a transition that is blurred with Sarah Parker and Ana Parejo Vadillo's superb collection, *Michael Field: Decadent Moderns*.[21] Drawing from an approach that privileges manuscript culture, my analysis extends beyond a solely poetical critical focus, pairing Michael Field's understudied verse dramas with their unpublished journals. Doing so contributes to an understanding of the couple's entire oeuvre as an enactment of communal sympathy invoking experimental forms.

Within poetry, the Fields publicly display a united consciousness, which stems from Baruch Spinoza's vision of the Greek term for "fellow-feeling," as they noted in a letter to Robert Browning. I must start with the couple's poetry because in it we see an insistence on the unified voice, but critics who have discussed Michael Field's poetry miss the ways in which the two women were deeply interested in separateness as a prerequisite for such unity. This prerequisite becomes apparent in their journals and verse drama via a sustained attention to the elements of sympathetic collaboration. Michael Field's collaboration is founded upon a model of sympathetic mirroring, which necessarily preserves separateness while entering into the other's feelings through Smith's idea of imaginative transport, a concept to which I will return. Setting up this foundation, the chapter next considers Michael Field's diaries as a construction of the couple's life, exposing the narrative techniques and interpretive frameworks that allow for this sympathetic transportation. The narrative dialogism within the life-writing allows for the duality of the two voices to become unified in a sympathetic concord – a dialogism witnessed throughout *Works and Days*, but particularly in the 1906 emotional retrospective narration of the loss of Whym Chow, the russet-coated Chow dog given by Cooper to Bradley, and, in 1889, their detailed description of their travels to Holyrood Palace in Edinburgh. This constructed dialogic space from the life-writing becomes inscribed in the form of Michael Field's verse drama, *The Tragic Mary* (1890). In line with the Victorian focus on adapting older poetic forms for the repurposing of contemporary needs, the poet-dramatists experiment with formal boundaries of Greek and Shakespearean dramatic traditions, blurring conventions of voice, rhythm, and structure. In *The Tragic Mary*, the Fields experiment with traditional ballad conventions to incorporate mimetic literature, founded on female community, and encouraged by contagious transference – or sympathetic transport. Such blurred boundaries within the literature embody their own sympathetic collaboration.

Crossing and Interlacing: Writing as Mosaic

"It cannot be too frequently repeated that belief in the unity of M. F. is absolutely necessary," wrote Michael Field to Vernon Lee (Violet Paget) in a letter dated January 29, 1890. It continues:

Alike for the advancement of his glory & attaining of his favour. He is in literature <u>one</u>. Where the secret of this chance dualism is not known, the wise and kind preserve it. And every public reference to him should be masculine. But I need scarcely warn Vernon Lee on this point?[22]

Reminding another pseudonymous female writer of the necessity of keeping their identity secret, the Fields explicitly reference the "belief" of a solitary unity – "I" – and male embodiment due to their contemporaries' ideas of the myth of a *masculine* solitary genius.[23] Michael Field, first and foremost, publicly presented themselves as a unified individual; the reality was a bit different. The couple's choice of "Michael Field," as Jill Ehnenn attests, may combat sexism in the nineteenth-century literary marketplace, and "[negotiate] Bradley and Cooper's internalization of Victorian ideologies regarding sex/gender."[24] Cloaked in a persona that they know will more likely succeed in the marketplace and comply to the demands of the literary press, Michael Field becomes: "a highly nuanced and contradictory performance for survival; it is a production of the self, a recycling of cultural and psychological structures ranging from the most social of conventions to the most private desire."[25] While Ehnenn locates the performative aspect of the pseudonym in a gendered means of production, Linda Hughes contests that perceived sexism in the marketplace began a movement toward a level playing field in the late nineteenth century, as women were able to join the Society of Authors (founded by Walter Besant in 1884 – the same year as Michael Field's first publication, *Callirhöe*). The purpose of the Society was to "assist authors in business arrangements and to give them greater bargaining power and protection against publishers through collective action."[26] Perhaps, then, the choice of the pseudonym is a sly invocation of sexual inversion, to use late nineteenth-century understandings of homosexuality. In any case, Michael Field found themselves in a double bind as female collaborators, as Bette London points out: "in the case of women, literary collaborators suffered from a double invisibility—the invisibility of collaboration and the invisibility of women's writing. Even where such collaborations were openly recognized, they tended to be represented in ways guaranteed to ensure their marginalization."[27] In the introduction, I briefly traced differing gendered accounts of the collaborative process. While late nineteenth-century male collaborators detail their attempt at achieving unity of expression in a writing process characterized by competition, the portrayal of female collaborators is strikingly different.

There are two specific instances within the Fields' correspondence that discuss their belief in the necessity of viewing themselves as one entity: their likening of their union to a marital bond in 1886 and their use of

Spinoza to clarify their understanding of unity in 1884. I begin with the latter, addressing Michael Field's invocation of Spinoza while continuing to argue that the couple's collaborative process is grounded within liberal sympathy. Just as conversations at the end of the century emphasize the individual within the community, Michael Field's collaborative process is founded upon separateness, upon the preservation of the self. This distinction underlies Bradley's rhetoric when appealing to Spinoza's *Ethics* in her letter to Robert Browning dated November 23, 1884:

> Spinoza with his fine grasp of unity says: "If two individuals of exactly the same nature are joined together, they make up a single individual, doubly stronger than each alone," i.e. Edith and I make a *veritable Michael*. And we humbly fear you are destroying this philosophic truth: it is said the *Athenaeum* was taught by you to use the feminine pronoun.[28]

In their construction of themselves as "a single individual," Michael Field emphasizes individuality, or oneness. The "philosophic truth" outlined by Bradley focuses on the preservation of their masculine pseudonym and the solitary authorship of one: Michael Field. This, as we know, is a socially constructed coauthorship. "This philosophic truth" of a "veritable Michael" remains the core of Michael Field's articulation of their unified persona; their collaboration is not only a process and a writing practice, but, in some respects, it constructs their very identity and their marriage union, an image described in an 1886 letter to Havelock Ellis. Certainly, when comparing the Fields' many instances of insisting upon their oneness, the Spinozan philosophy best accommodates their vision of unity rather than the heteronormative assumptions (and problematics) of nineteenth-century marriage. Their focus on the joining of "individuals of exactly the same nature" resembles Spinoza's claims for sympathy, a term which appears only once in *Ethics*. In Proposition 14, Spinoza argues that if we are affected by two things simultaneously, when we recollect one of those things, the other comes to mind. In this view of sympathy, there is a restriction: there must be both a resemblance to something and a prior experience.[29]

Interestingly, Spinoza's understanding of sympathy says nothing about *unity*; unlike the concord of Adam Smith, Spinoza's claims for sympathy are inspired by self-interest. For Spinoza, unity refers not to sympathy but to the dissolution of the mind-body duality, which may help to explain Bradley and Cooper's articulation of Michael Field as a doubled unity. In contrast to the eighteenth-century philosophers of moral sentiment, Spinoza locates in moral sentiments "certain occult qualities of things" – that is, the metaphysical connection or the affective concord between individuals described by Smith – and positions himself as providing a "manifest quality" of sympathy.[30] As *Ethics* progresses, we get a more "manifest" understanding of sympathy (even if the term is not used): sympathy leads us to associate our experience of emotions felt by others not only to convey those feelings but to feel certain pains or pleasures that motivate us to act in a specific way.[31] At first glance, Smithian sympathy seems aligned with Spinozan sympathy; however, the key difference lies in Spinoza's self-interestedness – the focus on individualism – in contrast to Smith's focus on the formation of social bonds. Spinozan sympathy, as Hanley clearly summarizes, "leads us to relieve the distress of others; in this sense it serves other-directed purposes. At the same time, the motive behind our doing so is self-interest: We seek to relieve the pain of others because of the pain we feel as a consequence of their distress."[32] While the end-result of Spinozan sympathy appears other-oriented, the motive underlying the action is egocentric.

Using Spinoza, therefore, as a model for Michael Field's collaborative process enables Bradley and Cooper to formulate their desire to preserve the idea of doubleness inherent in "Michael Field." While Michael Field is not interested in the formation of an aesthetic community of creative productivity, as explored in previous chapters, they are interested in the unity found within identification with another. By relying on a Spinozan unity to describe the significance of their pseudonym, we see the tension between "Michael Field" as a constructed persona and the reality of their collaborative process, which is defined by an other-oriented separateness. Spinoza's self-interest and self-preservation, therefore, makes sense in this context of unification and explains why they continue to publish as Michael Field until the end of their lives. Alongside the doubleness of "Michael Field," their identification with the other through sympathetic mirroring forms the basis of Michael Field's enactment of sympathetic collaboration.

If, as previous chapters have asserted, Smithian sympathy relies upon a social mirror by which individuals come to know themselves and the world around them, sympathy is fundamentally a social and epistemological process of understanding. This process, we recall, involves the assimilation and accommodation of one's feelings and principles with those surrounding us.[33] However, at the end of the century, a shift in Smithian understandings of sympathy occurs: maintaining a focus on individuals – on the distinct separateness that occurs even within circulating communities – coming together involves neither maintaining self-control and social order, nor self-modulation, but instead emphasizes individual parts, with their individualized perspectives, forming a whole. Sympathetic mirroring foregrounds that difference via the outward illusion of oneness that a mirror provides, while preserving individuation and selfhood. Through the other, we understand ourselves via imaginary transport, and yet the difference between the two remains.

Despite the Fields' insistence on unity, in their writing, we see a different focus on the process of coming together. In *Underneath the Bough* (1893), Michael Field describes their seamless, if eroticized, writing process in the sonnet "A Girl":

> A girl,
> Her soul a deep-wave pearl,
> Dim, lucent of all lovely mysteries;
>   A face flowered for heart's ease,
>   A brow's grace soft as seas   5
>   Seen through faint forest trees
>   A mouth, the lips apart
> Like aspen-leaflets trembling in the breeze
>   From her tempestuous heart.
>   Such: and our souls so knit,   10
>   I leave a page half-writ—
>   The work begun
> Will be to heaven's conception done,
>   If she come to it.[34]

The speaker remains unseen, observing the girl "through faint forest trees," and detailing the objectification of the female-object. The foregrounded deictic element of the poem – "A girl," rather than referencing a specific or "this" girl – creates emotional distance. Instead of establishing the poem as part of an implicit situation, deixis delineates the girl as an object. The poem's structural form, in fact, furthers this commodification through indenting lists of sensualized body parts: face, brow, and parted lips. Moreover, rather than the traditional 8/6 sonnet structure, "A Girl" utilizes a 9/5 structure. At line 10, the sonnet's volta occurs as readers realize that the writer and viewer are united, thus complicating the initial distancing of "A girl." This is not, it seems, an imaginary transportation into the other's situation, but a material transportation that takes place in the act of writing. In the quintain, Michael Field shifts the active male/passive female trope of the voyeuristic gaze by introducing a demonstrative followed by a colon: "Such: and our souls so knit, / I leave a page half-writ—"[35] The start of line 10 with "Such:" is striking, and suggests that this image of the girl in lines 1–9 is akin to the couple's uniting in verse on the page. "Such:" bridges the first and second half of the poem, and the strong punctuation of the colon commands a long pause, in the space of which the image of the girl, notably singular, is transformed into a plural "our" upon the written page. The colon's silence functions as demonstrative proof of the seamless interlacing of the couple's writing process. Suddenly, in line 10, the viewer and object are intertwined – "our souls" – awaiting the coming of the other. What does this transformation from the individual to the plural mean, then, for liberal sympathy? If we recall that Adam Smith's fellow-feeling is evoked as a means of identifying one's self in the other, then the accommodation of another occurs through the silence – or missing feet – of line 12. Moving from an awareness of a solitary presence with one voice speaking for another, as in traditional courtship poetry, the second half of the poem reveals the two as united with knit souls and indicates the importance of a shared work. Michael Field plays with formal history; even as the Fields name themselves male, this innovation places them in an experimental feminist literary history.

Importantly, "A Girl" situates the collaborative process as a completion: finishing the poem remains voluntary, noted by the weight of "if" in the poem's final line: "The work begun / Will be to heaven's conception done, / If she come to it."[36] The inspiration and actual writing come not from the Romantic ideal of literature created in solitude but from the sympathetic, affective connection that happens when two poets come together. Once again, true unity – or a unison – is improbable. Indeed, in this act of coming together, the Fields shift yet again to focus on individual work completed together – that is, an acknowledgment of individual desires for recognition as "our" devolves into "I" and "she."[37] The slippage of pronouns begs the question of whether accommodation has, in fact, occurred or whether what we witness in the sonnet's volta is the illusion of oneness as two individuals gaze upon each other and identify the strength of their work – "heaven's conception" – in the image of coauthorship rather than solitary authorship. This focus on individual parts forming a whole is evocative of the Fields' aesthetic and characteristic of the evolution of community-making at the end of the century. As this project has traced, this is a specifically nineteenth-century sensibility, versus the modern – and Romantic – sense of the subject in isolation. By drawing attention to the individual within a community in order to form a whole, this process of sympathetic collaboration remains aligned with Victorian conceptions of poetry as a means of reform, in contrast to Spinoza's conception of sympathy, which remains ego-centric: "each thing, in so far as it is in itself, endeavors to persist in its own being."[38] The motivating concern for individuals, in Spinoza's view, is the preservation of their own selves; it is, in other words, self-interested. This focus on self-interest is, indeed, in opposition to the Fields' reshaping of the traditional amatory sonnet, which reveals a defiance witnessed in the poem's closing lines.[39] The poem comes into being only through the intervention of a second poet, indicated by a dash (which depicts a silent pause, waiting for the arrival of the other), despite the irony of the sonnet's completion. The poem, as I read it, bears traces of a liberal view of sympathetic collaboration by demonstrating not an imaginary transportation but a material transportation that visibly shows the anxiety of waiting, the anxiety and hesitancy surrounding the identification of one's self in the other.

Edith Cooper and Katharine Bradley's physical, emotional, and spiritual connection is interrelated with their writing as Michael Field. Indeed, unlike the Shelley collaboration that foregrounded the radical nature of their union due to intellectual heritage, the Fields persist in assertions of the physicality of their desire, often figured through the language of nature or marriage. In a letter to Havelock Ellis, the couple claim that they perceive their authorial creation as a mosaic that derives authority not by genius but through their union, described in the language of a marital bond:[40]

> As to our work, let no man think he can put asunder what God has joined. [...] The work is a perfect mosaic. We cross and interlace like a company of dancing summer flies; if one begins a character, his companion seizes and possesses it; if one conceives a scene or situation, the other corrects, completes, or murderously cuts away.[41]

Often, this quotation is used to demonstrate the "oneness" of the Fields' union. Notice, however, that the reference to marriage refers back to "our work": that is, the collaborative production put on display to *fin de siècle* readers. The actual collaborative process, underscored by the natural imagery of dancing flies, is one of separated difference: "if one" does something, then "the other" follows through with the action. Such a description bears remarkable resemblance to the process described in "A Girl": "I leave a page half-writ—" with the expectation that the other will "come to it."[42] Indeed, an 1893 review in *The Athenaeum* for *Underneath the Bough*, a book of verse taken mostly from Field's plays, hints at this co-authored process, musing on the "strange poetic unison of two" and claims that "the peculiar interest [of the poems] will lie in the suggestion of the two lives, not twin, but with one heart."[43] Michael Field's contemporary readers were more likely to see this duality as a point of compositional interest due to the period's increasing conception of literary production as a social or communal activity than scholars are today, with our focus on canonical representations of the solitary author. The review, further, emphasizes the "poetic unison" of the two voices, which points to the role of poetry as a form most suited to the constructed unison, demonstrated above in the lyric form of "A Girl," merging from a solitary to a plural image and characterized by personal expression that is social origin – the ultimate coming together of the writers to form the poem. In both their literature and their correspondence, therefore, the Fields construct their work as a united and divinely ordained consciousness: inseparable from the other. Just as their joint pseudonym is characterized by a fluid merger, so too are the emblems they used on publications and stationery – the bramblebough and the thyrsus with interlinked golden rings – and the fondness with which they used nicknames.[44]

Michael Field indulged in a variety of nicknames throughout their lives; early on, their letters reveal a preference of Sim or Simorg (a mythical flying creature) for Bradley and Persian Puss for Cooper. Holly Laird suggests that their multiple nicknames indicate a sort of "radical free play," "suggesting a plurality of ways of interacting."[45] Reading these nicknames alongside the nicknames used by Mary and Percy Bysshe Shelley underscores the radical nature of their union, and its resonance with revolutionary Romantics. Their early choice of antagonistic animals – a bird and cat – is telling: in an excerpt from a letter to Havelock Ellis in 1891, Cooper suggests that their collaboration involves a sympathetic pluralism, evolving from various methods of coauthored practice: "P. [Puss, i.e. Cooper] and I have nearly killed one another with vain and cruel reproaches over the Romuald scene," Bradley intimates during their writing of *Stephania* (1892). "We are left," she continues, "with wasted eyes, reconciled hearts, and a humorous scene of the folly of alienation."[46] Integrating their bodies upon the written page, the Fields note how their texts perform their collaboration and construct an image of unity, while blurring the boundaries between the personal and the professional.

Evocations of this inseparable unity notwithstanding, the reality of the actual collaborative process is far different from the performative ideal. It is now well known that, generally, Bradley and Cooper worked in separate rooms.[47] When they moved to No. 1, The Paragon in Richmond, a home chosen for them by artistic and personal partners Charles Ricketts and Charles Shannon – affectionately nicknamed "the Artists" in *Works and Days* – the two women had individual work spaces, each designed after their own decorative manner. As a rule, they did not exchange a word between 9 a.m. and 1 p.m. out of the seriousness with which they took their work.[48] Ricketts further notes their separateness in his essay, "Michael Field":

Their habit of work was after long consultations and discussions to sketch out a rough scenario, and their separate work on the scenes of a play was compared, retouched and recast in the process, and overhauled at various times till finally amended and made smooth by Henry [nickname for Edith] [...] Matters of research, business, enquiry and letter writing rested with Michael [nickname for Katharine].[49]

This "habit of work" described by Ricketts becomes transformed into a personification of horticulture in a letter dated June 9, 1889 from Bradley to John Gray: "I weed Edith's garden she mine; then examining each other's withering heaps we exclaim—'Well, you might have spared that'—or, 'that weak twining thing had yet a grace'—but the presiding horticulturalist is ruthless, & it is borne away to the barrow."[50] In this personification, the Fields' garden becomes a collaborative production. Such a division of labor further suggests what Sharon Bickle previously noted about Michael Field's collaboration in her examination of the letters exchanged between Bradley and Cooper. "These letters," Bickle claims, "indicate that the poets had no static or singular model of collaborative practice to which they worked. Rather, it seems likely that [...] the process of collaboration was a fluid one, responsive to the particular needs and circumstances surrounding each work."[51] Thus, the couple's collaboration was subject to a continual negotiation designed to meet the demands of each text.

Sympathetic collaboration is reliant upon separateness. Sympathy does not dissolve the fundamental separateness of either party; there is an insistence on entering, through imaginative transport, into another person's *situation* (rather than emotions or sentiments). Like Pater's understanding of art as an *Andersstreben*, in which "arts are able, not to supply the place of each other but reciprocally to lend each other forces," sympathy extends subjective/objective boundaries through its ability to imaginatively feel with, and for, the other.[52] In this way, objectivity is preserved and individuals see themselves through the eyes of others and become mirrors to each other. Michael Field, then, is "doubly strong" due to their capability of seeing themselves in the other through the intertwining of their bodies upon the written page, enabled by their imaginary change of situations, as I will demonstrate in the following sections. The poets appeal to this sympathetic mirroring in their construction of "A Girl" and its reliance on the trope of watching and waiting. Further, this sympathetic mirroring – with its preservation of separateness – provides an ideal framework for understanding the couple's entries in *Works and Days*. Closely reading the journal entries showcases the collaborative depiction of separateness and anticipation in "A Girl": "I leave a page half-writ— / The work begun / Will be to heaven's conception done, / If she come to it."[53]

A Textured Approach to Life-Writing

So far I have examined the distinction between Michael Field's construction of their writing process as a united consciousness in contrast to the reality of their collaboration in order to understand their collaborative process as a model of sympathetic mirroring. I now wish to turn to the couple's life-writing to explore how this model of sympathetic collaboration, with its distinct preservation of a singular yet plural identity, becomes crafted within the diary pages. Their life-writing has been relatively understudied due, in part, to the relative inaccessibility of the manuscripts. The 28-volume set of large, hard-bound, handwritten volumes, comprising the years 1888–1914, are housed in their entirety at the British Library. With the Victorian Lives and Letters Consortium's 2015 launch of the digitized diaries of Michael Field, its crowd-sourcing of transcriptions, and the 2021 release of a new digital home at Dartmouth, hopefully the terrain of scholarship will shift to incorporate a fuller understanding of the couple's life, complex relationships with leading literary and artistic figures of the *fin de siècle*, and Michael Field's literary works.[54] The texture of the journals, however, is not merely comprised of two individuals at work on the same page. Rather, the diaries contain a mixture of mediums, including newspaper clippings, draft and fair copies of poems, transcriptions of letters, pressed flowers, and a number of loose insertions. This multivolume diary, then, is perhaps best considered a form of art. As Marion Thain posits, the diary should be read not as an intimate outpouring but as a well-crafted work. Incorporating various mediums into the journals and providing a title "are clear signs that Bradley and Cooper conceived of the diaries (not from the beginning, perhaps, but certainly from an early stage) as a 'work': a whole, public, narrative."[55] Thain's supposition supports Martin Hewitt's understanding of nineteenth century diaries as a "sustained and systematic concern with the management of" a public, or autobiographical, narrative.[56] Reinforcing elements of a performed narrative, Hewitt examines, among a number of other Victorian diaries, Beatrice Webb's diary to argue that her preoccupation with taking stock of her life within the diary pages manifests an "exegetic function" by "establishing and reinforcing her sense of her life as an entity: performing exegesis as well as mimesis."[57] Hewitt's understanding of a well-crafted diary with its various material and textual layers, therefore, facilitates our understanding of the Victorian diary as a means of managing one's public persona, with the diary itself operating "as the unifying nexus of an autobiographical presence."[58] Indeed, in the editorial preface of his heavily excised edition of *Works and Days*, Thomas Sturge Moore, as Michael Field's appointed literary executor, recalls that the Fields "left me instructions to open, at the end of 1929, their journal [...] to read it and then to publish so much and whatever parts of it I might think fit."[59] After the deaths of Cooper and Bradley, Michael Field waited fifteen years to publicly narrate their life and the community in which they participated because "we have many things to say that the world will not tolerate from a woman's lips."[60] This sentiment was prefaced by Bradley who claimed in 1900: "Michael will be discovered in the 20th Century."[61] Such a statement recalls, from the introduction to this chapter, the inevitability of the couple's fame: "Michael *will be* discovered." Despite this confidence, Michael Field lapsed into obscurity for most of the new century. The feminist recovery of marginalized literary works in the 1980s and 1990s marked the poet-dramatists' first resuscitation from anonymity, yet it has been only recently that scholarship has begun to recover the couple's works for its literary merits, rather than dissecting the specifics of Michael Field's collaboration by ascertaining the speaker/ writer in the couple's poetry and life-writing. Traditionally, the critique of early feminist recovery scholarship is that literary merit is secondary to the recovery itself: it is enough that the writers have been rescued. Instead, I posit that the binary is scholarship that discusses merit versus scholarship that only seeks to recover the collaborative relationship. There are three levels at work here: (1) feminist recovery; (2) interest in the collaborative process; and (3) arguments about literary merit. Within these approaches, this chapter seeks to resuscitate Michael Field's own construction of their collaborative process – witnessed in their poetry and in their life-writing – to draw marked attention to the influence of the social process upon the creative product, which asserts new claims of literary merit based upon innovative poetic forms and techniques. Examining the collaborative process as a whole, linking their life-writing with their literary oeuvre, sheds light on the experimental nature of Michael Field's works as an enactment of communal sympathy.

Not only do Bradley and Cooper wait for one another to come to the shared page (as in "A Girl"), but the introduction of various perspectives and multifaceted realities offer an innovative way of understanding the couple's life-writing. Such a view emphasizes an ever-changing understanding of and reflection on particular events that relies upon sympathetic observation and communal reading (whether their contemporaries or their future publics) of their journals. Partially fulfilling Laura Marcus's belief in the basic intention of life-writing to "understand the self and explain the self to others,"[62] Michael Field's diaries can best be described, following Hewitt, as *constructions* of their life, rather than a strict record.[63] Such narrations were, importantly, multilayered. As Thain argues, the persona of the signature Michael Field "mediates or expresses the women's *experience* of the world as distinguished from the unmediated raw reality of Bradley and Cooper, and allows them to communicate this to others."[64] It is this mediation that I find most applicable to the sympathetic process. Adam Smith argues that the act of sympathy depends upon the process of "transport": readers "transport ourselves in fancy" to the scene of a particular book and imagine ourselves within the scene in order to "sympathize with the highest transports" of the characters' feelings.[65] At the same time, "we feel ourselves naturally transported towards" other characters, scenes, situations, etc. to "move and feel with them, regardless of any will to do so."[66] The interpretive framework depicted within the pages of *Works and Days* allows for a transportation into the world as experienced by Michael Field. Often the entries were written retrospectively, as was normative in nineteenth-century life-writing, allowing for self-reflection and development of heightened narration. For instance, while traveling in northern Italy, Cooper recalls their visit to Vernon Lee, using a delayed narrative structure, followed by matter-of-fact description and interpretation, similar to that of Wilkie Collins's *The Woman in White* when Walter Hartwright meets Marian Halcombe for the first time. Cooper testifies: "We saw a *sibyl*, in a tailor-made black dress, vine-dresser's hat and apron, sowing seeds. We advanced—it was Vernon. She looks fifty; she is thirty-nine. She is very ugly; the face very long; the eyes with a look of greed for discussion."[67] Indeed, events of singular importance were often recorded multiple times in both women's hands, offering different perspectives. Such narrative technique provides a layered or palimpsestic approach.[68]

A notable example of a narrative written retrospectively and with repeated retellings is the death of Whym Chow in 1906. The formal layers and repetitions embedded within this narrative, which takes place over several entries, transport readers into the agony of the couple's experience. While it was Victorian mourning practice to record deaths of human beings, with multiple family members maintaining detailed accounts, what is unusual about the Fields' entries is that such detail should occur for a dog within a shared diary. In an entry written January 14, Cooper discusses Chow's need for a muzzle and notes his "dragging paw." She closes the entry with a parenthetical: "(Written after his death)," indicating the retrospective nature of this particular narrative.⁶⁹ What is innovative about the Michael Field diaries is the extreme use of retrospection and the diaries' collaborative aspects: its construction by two voices. Moreover, what is fascinating about the pages of *Works and Days* is their relatively clean nature, despite their textured construction, which, as Marion Thain has suggested, lends the assumption that the diaries are fair copies.⁷⁰ If, indeed, we assume this, then I argue that the couple *chooses* the fair copy as a way of demonstrating their choice to preserve independent reactions – and, more broadly, their life experiences – as a form of collaborative production. This focus on independence as a means toward interdependence also illustrates the shift in communal formation at the *fin de siècle*. Regenia Gagnier articulates one of the social tensions during this time:

> Socially, how did individual needs and desires relate to the needs and desires of others [...]? Many *fin-de-siècle* figures opposed narrow egoism, domesticity, and nationalism with larger social visions. This tension of independence versus interdependence, specifically of individual development threatening the functioning of the whole, constituted the anxiety of liberalism after a century of its development.⁷¹

Through the preservation of individualism within an interdependent form, the diaries recall Michael Field's awareness of shifting Victorian conceptions of social formation, and by extension, sympathetic experience. At the same time, *Works and Days* illustrates the couple's collaboration as dependent upon formal construction and experimentation, evident in the constructed blend of voices within the Whym Chow narrative.

In January 1906, over the course of a week, Whym Chow sickened and died. On January 15, during a visit with a Latin tutor, Cooper writes of taking Chow on a walk; by January 17, while Ricketts and Shannon visit, Cooper notes: "Chow hesitated long to spring into his chair. 'Whack him, Michael [nickname for Bradley]!' Fay [nickname for Ricketts] said with [...] impatience. 'No, Painter, we I must be patient; he is ill.'"⁷² By Friday, January 19, Cooper records anxiety over "Chow's stiffness in standing or climbing & the golden front paws lay out rather long."⁷³ Finally, on January 21, while reading in bed with "Michael," Cooper asserts that "Chow hardly comes up at all."⁷⁴ Cooper continues the entry for Monday the 22nd, and notes that the dog made no progress and calls the vet, who promises to return on Wednesday. Following this January 22 entry, there is a gap in the manuscript, a blank space of three lines, before Cooper resumes her Tuesday entry for January 23.⁷⁵ Such a gap suggests that Cooper left room for Bradley to record her perspective of Chow's illness, a gesture that Bradley declined, or withheld due to a lack of space.

The diary's narrative of Chow's illness resumes, still in Cooper's hand, on Wednesday, January 24th, as Bradley prepares to meet Ricketts for introduction to poet John Gray: "I have to press [Bradley] to go because the vet had not been: But she so needs change and I do not feel in any dread. As she leaves, Chow makes an effort with straight fore-paws to hold up to the window for his fond goodbye."[76] In the closing lines of the entry, Cooper relates her horror at realizing the extremity of Chow's illness: walking into the sun-room, Chow follows but "instead of turning downstairs he walks into the wall – It freezes me"[77] Squeezed into the corner of the page, the final phrase ends abruptly without punctuation. In fact, Cooper does not share the event of the vet's visit; the visit and subsequent news are recorded six pages later by Bradley.

The switch in both hand and narratorial perspective highlights the significance of the fatal day of January 24th. Rather than linearly continue the narrative, when Bradley takes over from Cooper in the journal, she decides to recount the same events, returning to January 21st: "Chow bad, Hen. in bed."[78] Interestingly, whereas Cooper's narrative focuses on Whym Chow, Bradley's entry for the 21st consists of four pages discussing her reading of Boccaccio, and providing drafts of passages that are revised into their play, *A Flower of Wrath* (1906). On the fifth page of Bradley's narrative, 13v, the manuscript is left blank, with only "<u>Chow</u>" written in Cooper's hand.[79] Turning the page, over half of the space is taken up with a continuation of *A Flower of Wrath*, before skipping a line and asserting, in the remaining quarter of the page: "What an entry I have now to make! On Wednesday [blank space in manuscript]^{find out day [in pencil]}."[80] Continuing her retelling of what is presumably January 24th, Bradley records her account of her visit with Gray and the news that awaited her return. Bradley's Friday entry, again missing an indication of the date, further narrates the diagnosis of the veterinary specialist: "'I am sorry, it is a bad case – I cannot say he will recover' – Yet if Chow were his dog, he would 'give him a month' – there is chance, though it is vague chance, for life."[81] The next entry on Sunday, January 28th is written by Cooper, narrating the "worst loss":

> How terrible Sundays are! Milestones of doom to us as a family. Today I have had the worst loss of my life—yes worse than that of beloved mother or the tragic father [...] My Whym Chow, my little Chow-Chow, my Flame of Love is dead & has died—O cruel God!—by our will!
> Wednesday after Michael started for the Palace I took my Delight a walk [...][82]

Interrupting the heart-breaking news, Cooper returns back to the pivotal Wednesday, January 24, when Whym Chow was given his diagnosis, effectively picking up where her initial narrative left off (and leaving Bradley's voice sandwiched in the middle). The narrative of Whym Chow, therefore, is both repetitive and circular (in sum, the narrative circles back upon itself: Cooper – January 15–January 24; Bradley – January 21–January 24; Cooper – January 28, return back to January 24). The loss of their dog haunted Michael Field for the remainder of their lives, with many of their 1906 entries trying to make sense of the dog's illness, and constitutes a pronounced version of the dramatization of their journal entries. Repeated retellings offer a variety of perspectives; indeed, the narrative trope of different points of view – not only Cooper and Bradley but speech from the specialist, and even Whym Chow's actions – offer a sense of the constructed blend of voices, a necessary separateness, that appear in their literary works. This dialogism allows for a means of processing and internalizing the traumatic ordeal – feeling with and for another by entering into her experience through transportation.

I have focused on the 1906 entries pertaining to Whym Chow as a demonstration of the narrative elements the couple uses in their dramatization of their lived experience and their reliance on repetition and dialogism as a means of publicly transporting the reader into their agony and privately making sense of their personal loss. These entries are representative of entries throughout *Works and Days*, as Bradley and Cooper recount and retell their experiences in a formal blending, matching the journal's crafted art form. As Hewitt noted, diaries often took the form of travel journal, as demonstrative of Mary Wollstonecraft Godwin and Percy Bysshe Shelley's joint elopement journal, and "produced a sustained dialogue between diarist and editor [...] But this sort of exchange was not merely a feature of [travel] publication, because even manuscript diaries were often layered texts, with original entries glossed by additions from friends, from family members or others to whom the diary came after the death of the diarist."[33] The nineteenth-century diary as travel writing, with multiple perspectives and layers, is suggestive of Michael Field's entries pertaining to Whym Chow; and indeed, the same form – with its participation in the Victorian practice of material textual revision (its material layers, pages cut and pasted in particular places) – was used by the Fields earlier, in October 1889, when they traveled to Scotland to research for *The Tragic Mary*. Whereas the 1906 Whym Chow passages use a circular structure of repetition to foreground multiplicity, the 1889 passages from the couple's Scottish tour utilize a vertical spatial division between Bradley and Cooper's respective individual perspectives and are self-referential, emphasizing the coming together of individual parts to reflect a whole and unified consciousness.

Sympathetic Transportation to Edinburgh

In 1889, Michael Field immersed themselves in Holyrood Palace, once the home of the ill-fated Queen of Scots, to research the queen's life for their verse drama, *The Tragic Mary* (1890). On October 10, the couple arrived and spent a fortnight in Edinburgh. Prior to their arrival at Holyrood on October 12, Cooper describes their "evening with Mr. Gray – much 'Michael' talk," in which they beheld Gray's reproductions of Dante Gabriel Rossetti's *Hamlet and Ophelia* (1858). Rossetti's depiction, in Cooper's estimation, is:

> a most-original reading from the scene of the returned letters. Ophelia/ Rossetti's wife is sitting in what looks much like a pew, over the back of which is stretched the despairing form of Hamlet, like as if a storm-cloud over her life—his mouth impotent in its anguish, the strong brows conceiving madness."[84]

Following this entry of artistic critique, the journal takes on a divided form, with each woman maintaining a distinct separateness. Cooper's entry, written on the right side of the page, literally leaves room for Bradley's impressions of her experience of Holyrood. Bradley's experience is pasted in at some unknown point. Dated October 12, the entry provides the couple's differing accounts of (and narrative approaches to) Holyrood:

[Pasted in; Bradley's hand]
Oct 12th. Holyrood.
"I will give you a peep unto your Box" quoth the custodian, & un at locked the Queen's work-box. It is her own work. Jacob's ladder --the lion & the lamb lying down together. delicate strawberry & flower embroidery on the sides. --Within a peculiar, antique cap- [cut off]
Lord Darnley's gloves—scraps of the old tapestries; Queen Mary's tear bottle.
Just above the work-box the Queen's mirror—the first Venetian mirror in England: the scallops engraved alternately with doves

[Cooper's hand]
The good promise of the morning was established in the day, whi came out of the mist with gentle shine, & that sudden revelation formed treetops or golden copses whi is one of the charms of October Holyrood—the very palace of our Art, the very centre of our Enthusiasm. We saw all the old points of ~~attraction~~ interest & objects of memorial attraction—also some new ones. The Work-box of the Queen lined with cherry-red & inside mirror of Venetian glass—outside & embroidered with Jacob's ladder at the base of whi the lion & lamb are lying down together in all the unquestionable Innocence of woodwork. Some of the finer designs round the box are most decorative-- especially the strawberry (Ruskin's "Rose of Venetia") leaves, blossom & fruit. On the wall above the box is a Venetian mirror edged by

& quatre-foils. dove & The Queen's bed hangings a flushing red. By the bed a baby-basket given to her by Elizabeth. The tapestry by the bedside Phaeton overthrown in his attempt to drive the courses of the sun, repeating the recklessness of the royal creature.	Scallops in whi are engraved alter-nately a quatre-foil. The Goblin tapestry is interesting in her bedroom. The design is spirited; it represents Phaeton falling from his chariot amid the tumultuous hoofs & grey sides of his red-harnessed horses.[85]

Following the visit with John Gray, the elaborate entries describing Bradley and Cooper's tour of Holyrood and their subsequent Edinburgh visit remain influenced by Decadent Aestheticism.[86]

Before returning to a closer analysis of the above passages, it is useful to recall Julia F. Saville's observation that in the early 1890s, the couple's journals are filled with references to eminent male thinkers: Robert Browning, George Meredith, Walter Pater, Oscar Wilde, and Arthur Symons, to name a few. As Sarah Parker recently pointed out in her chapter in *Michael Field: Decadent Moderns*, the Fields were "more likely to associate themselves with male aesthetes."[87] Very rarely are female associates mentioned in the journals; when visiting Vernon Lee, Michael Field describe Lee as a "sibyl" and remain unimpressed with Lee's aesthetic, reflecting that she was "very stupid in what she said about art."[38] Their relationships with women, though understudied, are, at best ambivalent.[89] The journals, then, reveal "their delight in the company of literati and aesthetes (most of whom are men), a wish to be respected participants in literary and aesthetic circles, and a resolute refusal of any conventions governing female behavior that might curtail that participation."[90] Significantly, despite their interactions with male and female literary networks, Michael Field is not interested in a collaborative community of creative productivity, as witnessed the Victorian models of sympathetic collaboration traced within this project. Certainly, their interactions with these circles, specifically with Bernard Berenson and Mary Costelloe and Charles Ricketts and Charles Shannon, inspire their aesthetic philosophies, but their inclusion within these communities remains complicated, and would certainly benefit from future research. The driving force of the Fields' involvement in these circulating communities is a desire for respect, a desire to be placed among the aesthetic and decadent celebrities – a desire, in other words, for creative renown.[91]

Aesthetic or intellectual recognition within these communities allowed Michael Field to fulfill their belief in the Paterian imperative to expand the interval of life in art. In the above narration of Holyrood, Bradley and Cooper's discursive articulation of their aesthetic viewpoints showcase their attempt to assimilate Decadent characteristics, and include as many points as the space would allow, recalling Pater's dictation of achieving "as many pulsations as possible into the given time."[92] Cooper, furthermore, assimilates "Michael talk" – what Cooper refers to as Bradley's aesthetic conversations with Gray – in her narrative, which takes the form of a decadent artistic critique, layering in Victorian voices: Alfred Lord Tennyson, with Holyrood becoming the "palace of our Art," and Ruskin's "Rose of Venetia." In other words, Bradley's sustained examination of Rossetti with a decadent poet on October 12 inflects Cooper's descriptions of Holyrood. Bradley's narrative, on the other hand, remains dramatically descriptive, taking less care to combine aesthetic philosophy with her depiction. Take, for example, the joint account of the queen's work-box. Bradley devotes little space to the box, preferring instead the Venetian mirror – "Just above the work-box the Queen's mirror—the first Venetian mirror in England" – while Cooper details the box's embroidery and the "unquestionable Innocence of woodwork. Some of the finer designs round the box are most decorative – especially the strawberry (Ruskin's "Rose of Venetia") leaves, blossom & fruit." Only by coming together on the shared page do the individual narratives form a whole, – form "Michael Field" – a whole which eventually becomes inscribed in the preface of *The Tragic Mary* and is reminiscent of the language of collaborative completion in "A Girl." In this way, the Michael Field diaries as a whole illustrate the process of sympathetic mirroring – identifying one's self in the other – and modulating the self for the betterment of the whole persona.

Sympathy was conceived, by Smith, as a social and cognitive process. As discussed in Chapter 1, the self was understood to engage with other selves over time to evolve into a social being. Thus sympathy is not a spontaneous emotional connection; it is not a "felt immediacy," as framed by aesthetic empathy in the next chapter. Instead, Smith is primarily concerned with the minimal requirements for social coordination. The social order is the focus of *The Theory of Moral Sentiments*: the "welfare and preservation of society" are "the favorite ends of nature."[93] As Fonna Forman-Barzilai discusses in her analysis of Smith's sympathetic self, sympathy is an activity of the mind that "takes place in a social context among other minds, mixing together in shared spaces, and [... this] has important implications for the role that sympathy plays in socialization, in the development of conscience, and in the creation and perpetuation of moral culture."[94] This self-referential process of participating in a sympathetic exchange takes form through a mirroring process: society provides a mirror through which the self mimics and judges itself and others. This constant modulation and affection, as we have seen throughout this project, lays the groundwork for considering Victorian liberalism's roots in Smithean sympathy, and it is this mirroring process that we see at work in the side-by-side comparison of the above Holyrood description.

Significantly, unlike my earlier discussion of Mary Wollstonecraft Godwin and Percy Bysshe Shelley's sympathetic assimilation, Cooper and Bradley maintain their distinct voices in their life-writing; each portion of their narrative respects separateness, which is indicative of the tendency toward individualism as a hallmark of aesthetic empathy. And yet, laid side-by-side, the individual parts form a whole – the two merge into a united consciousness for that one moment, just as Smith's sympathetic exchange allows for an immersion into the other's experience through imaginative transportation, through the social mirror. Viewing the nineteenth century under the influence of Smithean sympathy indicates an interesting progression: assimilation models for social coordination give way, at the end of the century, to a model of "parts forming a whole." Such a progression is a process of liberalism and its attention to a universal lived experience that aligns with the creation of a feeling community.

Through the realm of aesthetic philosophy, then, Michael Field recreates their experience of Holyrood, "the very palace of our Art, the very centre of our Enthusiasm." With a sustained focus on lavish descriptions of objects encountered in Mary Stuart's bedroom, the couple transports themselves and readers into the past. This interlinked function of travel writing and diary takes on particular prominence in their later visits to art galleries for *Sight and Song* (1892). In *Sight and Song,* Thain suggests that "the women's notes on paintings, made soon after the visit to the gallery if not in the galleries themselves, gradually metamorphoses into the published poems."[95] This metamorphosis occurs also for *The Tragic Mary* (1890), in which the dramatized narration of Holyrood becomes transformed in verse drama, a dramatic form that experiments with voice and meter to blur the boundaries of personal and public. Further, the diary's dramatized narration of the bedroom begins, for Bradley, by inserting another voice: the custodian. "'I will give you a peep unto your Box' quoth the custodian, & un locked the Queen's work-box," writes Bradley. The quoted language remains interesting for its use of "your," drawing attention to a shared aspect of the Queen's box. No longer is the box for the private use of Mary Stuart; it has become a public object, always on display. At the same time, Bradley underscores the custodian's use of "peep": given only a small look, in some ways the box remains private. Within the shared private setting of Michael

Field's journals, the public custodian's voice acts as an interruption. Here the couple enacts the blurred private/public boundaries in their own *Works and Days*. Crafting this dramatized retelling of their guided tour of the palace within their diary, Michael Field creates a dialogic space through the blending of voices and the merger of histories. Using the metaphor of the box, a personal possession, which becomes a shared national object because it is on display, the couple dramatize that Queen Mary's history has become, in a sense, *their* history – a national and universal history – and a shared space in which Michael Field and their readers are transported into a historical community founded upon a participatory observation and response. It is this constructed dialogic space from their life-writing that becomes inscribed in the form of *The Tragic Mary*.

Collaborating with the Past in Decadent Drama and Balladry

Whereas the diaries offer one material/textual example of female community and even an erotically charged space, their verse drama, *The Tragic Mary* (published in 1890, though never performed on stage), offers another with its inclusion of ballad meter as a means of formally and sonically binding women together through transport. The drama, by its very nature, allows for and relies upon the parts making up a whole – following the aforementioned model of social coordination. In Michael Field's poetry, they adhere to the conception of the singular "I" – a voice reminiscent of the Romantic genius poet. Turning to a more lyrical mode in *The Tragic Mary*, the poet-dramatists incorporate the ballad, with its metrical and rhythmical repetition – like the narrative techniques used in *Works and Days* – to enact the role of sympathetic and affective transport. Before beginning a close reading of the use of ballad form, it is first necessary to consider drama as a form of contagion. Edinburgh, allegorized as a woman in the opening lines of the preface to *The Tragic Mary*, fascinates the couple and draws them to her:

> Beautiful for situation, happy in the way the light visits her, noble in natural outline, and favoured even in the rise and declivity of her streets, it is nevertheless as the repository of her Queen's tragedy that Edinburgh fascinates us to herself.[96]

Michael Field's language of transport and suspension of volition as the city "fascinates" them and draws them toward its historically tragic queen are reminiscent of Walter Pater's description of the collective contagion of dramatic form, and has traces of eighteenth-century sentimental language and moral philosophy. We can draw parallels between Michael Field's approach to verse drama and Pater's aesthetic narrative of the "swarming" that occurs in Bacchic or Dionysian drama, with wild desire exciting passions within the collective through bodily ritualistic dance: "the sympathies of mere numbers, as such, the random catching on fire [...] when people are collected together, generates as if by mere contact, some new and rapturous spirit, not traceable in the individual units of a multitude."97 Pater's understanding of drama as a form of contagion informs Gustave Le Bon's *La psychologie des foules* (1895), the pioneering text for interpreting physiological and psychological understandings of crowd theory. Le Bon's belief in the "collective mind" or "single being" of the crowd reflects his understanding – as Phyllis Weliver details in her application of Le Bon to her discussion of George Du Maurier's *Trilby* – that "human beings seem most like one another in their unconscious states of being."98 Pater's sense of a collective contagious quality within drama's mimetic form inspires a heightened sense of emotion and rhythmic force generated by collective contact.

The material relics at Holyrood facilitate a similar sort of contagious contact, inspiring the poets to offer a glimpse into Mary Stuart's life in order to arouse sympathy for the queen's tragic life, and recreate, through dramatic form, a heightened experience of "rapturous" emotion and historic transport. Beholding objects of the Queen's past, the couple "are seized," they write, "with a passionate desire of access, an eagerness of approach: We cannot pause to wonder, or debate, or condemn; an impulse transports us: we are started on an inevitable quest."99 Drawing from their aforementioned notes and descriptions of Holyrood in *Works and Days*, in this preface to *The Tragic Mary*, Michael Field writes of encountering material relics – silks, mirrors, curtains – before visiting the "sculptured" body of the queen at Westminster. The compulsory attraction that enables the Fields' impressions of Mary Stuart can best be described via the sympathetic process of imaginative transport: by revisiting the relics of Mary Stuart's past, the Fields become transported to the past, fueled by their quest to (re)write the Queen of Scot's tragedy.

Indeed, when Michael Field turned to writing historical verse drama, they entered that form's tradition of recuperating and bringing to life the legends of mythic women in order to dramatize contemporary female sexuality. Combining prose, poetry, and song in their verse drama to revive the female history of Mary Stuart, the couple assert their perception of aesthetic modernity and renewal, as Andrew Eastham has posited in his discussion of the couple's first verse drama, *Callirrhoë* (1884).[100] Drama – as a mimetic form – relies on, as Eastham argues, "the translation and transference of expressive energies" and is "essential to both Pater and Field's Hellenist visions that the contagious and excessive energy of Dionysus provided the first impulse towards theatre."[101] Beginning with *Callirrhoë*, Michael Field experimented with various formal boundaries in their verse dramas to refashion a longer, and notably masculine, tradition of drama – fifth-century Greek and Shakespearian. If Aristotle believed drama to be an imitation of action, and mimesis to be a showing (or representation) versus a narrative retelling of that action, in *The Tragic Mary*, the Fields continue the formal history of drama by playing with voice, rhythm, and structure, mirroring their own sympathetic collaboration, their blend of voice from their life-writing.

Representations of Mary Stuart became profuse during the Victorian period. At least nineteen published dramas show writers repurposing her tragedy to contest the essentialist readings of feminism put forth by John Ruskin in "Of Queen's Gardens" and Coventry Patmore in "The Angel of the House."[102] The unanswerable questions surrounding the queen's possible involvement in the murder of her second husband, Darnley, made her an appealing dramatic figure. *The Tragic Mary* traces the events of Mary Stuart's life between March 9, 1566 and June 15, 1567. Beginning on the night of the murder of her Italian secretary Riccio, the plot traces the machinations of her advisors and her marriage to Lord Darnley in light of his role in Riccio's murder. Michael Field envisions a queen who loves her husband, despite her frustration with his weakness and jealousy. The play's central crisis comes when James Hepburn, Earl of Bothwell, leads a successful plot to murder Darnley, which ultimately forces the queen to marry Bothwell. The play concludes with Mary's defeat, as she is captured amidst cries for her execution on the grounds of adultery and murder. From the outset, Mary is depicted as a political and sexual *femme fatale*. As Jill Ehnenn argues in "Collaborating with History," Mary's political and erotic power – and the frustrated confusion that power inspires – denies the men surrounding her and plotting against her the ability to control her. Like the traditional conflict of *polis* versus *oikos* in Greek drama, this charged political environment is juxtaposed with a positive domestic one – Mary's community with her ladies in waiting: Mary Seton, Mary Fleming, Mary Livingstone, and Margaret Carwood (known collectively as "the Maries"). This community presents a space of sympathy and love, a space in which women are bound together, as we see, a binding sonically communicated and felt through ballad meter; it is an embodied sensual communication.

Throughout the drama Michael Field uses the lyric to play with voice and highlight shifts in sense of community. In the idyllic world of female community, "the Maries" often discuss life before political scheming interrupted their personal time with Mary Stuart. Act II, Scene IV of *The Tragic Mary* illustrates such experimentation of voice. Before the queen's entrance, her women use prose to discuss prior intimacy with Mary Stuart, as Mary Seton joyfully exclaims: "Is it not happy that our queen is restored to us? Since the Lord Darnley hath denied her his company, she is as fond and familiar as in her teens."[103] Mary Fleming continues to elaborate the queen's familiarity with her women: "Or when, a widow of twenty, she took us in turn to be bed-fellows. And we watched her waking in the early light; it was more regal than a sunrise."[104] Upon the queen's entrance, however, the meter of the drama shifts to greater formality in English speech rhythms as she complains that she has "caught disease / From the close air and crowding of the courts."[105] Contrasting the diseased world of public courtiers with the insular tranquility provided by her palace and its communal sanctuary of women, Queen Mary asks for her lute and begins her ballad to the ladies: "She was a royal lady born." The shift from the women's use of prose to Mary's poetry – and the Queen's subsequent shift from poetry to ballad meter in her song – signifies the influence of Greek tragedy, in which spoken sections are juxtaposed with song in the role of the chorus. The choral song – repurposed in *The Tragic Mary* as the queen's song – functions as the core of dramatic performance and provides cohesion for overarching themes and plots. The Fields' recasting of the choral song as the queen's ballad allows for an intimate and lyrical expression of nostalgia and transgressive desire, which ultimately becomes a cohesive element in depicting the queen's tragedy. In addition, this shift to song signifies a concord within the female community, drawing the women into familiar intimacy through the ritual of collective music, away from the diseased royal court. This music takes the form of ballad meter – a form that is familiar, more conversational, intimate, and community-minded.

The ballad's regularly alternating 4/3 is itself an irregularity of rhythm. This rhythm enables a simultaneity of experience, which links communities of people together in a sociable network of feeling, both psychically and bodily. Poetry, Meredith Martin believes, recreates a nostalgic projection of a connected society. Historical discussions of balladization in literary scholarship support notions of the ballad as forming community through affective experience.[106] Indeed, Marjorie Stone argues that the ballad, with "its energy, its frank physicality, its elemental passions, its strong heroines, and its sinewy narrative conflicts allowed [Elizabeth Barrett Browning] to circumvent the passionless purity conventionally ascribed to the middle class Victorian woman."[107] The ballad's ability to "circumvent the passionless purity" of Victorian gender ideologies, then, affords Michael Field a formal construct within their verse drama to imagine a space of female desire. Thus, like the artifacts envisioned in the verse drama's preface – objects which facilitate Field's transportation into the past and into an affective sympathy with an idealized Mary Stuart – the women serving Queen Mary become the means to create sympathy for the mythic heroine.

It is within this community that readers are given insight into what may initially seem like Mary's flightiness in her responses to the men surrounding her. Mary's ladies in waiting, the four "Maries," converse among themselves, understanding Queen Mary's balancing of her public duty as queen with her personal feelings. Discussing Queen Mary's "reputed marriage-day," Mary Seton observes this dichotomy known to none but her community of women:

> [...] She gave
> Her head a sportive and capricious arch,
> As she were playing queenship and no queen;
> Yet, when he entered, with a heaving bosom
> She kept her ground so regnantly he bent
> Irresolute, subjected.[108]

This ability to read their queen is reserved for those who understand Mary Stuart, who are able to, "sympathize[e] with the highest transports," to imagine themselves in concord with their queen.[109] While the modal marker, "as [if] she were playing queenship," illuminates uncertainty, begging the question of whether Mary Seton has correctly interpreted her queen, the ballads sung by Queen Mary facilitate the understanding of concord between the women, asserting their sympathetic bond. Simultaneously linking individuals (whether the poet and his/her publics, or, as we will see in *The Tragic Mary*, the singer and her community) through rhythm and shared experience, the ballad meter's familiarity facilitates concord and community, at the same time as it transforms and transports female desire through visceral poetic experience.

Returning from a morning in the council chamber, Michael Field's Mary Stuart retires with her ladies in waiting and describes her embroidered depiction of the judgment of King Solomon. She hopes that her stitching will give contentment: "Every stitch is a caress."[110] It is, however, not in the embroidered arts but rather in song and lyric that the queen finds solace, as the preface to "She was a royal lady born" dictates. Music, she says, "draws reluctant lovers to its course, / As a lone, female dove with luring note, / Draws her mate homeward on firm, open wings."[111] The published text of the song is set apart through its italics. Expressing herself in ballad form, Mary Stuart signals the first of several shifts toward a non-normalized view of community presented by the play; the lyrical form allows for a heightened sense of emotion and affirmation of private love. Further, in this scene of female community, readers are given a glimpse of the imagined sympathetic concord between Mary Stuart and her ladies.[112]

At the same time, readers are given insight into the concord between collaborators, between Michael Field and their revisioning of the past. Just as Michael Field writes the tragedy of the Queen of Scots, Mary uses song to write her own history in this poignant scene. Here, then, we are provided a peep – to mirror Bradley's quoted language of the custodian from *Works and Days* – into the collaborative writing process. Pater asserts in "The School of Giorgione" that music is life and that "[a]*ll art constantly aspires towards the condition of music*.[113]" Aligning themselves with Pater, the Fields use song to allow the queen to express her frustration with the "crowding of the courts," the machinations of the men surrounding her, in direct contrast to the energizing properties of music. In her ballad, Queen Mary rewrites the life of a royal lady as shepherdess who is brought the bloody crook of her "shepherd lad" by his murderers. To escape into tranquility, she devotes herself to her lambs, acknowledging her preference for them – her community of women. Accompanying herself on the lute, suggesting that music allows for imaginative play-acting and assumption of another guise – much like sympathy's imaginative transportation – Mary sings her first ballad to her ladies:

> *She was a royal lady born,*
> *Who loved a shepherd lad;*
> *To bring the smile into his face*
> *Was all the care she had.*
>
> *His murderers brought a bloody crook*   5
> *To shew her of their deed;*
> *She eyed it with a queenly eye,*
> *And leapt into the mead.*
>
> *And there she settled with the lambs,*
> *And felt their woolly fleece;*   10
> *It was their cry among the hills*
> *That brought her to her peace.*

> *And when at night she folded them*
> *Outside the wattle-fold,*
> *She took her lute and sang to them*   15
> *To keep them from the cold.*
>
> *She was a happy innocent*
> *Whom men had sought to spite.*
> *Alack, no sovereign lady lives*
> *A life of such delight.*   20
>
> *For no one crossed her any more,*
> *Or sought to bend her will;*
> *She watched the ewes at lambing-time,*
> *And in the winter chill.*
>
> *And when her flock was scattered far*   25
> *One day beside the brook,*
> *They came and found that she had died,*
> *Her arms about her crook.*
>
> *She had no memories to forget,*
> *Nor any sins to weep;*   30
> *O God, that I might be like her,*
> *And live among the sheep!*[114]

Upon first glance, the structured rhythm tells the story of a woman's love for a man: the royal lady falls in love with a shepherd and, upon his murder, leaps "into the mead" to become a shepherdess and later dies contentedly. However, the first lines of the second and final stanzas alter the traditional rhythm by adding an extra stress and, in doing so, affect what Linda K. Hughes describes as a "double poem: one that expresses an emotion or point of view yet, through formal means, simultaneously calls into question the poem's grounds for representing its subject and who or what should figure in poetry."[115] Rather than the regular iambic pattern, line five causes the narrator to stumble with its additional "er" in murderers: "His murderers brought a bloody crook" (U/ | UU/ | U/ | U/). The line's iambs are broken up by an anapest on "murderers brought," to give emphasis and pause to the action of murder. A similar pattern of stress happens in line 29, a line beginning with iambs and ending with an anapest: "She had no memories to forget" (U/ | // | U/ | UU/). Ending the line with an extra slack, the function of the anapest serves to elongate the rhythm of the line, drawing out "forget" before continuing with the ballad's regular iambic trimeter. In doing so, the singer emphasizes a longing for forgetfulness, echoing the death of the royal lady in the previous quatrain.

Mary Stuart's ballad is a double poem that questions the story of heterosexual love developed in the poem's opening lines. If, as the ballad's preface suggests, music "draws her mate homeward," the queen draws her women into intimacy with her – suggested by the sensual and tactile image of the Mary touching the "woolly fleece" of her lambs – by recasting heterosexual love as female desire. Stressing the murder of the shepherd, line five elicits a stutter, creating an elongated pause through anapestic meter. Such emphatic accent projects the indictment of murder and foreshadows Darnley's murder at the hands of Bothwell, who has his own plot for the marital crown. This pause suggests a connection between the murder and the politicization of marriage. The distortion of "his murderers" strikes discord in the otherwise ebb and flow of iambs to stress the royal lady's desire to rid herself of heterosexual love, in preference to the devotion of the lambs, or her ladies in waiting. Moving from this dissonance, the ballad continues with the rising rhythm of iambic meter, mimicking the speaker's movement of leaping and falling into the mead with her lambs. Line five, then, creates a shift in the ballad, moving the speaker from her lofty status as royal lady to her role as shepherdess, echoed in the regularity of the rise and fall of iambic meter that returns in line six. Such consistent repeated patterns of accented and unaccented beats enact an affective experience that brings its listeners together through its rhythm. As Jason R. Rudy argues in *Electric Meters*, rhythm "becomes a key element for poetic communication, suggesting through its stress and release a physiological give and take that [...] connects individuals via a bodily sensation."[116] Such patterned rhythm of iambic tetrameter and trimeter occurs in the fourth stanza: "And when at night she folded them / outside the wattle-fold, / She took her lute and sang to them / To keep them from the cold."[117] The rise and fall of the iamb mirrors the bodily rhythmic experience of breath or heartbeat, as Kirstie Blair discusses in *Victorian Poetry and Culture of the Heart*, which associates poetic rhythm with bodily rhythms, such as the pulse or heartbeat.

As listeners, the ladies in waiting are "folded" into the queen's embrace with the patterned rhythm of the ballad, mirroring the royal lady's intimate embrace. Distancing herself from the machinations of the murderers, the royal lady normalizes her bodily rhythm to live a "natural" life – both in nature and refiguring the community of women as normative – among her lambs as a shepherdess. In the final stanza, the heartbeat stops with the metrical irregularity of line 29: "She had no memories to forget." At the royal lady's death, the ballad comes to a subdued, yet rolling halt. Ending her life with the delight of her lambs, the royal lady has no regrets, unveiling the ballad's tragedy and transforming, as Emily Harrington notes, the "lyric 'I' to a dramatic 'I' in the penultimate line."[118] In other words, in the final lines Mary Stuart inserts herself into the tragedy, her voice pleading for her desire to be with her lambs (and her iambs). It is for this reason that the poem maintains stress on the past tense in the initial line of iambic tetrameter: "She was a royal lady born." Traditionally, perhaps, the stress would remain on the personal pronoun, but here, the accent remains on the past. By the reversal at the end of the ballad, her ladies – and the dramatic audience – understand why: Mary Stuart sings her story, substituting the royal lady for herself and transporting herself to the idyllic past, a past where she was surrounded by her ladies, without care for a contrived marriage plot.

Metrical Transport and Transgressive Remembrance

If the ballad, for Michael Field, enables the intimacy of female community and expressions of same-sex desire, the metrical familiarity of the ballad lulls Mary Seton and the Queen into intimate recollections of former embraces. Such metrical measures transports the women to scenes of their past – echoing the transport described by Bradley and Cooper in their distinct descriptions of Holyrood and their rewriting of Whym Chow's tragedy in *Works and Days* – as they speak in lines of iambic pentameter:

> Queen. (*Stooping over the rose-bushes*) How I stood
> On tip-toe, and with prickled hand drew down
> The roses in the bower at Inchmahome!
> We were so happy 'neath the filbert-trees
> In the old monkish garden.
> Mary Seton.   I remember
> The rows of boxwood hid us from each other;
> You struggled to get out into the sun,
> Transgressing the due limits.
> Queen.   I was free
> Those last few weeks before we went to France;
> I could be naughty at my pleasure then.[119]

Significantly, the women recall their time in a different female community: the convent at Inchmahome and the "monkish garden" that allowed for transgression and "naughty [...] pleasure." Such nostalgia occurs after the queen has sung her second ballad, "Ah, I, if I grew sweet to man," to her ladies in waiting in Act III. This ballad depicts the involuntary attraction that a woman feels for a man and asserts that heterosexual love disempowers a woman due to her lack of agency. Using the metaphor of a rose's inability to control its scent, the Queen sighs to emphasize her conditional statement: "Ah, I, if I grew sweet to man, / It was but as a rose that can / No longer keep the sweet that heaves /And swells among its fluttering leaves."[120] Such a "sweetness" is involuntary, like a rose's inability to control its heaving and swelling fragrance. The sensuality of the rose raises a sensate, or nonverbal, communication, much like the earlier sonic communication of the ballad.[121] Mirroring an uncontrollable transport and emotional contagion of drama's mimetic form, inspired both by Pater and eighteenth-century moral philosophy, this ballad asserts the queen has no control over the love that she inspires within men: "no art I used men's love to draw."[122] This lack of volition, then, becomes the ballad's lament. The ballad allows not only for an expression of same-sex desire – as we have seen in the initial ballad within the drama – but, here, also expresses the compulsory attraction that the woman inspires, an attraction that mirrors the compulsion felt by Michael Field for the historical Mary Stuart. If, as Meredith Martin believes, the ballad's overall form "is transformed to a family hearth where stories of the community's history are told," then Michael Field refashions Martin's hearth into an enclosed, and almost secret, garden, where memories of the women's past are confronted and retold.[123] This is a different "Queen's Garden" than that imagined by Ruskin.

The rhythmic familiarity of the second ballad's iambic tetrameter brings the women together in an erotically charged space that enables a sympathetic transport, imagined in the queen's conversation with her lady in waiting. The formal use of iambic pentameter in the above dialogue between the queen and Seton among the rose bushes maintains what is generally regarded as the closest approximation of English speech rhythm and is conventionally used in the expression of a public poetry. The Fields refashion the conventions of iambic pentameter by using it in private dialogue to continue the ballad's erotic and transgressive content. Using these dramatic lines of iambic pentameter, the women feel with and for the other as they share their nostalgic memories: "[Mary Seton] Transgressing the due limits. [Queen] I was free." This enjambed line equates transgression and freedom, suggesting that while society may label their love transgressive, this love maintains their freedom. Using metrical repetition and the structure of the ballad, Michael Field refigures the ballad to allow for expression of the passionate impulses drawing the women together, effecting sympathetic concord.

Shortly following the metrical transportation of the ballad "Ah, I, if I grew sweet to man," the queen asks to be left alone with her reverie. Such solitude, however, seems impossible as Darnley interrupts his wife to remind her of his drunkenness and adultery. With his departure, again in solitude, the queen's tone shifts to anger as she sings her final, and most irregular, ballad:

> *I could wish to be dead!*
> *Too quick with life were the tears I shed,*
> *Too sweet for tears is the life I led;*
> *And, ah, too lonesome my marriage-bed!*
> *I could wish to be dead.* 5
>
> *I could wish to be dead,*
> *For just a word that rings in my head;*
> *Too dear, too dear are the words he said,*
> *They must never be rememberèd.*
> *I could wish to be dead,* 10
>
> *I could wish to be dead:*
> *The wish to be loved is all mis-read,*
> *And to love, one learns when one is wed,*
> *Is to suffer bitter shame; instead*
> *I could wish to be dead.*[124] 15

This song, like the queen's prior songs, is italicized and thus set apart in the printed edition of *The Tragic Mary*, and arguably should be read, like the others, as a ballad. This time, it contains a refrain. If both the lyric and the dramatic forms allow for expressions of intense emotion, "I could wish to be dead!" enacts traumatic experience with the loss of the queen's power to speak, as the song falls out of ballad structure and merges with Greek Tragedy's lament structure. Using trochaic tetrameter, the ballad's falling rhythm accentuates the repetition of death echoed in the refrain. The echo of anapestic dimeter (itself a play on two within a marriage) in the refrain – "I could wish to be dead" (UU/ | UU/) – portrays the suicidal thoughts of a woman trapped within her marriage as its meter stresses a wish for death.

Michael Field refashion the choral refrain as an embodiment of trauma, indicating the queen's loss of speech with the inclusion of a repetitive and dulling echo. Like the folk ballad, the Greek choral lament uses refrain to build emotional intensity, increasing the frequency of grief and establishing contact with the dead.[125] Such intensity furthers the drama's mimetic form and its transference of expressive energy. In the first line of the ballad, however, the refrain is exclaimed, but as it becomes repeated, its exclamation is dulled through the varying lengths of pauses indicated by commas, colons, and periods. Such a numbing echo becomes repeated through the ballad in the abnormality of a poem with monorhyme: dead. Since each stanza begins and ends with the refrain, each stanza – and indeed, the poem as whole – is trapped within this death wish. Aside from the refrain, the ballad maintains a variation on iambic tetrameter, with an anapestic substitution in each line:

I could wish to be dead!	UU/ | UU/
Too quick with life were the tears I shed,	// | U/ | UU/ | U/
Too sweet for tears is the life I led;	// | U/ | UU/ | U/
And, ah, too lonesome my marriage-bed!	U/ | //U | // | U/
I could wish to be dead[126]	UU/ | UU/

While the recurrence of "too" attempts to quicken the rhythm, beginning with spondees in lines 2–3 slows the rhythm down, working against "too quick." Further, the single triplet rhyme and ending punctuation of all lines eliminates any forward motion, creating the effect of a spiral: starting and stopping; starting and stopping. Reading the ballad as an affective expression of sorrow, the lines feel metrically contained, with each line doubling back upon itself at the verb – "were" and "is" – to suggest a completely trapped state of being. This alternating back and forth 3/4 rhythm, in fact, creates a formal incantation, a rocking forwards and backwards, reminiscent of the tragic keen, increasing in intensity as it builds emotional and bodily tension.[127] As such, the ballad's form enables a reading of Mary Stuart's ballad as a keen for herself, a woman who is "mis-read."

Isolated, the queen reaches a tragic climax, spiraling out of control and lapsing into repetition in her heightened desire for death rather than the poisonous atmosphere of marriage. Contrasting the life she once led (with her ladies) and her "lonesome [...] marriage-bed," Mary Stuart realizes in the final stanza that she has been misread: "The wish to be loved is all misread, / And to love, one learns when one is wed, / Is to suffer bitter shame; instead / I could wish to be dead."[128] The mixture of shame with misreading accentuates the misreading of love that the play presents to the public through its innovative use of ballad form: Mary Stuart's tragedy is not her capture or the accusations of matricide leveled against her; rather, her tragedy is her inability to love freely. If her prior ballads offered an admission of same-sex desire and transported the queen to the "sweetness" of her past life, then this final ballad emphasizes the misreading of her present tragic life and the shame suffered by her marriage, not only because of its abusive nature but also because of its dishonesty: "The wish to be loved is all misread."[129] Indeed, I suggest that this reference to misreading is metatextual: that Michael Field is pointing out a historical misreading of Mary's tragedy. The only freedom that Michael Field's Mary Stuart can grasp is within her female community; negating marriage as a misreading, the queen sings of her desire for a different kind of freedom, a release in death.

Despite the "prosaic [...] and affected [...] [as well as] 'ludicrous' and 'distasteful'" language of some of the play's passages, *The Academy* praised

Michael Field's skill for their dramatic presentation of character: "[t]he approaches to each decisive act, and the memories, regrets, and apprehensions following it; it is that, which Michael Field is careful and skilled to expose."[130] Such crafted skill is most evident in the couple's use of ballad form. Their innovative use of ballad structure and meter, itself a versatile poetic form, allows for the presentation of character and interiority. Seeing these embedded ballads as double poems helps us apprehend the ballad as an ideal vehicle not only for the expression of communal nostalgia but also for formal innovation: form and content together facilitate a sympathetic concord across time. Michael Field integrates duplicity and asks readers to shift toward a polymorphic reading of the text, revealed in the formal structure of the ballads. As such, they use the ballad as lyric – capable of expressing both communal and private sentiment – in order to encourage a doubled reading practice. It is precisely because the ballad is a form understood as communal, public, and straightforward that making it, as Michael Field does, a layered, experimental, and private lyric is so innovative.[131] The discomfort with generic form experienced by contemporary reviewers suggests, in fact, that the affective play within *The Tragic Mary* was doing its job. Refiguring ballad conventions to allow for the transportative and passionate impulses that draw communities together, Michael Field effects an affective experience of sympathetic concord. In this way, the ballad becomes a transgressive form, allowing for a transference, or transportation, of transgressive desires. Such transgression is part of Michael Field's innovation: it is the transgressive nature of what is being communally disseminated.

From their poetry to their prose, to the combination of forms within their verse drama, Michael Field's writing enacts a sympathetic concord in its creation of a dialogue – a sympathetic exchange – between "Michael" and "Field," or "Sim" and "Puss." "Cleav[ing] to art," as Bradley writes to Cooper in July 1892, the couple's life and writing become intertwined social processes that only become illuminated through a careful examination of their collaboration. It is this new art – this invigorated formal experimentation apparent throughout the extensive oeuvre of Michael Field – that Bradley references in October 1892, following the couple's attendance at Tennyson's funeral:

> And so closes the Victorian epoch.—It is an epoch already yesterday: it is for us, England's living, & yet unspent poets to make all things new. We are for the morning—the nineteenth century thinks it has no poets—nothing to lose—verily it has nothing: for we are not of it—we shake the dust of our feet from it, & pass on into the 20th century.

CHAPTER 6

Towards Empathy
Vernon Lee's Psychological Aesthetics

In the summer of 1887, while staying with Scottish artist Clementina "Kit" Anstruther-Thomson, "Vernon Lee" (a pseudonym for Violet Paget) received the news of poet A. Mary F. Robinson's engagement to Orientalist and University Professor, James Darmesteter. Suffering a nervous breakdown, Lee relied upon Anstruther-Thomson during her convalescence and subsequently formed a romantic and professional attachment. In a journal entry dated August 28, 1887, Lee describes finding a white rose on her pillow: "It was a rose, scarcely more than a bud, lying very gently, white on whiteness. The scent of that rose will cling, I believe, as long as I live, in the corners of my soul."[1] This budding flower, as many have noted, became the symbol of the women's relationship and collaborative partnership; it was preserved in an envelope labeled "Kit/Charleton, Aug. 24 / *Neue Liebe, Neues Leben* [New Love, New Life]."[2] This reliquary of sorts also contains letters written by Lee to Anstruther-Thomson during 1887 and 1888. The importance of that moment in 1887 is clearly underscored by Lee's German inscription, alluding to Goethe's poem of the same name, and reverberates in a subsequent letter, written to Anstruther-Thomson six years after the dissolution of their relationship. Visiting Charleton alone in 1904, Lee recalls her initial visit:

> At Kilconquhar you came to fetch me, now just seventeen years ago, the first time I came to Charleton; you had a beret deep over your head, and we picked up an old lady's blue hat box, somewhere near the big willows on the road. And at the Largo, on the pier, they were dancing, that evening (there was a fire balloon, and we took it for the moon) on which, coming home, I got the news that the first great friendship and love of my life had come to an end; that evening when the little white rose on my pillow told me that a new, greater, eternal (I think, dear Kit!) one had begun ... and every turn of the roads tells me of those strange dreamlike months of illness and hopelessness, of misery and of such enveloping happiness, out of which your patience and loving kindness drew me, a new creature.[3]

In recalling these events with great detail, the rose, therefore, is more than a familiar token of love; it suggests both love and life – that is, the new collaborative partnership created out of Lee and Anstruther-Thomson's love for one another, a collaboration following upon the heels of Lee's loss of Robinson, "the first great friendship and love of my life." These recollections also situate the women as a sort of triad – a triangulated relationship that seems to refract and reflect different points of Lee's professional career.

When scholarship has focused on Vernon Lee and collaboration, critics turn to Lee's relationship with Anstruther-Thomson. After all, their partnership resulted in the publication of the collaborative essay "Beauty and Ugliness" in the *Contemporary Review* in autumn 1897.[4] And yet, in terms of sympathetic collaboration, the choice to study Vernon Lee and Kit Anstruther-Thomson remains a curious one. For, after all, it might be considered an instance of failed collaboration: in 1912, Lee revises the joint publication of 1897 to include contributions portioned out by brackets in an effort to distance herself from the physiological ties of aesthetic empathy.[5] Occurring during the wane of the nineteenth century, their collaboration cements the shift noted in the previous chapter: the transition from community development and its emphasis on moral sensibility and sympathetic assimilation to a modern sense of separateness, a prevailing sense of individuality. In other words, rather than a wholly sympathetic collaboration, this chapter traces a model that is not necessarily reliant upon individuals coming together in concord but is founded on the privatization of the aesthetic experience and the discord that arises due to the individualist qualities advanced by the aesthetic imperative.

The collaborations traced thus far in this book have argued for a model of collaborative process reliant upon Smithean sympathy. However, by the close of the nineteenth century and the introduction, from German aesthetics, of empathy, a change occurs in understandings of collaboration. To open this topic, I consider what happens to sympathetic concord at the *fin de siècle* by focusing on the partnerships established by Lee. This chapter establishes an overview of the shift from sympathy to empathy before questioning Lee and Anstruther-Thomson's collaboration, looking briefly at the inequitable standards of their collaboration, which resulted in the 1897 essay publication of "Beauty and Ugliness." In terms of aesthetics, scholarship often draws from Lee's work beginning in the 1890s; recently more attention has been paid to the aesthetic work undertaken in the 1880s during her synergetic relationship with poet A. Mary F. Robinson. Emily Harrington has illuminated Robinson's lasting influence on Lee's aesthetic works and later formulation of aesthetic empathy, demonstrating their joint aim to establish an alternative to the accusations of solipsism leveled against Paterian aestheticism.[6] At times, however, Harrington misreads Pater and Robinson. Lee's empathy is a version of Paterian sympathy or, as Sarah Townley has argued, a rewriting of it.[7] Nonetheless, I, like Harrington, turn from the 1890s to the 1880s to fully understand the discord that arises in the Lee-Anstruther-Thomson collaborative endeavor. Lee first attempted to explore questions of aesthetics with Robinson; together they wrestled with contemporary formulations of aestheticism, primarily the so-called "missionary aestheticism" associated with Ruskin and the pleasurable aestheticism associated with Pater. Exploring the Lee-Robinson correspondence and *Belcaro* (1881), Lee's collection of aesthetic essays dedicated to Robinson, I view these dialogue essays as a form of sympathetic collaboration. This partnership and aesthetic viewpoint lie in contrast to Lee's later development of psychological aesthetics, with which the chapter closes. As the century progresses, Lee's thinking on aesthetic discourse shifts and changes.[8] Lee's relationship and creative production with Robinson, followed by her collaboration with Anstruther-Thomson, embodies the late nineteenth-century shift away from sympathy in favor of empathy. Thus in breaking from Robinson and wrestling with the sympathy developed in the dialogues of *Belcaro*, Lee progresses from moral or ethical aesthetics to psychological aesthetics.

Fluidity of Transition: From Sympathy to Empathy

Today, the lines between sympathy and empathy are blurred; the two terms seemingly interchangeable. This, however, was not the case in the long nineteenth century: "empathy" was not translated into English until 1909 by Edward Bradford Titchener.[9] Empathy was originally, as Benjamin Morgan succinctly defines, "a term denoting an unconscious physiological reaction to an object that involved either ego projection into it or physical mimicry of it."[10] In the first half of the twentieth century, empathy retained its bodily connections; sympathy retained its cognitive associations. Such a linguistic shift is mirrored in the literary transition into Modernism. As rehearsed in Chapter 2, the inheritance of moral sentiment and the culture of feeling – along with notions of beauty and goodness – bequeathed by Romanticism upon Victorian writers, established a close association between aesthetics and moral feeling in the nineteenth century.[11] Victorian aesthetics "foregrounds a sensory, feeling body and was quickly associated with ideas of right feeling or taste and aligned with moral forms of right feeling."[12] Late-Victorian aestheticism and Modernism organized against the association between aesthetic taste and morally directed feelings, cultivating a critique of sentimentality. The rise of Modernism is often seen as a shift away from sympathy, as Stephen Arata argues: the "turn away from sympathy [...] was perceived by many as the defining feature of late-Victorian realism."[13] And what does this mean for liberalism? With "the strange death of moral England," disaffection from the public became more pronounced, and, increasingly, liberal values of character, self-restraint, and duty no longer seemed relevant, particularly in the face of World War I.[14] Although a lived sense of liberalism – a liberal idealism founded upon moral collectivism – becomes diluted in the shift toward realism, the optimism of liberal proponents remained. In the post-war world, there remains evidence of Progress and Reform (to recall the Liberal slogan): the position of women, the welfare of the working classes.[15] This division, however, is more complex, as Carolyn Burdett argues in "Is Empathy the End of Sentimentality?" – a view to which I also subscribe.

Certainly, the end of the nineteenth century marks some kind of end to Victorian sentimentality, but that ending is more fluid than the accounts permitted by designations of literary historical periods. Such fluidity becomes visible when looking at the introduction of empathy: "questions of the relation between internal feeling and behaviour towards others, of the humanly educative role of art, of the power of identification with the plight of others, all remain issues of importance" to Modernist writers, and continue to be crucial in the present day.[16] During the twentieth century, sympathy creates confusion in distinguishing itself from similar sentiments: compassion, altruism, empathy. Kirsty Martin addresses such confusion by drawing a distinction between empathy and sympathy, with the latter "involving a more distanced 'feeling for' others and empathy amounting to an absolute inhabiting of another's experience, 'feeling with.'"[17] We arrive at the distinction between sympathy and empathy: sympathy necessitates distance; empathy is perceived as "absolute" inhabitation. Or, perhaps, sympathy requires reflection, while empathy is a somatic immediacy. Moreover, as I have suggested throughout this study, sympathy, for Smith, is much more than "fellow-feeling" or "feeling for" due to its processes of judgment and its impact on community formation. *The Theory of Moral Sentiments* underscores an appropriate bodily "pitch" for the passions that one experiences, a qualifier established by the corresponding reactions viewed within society. Additionally, I appreciate Martin's distinction of empathy as an inhabitation of the experience of another because of its focus on the aesthetic experience, derived from Lee's and Anstruther-Thomson's usage of *Einfühlung*, or "empathy."[18]

As traditional terms of Victorian feeling – such as sympathy and sentiment – underwent great strain, a new term was adopted from German aesthetic traditions: empathy, which emphasized not a mental or imaginative attitude toward others, but a specific aesthetic responsiveness. The causes for such a strain are, as Burdett points out, various, but include: the effects of political democratization, impacts of secularization, and the rise of scientific naturalism and psychological theories.[19] In the 1890s, at the same time as Lee and Anstruther-Thomson indulged in their "gallery experiments," late-Victorian critics "perceived that the much-touted but ultimately clichéd orthodoxy of '*l'art pour l'art*'—which prized aesthetic experience above all moral questions—retained little theoretical advisability."[20] Throughout the 1880s, Lee examined this pioneering orthodoxy while engaging with associationist psychologist William James's arguments for the body's connection with aesthetic responses. Initially, Lee was influenced by Ruskin; however, her encounters with aesthetic leaders – particularly the influence of Walter Pater – resulted in her rejection of the moral presuppositions of Ruskin's works. In its place, she would eventually offer the concept of aesthetic empathy.[21]

A Partnership of "Loose End[s]"

In 1897, "Beauty and Ugliness" was published as a collaborative text. The publication uses the plural voice – the inclusive "we" – yet persists in conveying distance with the couple's authorial decision to include separate names in the *Contemporary Review*'s list of contents: Vernon Lee and C. Anstruther-Thomson. Perhaps this separation occurs because of Lee's prior publications in the *Contemporary Review*: two essays on *The Renaissance* (1879) and another on comparative aesthetics (1880). Or, it may be that this collaboration resonates with the bipartite understanding of Michael Field's collaborative process, noted in the previous chapter. Although Michael Field generated a pseudonym of public unity, privately, Katharine Bradley and Edith Cooper maintain their distinct separateness. With "Beauty and Ugliness," there is a marked difference, or separation, in the individualism asserted by an insistence on dual authorship: Lee and Anstruther-Thomson are two *authors* writing *together*, a separation further established by the 1912 revisions. While Michael Field maintain a distinct separateness, they still find identification within the other and continually assert their public unity, identified in their singular pseudonym. By foregrounding the coauthored text, Lee and Anstruther-Thomson present a complicated view of their collaboration: despite this publicly printed assertion of individuality, the methodology outlined in their aesthetic theory emphasizes a desire of bodily merger, that is, to present themselves in the same seamless union as Michael Field. Theirs is a desire to feel and experience as a unified body – to "obliterate the physical and mental barriers between them (and the art work)."[22] And yet, witnessed in this printed declaration of separateness, the relationship between Lee and Anstruther-Thomson is marked by the conflict over dependence upon one another and the loneliness experienced upon separation. Within the very foundation of their collaboration, then, we witness not a sympathetic concord, but a discord. Articulating this conflict, Anstruther-Thomson writes to Lee in an imprecisely dated letter (either 1887 or 1888): "I am still pondering over the fact of our all not being separete [sic] units, this particular unit Me feels as if it were united very closely to *you* but not to most other units the least—as yet, but I'm going to try to."[23] Separateness and individuality – "our" versus "Me" – marks the conflict; yet, Anstruther-Thomson asserts her union with Lee over "most other units." What seems to bother Anstruther-Thomson is her lack of connection with the community, but she is willing to "try."[24] Suggestive of growing tensions between individualism and interdependence at the end of the century, overcoming this obstacle of the individual over the collective – personal versus communal – would remain the goal of their collaborative endeavor.[25]

In a letter dated June 13, 1895, Lee articulates her reliance upon their partnership and of the "living atmosphere" created by their ideas:

> [...] I feel very curiously at a loose end without you. I don't think its mere affection of me [...] in the ordinary sense for heaven knows I've done that often enough before. This is a sense of enforced silence and at the same time a sort of deafness, which really comes. I feel sure, of the fact that so many of my thoughts and feelings nowadays are connected with yr discoveries, that your ideas have come to form a sort of living atmosphere for me. I find I cannot give my real reactions for so many things, to others, and that life, which is so synthetic, seems all in bits.[26]

As their correspondence indicates, within their life-writing, Lee and Anstruther-Thomson seem to achieve their desire for unity: they feel and experience as one, "form[ing] a sort of living atmosphere." Separation is equated to debilitation – "enforced silence" or "deafness" – or a half-felt presence – a "loose end" – because of the intensity of the connection between the couple's minds and bodies. Their relationship, she asserts, is more than feeling (more than the "mere affection" felt in her prior relationships) because it is, truly, a lived experience, a shared experience. Notably, Lee identifies the interconnectedness of her thoughts with "yr discoveries," highlighting what Dennis Denisoff sees as a meditation on "queer ecology" that runs throughout Lee's works: "one's emotional experiences of the ecological network arise not through individual perception, but through influences and interconnections among various emotional threads."[27] The intermingling of ideas and associations are "at a loose end" and the world – life as Lee experiences it – "seems all in bits" without Anstruther-Thomson's presence. Because of the disorder of her mind, Lee's interpretation of the world around her becomes just as chaotic: she is unable to share with others the life shared with Anstruther-Thomson. Such a life is made up of bodily responses and interpretations of art and perception of form – a unique theoretical language developed with Anstruther-Thomson.

While acclaiming their metaphysical connection, Lee asserts that, in their work, they have integrated both their private and professional selves. But is this truly the case? If the letter asserts Lee's reliance upon her partner, it also indicates the separate nature of their writing process: theirs is not a shared writing task – it is not the filling in of gaps or the completion of the other's sentences, as witnessed in previous collaborations. Theirs is not a sympathetic assimilation or accommodation of the other; their collaboration is a distinct act of isolation – a private act. In the "silence" and "deafness," we perceive a loss of conversation – of the dialogue that characterized sympathetic collaboration. This loss has, in fact, dire consequences: Lee writes of the isolation she feels at their separation and the impact that such seclusion has upon her craft – an inability to produce her "real" interpretations. For, as we come to realize, Lee, during the period of this letter, is at work on her interpretations of Anstruther-Thomson's bodily responsiveness to art.

"Beauty and Ugliness" begins with the claim of providing an empirical account of aesthetic experience in order to provoke a "new method of study." Such an account was possible, claimed the authors, because of recent psychological theories: aesthetics, "if treated by the method of recent psychology, will be recognised as one of the most important and most suggestive parts of the great science of perception and emotion."[28] Lee and Anstruther-Thomson believed they had discovered "one of the Keys to the Universe, a key which would instantly turn in the lock and reveal all the mysteries of art psychology to every observer."[29] In their essay, the partners expound upon a specific type of person capable of registering bodily and mental responses, like the "alteration in our respiratory and equilibratory processes, and by initiated movements of various parts of the body," as a response to one's gaze upon the art object.[30] When viewing an object, they argue, physical changes occur in the body. Muscles relax or tense; shifts in balance occur; respiration increases or decreases. As a form of evidence, the essay includes detailed notes taken from the "gallery experiments" conducted by Lee and Anstruther-Thomson, and argues that these somatic reactions to the observed forms within the aesthetic object arouse specific feelings within the viewer. These feelings are the source of what we experience as beauty or ugliness: "how the subjective inside us can turn into the objective outside."[31] This transformative process of subjectivity to objectivity would, in the 1912 publication, be defined as "empathy."

Such an embodied approach to the study of art and beauty was not unusual at the end of the century. As Kirsty Bunting succinctly points out: the "key psychological aesthete commentators of the age, including, amongst others, George Henry Lewes, Bernard Berenson, William James, Karl Groose, Grant Allen and Theodore Lipps, talk of lone, not shared aesthetic experience or connoisseurship."[32] What was innovative about Lee and Anstruther-Thomson's approach to art was not only the transformation of "abstract theory into critical practice" through their turn to language and metaphor,[33] but their desire to experience these effects simultaneously – in concord together. During the 1890s, the female partners (in contrast to the male circle of aesthetic critics) created a series of private and public gallery experiments in order to note the bodily, emotional, and psychological effects felt by specific individuals – of which they believed themselves capable – when looking at art. Their theory revolves around voyeurism, what Jill Ehnenn terms a "triangulated gaze." Anstruther-Thomson would gaze upon the work of art while Lee gazed upon Anstruther-Thomson, "often holding onto her arm." Aloud, Anstruther-Thomson would describe her sensations as she looked upon the object, and these "responses, in turn affected (her perception of) the object through what they termed *aesthetic empathy* [in 1912]."[34] Such a triangulated spectatorial experience of art was inventive because "Beauty and Ugliness" records the intimate somatic, mental, and, as some critics have argued, erotic experiences of the couple. This triangulation – the desire to identify with one another's feelings simultaneously through the shared act of looking – captures, also, the ideal of the couple's attempted collaboration. Empathy, as Lee later describes in *The Beautiful* (1913), involves "the merging of the perceptive activities of the subject in the qualities of the object of perception."[35] This focus on merger identifies, indeed, that detachment is not required and that there is, in fact, an absorption of the self within the object.

In the essay that appears in the *Contemporary Review*, Lee and Anstruther-Thomson claim that they are both "specially developed persons" with "highly aesthetic natures" capable of perceiving internal transformations resulting in enhanced bodily functions and corresponding emotions."³⁶ In actuality, however, Lee knew that she was not one of these individuals. In her introduction to *Art and Man* (1924), a collection of essays written by Anstruther-Thomson and published posthumously, Lee confesses publicly: "A whole set of Kit's experiments I was indeed (as I have explained in our joint volume, *Beauty and Ugliness*) quite unable to join in [...] I had neither the bodily strength for such experiments nor any of the steady power of looking which is part of a draughtsman's training and habit."³⁷ In her confession, Lee draws a line between their collaborative labor, a distinction previously hinted at in her 1895 letter: her tendency to, perhaps unintentionally, reduce Anstruther-Thomson's involvement to a performative role while allocating the intellectual labor of writing and interpretation to herself.

When analyzing "Beauty and Ugliness" as a form of collaborative life-writing, Kirsty Bunting draws attention to the inequitable standards of the Lee-Anstruther-Thomson collaboration. She demonstrates the collaborative nature of "Old Lombard and Venetian Villas," an essay that remained unpublished until April 1896. "Old Lombard' follows a first-person narrator and her companion in their walks around famous Italian villas and landscapes. Until the penultimate paragraph, however, the companion's identity remains unclear. In this paragraph, the companion interrupts the narrator: "'Look at this composition,' says my friend K___."³⁸ Bunting notes that this interruption is indicative of the way in which Anstruther-Thomson's responsiveness to art commanded Lee's attention and impressed her; however, the essay as a whole – with its ambiguity and silencing of Anstruther-Thomson as a companion – "highlights the ways in which Lee was careful to frame Anstruther-Thomson's unapologetic, dynamic, and performative aesthetics. She contains her partner's 'notes' as a short, clearly delineated interlude in *her* work."³⁹ Such delineation – with its failure to harmonize or sympathize – results in communal discord and unequal labor. Indeed, when "Beauty and Ugliness" was reprinted in 1912, once again Lee marginalized her partner's contributions. When revising, Lee divides Anstruther-Thomson's physiological responses from her own interpretive language, using brackets to indicate portions written by Anstruther-Thomson. Furthermore, in her footnotes to this revision, she provides a startling statement recanting her belief in Anstruther-Thomson's abilities: "I no longer consider such sensations as explaining or even necessarily accompanying the activity of form perception."[40] By 1912, Anstruther-Thomson had become a sort of "loose end" for Lee – at least in terms of their aesthetic differences.[41] These differences – a shift in intellectual ideas and aesthetic discourse – constitute the failed sympathetic collaboration, offering not a coming together but a growing apart.

In her attempt to constrain and limit Anstruther-Thomson's contributions to their gallery experiments and subsequent aesthetic theories, Lee distinguishes her own intellectual prose from Anstruther-Thomson's bodily, performative responses. Bunting posits that such a distinction results from embarrassment over Anstruther-Thomson's "non-scientific, conjectural, and ambiguous language."[42] This shift in collaborative unity from 1897 to 1912 arises not necessarily from embarrassment but from Lee's return to earlier definitions of sympathetic partnership. Lee's aforementioned June 13, 1895 letter asserts her need for a "living atmosphere" – a need for conversation – not "deafness" – the shared circulation of ideas; indeed, the same liberal circulation that this study has traced as an undercurrent of nineteenth-century sympathetic collaboration. With her inability to feel as Anstruther-Thomson felt, to partake in the same sympathetic sensations as her partner, Lee's "living atmosphere" falls short as boundaries are drawn: physical performance versus intellectual labor. By 1912, their unsuccessful collaboration becomes public knowledge with the segmentation of voices in the printed revision of "Beauty and Ugliness." With Anstruther-Thomson, Lee maintains a discord – a discord privately felt, but not publicly expressed. Moreover, after the demise of her collaboration with Anstruther-Thomson, Lee returns to moral aesthetics, conveying how aesthetic appreciation could result in a social good. This mixture of moralism and aestheticism is similar to earlier beliefs espoused in her dialogues with A. Mary F. Robinson. In other words, to fully explore the fissures leading to Lee and Anstruther-Thomson's collaborative undoing, it is essential to frame Lee's aesthetic theories within an earlier context. Doing so will illuminate, more broadly, Lee's ongoing struggle to place herself within dissonant aesthetic threads. Her turn to aesthetic empathy with Anstruther-Thomson results from a movement away from ethical aestheticism, a transition that continued to haunt Lee during the gallery experiments and subsequent collaborative production, culminating in her 1912 *volte-face*.

Individual or Communal?: Waking from "False Aestheticism"

Vernon Lee has come to be recognized as a key figure in late nineteenth-century British aestheticism, with critical attention in the 2000s devoted primarily to her supernatural tales – *Hauntings* (1890) – and her collaborative work in psychological aesthetics at the turn of the century.[43] Her interest in, and engagement with, aestheticism, however, was threaded throughout her professional ambition, and, arguably, reached a climax upon meeting A. Mary F. Robinson. In 1881, as Robinson gained respect as a rising female poet, she introduced Lee to the well-known aesthetes and female poets of her family's London salon. Included in this circle were Walter Pater, Oscar Wilde, John Addington Symonds, Mathilde Blind, Amy Levy, and Augusta Webster.[44] In the 1880s, these figures diverged in their attitudes of political and moral concern, generating multiple strands of aestheticism. On the one hand, aestheticism is often characterized by its tenet of art and beauty to the exclusion of everything else, as in the phrase "art for art's sake." Sarah Townley notes in her comparative study of Paterian sympathy and Lee's aesthetic empathy, that "Pater's emphasis on the individual and the private nature of his response to art has led to various accounts which view Paterian aestheticism as ethically—or socially—disengaged and as demonstrating a lack of concern for anything but the individual critic's pursuit of pleasure."[45] On the other hand, aestheticism emerges with a political position, characterized by the earlier values of John Ruskin and espoused by William Morris: the exposure of art and beauty as means of rescue from mechanical and industrial ugliness, and as an enlivening of moral sensibility and sympathy, discussed in Chapter 4. Although critics like Linda Dowling argue for the implicit liberalism and democratization in Pater's position, as Harrington acknowledges, the famed conclusion to *Studies in the History of the Renaissance* (1873) pays no direct attention to how art might address social advocacy or the compulsion to aid the less fortunate.[46] This tension between "missionary aestheticism" or "aesthetic philanthropy" and the isolation inherent in "art for art's sake" deeply affected Robinson – and, by extension, Lee.[47] Indeed, Townley argues that Lee's aesthetic empathy "sharpen[s] the social conscience of Pather's aesthetic theory" in her belief that empathy does not remove us from the world – the external environment – when we engage with art.[48] The dissident public debates surrounding aestheticism at the *fin de siècle* developed what Harrington traces as an initially private and, eventually, public dialogue between the couple as they attempt to establish an alternative to Paterian aestheticism by merging the pleasures of art with a more accessible and inclusive aestheticism.

Feeling her poetic impulse to be at odds with her sense of altruism, Robinson first writes of her internal struggle to her mentor, John Addington Symonds, on March 4, 1879:

> I only want to be good and some use in the world. [...] I think I am growing more thoughtful for others. At least I know I often feel the love of the whole unhappy world and a passionate longing to help it that burns like a fire in me like a real physical fever. But it is so easy to feel unselfish. I often feel passionately unselfish but I live a life that is narrow, selfish, self-centered so that I hate myself.[49]

Perceiving herself in an aesthetic crisis, Robinson feels her poetic impulse for art and beauty in conflict with her desire "to be good and [of] some use in the world." Here, we read a strong sense of Morrisian conflict – the utilitarian aspects of Morris's encouragement of both beauty and usefulness. Echoing the dissonant views of aestheticism within London circles, Robinson here acknowledges her desire to alleviate the suffering she witnesses around her in terminology that begins as an abstract emotion before moving into physical embodiment: she feels "the love of the whole unhappy world" so strongly that it "burns like a fire in me like a real physical fever." This feverish manifestation of sympathy and social concern resonates with the question of whether aesthetic responsiveness is physical or mental – a question often associated with "Beauty and Ugliness." And yet, as early as 1879, we see Robinson first grappling with such a question in terms of not only aesthetics, but morality: her desire to be good and unselfish is often marred by "a life that is narrow, selfish, self-centered." Robinson, therefore, engages with the same concerns preoccupying many at the end of the century: the role of the individual in relation to the whole, or the community.

In the following year, Lee writes to Robinson and affirms that beautiful poetry could be useful. She encourages Robinson to continue writing, despite her increasing skepticism of both Paterian and Ruskinian aestheticism. Harrington argues that "[a]s they wrote together and responded to each other's work, the passionate relationship between Robinson and Lee became a crucible for their bold attempt to establish an ethical aesthetics."[50] Robinson has waken from "false aestheticism," Lee claims on November 20, 1880, in a letter responding with praise of an indeterminable poem most likely published in *The Crowned Hippolytus* (1881), and urges Robinson to fulfill her vocation:

The poem you have sent me is very charming & has a sort of pathos. But why will you go on doubting of yourself? No person of any sense could doubt what you are & will be. Why in heaven's name do you not feel sure of your vocation, when it must be so evident to everyone else? [...] You have woken up from false aestheticism, you have recognised the opposite danger of wasting your artistic gifts from ardour to be practically useful; they why do you not calmly take up your position, & make up your mind to do your utmost in the line for which you are appointed.⁵¹

In her frank encouragement of Robinson, Lee's usage of utilitarian terms is striking. Her emphasis on poetry as a "vocation," a "position" that is "appointed," recalls Ruskin's discussion of the artist's vocation of service to the public. Such a position lies in stark contrast to the "false aestheticism" privileged by the Pre-Raphaelites, as denounced in Lee's *Miss Brown* (1884), which criticizes the subversive sexuality of, particularly, Swinburne and Baudelaire. In this private conversation with Robinson, Lee reveals her engagement with ongoing discussions about aestheticism. Is art for the "select few" – the elite – or is it for the masses, for the general public? Townley traces the recovery of Vernon Lee's writings and its impact on conversations seeking to redefine British Aestheticism. Much feminist recovery of Lee's work has emphasized that her revision of Paterian aestheticism incorporates more social engagement, arguing that her aesthetic appreciation is more inclusive, more communal.⁵² Certainly, her letter to Robinson in 1880 gestures toward an engagement in contemporary aesthetic discussions by contributing ethical values to aesthetic ideologies. But is this truly what Lee means by "false aestheticism?" Is, perhaps, this delineation too simplistic?

Begging Robinson for "patience with my preachings," Lee continues, in the following paragraph, to expound upon her integration of Ruskinian and Paterian aestheticism. Here, we see the germination of her formulation of ethical aesthetics. In an extended quotation that sheds light on Lee's confrontation of aesthetic difficulty and what constitutes aesthetic value, she privileges the artist's creation of good over what might be considered one's duty of performing good:

> When I said that some are sent to get rid of evil & others to create good, I was thinking of artists only in the second class. A man who builds a hospital is *doing* good, but not creating it; a man who discovers error is doing good, but not creating it; they are in reality only getting rid of evil. But a man who paints a beautiful picture, or composes a beautiful opera or writes a beautiful poem, is positively *creating* good: *he is* not diminishing pain, he is bestowing pleasure. And the mere removing pain is not enough (though Heaven knows it is enough work for all time to come)[;] a painless world would be but a

poor world, & the mere pleasure of removing pain is but negative, duty, not pleasure. Now you artists do create good, give absolute pleasure. And artistic pleasure is the only real pleasure except pleasure in affection: the rest is all duty work, which if pursued for the sake of pleasure, would become next to worthless: it is the only pleasure which is not limited to one individual & one moment: it is given to all & lasts for ever. Is it not enough then to create this sort of good, when you have been fitted out for the purpose? As a human being you may do more; but you must listen to your vocation. If you have received the brain of a poet, which means that you are a machine for producing poetry, why must you neglect your work & seek for that which requires the muscle & fibre given to a sister of charity or a social reformer?[53]

This passage is emblematic of the skepticism shared by Robinson and Lee over perceptions of aestheticism. She notes the difference between the pleasures associated with the creation of good and the duty of ridding the world of evil, a task reserved for "a sister of charity or a social reformer." It is not enough to eliminate evil in the world, Lee argues, because such a duty is limited to the good of "one individual & one moment." Yet, the creation of "a beautiful picture [...or] a beautiful opera [...or] a beautiful poem" bestows pleasure "to all & lasts for ever." In contrast to Pater's preference for the individual aesthetic moment,[54] Lee attempts to formulate her reworking of aesthetic values by not only departing from the interiority of Pater's "imaginative access," as Benjamin Morgan describes it,[55] but by emphasizing the pleasures that art, music, and poetry afford to the wider world. Her emphasis on production and creation as a means of social engagement resonates with the liberal sympathetic values that I have traced throughout this book. Indeed, it must be noted that Lee's preferred vehicle for carrying out revisions of British aestheticism is in the form of dialogue, reserved here in private correspondence to Robinson. Such a dialogue is suggestive of ideas circulated and discussed together either in intimate conversation or, more publicly, within their wider aesthetic circle. In addition, the dialogue becomes a crucial form for Lee's early aesthetic theories, written while working alongside Robinson. It is, therefore, significant that Lee closes her letter with a reference to *Belcaro*: "I am trying to carry out an old plan of mine of an Essay on Ruskin; strange to say, on the very points of the morality of artistic work which you have so strongly brought home to me."[56]

The Companionate Nature of *Belcaro*

I have been discussing the swirling strands of aesthetic ideologies with which Lee and Robinson engaged as they were writing their respective works: *Belcaro* (1881) and *The New Arcadia* (1884), a socially informed collection of poetry. Both authors dedicated these works to the other, forming an intertextual dialogue and, as Harrington asserts, making "their private intimate relationship part of the public lives of their works."[37] In their correspondence, Lee and Robinson participated in a mutual exchange of ideas, considering the moral or ethical implications of aesthetics as they struggled with competing desires for a life – paraphrasing Robinson's aforementioned letter to Symonds – of selfishness or unselfishness. Harrington argues that the couple "forge[d] their intimacy around questions of ethical aesthetics" and traces the sympathetic strain carried across their literary texts, recognizing their differences in how the aesthetic could be ethical.[58] I remain indebted to Harrington's argument and her illumination of these texts in dialogue with one another. Indeed, the concept of dialogue here remains central to my argument, which reads *Belcaro* as a collaborative text, influenced by the model of sympathetic collaboration – but with a slight twist. For, as we know, *Belcaro* publicly asserts itself as having a solitary author; yet reading Lee's early entrance into aesthetics as a form of sympathetic collaboration illuminates the influence of lived communal experience upon her writing as an undercurrent of her lifelong attempt at revising aesthetic value to be more companionate and socially aware.

Lee's introduction to *Belcaro* – "The Book and Its Title" – includes its own dedicatory phrase: "To one of my readers—the first and earliest."[59] In fact, all dedications included in the book, the final being "A Dialogue on Poetic Morality," pertain to Robinson. This is a collection for a specific audience: a private reader, whose thoughts and dialogues shaped, nay, helped to create the text of *Belcaro*. If sympathetic collaboration is defined as a shared creation arising from sympathetic identification with the other, the paratext of *Belcaro* asserts the text's shared nature. Of course, this could be said of any text dedicated to another individual. Combining the paratext with the introduction, however, suggests that *Belcaro* is, in fact, a form of sympathetic collaboration, for it is a companionate text, compiled of various dialogues. Additionally, this air of collaboration is further underscored by the point of view: first person plural – "we."

The opening paragraph is written with the aim of presenting a manuscript to its reader – to, specifically, Robinson. Lee establishes a sense of intimacy with Robinson and recollects phrasing from their correspondence, while also acknowledging the book's public role and the involvement of an external reader:

> A little while ago I told you that I wished this collection of studies to be more especially yours: so now I send it to you, a bundle of proofs and of MS., to know whether you will have it. I wish I could give you what I have

written in the same complete way that a painter would give you one of his sketches; that a singer, singing for you alone, might give you his voice and his art; for a dedication is but a drop of ink on a large white sheet, and conveys but a sorry notion of property. Now, this book is intended to be really yours; yours in the sense that, were it impossible for more than one copy to exist, that one copy I should certainly give to you. Because these studies represent the ideas I have so far been able to work out for myself about art, considered not historically, but in its double relation to the artist and the world for whom he works; ideas which it is my highest ambition should influence those young enough and powerful enough to act upon them; and, this being the case, my first thought is to place them before you: it is, you see, a matter of conversion, and the nearest, most difficult, most desired convert is yourself.[60]

Placing *Belcaro* in Robinson's hands, Lee questions whether she will maintain ownership: "whether you will have it." If the book is to be "especially yours" and "really yours," with "yours" referring to Robinson, we — as public readers — find ourselves in something of a quandary. In some ways, the reader becomes an outside voyeur of Lee and Robinson's private relationship. After all, in saying that "I wish I could give you what I have written in the same complete way that a painter would give you one of his sketches" or a singer "might give you his voice and his art," Lee recalls to Robinson's mind her earlier words on the importance of artistic creation. The similarity in syntax and phrasing between the artists listed here, and the "man who paints a beautiful picture, or composes a beautiful opera or writes a beautiful poem" from her November 20, 1880 letter to Robinson should not be dismissed. *Belcaro* is, on the one hand, a private text that opens wide Lee's lived communal experience with Robinson, noting the influence of their conversations and shared experiences. And yet, it is also a public text: offering its readers the opportunity to be influenced and to act upon that influence. In fact, we find ourselves in a triangulated relationship — akin to the triangulated gaze for which Lee and Anstruther-Thomson are known. Eliminating the boundaries between private and public, inclusive and communal, Lee communicates the shared act of writing and, importantly, the purpose of that shared nature: *Belcaro* is meant to be an act of conversion. In making public the private dialogues between herself and Robinson, Lee hopes to convert her reader — both Robinson and the public — so that conversion to Lee's brand of aestheticism becomes an act of shared circulation.

Claiming to have "gone to school as a student of aesthetics," Lee narrates her means of acquiring knowledge, noting the influence of Robinson and the importance of discussion and dialogue. "To school, where, and with whom?," she asks, and answers: "mainly to art itself, to pictures and statues and music and poetry, to my own feelings and my own thoughts; studying, in seemingly desultory fashion, in discussions with my friends and with myself."⁶¹ Expanding Pater's model of disinterested aesthetic appreciation – in which the aesthetic critic regards "all the objects with which he has to do [...] as powers or forces producing pleasurable sensations" which must be "explain[ed], by analysing and reducing it to its elements"⁶² – Lee asserts a social mode of aesthetic engagement, a mode requiring not only analysis but shared discussion.⁶³ In light of these dialogues, Lee notes her difficulty in compiling *Belcaro*. It is presented in the form of notes, removed from the "living frame-work; to be written down, that is to say, to be made quite lifeless and inorganic."⁶⁴ Despite the lifelessness that occurs in the writing process, Lee affirms the collaborative nature of her writing:

> I have always thought, in arranging these discussions, of the real individuals with whom I should most willingly have them: I have always felt that some one else was by my side to whom I was showing, explaining, answering; hence the use of the second person plural, of which I have vainly tried to be rid: it is not the oracular *we* of the printed book, it is the *we* of myself and those with whom, for whom, I am speaking; it is the constantly felt dualism of myself and my companion.⁶⁵

Lee's aesthetic theories, therefore, are not her own: they have evolved out of a communal effort. Not content with what she would later denounce in *Miss Brown* (1884) as Pater's emphasis on the Decadent individual as hedonistic, Lee offers here an alternative in the form of the communal "we": "the constantly felt dualism of myself and my companion." In repeating "felt," Lee also draws attention to the sensation of the communal: she feels "someone else [...] by my side" and the "dualism of myself and my companion." It is worth emphasizing here that in these early formulations of an ethical aesthetics, Lee concentrates on how people feel for each other: on the dualism of interdependency, on the social nature of collaboration. In *Belcaro*, Lee uses the "we" of the shared text, participating in the same shared circulation of private life-writing as Mary Wollstonecraft Godwin and Percy Bysshe Shelley. In uniting the communal act of writing with pleasure and beauty, Lee provides a practical answer to the conflict over aesthetic value in private correspondence with Robinson: the value lies in social pleasure.

Robinson, too, would later comment on the creative influence of Lee and the pleasures derived from the act of creating together. In memoriam to Lee's brother, Eugene Lee-Hamilton, Robinson wrote "In Casa Paget" (1907) and emphasized the importance of dialogue in creative stimulation:

> We were always writing in corners, Violet and I. She at a carved table on large vellum-like sheets; I huddled in a shawl on the chimney step, my inkpot neighboring the firedogs, a blotting-pad upon my knee. I cannot say we wrote in solemn silence. Impressions, forecasts, reminiscences, quotations from Michelet or Matarazzo, subjects for ballads, problems for essays, aesthetical debates and moral discussions would burst forth, in the midst of our occupations, from the couch in the corner, from the writing table, or (much more rarely) from the warm seclusion of the chimney step.[66]

Although not upon the same page, Robinson and Lee write together while exchanging ideas. Robinson's memory of "writing in corners," punctuated by "burst[s]" of conversation is suggestive of the "living atmosphere" that Lee sought to create with Anstruther-Thomson. Such a suggestion indicates that Lee, like Shelley and Morris, continually strived to formulate a community of fellow thinkers. Moreover, this representation of Lee's and Robinson's writing process foregrounds the environment in which Lee believed aesthetic pleasure could thrive: not in isolation or individual experience, but in Fraternity, within a sympathetic exchange of ideas.

If this collaborative community enriches aesthetic pleasure, it makes sense that Lee's chosen form is the dialogue essay. Importantly, the final essay in *Belcaro* resumes the debate begun in the Lee-Robinson correspondence. In "A Dialogue on Poetic Morality," Cyril and Baldwin stage the conflict between the couple: is poetry a contribution to aesthetic sensuality and individual gratification, or can poetry be used as an influence to stimulate curiosity and moral concern? Harrington emphasizes the difficulty of this dialogue, pinpointing the contradictions and destabilizing accounts of aestheticism that Cyril and Baldwin create in an effort to resolve their conflicting viewpoints. Such contradiction, Harrington notes, "testifies to the difficulty of finding a middle ground where debates around aesthetics were so highly polarized."[67] "A Dialogue on Poetic Morality" does not attempt a resolution to these polarized accounts, but it does – as Harrington also argues – provide the intellectual intimacy of Robinson and Lee in full force as the couple attempt to sympathetically assimilate and accommodate the other's viewpoints. In the true form of a Platonic dialogue, however, complete assimilation or accommodation is impossible – but the *possibility* of the influence of conversion remains for both Robinson and the public.

In a Platonic dialogue, the protagonist performs an interrogation to ascertain the other's understanding of moral issues. The purpose is to influence the readers to think for themselves about the issues raised – hence, the contradictory responses of Baldwin (Lee) and Cyril (Robinson) create distance, enabling the "converted reader" of *Belcaro* to formulate their own opinion. In discussing the vocation of the poet, Cyril asserts that Baldwin's philosophy is accurate, and yet cannot suit his "moral condition" – in other words, there are limits to his assimilation of his friend's viewpoints:

> "I think your philosophy is quite right, Baldwin, only—only, somehow, I can't get it to suit my moral condition," answered Cyril. "I do feel quite persuaded that sculptors must not try to be painters, nor musicians try to be poets, nor any of them try to be anything beyond what they are. It is all quite rational, and right, and moral, but still I am not satisfied about poetry. [...] But a poet, inasmuch as he is a poet, knows sees, feels a great many things which have a practical and moral meaning: just because he is a poet, he knows that there is something beyond poetry; he knows that there are in the world such things as justice and injustice, good, and evil, purity and foulness: he knows all this [...] and knowing it, perceiving, feeling, understanding it, with more intensity than other men, is he to sweep it all out of his sight? [...] Oh Baldwin, if he be a man and an honest one, he surely cannot [...]
>
> [Baldwin responds,] "He will not set aside the ideas of justice and injustice, of good and evil, of purity and impurity, Cyril. He will make use of them [...] I have always laughed at the Ruskinian idea of morality or immorality in architecture, or painting, or music, and said that their morality and immorality were beauty and ugliness. I have done so because moral ideas don't enter into the arts of line, or colour, or sound, but only into the subjects to which their visible and audible works are (usually arbitrarily) attached. But with poetry the case is different; and if the poet has got a keener perception (or ought to have) of right and wrong than other men, it is because a sense of moral right and wrong is required in his art, as a sense of colour is required in painting. I have said 'art for art's sake,' but I should been more precise in saying 'art for beauty's sake.'[...]⁵⁸

Poetry is given a higher standing than other arts, providing the requirement of "a sense of moral right and wrong." As Kristin Mahoney argues, Lee "turned to literature with an interest in its capacity to render the human subject more ethical."⁶⁹ Dismissing the dominant strand of aestheticism – *l'art pour l'art* – Baldwin inserts subjective aesthetic value: beauty. This might seem a contradiction, posing a harsh critique of aestheticism while laughing at Ruskinian thought. And yet, when returning almost twenty pages later to his central assertion that the poet must have a "keener" sense of morality, Baldwin rephrases his tenet of aestheticism:

> I do not think that the poet's object is to moralize mankind; but I think that the materials with which he must work are such that, while practising his art, he may unconsciously do more mischief than all the professed

> moralists in Christendom can consciously do good. The poet is the artist, remember, who deliberately chooses as material for his art the feelings and actions of man; he is the artist who plays his melodies, not on catgut strings or metal stops, but upon human passions; and whose playing touches not a mere mechanism of fibres and membranes like the ear, but the human soul, which in its turn feels and acts […]⁷⁰

In Baldwin's (or Lee's) view, the poet retains a moral, or ethical, obligation – not by preaching what is right or wrong – but through influence. Again, returning to the Lee-Robinson correspondence, the poet is able to influence a wider public with his creation rather than the action of a solitary figure. Lee claims that poetry – art – can have moral value, without specific moral meaning. The value lies in the dialogue – in the communal influence of shared ideas and feeling.

In reading *Belcaro* as a variation on sympathetic collaboration, what, specifically, do we gain? Within its formal construct, we witness the influence of private dialogue – the life-writing between Lee and Robinson – in the formulation of the published text's first-person plural. Such a reading also foregrounds the communal aspect of togetherness: despite their differing approaches to aesthetic value, what remains central in *Belcaro* is the intellectual exchange, the shared circulation of feeling – sympathy, and the ability to enter into the other's situation, yet retain a difference in opinion. Moreover, if sympathy is a social process, concerned with the formation of community, Lee's introduction as a means of conversion takes on new meaning. As readers, we are given the choice to convert: to enter into Lee's aesthetic community. Such an experience of conversion requires the "untutored learning" that Lee espouses in her introduction, in which, as Stefano Evangelista argues, "art, emotionally experienced and organically integrated in the texture of everyday life, is a stimulus for pleasure and companionship."⁷¹ *Belcaro* becomes that companionate community: it becomes the redefinition of aestheticism as that which must find value in the social, rather than the strains of Decadent, sensorial gratification.

Isolating Effects of Empathy

Lee's criticism of Paterian aestheticism involved its tendency to lapse into Decadence, its tendency toward self-absorption. As Catherine Maxwell and Patricia Pulham assert, "Lee claimed to be repelled by Decadent formulations and to disapprove of their unwholesomeness and lack of moral health."⁷² Therefore, it makes sense that in revising definitions of aestheticism, Lee incorporates ethical concerns. Lois Agnew suggests that this revision highlights Lee's "appreciation for subjective criticism" which "co-exists with a social conscience that leads her to insist that artistic appreciation is ultimately an ethical act."[73] By the time Lee writes *Miss Brown* (1884), her increasingly ethical response informs her condemnation of aestheticism and its followers, straining, in particular, her relationship with the Pre-Raphaelites. Yet such a narrative takes a striking turn by 1887, with the introduction of Anstruther-Thomson.

The difficulty traced in Lee and Anstruther-Thomson's collaborative process arises from the tension experienced by Lee as she confronts ethical or moral aesthetics while countering Decadent formulations. Diana Maltz argues that Lee "stifled" her initial social imperative because she was "bent on enabling others to revere Anstruther-Thomson's sentient body as she did."[74] Informed by the nineteenth-century emphasis on sociability and reform that characterized her initial framing of aesthetic dialogue, Lee's transition into psychological aesthetics certainly seems an abrupt shift with its emphasis on the corporeality of intellect. Maltz carries her argument further, asserting that "[i]n the spirit of the fin de siècle, Anstruther-Thomson used her decadent focus on bodily sensations to subvert Lee's social and educational agendas, in effect producing a new version of psychological aesthetics, one in which social service was subordinated to sexuality."[75] I remain unconvinced that Anstruther-Thomson "subverts" Lee's moral agenda; however, in removing Victorian sentimentality and liberal reform from her conceptions of aestheticism, Lee signals her participation in the empathetic transition toward Modernism, and a larger integration of British psychology and Associationist terminology.

"Beauty and Ugliness" sets out to understand how art produces bodily feeling. Notably, after Robinson leaves Lee in 1887, Lee turns from poetry to visual art, noticing lines, shapes, and colors. Such a transition recalls Baldwin's laughing at whether there is morality or immorality in lines, color, and sound, and begs the question: has Lee, after all, moved so very far from her initial aesthetic conceptions? The collaborative essay seeks to establish how "the aesthetic phenomenon as a whole is the function which regulates the perception of Form, and that the perception of Form, in visual cases certainly, and with reference to hearing presumably, implies an active participation of the most important organs of animal life."[76] Central to this active participation are the emotions that arise when observing art: "*Why should a specific kind of condition, either agreeable or disagreeable, accompany the recognition of those co-related qualities of form called respectively Beauty and Ugliness?*"[77] To answer this question, Anstruther-Thomson records, in great detail, her respiratory and ocular movements in conjunction with "alterations in the equilibrium of various parts of the body."[78] To demonstrate, in a succinct example, Anstruther-Thomson records her sensations when observing a triangle:

> A *triangle* one can focus as a whole without moving the eye perpetually about. The thoracic movements come into play, and seem to make three little pinches at the three corners. There is a sense of resistance being offered all round, and of the *chest having something to lean against*. We have now got to *complete Form*. And with *Form* we get to the possibility of aesthetic agreeableness or disagreeableness, in other words, of beauty or ugliness.[79]

As critics like Maltz and Joseph Bristow have noted, Anstruther-Thomson's descriptions amount to imitation or mimicry of the formal elements of the art object. And to what effect? Anticipating her audience's question, Anstruther-Thomson concludes that such mimicry leads to "a sense of increased vitality and of marvelous harmony of existence."[80] The bodily imitation of the perceived form results in an appreciation of subjective impression. In this sensorial recording, we see influences of Alexander Bain's understanding of the body as inextricably linked to intellect. Bain "develops a new interest in the way intellectual life is located within the physiology of the brain and, in turn, the body in general."[81] Significantly, this turn toward physiology and corporeality is, for Anstruther-Thomson, experienced in isolation. The "thoracic movements" and "resistance" are felt not by the "we" identified in the passage above, but in the individual physiological perceptions of Anstruther-Thomson – Lee, by her own admission, failed to experience the same bodily sensations.

In documenting Anstruther-Thomson's individual perceptions, Lee asserts in her introduction to the collected volume, *Beauty and Ugliness*, that the "essay on *Beauty and Ugliness* has an undeniable importance—that of originating not in psychological speculations, but in the study of the individual work of art and its individual effects; and thereby attacking the central problem of aesthetics, and arriving at the fact of *Einfühlung* or *Empathy* from sides other than those which Lipps, Groos and their followers have started."[82] In her turn away from the metaphysical aspects of Theodor Lipps' empathy, curiously, Lee upholds that which she had previously condemned as decadent: the individual focus on the pleasures afforded by the body. This suggestion, furthermore, is foregrounded in Ethel Smyth's descriptions of the couple's "gallery experiments:"

> some few years ago I had gone with [Vernon Lee] and Kit to the Vatican, when, pulling up before what Baedeker rather unnecessarily described as a Roman copy of a Greek bust of Apollo, but which Il Palmerino [Lee] had decided was a Greek original, Vernon suddenly said, "Kit! show us that

bust!" Kit's proceedings were remarkable; in dead silence she advanced, then retreated, shaded her eyes, and then ejaculated, "Look at that Johnny! how he sings! [...] how he sings!" Various technical details were then pointed out as proving their contention, though Vernon considered these less important than the singing quality discovered by her friend.[83]

Focusing on the materiality of the body ensures that individuals "are susceptible to art's influence and facilitates the subordination of our self-interest."[84] This receptivity to external influences aligns the couple with models of Associationist psychology, which proposes a keen awareness of how our environments shape us. While Maltz identifies the erotic subtext of Smyth's narrative and emphasizes the mastery of Anstruther-Thomson's performance as transforming "Lee's aesthetic mission into a decadent amusement," to my mind, this passage indicates – once again – the delineation of roles. Far earlier than the division of labor in the 1912 collected volume, Lee and Anstruther-Thomson's collaborative endeavor is marked by a tension between performance and intellect. Lee seems to admire Anstruther-Thomson's performance – the singing – over the "technical details" advanced as proof. This difference becomes a public tension in Lee's introductory remarks to "Beauty and Ugliness' in 1912 and her insistence that aesthetic empathy remains her contribution, rather than a collaborative production.

By contributing empathy to the couple's gallery experiments, Lee attempts to differentiate herself from the strains of decadence associated with Anstruther-Thomson's performance. Empathy, therefore, becomes an intellectual frame that establishes distance: empathy becomes a means of interpretation. She clarifies this position, while dividing labor and asserting difference, in her opening statement to the revised essay:

> While admitting the secondary importance of such organic and mimetic sensations, I am more and more inclined to consider that mere formal-dynamic empathy as such, that is to say, considered as a mere mental phenomenon (whatever its physiological origin or connexions) is the direct, the primary explanation of the aesthetic phenomenon; and, in taking up this position, I have evidently followed along the lines of Lipps's hypothesis of *Einfühlung*. My collaborator, on the contrary, adheres to our original point of view as expressed in the following pages; and in so far she must be grouped rather with Groos and those more recent aestheticians who [...] lay stress especially upon mimetic processes and organic accompaniments.[85]

Relegating Anstruther-Thomson's contributions to parentheticals, Lee asserts her revised inclination to view their experiments as a form of empathy, following German philosophers Theodor Lipps and Robert Vischer. Converted to aesthetic empathy, Lee is able to divorce the somatic sensations and performative aspects of Anstruther-Thomson's body from "mental phenomenon" and focus instead on the central role that associations play in allowing an individual to maintain an empathic relationship with art. By 1912, Lee believes the aesthetic response to be mental rather than physical. Rae Greiner's analysis of sympathy versus empathy is particularly useful here. "In Vischer's view," Greiner summarizes, *Einfühlung* "described the ways humans projected emotion into aesthetic objects so as to animate our relationship to the phenomenal world: it was a 'feeling into' of the self into aesthetic form." For Lipps, empathy is the "process in which the boundary between subject and object [...] disappeared."[86] Here, then, is the prime difference between empathy and sympathy: in eliminating the boundaries, empathy might be considered to be a more intimate encounter. And yet, for Lee, empathy remains a form of specific aesthetic response: it remains intimate due to the encounter between one's self and the art object. And at the same time, it remains individualistic and introspective.

Whereas Smithian sympathy remains distanced in an effort to include impartial judgement as a means of forming community, aesthetic empathy retains its focus on the individual and transitions to assert the merger of the individual with the external environment via associations. The primary obstacle to Lee's collaborative production with Anstruther-Thomson lies in her struggle to reconcile her earlier view of aestheticism as deriving pleasure from intellectual dialogue, from the establishment of a converted community. "Beauty and Ugliness" publicizes Lee's inability to overcome the aesthetic differences between herself and Anstruther-Thomson, yet fails to resolve the conflict between individual and communal aesthetics, in part, because of her reliance on empathy. In arguing that "sympathy belongs to the Victorians, empathy to us" Greiner asserts that empathy is, in a sense, the formulation of "remak[ing] sympathy for aesthetics."[87] For Lee, aesthetic empathy marks an attempt to find a solution to the impossibility of separating bodily and emotional – subjective and objective – boundaries. Indeed, by 1912, Lee asserts that empathy is "analogous to that of moral sympathy": "Just as when we 'put ourselves in the place' or, more vulgarly, 'in the skin' of a fellow-creature, we are, in fact, attributing to him the feelings we should have in similar circumstances."[88] This understanding suggests that, for Lee, the relationship between feeling and aesthetics is similar to the sympathetic exchange of one person entering into the other's experience. But with a key difference: for Smith, sympathy is a social process of communal formation; for Lee, sympathy is merely a relational exchange – an attribution of similar feelings that allows for greater intimacy.

Lee's early aesthetic essays establish her commitment to confront the issue of aesthetic difficulty. Her wavering between the individual and the social is a result of Lee being a product of her time: she is both of the Victorian period and of the Modern period, or, as Mahoney says, Lee is a "Victorian Modern."[89] She, like Michael Field, exists in a liminal space, and her aesthetic theories align with late nineteenth-century debates over the values inherent in aestheticism and the emergence of Associationist psychology. In tracing the tension of Lee's early aesthetics and the implications of that tension upon Lee's participation in collaboration, I have marked the difference between the companionate collaboration with Robinson and the bipartite collaboration with Anstruther-Thomson. In moving away from models of dialogue and sympathetic collaboration in favor of the privatization of the aesthetic experience, Lee experiences the discord that arises due to the individual difference advanced by the aesthetic imperative. In the late 1890s, Lee was unable to reconcile the importance of difference; only later would she realize the "similar yet different" approach espoused in *Laurus Nobilis* (1909):

> Final fulfillment of that dream of absolute union? No; [...] We have seen that by one of the most gracious coincidences between beauty and kindliness, the aesthetic emotion is even intensified by the knowledge of coexistence in others: the delight in each person communicating itself [...] to the similar yet different delight in his neighbour, harmonic enriching harmonic by stimulating fresh vibration.[90]

Conclusion

Sympathy, fellow-feeling, enables nineteenth-century collaboration. Throughout *Collaborative Writing in the Long Nineteenth Century*, my conception of sympathetic collaboration relies not only on the "joint creation," but also on the associations and networks that make up the artistic process in order to trace the coming together of individuals both interpersonally and intertextually. Sympathetic collaboration is an exploratory, liberal, and necessarily social interaction and, in the nineteenth century, aesthetic, moral, and social judgments are interrelated. Sympathetic collaboration reconsiders the collective nature of nineteenth-century literary production and its reliance upon lived experience and communal relations as a means of constructing shared expression through formal experimentation. Demonstrating the extent to which Smithean sympathy influenced the Victorian establishment of liberal community, my model of collaboration illuminates an innovative argument about the nineteenth century: namely, that sympathetic communities are implicated in formal experimentation.

As we have seen, conceptions of sympathy do not remain static across the century, due, in part, to changing conceptions of social formation. To conclude, I look forward to sympathy's evolution at the end of the nineteenth century, expanding on the claims of Modernism and empathy made in the final chapters on Michael Field and Vernon Lee. From its Romantic heritage in eighteenth-century philosophy, sympathy began as an ethics, as a moral imperative between people. During the last quarter of the nineteenth century, however, sympathy and empathy are inextricably woven together in cultural discourse, despite being completely separate concepts.[1] Moreover, as these discourses circulate in the latter half of the century, Victorians struggle to conceptualize the role of the individual within social relations. In an era marked by morality and reform, in which sympathy underlies the coming together of individuals, it therefore makes sense that as investigations into sympathy and empathy evolve, so too does the dynamic function of society.

In 1889, French philosopher Henri Bergson set forth his understanding of sympathy in *Time and Free Will*, a theory that would be expanded in 1903 with the publication of *Creative Mind: An Introduction to Metaphysics*. Sympathy, for Bergson, is identified as intuition, and is capable of existing beyond individual relations to incorporate a relationship between things:

> An absolute can only be given in an intuition, while all the rest has to do with analysis. We call intuition here the sympathy by which one is transported into the interior of an object in order to coincide with what there is unique and consequently inexpressible in it. Analysis, on the contrary, is the operation which reduces the object to elements already known.[2]

At first glance, the language that Bergson chooses is reminiscent of Smith's transportation: sympathy allows for an exchange of feeling between situations. Importantly, however, Bergsonian sympathy shifts away from Smithian sympathy in its concern for objects; that is, sympathy is no longer reserved exclusively for the relations between individuals, and thus contingent upon social formation. Here, sympathy is more of a feeling, rather than a form of critical reflection, or thought. Moreover, it "is a feeling that is unspecified" and capable of branching out into all dimensions of life.[3] Penetrating all things, sympathy transports through intuition, immediacy, and synchrony, as exemplified in Bergson's example of a wasp: "The Ammophilia, no doubt, discerns but very little of that force, but what concerns itself; but at least it discerns it from within, quite otherwise than by a process of knowledge—by an intuition (*lived* rather than *represented*), which is probably like what we call divining sympathy."[4] As sympathy evolves at the end of the century, we witness a self-interested interiority between a vast host of relations, moving outward to consider a transformation that occurs when individuals or things synchronize their behavior with another. As Spuybroek succinctly summarizes, sympathy is an abstract feeling, localized not in the brain, but in the entire body as an "experiential fabric," an "interiorized form of motion, a preparing and tensing of muscles, and the integration of such tensing provides orientation."[5] In abstracting humans as things among others, Bergsonian sympathy illustrates a network of interconnected things, resonating, synchronizing, and existing in sympathy.

Bergson's network may recall the unconscious processes theorized by Charles Darwin in the 1859 and 1860 editions of *The Origin of Species*. Darwin's theory of evolution relies on the relations between a variety of organisms: "'a web of complex relations'—rather than competition alone."[6] Emphasizing organic interdependence, Darwin follows the tradition of

Charles Lyell's *Principles of Geology* (1833). Indeed, by mid-century, views of interdependency were so widespread that Henry Mayhew's *London Labour and the London Poor* (1861–1862) upholds "universal compensation" to reveal "each mutually dependent on the other, and so contributing each to the other's support."[7] In an interdisciplinary dialogue between scientists, social theorists, and philosophers, then, we witness a growing tendency toward explorations of the self in relation to the whole as a model of sociability. Ultimately, these dialogues err on the side of favoring social cooperation over individualistic struggle, as Gagnier traces in her overview of Victorian models of life. But by the end of the century, abstraction takes hold, as demonstrated by Bergson above and Theodor Lipps below, resulting in a contrasting view that aligns with a transition from the ethics of sympathy to underscore the relationality between a variety of things, both human and non-human: "Whereas mainstream Victorian literature concerned itself with how to harness the individual's energy for social purposes, polygenetic fiction towards the end of the century 'explores the alternative possibility that humanity is nothing but points of intensification through which desires circulate to form one all-encompassing and mindless [...] mass of humanity.'"[8]

Tracing the "points of intensification" forming a "mass of humanity," in 1905, Theodor Lipps foregrounds the abstracting tendency of intensity in his conception of empathy: "What I empathize into it is quite generally life. And life is energy, inner working, striving and accomplishing. In a word, life is activity. But activity is that in which I experience an expenditure of energy."[9] Lipps' *Einfühlung*, from which Vernon Lee draws, is differentiated from moral and social conceptions of sympathy in its understanding of the relationship between movement and form. Questioning his feeling of anger during a storm, Lipps arrives at the underlying resonance between the nature of movement – the activity of the storm – and feelings that one experiences: "We immediately—that is, without reflection—project ourselves into the other, the living (or non-living but moving) thing."[10] Of concern to Lipps – as well as Lee and Kit Anstruther-Thomson – is the external movement of something beyond our bodies and the evocation of a specific feeling within the body:

> In a word, I am now with my feeling of activity entirely and wholly in the moving figure. Even spatially, if we can speak of the spatial extent of the ego, I am in its place. I am transported into it. I am, as far as my consciousness is concerned, entirely and wholly identical with it. Thus feeling myself active in the observed figure, I feel also in it free, facile, and proud. This is the aesthetic imitation, and this imitation is at the same time aesthetic *Einfühlung*.[11]

In moving away from a reliance on social cooperation – on sympathetic collaboration as traced in this book – aesthetic empathy demonstrates a transportation that is wholly self-interested, an "aesthetic imitation" that allows for an "identical" consciousness between the internal self and the external world.

I am not, in the end, arguing that collaboration and community dissolve at the end of the nineteenth century. Rather, differing forms of collaboration take root in what I perceive as a shift from the social intimacy of sympathy and the impersonality of empathy, with its individual bodily connotation.[12] I suggest that this shift is rooted in a preoccupation, at the *fin de siècle*, concerning the individual's role within a larger social whole. In this way, empathy fills in the essential gap that makes sympathy situational and liberal in origin – the gap between individuals is necessary for the purpose of disinterested reflection, assimilation, and accommodation.

Notes

Introduction

1. Somerville and Ross, "Two of a Trade," 85.
2. Ehnenn, *Women's Literary Collaboration, Queerness, and Late Victorian Culture*, 32.
3. Take, for example, an 1890 article in *Longman's Magazine* and *the Living Age*, which asserts that the first question asked of collaborative works is "'what was the part of each partner in the writing of the book?' (Matthews, 167); yet the article goes to great lengths to explain how two writers can (and must) achieve 'unity of expression' (Matthews, 168)" (qtd. in Ehnenn, *Women's Literary Collaboration, Queerness, and Late-Victorian Culture*, 28–9).
4. See Greiner, *Sympathetic Realism in Nineteenth-Century British Fiction*.
5. See Bednarz, "The Collaborator as Thief," 279; 281; Brooker, "Common Ground and Collaboration in T.S. Eliot," 231; Stillinger, *Multiple Authorship*, 185.
6. Inge, "Collaboration and Concepts of Authorship," 629.
7. Hines, *Collaborative Form*, 4. Hines's primary focus is on artistic forms such as opera, which involves collaboration. His focus is not on collaborative authorship.
8. Ede and Lunsford, *Singular Texts/Plural Authors*, 14.
9. As will become clear with the chapter outlines at the end of this Introduction, I am also interested in expanding understandings of collaboration across disciplinary boundaries and a wide range of personal relationships.
10. Latour, *Reassembling the Social*, 5.
11. Ibid.
12. Ibid., 8.
13. I am grateful to Dr Nathaniel Rivers for introducing me to Latour's theories and helping me to see my modeling of collaboration as Latourian.
14. Ede and Lunsford, *Singular Texts/Plural Authors*, 5.
15. Stillinger, *Multiple Authorship*, v.
16. McGann, *The Textual Condition*, 60.
17. Ibid., 100.
18. Ehnenn's work is one exception: her focus on collaboration as a "coming together" pairs descriptions of collaboration as eating or cooking together,

conversation, and dialogic dialogue with acts traditionally associated with female experience and domestication. In so doing, Ehnenn elaborates on learning theorist Kenneth Bruffee's claim that writing is a social act (4).
19. Laird, *Women Coautnors*, 5.
20. Stone and Thompson, *Literary Couplings*, 4.
21. Ibid., 5.
22. Morgan, *The Outward Mind*, 5.
23. Stone and Thompson, *Literary Couplings*, 14.
24. See Potolsky, *The Decadent Republic of Letters*. Chapter 4 also draws from Potolsky's understanding of decadent communities as maintaining an "imagined community of sympathetic readers and writers" not to produce an affiliation with – as it was for the Victorians – the public, but to admire and exchange texts (8–9).
25. Wilson, *Shelley and the Apprehension of Life*, 162.
26. Collini, *Liberalism and Sociology*, 38.
27. I am not alone in regarding Vernon Lee as a modernist. See, among others, Denisoff's "The Queer Ecology of Vernon Lee's Transient Affections"; Martin's *Modernism and the Rhythms of Sympathy*; and Leighton's "Ghosts, Aestheticism, and Vernon Lee."

1 Adam Smith's Liberal Sympathy

1. See, for instance, Prins and Jackson, *The Lyric Theory Reader*; Thain, *The Lyric Poem*; Attridge, *Moving Words: Forms of English Poetry*; and Culler, *Theory of the Lyric*.
2. Prins and Jackson, *The Lyric Theory Reader*, 2.
3. See Stillinger, *Multiple Authorship and the Myth of the Solitary Genius*.
4. Prins and Jackson, *The Lyric Theory Reader*, 3.
5. Ibid.
6. Ibid., 4.
7. Thain, *Lyric Poem*, 2.
8. Ibid., 166.
9. Rossetti, *Goblin Market*, ll. 562–5.
10. Smith, *Theory of Moral Sentiments*, 13; 53.
11. Ibid., 22; 27.
12. Frazer, *The Enlightenment of Sympathy*, 8.
13. Ibid., 4.
14. Ibid., 8.
15. This aspect of judgment is further elucidated in discussions of the social mirror and the impartial spectator, discussed at length below.
16. Smith, *The Theory of Moral Sentiments*, 20. The opposite is also true – disapproving showcases a lack of sympathy: "and not approve of them as such, is the same thing as to observe that we do not entirely sympathize with them."
17. Ibid., 27.

18. Ibid., 13.
19. Ibid., 11–2.
20. Darwall, "Empathy, Sympathy," 60; original emphasis.
21. Griswold, "Imagination: Morals, Science, and Arts," 25.
22. Smith, *The Theory of Moral Sentiments,* 27. During the early eighteenth century, "concord" meant "agreement between persons; concurrence in feeling and opinion; harmony, accord" (concord, n.1). The *OED* attributes this usage to Edmund Burke's *Observations on a Late State of the Nation* (1769): "No projects of theirs could endanger the concord of the empire." Thus, this terminology is quite common in the eighteenth-century economic and moral philosophy, and engages with the affective circulation of feeling.
23. Smith, *The Theory of Moral Sentiments,* 129.
24. Ibid.
25. Ibid., 263.
26. Hanley, "The Eighteenth-Century Context of Sympathy from Spinoza to Kant," 173.
27. Weinstein, *Adam Smith's Pluralism,* 69.
28. Ibid., 72.
29. For the "theatricality" of sympathy, see Marshall, "Adam Smith and the Theatricality of Moral Sentiments," 592–613; Marshall, *The Figure of Theatre*; and Marshall, *The Surprising Effects of Sympathy*.
30. Smith, *The Theory of Moral Sentiments,* 12.
31. Jervis, *Sympathetic Sentiments,* 96.
32. Griswold, "Imagination," 25; 27.
33. Jervis, *Sympathetic Sentiments,* 101.
34. Smith, *The Theory of Moral Sentiments,* 131; 158.
35. Griswold, "Imagination," 38.
36. Forman-Barzilai, *Adam Smith and the Circles of Sympathy,* 13.
37. Smith, *The Theory of Moral Sentiments,* 101.
38. Ibid., 90.
39. See, for example, Weliver's *Mary Gladstone and the Victorian Salon*; Winckles et al. (eds.), *Women's Literary Networks and Romanticism*; and Alfano and Stauffer (eds.), *Virtual Victorians: Networks, Connections, Technologies*.
40. See Chandler, *An Archaeology of Sympathy* and Duncan's Introduction to *The Private Memoirs and Confessions of a Justified Sinner*.
41. Chandler, "The Languages of Sentiment," 26. Perhaps this is a result of contemporary scholarship on emotions and sympathy emerging from *Das Adam Smith Problem*, which "concerns the ostensible tension between the supposedly self-interested moral psychology of Smith's *Wealth of Nations* and the other-directed moral psychology described in his *Theory of Moral Sentiments*" (Hanley, "The Eighteenth-Century Context of Sympathy from Spinoza to Kant," 177). It is not my intention to engage in this debate, besides pointing to recent re-evaluations that indicate this "problem" as founded upon a false dichotomy between self-interest and sympathy. See Montes, "Das Adam Smith Problem," 63–90.

42. Greiner, *Sympathetic Realism in Nineteenth-Century British Fiction*, 6.
43. Greiner notes this influence in her work on sympathy's influence on nineteenth-century realism: "In Maria Edgeworth's *Belinda* (1801), *TMS* sits alongside La Bruyere and John Moore on a reading table, and *Wealth* – along with a slew of invisible hands – is referenced openly in such texts as Harriet Martineau's *Illustrations of Political Economy* (1832–34) and George Eliot's *Middlemarch* (1871–72)" (7).
44. See Morrison, "Conduct (Un)Becoming to Ladies of Literature," 202–28.
45. See Leps, *Apprehending the Criminal*.
46. Greiner, *Sympathetic Realism in Nineteenth-Century British Fiction*, 3.
47. Qtd. in Greiner, 3.
48. Ablow, *The Marriage of Minds*, 3.
49. Potolsky, *The Decadent Republic of Letters*, 9–10.
50. Crowell, "Matthew Potolsky," 277.
51. Noble, *Rethinking Sympathy and Human Contact*, 33.
52. Pinch, *Thinking About Other People*, 7.
53. Ibid., 47.
54. See Draucker, "Hearing, Sensing, Feeling Sound."
55. Morgan, *The Outward Mind*, 223.
56. Ibid., 227.
57. Smith, *The Theory of Moral Sentiments*, 27.
58. See Weinstein, *Adam Smith's Pluralism*; Darwall, "Sympathetic Liberalism," 139–64; and Frazer, *The Enlightenment of Sympathy*.
59. Weinstein, *Adam Smith's Pluralism*, 13.
60. Ibid., 2.
61. Ibid., 267.
62. Barton, *Nineteenth-Century Poetry and Liberal Thought*, 29–30.
63. Qtd. in Barton, *Nineteenth-Century Poetry and Liberal Thought*, 31.
64. See Mandler's Review of Elaine Hadley's *Living Liberalism*, 871–2.
65. Barton follows recent trends in studies connecting liberalism to Victorian literature by foregrounding the instability of the term: "Nineteenth-century liberalism is an ideology in the making" (16).
66. See Hadley, *Living Liberalism*; Weliver, *Mary Gladstone and the Victorian Salon*; Barton, *Nineteenth-Century Poetry and Liberal Thought*; and Clark, *Liberals and Social Democrats*. I also depart from these scholars in significant ways with my reliance on a sympathetic underpinning.
67. Anderson, *Bleak Liberalism*, 1.
68. Ibid., 4.
69. Ibid., 14.
70. Ibid., 4.
71. Weliver, *Mary Gladstone and the Victorian Salon*, 63.
72. Ibid., 64.
73. Ibid., 64–5.
74. Bristow, "Reforming Victorian Poetry," 4.
75. See Barton for an excellent monograph exploring poetry's participation in liberal practice. Barton reads the formal discipline of Victorian poetics as

"analogous to and also frequently identical with liberalism's ongoing mediation between law and liberty" (2).
76. Slinn, "Experimental Form in Victorian Poetry," 46.
77. Of course, Romantic poetry had already begun this kind of cultural experimentation, challenging generic categories and adapting/reshaping older poetic forms (ballads, pastorals, and odes). Thus, the lineage of the "lyrical ballad" by William Wordsworth and Samuel Taylor Coleridge alongside the verse dramas of Percy Bysshe Shelley and Lord Byron is sustained in the Victorian period.
78. See Weliver, *The Figure of Music in Nineteenth-Century British Poetry*.
79. Ibid., 11–2.
80. Slinn, "Experimental Form in Victorian Poetry," 47.
81. Ibid., 48.

2 "O You Pretty Pecksie!"

1. A note on naming: throughout, I alternate between Mary Wollstonecraft Godwin and Mary Wollstonecraft Shelley, as appropriate. Wollstonecraft Godwin and Percy Bysshe Shelley were married in late 1816, after the suicide of Shelley's first wife, Harriet Shelley.
2. Sunstein, *Mary Shelley: Romance and Reality*, 384–5.
3. Carlson, *England's First Family of Writers*, 195.
4. Feldman and Scott-Kilvert (eds.), *The Journals of Mary Shelley, 1814–1844*, 435.
5. The Bodleian Libraries, MS Abinger, d. 27 fol 2r.
6. Mary Wollstonecraft Shelley's five journals (spanning 1814–1844) are housed in the Bodleian Library's Abinger Collection. The first journal covers the years 1814–1815 and is the first of the shared journals. The second journal, covering 1816–1819, completes the shared journal entries, with Shelley's entries occurring less frequently.
7. The first volume of the journal is titled in Wollstonecraft Godwin's hand as "Shelley and Mary's Journal Book." At a later date, however, "not" is inserted above Shelley's name, presumably by Wollstonecraft Godwin. The exact dating of this insertion is unknown.
8. Flint, *Family Fictions*, 251.
9. See the introduction to the papers on Joseph Johnson that arose from the 2008 MLA Division on the English Romantic Period: Cox and Galperin, "Joseph Johnson," 93–5. This MLA session was the most recent discussion of Joseph Johnson in literary circles and derived from two prior MLA sessions sponsored by the Wordsworth-Coleridge Association (2001). Joseph Byrne also expanded the Johnson Circle to examine William Blake's role and the circle's influence on *The Gates of Paradise*; see Byrne, "Blake, Joseph Johnson, and *The Gates of Paradise*," 131–6. More broadly, four recent monographs have been devoted to "social authorship" in the Romantic period. See Ferris, *Book-Men, Book Clubs, and the Romantic Literary Sphere*; Fulford, *Romantic Poetry and the Literary Coteries*; Orr, *Literary Networks*

and Dissenting Print Culture in Romantic-Period Ireland; and Whelan, *Other British Voices: Women, Poetry, and Religion, 1766–1840*.
10. Butler, "Shelley and the Question of Joint Authorship," 42–5.
11. Pujol, *Political Fraternity*, 5.
12. Ibid., 6.
13. Cox and Galperin, "Joseph Johnson," 94. Furthermore, recent work has been done to establish a growing sense of female networks in the period, pointing to an overall dearth in literary studies surrounding the complexity of the term "network." See Winckles et al. (eds.), *Women's Literary Networks and Romanticism*.
14. Gaull, "Joseph Johnson: Webmaster," 108.
15. Cox and Galperin, "Joseph Johnson," 95.
16. Feldman and Scott-Kilvert, *The Journals of Mary Shelley, 1814–1844*, 30. I refer here to Coleridge's utopian scheme to set up a pantisocracy in America with Robert Southey. See Newlyn, "Pantisocracy."
17. Stocking, *The Journals of Claire Clairmont*, 48.
18. Cameron (ed.), *Shelley and His Circle, 1773–1822*, 431.
19. Ibid.
20. Feldman and Scott-Kilvert, *The Journals of Mary Shelley, 1814–1844*, 7.
21. Robinson, *Notebooks*, lxx.
22. The Bodleian Libraries, MS Abinger d. 27 fol. 2r. I use the manuscript for this quotation in order to distinguish the couple's hands. As I have previously argued, Feldman and Scott-Kilvert attribute Wollstonecraft Godwin's hand as "S.helley was also with me"; however, the manuscript reveals that she only completes the final two words.
23. For a fuller discussion of the collaborative nature of the couple's 1814 elopement journal, see Witcher, "'with me': The Sympathetic Collaboration of Mary Godwin and Percy Bysshe Shelley," 144–59.
24. I use the term "initially shared" because, ultimately, the journal became Wollstonecraft Shelley's private journal, with Shelley's contributions ending in the second journal book, covering July 21, 1816–June 7, 1819.
25. Feldman and Scott-Kilvert, *The Journals of Mary Shelley, 1814–1844*, xv.
26. Corbett, "Reading Mary Shelley's Journals," 79.
27. Of course, as common in the period, the dash also indicates a break in action in many of the entries as well.
28. Corbett, "Reading Mary Shelley's Journals," 77.
29. Feldman and Scott-Kilvert, *The Journals of Mary Shelley, 1814–1844*, 8–9.
30. Such arguments are further addressed in the final section of this chapter, which takes into consideration Shelley's role in the compilation of Mary Wollstonecraft Shelley's *Frankenstein*.
31. Shelley, *PBS Letters*, vol. I, 402.
32. In 1810, when Harriet Westbrook (fifteen years old) met Shelley (eighteen years old), she was a pupil at a boarding school in Clapham and friends with Shelley's sister, Hellen. Although unsettled by Shelley's radical atheism, she befriended him and, after an acquaintance of only six months, turned to him when her father insisted she remain in school. Desirous of helping her,

Shelley offered advice, assuring Hogg that he was not in love. However, after Harriet wrote to Shelley threatening suicide, Shelley suggested they elope to Edinburgh. On August 29, 1811, they were married under Scots Law. See Cameron, *Shelley and His Circle, 1773–1822*.
33. Shelley, *PBS Letters*, vol. I, 395.
34. Corbett, "Reading Mary Shelley's Journals," 79.
35. Ibid., 80.
36. Feldman and Scott-Kilvert, *The Journals of Mary Shelley, 1814–1844*, 18.
37. Ibid., 16–17.
38. The Rossetti family also played games of bouts-rimés.
39. Feldman and Scott-Kilvert, *The Journals of Mary Shelley, 1814–1844*, 19.
40. Ibid., 44.
41. Shelley, Introduction to the 1831 edition (of *Frankenstein*), 438.
42. Feldman and Scott-Kilvert, *The Journals of Mary Shelley, 1814–1844*, 24.
43. Krawczyk, *Romantic Literary Families*, 137.
44. Godwin, *Political Justice*, 338–9.
45. Taussig, *Coleridge and the Idea of Friendship*, 116–17.
46. Qtd. in Taussig, *Coleridge and the Idea of Friendship*, 17.
47. Ibid., 44.
48. Ibid.
49. Shelley, *Laon and Cyntha*, ll. 58–9.
50. Hays, *Young Romantics*, 35.
51. Godwin, *Political Justice*, 338.
52. Shelley, *MWS Letters*, vol. I, 9.
53. Ibid.
54. Ibid.
55. Feldman and Scott-Kilvert, *The Journals of Mary Shelley, 1814–1844*, 79.
56. Shelley, *MWS Letters*, vol. I, 29.
57. Feldman and Scott-Kilvert, *The Journals of Mary Shelley, 1814–1844*, 25.
58. Hays, *Young Romantics*, 67.
59. Shelley, *Laon and Cyntha*, ll. 2.
60. Ibid., ll. 5–9.
61. Ibid., l. 101.
62. Ibid., ll. 55–63.
63. Ibid., l. 57 and 60.
64. Ibid., ll. 62–3.
65. For a comprehensive account of Edmund Spenser's influence on Romantic forms, images, and styles, see Kucich, *Keats, Shelley, and Romantic Spenserianism*.
66. For the most detailed chronology of the conception, drafting, and revision of *Frankenstein*, see Robinson, "*Frankenstein* Chronology," in *The Frankenstein Notebooks*, pp. lxxvi–cx. Robinson's chronology includes references to various early circumstances anticipating her novel, recorded by Mary in her life-writing.
67. Shelley, "Introduction to 1831," in *Frankenstein*, 442.
68. Smith, "Hideous Progenies," 122.

69. This is a brief overview of the major published editions of *Frankenstein*. See Robinson's larger outline indicating how each text, in all of its forms (ur-text, proofs, revisions, etc.) lead directly to another in "Texts in Search of an Editor: Reflections on *The* Frankenstein *Notebooks* and on Editorial Authority."
70. See Rieger's Introduction to *Frankenstein; or, the Modern Prometheus* (The 1818 Text).
71. Smith, "Hideous Progenies," 125.
72. Shelley, *MWS Letters*, 42.
73. Smith, "Hideous Progenies," 126. See also Poovey, *The Proper Lady and the Woman Writer*.
74. Robinson, "Introduction," lxvii–lxix.
75. Ibid., lxvii.
76. For a detailed description of the changes made by Shelley, see Charles Robinson's abundant scholarship, including: his Introduction to *The Frankenstein Notebooks* (1996), edition of the novel, *The Original Frankenstein* (2008), and "Collaboration and Ventriloquism in Mary Shelley's *Frankenstein*" (*La Questione Romantica*, 2009).
77. Shelley, *Frankenstein*, 442.
78. Hays, *Young Romantics*, 88.
79. Robinson, *Notebooks*, 301.
80. Ibid., 461.
81. Mellor, *Mary Shelley*, 69.
82. Feldman and Scott-Kilvert, *The Journals of Mary Shelley, 1814–1844*, 80.
83. Robinson, "Introduction," 25.
84. Robinson, *Notebooks*, 424–5.
85. Ibid., 418–19.
86. Murray, "Shelley's Contribution to Mary's *Frankenstein*," 56.
87. Qtd. in Forman-Barzilai, *Adam Smith and the Circles of Sympathy*, 67.
88. Smith, 129.
89. Robinson, "Introduction," lxx.
90. Robinson, "Reflections," 92.
91. Ibid., 107.
92. Britton, "Novelistic Sympathy in Mary Shelley's *Frankenstein*," 3.
93. See Hatch, "Disruptive Affects," 33–49.
94. Britton, "Novelistic Sympathy in Mary Shelley's *Frankenstein*," 3–4.
95. All references to *Frankenstein* are from Robinson's edition of the novel, utilizing the two-volume 1816–1817 manuscripts, and containing, for the first time two versions: a representation of Wollstonecraft Shelley's earliest draft and a corrected version of that draft, with Shelley's incorporations.
96. Shelley, *Frankenstein*, 48.
97. Ibid., 56. Wollstonecraft Shelley slightly revises Walton's appeal to Frankenstein in the 1831 edition, which further privileges the intimacy of a sympathetic union: "I spoke of my desire of finding a friend—of my thirst for a more intimate sympathy with a fellow mind than had ever fallen to my lot" (Hindle [ed.], 29–30).
98. Shelley, *Frankenstein*, 58.

99. Ibid.
100. Ibid., 124.
101. Ibid.
102. Ibid., 125.
103. Ibid.
104. Ibid., 168.
105. Ibid., 191.
106. Ibid., 239. Wollstonecraft Shelley revises Frankenstein's appeal in the 1831 version, focusing on vengeance and duty: "swear to me, Walton, that he shall not escape; that you will seek him, and satisfy my vengeance in his death" (Hindle [ed.] *Frankenstein*, 212).
107. Shelley, *Frankenstein*, 241.
108. Ibid.
109. Ibid.
110. Ibid., 242.
111. Ibid., 245.
112. Ibid., 58.
113. Ibid., 232.
114. Shelley, "Introduction to 1831," in *Frankenstein*, 32.
115. Britton, "Novelistic Sympathy in Mary Shelley's *Frankenstein*," 13.
116. Smith, *Theory of Moral Sentiments*, 129.
117. I am grateful to the external reader for Cambridge University Press for pointing out the allegorical implications of the novel and this question on materiality after reviewing this chapter for publication.
118. Robinson (ed.), The Frankenstein Notebooks, 608–9. For ease of reading, I offer a transcription: "My thoughts and every feeling of my soul *have* been drunk up by the interest *for* my guest *which this tale and his own elevated and gentle manners have created*. I wish to soothe him, yet *can I counsel* one so infinitely miserable, so destitute of every hope of consolation, to live? Oh, no! the only joy he *can now know will be when he* composes his shattered feelings to peace and death. Yet he enjoys one comfort, the *offspring* of solitude and delirium: he believe*s* that when in dreams he *holds converse with* his friends, *and derives from that communion consolation for* his miseries or *excitement* to *his* vengeance, that they *are* not the creations of his fancy but real beings *who visit him from the regions of a remoter world. This faith* gives a solemnity to his reveries that renders them *to me almost as imposing and interesting as truth*" (Shelley, *Frankenstein*, 232).
119. Bennett, *MWS: An Introduction*, 48.
120. Feldman and Scott-Kilvert, *The Journals of Mary Shelley, 1814–1844*, 429.

3 Written–Visual Aesthetics

1. Rossetti, *Ruskin*, 49.
2. Ibid.
3. William Michael Rossetti arranges and edits what he terms "Pre-Raphaelite Papers" from 1854 to 1862. In his annotation to Christina's dream, he

provides imprecise dating: "I cannot say what is the real date of this note but put it in as if proper to 1855. The last paragraph, 'This *real* dream,' &c., is evidently of much later date—say 1880" (48).
4. William Michael Rossetti, "Notes," *Poetical Works of Christina Rossetti*, 464.
5. The Royal Academy of Art did not admit female pupils until the late 1860s, admitting women artists on a restricted basis. However, life study was not permitted until 1903. See Kooistra, *Christina Rossetti and Illustration*.
6. Qtd. in Kooistra, *Christina Rossetti and Illustration*, 23.
7. Rossetti, *Letters*, vol. 1, 71.
8. Most literary scholars are familiar with the illustrations completed by other artists for Christina's works; however, she also illustrated her own works – notably, her illustrations for *Sing-Song* (1872), which appear in a manuscript draft. See Kooistra, *Christina Rossetti and Illustration*.
9. Kooistra, *Christina Rossetti and Illustration*, 1.
10. Ibid., 7.
11. Kooistra, *Poetry, Pictures, and Popular Publishing*, 5.
12. Kooistra, *Christina Rossetti and Illustration*, 76.
13. Christina, herself, comments on her brother's "revising hand" in a note dated December 7, 1893, inscribed in a copy of *Goblin Market*: "And here I like to acknowledge the general indebtedness of my first and second volumes to his suggestive wit and revising hand" (qtd. in Goldberg, "Dante Gabriel Rossetti's 'Revising Hand,'" 145).
14. Christina was concerned about her mother, Frances Mary Lavinia Rossetti's, death, which did not occur until April 8, 1886.
15. *LCR*, Letter 250. *The Letters of Christina Rossetti* have been compiled into a digital edition by the University of Virginia Press, which incorporates the complete text of the Antony H. Harrison's four-volume print edition (2000–2004). All subsequent references to letters will use this edition.
16. Marsh, *Christina Rossetti*, 26.
17. Ibid., 26–7.
18. *LCR*, Letter 250.
19. *LCR*, Letter 253.
20. The extent of D.G. Rossetti's "revising hand" is now apparent with Rebecca Crump's variorum edition of Christina's poetry and has been discussed in scholarship. See Chapman, *The Afterlife of Christina Rossetti*; as well as the literary biographies of Christina Rossetti by Lona Mosk Packer and Jan Marsh.
21. I am grateful to the reader for Cambridge University Press for pointing this out in the reader report.
22. *LCR*, Letter 255; original emphasis.
23. There are also differences between Tennyson and Christina's poetic style: whereas Tennyson's poetic style is oral and textual, Christina's poetic style is visual and textual.
24. Arseneau, "Pilgrimage and Postponement," 292–3.
25. Ibid., 293. See also Hurley's *Faith in Poetry* for an exploration of how Christina Rossetti engaged her religious faith within the form of poetical expression.

26. The PRB was formed in 1848, and the original Brotherhood was virtually dissolved by 1853. The term "Pre-Raphaelite" began to be associated with a much wider and longer-lived literary and artistic movement.
27. See Witcher, "Brainwork and Community in 'Eden Bower'," 90–107.
28. Rossetti, *The Correspondence of Dante Gabriel Rossetti*, 248.
29. *LCR*, Letter 256.
30. Rossetti, *Rossetti Papers*, 83–4.
31. Marsh also notes Christina's forwardness and initiative when it came to her publications. In January 1860, C. Rossetti renewed her desire for poetic acclaim and set about getting her work published, sending shorter poems to David Masson, editor of *Macmillan's Magazine*, who responded favorably, publishing "Up-Hill" in the February issue. At the same time, D.G. Rossetti reached out to Ruskin and sent along his sister's notebook with *Goblin Market*, asking him to put in a word with Thackeray, editor of *Cornhill*. While he was addressing Ruskin, who responded unfavorably, Christina was far more successful with Masson. In this way, her poetry – through Masson – came to the attention of Alexander Macmillan, who subsequently asked D.G. Rossetti to see more of his sister's work. Thus, *Goblin Market, and Other Poems* was published by Macmillan (Marsh, *Christina Rossetti*, 267–9).
32. *LCR*, Letter 257.
33. *LCR*, Letter 258.
34. *LCR*, Letter 266.
35. See Goldberg, "Dante Gabriel Rossetti's 'Revising Hand': His Illustrations for Christina Rossetti's Poems," 145–59.
36. *LCR*, Letter 266, original emphasis. William Michael Rossetti notes that "Come & See" possibly referred to "I Will Lift Up Mine Eyes Unto the Hills," which remained unpublished until WMR's posthumous compilation, *Poems of Christina Rossetti* (1904).
37. Barret Browning refers to *Aurora Leigh* as an innovative hybrid form – "novel-poem" – in a letter to Robert Browning on February 27, 1845 (*Letters of Robert Browning and Elizabeth Barrett Browning, 1845–1846*, 53).
38. Barrett Browning, *Aurora Leigh*, Book I, ll. 2–9.
39. Prins and Jackson, "Lyrical Studies," 523.
40. Ibid., 524.
41. Thomas, in *Cultivating Victorians: Liberal Culture and the Aesthetic*, pays sustained attention to D.G. Rossetti's replication process in terms of his painting, arguing that the replica became a scene of anxiety for the artist, displaying "a disconcerting index of art's relation to money" (142). As I suggest below, D.G. Rossetti's poetry is similarly multiple, an aspect of replication left unconsidered by Thomas.
42. Rossetti, *Poetical Works*, lxviii.
43. Ibid., lxviii–lxix.
44. These six notebooks (1856–1866) are now digitized in the "Romantics and Victorians" collection on the British Library's website: www.bl.uk/collection-items/notebook-of-christina-rossetti-one-of-six.

45. John Ruskin to Dante Gabriel Rossetti, January 24, 1861.
46. Kooistra, *Christina Rossetti and Illustration*, 11.
47. Hill, *Letters*, 97.
48. Qtd. in Suriano, *British Pre-Raphaelite Illustrators*, 42.
49. Hill, 113–15.
50. For further discussion on the communal aspects of literary Pre-Raphaelitism and the effects of sociability upon Pre-Raphaelite poetic style, see Witcher and Huseby (eds.), *Defining Pre-Raphaelite Poetics*.
51. Kooistra, *Christina Rossetti and Illustration*, 58.
52. For a further discussion of Blake's visionary interpretations, see Rowland, *Blake and the Bible*.
53. Qtd. in Kooistra, *Christina Rossetti and Illustration*, 62.
54. Rossetti, *Letters*, vol. I, 224.
55. Digitized images of Dante Gabriel Rossetti's illustrations for *Goblin Market* can be found in the British Library's online exhibition, "Discovering Literature: Romantics and Victorians," February 2014: www.bl.uk/collection-items/second-edition-of-goblin-market-by-christina-rossetti-with-original-covers.
56. Rossetti, *Goblin Market*, ll. 1–14.
57. For a brilliant account of the "goblin metrics" of *Goblin Market*, and the modernist reception, rejection, and repression of experimental form, see Jamison's *Poetics en Passant*. 145–77.
58. Rossetti, *Goblin Market*, ll. 64–8.
59. Ibid., ll. 69–70.
60. Ibid., ll. 77–80.
61. Ibid., l. 30.
62. Ibid., l. 543.
63. Ibid., ll. 30–1.
64. Ibid., ll. 554–6.
65. Ibid., l. 559.
66. Ibid., ll. 562–7.
67. Smulders, *Christina Rossetti Revisited*, 40.
68. Cameron worked closely with George Frederic Watts and derived inspiration from D.G. Rossetti's *The Blue Closet* (1857) for her photograph *The Minstrel Group* (1866). Many of her photographs reveal Pre-Raphaelite inspiration, a theme recently explored in the Tate's exhibition *Painting with Light: Art and Photography from the Pre-Raphaelites to the Modern Age* (May–September 2016).
69. Goldberg, "Dante Gabriel Rossetti's 'Revising Hand.'" 147.
70. Jamison, *Poetics en Passant*, 176.
71. Ibid., 158.
72. Indeed, throughout the 1850s, feminist writers (such as Harriet Martineau, Mary Howitt, Anna Jameson, and a number of writers for the *English Woman's Journal*) encouraged women to undertake more purposeful work for themselves, but more importantly, for society.

73. Qtd. in Marsh, *Christina Rossetti*, 220. This language comes from the institution's first annual report, now located in the Guildhall Library. For more detail on the penitentiary, see Jan Marsh's literary biography of Christina Rossetti.
74. Sawtell, *Christina Rossetti*, 51.
75. Rossetti, *Family Letters*, 26.
76. See Margaret Lonsdale's biography, *Sister Dora* (1880). The biography describes Sister Dora's vocation to a life of good works, rather than that of a wife or mother, focusing on her love of the poor and her combination of nursing and religious fervor. Her service to her patients enabled a stronger devotion to God, not only for Sister Dora but also for her patients.
77. Marsh, *Christina Rossetti*, 235.
78. Kent, *The Achievement of Christina Rossetti*, 62.
79. Ibid., 4.
80. *Goblin Market* was initially titled "A Peep at the Goblins." As Crump's annotations note, the title revision was suggested by D.G. Rossetti.
81. Green, *Prolegomena to Ethics*, 297.
82. Greengarten, *Thomas Hill Green*, 4.
83. See Weliver, *Mary Gladstone and the Victorian Salon*.
84. Tyler, "Thomas Hill Green."
85. The Introduction to the "Jenny" Collection on the Rossetti Archive provides an overview of the compositional process. According to W.M. Rossetti, this first version was reflective and nondramatic. See www.rossettiarchive.org/docs/3-1848.raw.html.
86. D.G. Rossetti, "Jenny," *Collected Poetry and Prose*, ll. 339–41. In the Bancroft MS (1847–1948), the lines pertaining to golden hair allude to the perils of eroticism and the bodily temptation that men experience when gazing upon a "fallen" woman's body: "And the thigh from thy rich side slopes oblique, / And thy lips are full, and thy brows are fair, / And the gold makes a daylight in thine hair" (ll. 114–116). Thus the same tension between golden hair/golden coin occurs in the extant first draft of the poem.
87. D.G. Rossetti used the phrase "inner standing-point" in his defense of "Jenny" against the notorious attack of Robert Buchanan in "The Fleshly School": "Neither some thirteen years ago, when I wrote this poem, nor last years when I published it, did I fail to forsee impending charges of recklessness and aggressiveness, or to perceive that even some among those who could really read the poem and acquit me on these grounds, might still hold that the thought in it had better have dispensed with the situation (prostitution) which serves it for framework. Nor did I omit to consider how far a treatment from without might here be possible. But the motive powers of art reverse the requirement of science, and demand first of all an *inner* standing-point. The heart of such a mystery as this must be plucked from the very world in which it beats or bleeds; and the beauty and pity, the self-questionings an all-questionings which it brings with it, can come with full force only from the mouth of one alive to its whole appeal, such as the speaker put forward in the poem" (*Collected Poetry and Prose*, 337–8).
88. D.G. Rossetti, "Jenny," Collected Poetry and Prose, ll. 203–8.

89. "Jenny" also includes a market scene when the narrator speaks of Jenny's knowledge of the city, in homage – perhaps – to his sister's poem (lines 135–154). This market would also serve as the basis for D.G. Rossetti's painting *Found*, which depicts a prostitute meeting her former lover. The painting depicts the description of the dawn from "Jenny": "And there's an early wagon drawn / To market, and some sheep that job / Bleating before a barking dog; And the old streets come peering through / Another night that London knew; / And all as ghostlike as the lamps" (lines 304–9).
90. W.M. Rossetti, *Poetical Works*, lxvi.
91. McGann, *The Game That Must Be Lost*, 66.
92. Jensen, *Marketing Modernism*, 43. *Gesamtkunstwerk* refers to Wagner's credo for the unification of art through opera (see "Art and Revolution" [1849] and "The Artwork of the Future" [1849]). Jensen's quote, therefore, does not truly refer to Wagner's sense of the German term, but instead looks more broadly at what Whistler conceived as "a total work of art."
93. McGann, *Game*, 67.
94. Ibid.
95. Ibid., 68.
96. Indeed, tracing D.G. Rossetti's experimentation in illustrations begins not in the publicly published illustrations mentioned here, but with his pencil illustrations for Christina's privately printed *Verses* (1847). Her first publication – albeit private – was printed by her grandfather Gaetano Polidori and is dedicated to her mother. The Harry Ransom Center holds the manuscript, which includes D G. Rossetti's pencil drawings produced on art paper sized to the text and later bound with the printed leaves.
97. For a digitized image of *Lady Lilith* and scholarly commentary on the painting, see *The Rossetti Archive*: www.rossettiarchive.org/docs/s205.rap.html.
98. April 21, 1870, Doughty and Wahl, vol. II, 850.
99. Rossetti, *Collected Poetry*, 161.
100. See *Rossetti Archive*: www.rossettiarchive.org/docs/nb0002.duke.rad.html#p5.

4 Typographical Adventures

1. Qtd. in Colebrook, *William Morris*, 2.
2. Peterson, *The Kelmscott Press*, 101.
3. Recent exhibitions and conferences have perpetuated the image of William Morris's extensive accomplishments and enduring legacy. See, for example, the William Morris Gallery's May Morris Conference (2015), devoted to the life of May Morris and her contribution to the Arts and Crafts aesthetic, the National Portrait Gallery's 2014 exhibition, "Anarchy & Beauty: William Morris and his Legacy, 1860–1960)," and the 2013 restoration and curation of the Albion press used at the Kelmscott Press, and later used at the Goudy Press. It is currently housed and in use at the Rochester Institute of Technology (Rochester, NY).
4. Morris, *Aims*, 1.
5. Peterson, *The Kelmscott Press*, 165.

6. MacCarthy's biography, *William Morris*, pays close attention to the relationships of William Morris, noting that "Morris's formations and renewals of male brotherhoods are the recurring pattern of his life" (xiv).
7. See Spuybroek, *The Sympathy of Things*.
8. In the *Sympathy of Things*, Spuybroek differs from Dowling, reading Ruskin's sympathy as an "ethereal, indeed *asensual aesthetics* that offers no pleasure whatsoever in sharing appearances or tastes but only in sharing each other's life and actions" (175). More will be said later in the chapter to explicate this contrast and Morris's difference from Ruskin's conception of sympathy as argued by Spuybroek.
9. Peterson, *The Kelmscott Press*, 50.
10. Pevsner, *Pioneers of Modern Design*, 16.
11. Ibid.
12. In "How I Became a Socialist" (1894), Morris begins with a definition of Socialism and maintains that this view "which I hold to-day, and hope to die holding, is what I began with; I had no transitional period" (379).
13. Vaninskaya, *William Morris and the Idea of Community*, 45.
14. MacCarthy, *William Morris*, 624.
15. Qtd. in Miller, "Sustainable Socialism: William Morris on Waste," 10.
16. Vaninskaya, *William Morris and the Idea of Community*, 45.
17. I am grateful to Florence Boos for pointing out this silencing of Morris's role in providing propaganda to the masses.
18. Morris, "How I Became a Socialist," 379.
19. Ibid., 380.
20. Ibid., 381.
21. Pevsner, *Pioneers of Modern Design*, 16. Pevsner's early twentieth century scholarship maintained efforts to downplay Morris's politics. While current scholarship has rectified this omission by highlighting the complexity of Morris's politics, I include Pevsner as a means of exploring the communitarian aspects of Morris's politics.
22. Morris, "Art and Socialism (1884)," 194; 201.
23. Vaninskaya, *William Morris and the Idea of Community*, 6.
24. Weliver, *Mary Gladstone and the Victorian Salon*, 12.
25. See Collini, *Liberalism and Sociology*.
26. See Morris's "How I Became a Socialist" and Glasier's *William Morris and the Early Days of the Socialist Movement*.
27. Smith, *Theory of Moral Sentiments*, 129.
28. Ibid.
29. This perspective has led philosophers to argue against the belief that Smith's sympathy is fundamentally self-centered, "founded on self-love" (Sugden, "Beyond Sympathy and Empathy," 75). See Nieli, "Sphere of Intimacy and the Adam Smith Problem" and Sugden, "Beyond Sympathy and Empathy."
30. Haakonssen, "Introduction," xiv.
31. Fleischacker, *A Third Concept of Liberty*, 49.
32. Weinstein, "Sympathy, Difference, and Education," 84.

33. Ibid., 86.
34. Smith, *The Theory of Moral Sentiments*, 374.
35. Ibid., 268.
36. Nieli, "Spheres of Intimacy."
37. Griswold, "Imagination."
38. Smith, *The Theory of Moral Sentiments*, 158.
39. Weinstein, "Sympathy, Difference, and Education," 90.
40. Smith, *The Theory of Moral Sentiments*, 259–60.
41. Ibid., 12.
42. Frazer, *The Enlightenment of Sympathy*, 105.
43. Dowling, *The Vulgarization of Art*, ix.
44. Compton-Rickett, *William Morris*, 21.
45. Morris, *Unpublished Lectures*, 231–2.
46. As just one example of these overlapping communities, consider that Henry Halliday Spalding, Emery Walker, Robert Catterson-Smith, and William Harcourt Hooper were part of both the Kelmscott Press and the Socialist League. In this way Morris's communities enriched and interrelated with one another.
47. See MacCarthy, *William Morris* and Mackail and William, *The Life of William Morris*.
48. Ibid.
49. MacCarthy, *William Morris*, 58.
50. Ibid.
51. Ibid.
52. Peterson notes that the Press was "created, in part, as an outlet for Morris's antiquarian enthusiasm for England's first printer [...before he] turned his attention to writers of the nineteenth century as well" (178–9).
53. Miller, in *Slow Print*, also uses Morris's work at *The Commonweal* and the Kelmscott Press as a launching point for her exploration of the radical press movement in the late nineteenth century.
54. Morris, *Aims*, 1.
55. Spuybroek, *The Sympathy of Things*, 175.
56. Ibid., 174.
57. Ibid., 108.
58. Ibid.
59. Morris, "Some Thoughts," 1–2.
60. This complaint has led to the erroneous conjecture that Morris held all technology in contempt. As the processes at work in Kelmscott production prove, however, Morris used technology when it could simplify the task of the designer. As Peterson points out in his history of the Kelmscott Press – and as this chapter will discuss in further detail, "the Kelmscott Press, the quintessential example of an arts-and-crafts longing for the pre-industrial age, was paradoxically built upon a foundation of photography, one of the most sophisticated forms of technology in late-Victorian England" (82).
61. Morris, "Some Thoughts," 2.

62. Dowling, *The Vulgarization of Art*, 51.
63. Ibid.
64. McGann, *Black Riders*, 74.
65. Skoblow, "Beyond Reading," 241.
66. Morris, "Woodcuts," 248.
67. Kooistra, *Poetry, Pictures, and Popular Publishing*, 43.
68. Morris, "Woodcuts," 255–7.
69. Colebrook, *William Morris*, 13.
70. Morris, "Art, Craft, and Life."
71. DeSpain, "A Book Arts Pilgrimage," 74.
72. Morris, "Art, Craft, and Life."
73. Miller, *Slow Print*, 54.
74. Peterson, *The Kelmscott Press*, 182.
75. Colebrook, *William Morris*, 9.
76. Peterson, *The Kelmscott Press*, 203.
77. Ibid., 211.
78. Peterson briefly mentions Robert Catterson-Smith's role in translating Burne-Jones's illustrations for wood-engraving and touches on the collaborations between Morris and Charles M. Gere or Arthur Gaskin, illustrators from the Birmingham School.
79. Morris, *Ideal Book*, 40.
80. Peterson, *The Kelmscott Press*, 147.
81. Kelvin, *Collected Letters* (1996), 374.
82. Ibid.
83. Ibid., 375.
84. Morris, "The Lesser Arts," 241.
85. Sympathetic, here, also carries on William Blake's ideal, carried over from the previous chapter, where fidelity remains unnecessary, with Rossetti preferring instead to "allegorize one's own hook." Since Rossetti was Morris's teacher, this Blakean ideal establishes an aesthetic lineage between the men.
86. Kelvin, *Collected Letters*, vol. III, 397. Kelvin notes that the reference to the proof is unclear, but bases his suggestion of its reference to *A Dream of John Ball* on prior letters between Walker and Morris.
87. Morris to Catterson-Smith, January 8, 1894, Mark Samuels Lasner Collection, University of Delaware.
88. "Fine Art Gossip," 559–60.
89. Qtd. in Peterson, *The Kelmscott Press*, 246–7.
90. Ibid., 247.
91. Morris, *Ideal Book*, 67.
92. Peterson, *The Kelmscott Press*, 148.
93. Vallance, "Revival," 101.
94. Vallance, "Designs for Painted Glass," 100.
95. Peterson, *The Kelmscott Press*, 148.
96. Bernard Quaritch, The Morgan Library (New York), PML 76853.

97. Ibid. Peterson, too, notes that Emery Walker (perhaps exaggerating) claimed that it took Murray three months to finish one illustration (149).
98. Peterson, *The Kelmscott Press*, 149–51. Peterson references a note made by May Morris in a 1922 letter from Laurence W. Hodson, of Bradbourne Hall, Derbyshire (British Library Add. MS. 45347, fo. 171).
99. Catterson-Smith's name was not included in the colophon of the published *Chaucer*.
100. Responding to the *Short Description of the Kelmscott Press*, the contributor noted that in "this little-known volume proper credit is incidentally given to Mr Catterson-Smith and Mr C. Fairfax-Murray for the large share they had in illustrating the Kelmscott 'Chaucer', but I think it would have been more interesting if their services had been acknowledged on the 'Chaucer' itself by Mr. William Morris" (qtd. in Robinson, *William Morris, Edward Burne-Jones, and the Kelmscott Chaucer*, 34).
101. Qtd. in Robinson, *William Morris, Edward Burne-Jones and the Kelmscott Chaucer*, 34.
102. Qtd. in Peterson, *The Kelmscott Press*, 152.
103. Peterson, *The Kelmscott Press*, 152.
104. Robinson, *William Morris, Edward Burne-Jones, and the Kelmscott Chaucer*, 34.
105. I have been fortunate to track down elements of this lot in the Mark Samuels Lasner Collection at the University of Delaware (Newark, DE) and in the British Library (London). Prior to the auction, Ronald Sly, a descendant of Catterson-Smith, published a memoir of Catterson-Smith's work, including facsimiles of the archival material, material which was presumably then offered to auction. The Family Archive intends also to produce the materials digitally, but, as of this writing, has not made the materials publicly available: www.rcscollection.co.uk/.
106. Catterson-Smith, unpublished lecture, Mark Samuels Lasner Collection at the University of Delaware.
107. Size is a glutinous material commonly used as a binder medium.
108. Catterson-Smith, The Morgan Library, MA 8593.
109. Sparling, *The Kelmscott Press*, 66.
110. Ibid., 67.
111. Ibid.
112. Ibid.
113. Catterson-Smith, unpublished lecture, Mark Samuels Lasner Collection at University of Delaware.
114. Ibid.
115. See Spuybroek for a fuller discussion of Ruskin's sympathy as a driving force of twentieth- and twenty-first-century aesthetics.
116. Sparling, *The Kelmscott Press*, 67.
117. Ross, *Aubrey Beardsley*, 71.
118. Peterson, *The Kelmscott Press*, 154.
119. Kelvin, *Collected Letters*, vol. III, 390.
120. Crane, "The Work of Walter Crane," 10.

121. See Crawford (ed.), *By Hammer and Hand* and "The Birmingham Municipal School of Art. With Many Illustrations of its Students' Work—I," 90–9.
122. Morris, *Daily Chronicle*.
123. Morris, *Ideal Book*, 110.
124. Kelvin, *Collected Letters*, vol. III, 463. The Kelmscott edition of *News from Nowhere* began printing in June 1892, but was delayed over questions of a frontispiece. Kelvin documents that Sydney Cockerell wrote in his diary for October 17, 1892 that he suggested to Morris the idea of a house for the illustration. On November 11, after Gere's invitation, Cockerell notes: "Saw proofs of some drawings of Kelmscott made by Gere, who is to make an illustration for News from Nowhere" (Kelvin, *Collected Letters*, vol. III, 463).
125. Morris, *Ideal Book*, 72–3.
126. Kelvin, *Collected Letters*, vol. III, 466.
127. Ibid.
128. Ibid., 482.
129. Ibid., 483.
130. Ibid., 482.
131. Peterson, *The Kelmscott Press*, 157.
132. Kelvin, "News from Nowhere," 117.
133. Morris's *A Dream of John Ball* was also serialized in the *Commonweal* (1886–1887) prior to publication as a Kelmscott edition (1892).
134. Miller, *Slow Print*, 26.
135. Goodlad, "Beyond the Panopticon," 14.
136. Crane, "The Work of Walter Crane," 29.
137. Miller, *Slow Print*, 50.
138. Ibid., 59.
139. Ibid., 66.
140. Dowling, *The Vulgarization of Art*, 55.
141. Ibid., 62.
142. Morris, *News from Nowhere*, 112.
143. Mackail and William, *Life of William Morris*, vol. I, 338.
144. Dowling, *The Vulgarization of Art*, 53.
145. Morris, "The Lesser Arts," 234. This lecture was not published until 1882, where it was printed in *Hopes and Fears for Art*, a collection of Morris's lectures published by Ellis and White.
146. Ibid., 233–4.
147. Ibid., 243.
148. Ibid., 244.
149. Ibid., 235.
150. Morris, "The Lesser Arts of Life," 77.
151. Dowling, *The Vulgarization of Art*, 50.
152. Ibid.
153. Morris, "Lesser Arts of Life," 77.
154. Peterson, *The Kelmscott Press*, 182.
155. Ibid., 184.
156. Sparling, *The Kelmscott Press*, 83.

5 Sim and Puss

1. Thain and Vadillo, *Michael Field*, ll. 1–4.
2. Donoghue, *We Are Michael Field*, 139.
3. Qtd. in Donoghue, *We Are Michael Field*, 139.
4. For a deconstruction of the tendency toward myth-making, see Blain, "'Michael Field, the two-headed nightingale'," 239–57.
5. Symons, "The Decadent Movement," 858.
6. Ibid.
7. Potolsky, *Decadent Republic of Letters*, 2.
8. Ibid., 6.
9. Ibid.
10. Ibid., 5.
11. Crowell, "Matthew Potolsky," 232.
12. Potolsky, *Decadent Republic of Letters*, 10.
13. Kristin Mahoney, too, recognizes the rich possibilities Michael Field offers to reconsider Modernism in her reading of Eric Gill through Michael Field in *Michael Field: Decadent Moderns* (2019).
14. Like Regenia Gagnier's exploration of "individuals-in-relation" at the *fin de siècle*, I too take the approach of tracing the ways in which individuals come together to form a whole. Gagnier's *Individualism, Decadence and Globalization* (2010) is a "genealogy of liberalism" that conceptualizes the relation of individuals to larger social units.
15. Moore and Sturge, *Works and Days*, 20.
16. Thomas, "What Time We Kiss," 329.
17. Ibid.
18. Ibid., 330.
19. Ibid., 348.
20. Examples of such scholarship include: London, *Writing Double*; Laird, *Women Coauthors*; Thain, *Michael Field (1880–1914)*; and, Ehnenn, *Women's Literary Collaboration, Queerness, and Late-Victorian Culture*.
21. See, for instance, Stetz and Wilson (eds.), *Michael Field and Their World*, and, more recently, Parker and Vadillo (eds.), *Michael Field*.
22. Qtd. in Ehnenn, *Women's Literary Collaboration*, 33.
23. Ibid., 33–4.
24. Ibid., 34.
25. Ibid.
26. Hughes, "A Club of Their Own," 235.
27. London, *Writing Double*, 9.
28. Moore and Sturge, *Works and Days*, 6.
29. Spinoza, *Ethics*, trans. C.H.R. Parkinson.
30. Ibid.
31. Hanley, "The Eighteenth-Century Context of Sympathy from Spinoza to Kant," 176.
32. Ibid.
33. Smith, *Theory of Moral Sentiments*, 263.

34. Field, *Underneath the Bough*, 51.
35. Ibid., ll. 10–11.
36. Ibid., ll. 12–14.
37. Ibid., ll. 10–14.
38. Qtd. in Hanley, "The Eighteenth-Century Context of Sympathy from Spinoza to Kant," 175.
39. Further, they avoid the traditional closing couplet of the sonnet. Rather than the customary moralization, the last line rhymes with line 11: "writ," which contains the poem's final word: "it."
40. See Ehnenn, *Women's Literary Collaboration* and Malfait, "'Against the World': Michael Field, Female Marriage, and the Aura of Amateurism" for fuller explorations of Michael Field's female marriage.
41. Qtd. in Sturgeon, *Michael Field*, 47.
42. Field, "A Girl," *Underneath the Bough*, ll. 11; 14.
43. Qtd. in Blain, "Michael Field," 248.
44. Their earliest insignia was the bramblebough, described to Robert Browning as: "pale-cheeked bloom / Fondling by purple berry loves to lie / …fruit and flower in living unity" (qtd. in Ehnenn, *Women's Literary Collaboration*, 32). The bramblebough was originally designed c. 1881, possibly by James Robert Cooper. Their later emblem was the thyrsus interlinked with rings, designed by Selwyn Image in the early 1890s, and first appearing on the cover of *Underneath the Bough*.
45. Laird, *Women Coauthors*, 87.
46. Qtd. in Bickle, *Fowl and Pussycat*, xxviii.
47. This separateness is depicted in Donoghue's *We Are Michael Field* (1998), a "short, personal study" of Michael Field, as well as Moore and Sturge's introduction to his edited collection, *Works and Days: From the Journal of Michael Field* (1933). In a critical context, Jill Ehnenn explores the implications of Michael Field's separateness in her chapter, "'Our Brains Struck Fire Each from Each': Disidentification, Difference, and Desire in the Collaborative Aesthetics of Michael Field."
48. Moore and Sturge, *Works and Days*, xix.
49. Ricketts, "Michael Field," 4.
50. Field, *Binary Star*, 50.
51. Bickle, *Fowl and Pussycat*, xxix.
52. Pater, *The Renaissance*, 105.
53. Field, "A Girl," *Underneath the Bough*, ll. 11–14.
54. See The Victorian Lives and Letters Consortium and the new digital home of the Michael Field Diaries at Dartmouth. https://michaelfielddiary.dartmouth.edu/home
55. Thain, *Michael Field*, 22–3.
56. Hewitt, "Diary, Autobiography and the Practice of Life History," 24.
57. Ibid., 31.
58. Ibid., 35.
59. Moore and Sturge, *Works and Days*, xv.

60. Ibid., 6.
61. Field, *Binary Star*, 38.
62. Marcus, *Auto/Biographical Discourses*, 231.
63. Hewitt, "Diary, Autobiography and the Practice of Life History," 31–5.
64. Thain, *Michael Field*, 23.
65. Smith, *The Theory of Moral Sentiments*, 87–9.
66. Ibid., 88.
67. Moore and Sturge, *Works and Days*, 263–5.
68. This approach recalls Michael Field's poem, "Palimpsest" (1908), which records another model of their collaboration.
69. Add. MS. 46795 8v. My citations of *Works and Days* refer to the original manuscript, including the British Library references. The journals are part of an ongoing digital humanities project, *The Michael Field Diaries*, with transcription of the volume ongoing at the time of this writing.
70. My thanks to Marion Thain for discussing the Michael Field diaries with me.
71. Gagnier, *Individualism, Decadence and Globalization*, 3.
72. Add. MS. 46795 9r-9v.
73. Add. MS. 46795 9v.
74. Add. MS. 46795 9v-10r.
75. Add. MS. 46795 10r.
76. Ibid.
77. Add. MS. 46795 10v.
78. Add. MS. 46795 11r.
79. Add. MS. 46795 13v.
80. Add. MS. 46795 14r.
81. Add. MS. 46795 14v.
82. Add. MS. 46795 14v-15r.
83. Hewitt, "Diary, Autobiography and the Practice of Life History," 29.
84. Add. MS. 46777 108v.
85. Add. MS. 46777 109r.
86. Many scholars, notably Ana Parejo Vadillo, have discussed how Walter Pater, Oscar Wilde, and Ricketts and Shannon, among others inspired Michael Field's Aesthetic philosophy. See, for instance, Vadillo's "Walter Pater and Michael Field: The Correspondence, with Other Unpublished Manuscript Materials"; "Aestheticism and Decoration: At Home with Michael Field"; and "Outmoded Dramas: History and Modernity in Michael Field's Aesthetic Plays," in *Michael Field and Their World* (2007).
87. Parker and Vadillo, *Michael Field*, 100.
88. Moore and Sturge, *Works and Days*, 263–5. Sarah Parker draws attention to the complicated relationship Michael Field has with female associates, noting that scholarship is sparse on these female networks. Parker focuses on the Fields relationship with Mary Costelloe in her chapter in *Michael Field: Decadent Moderns* (2020).
89. Parker and Vadillo, *Michael Field*, 101.
90. Saville, "The Poetic Imaging of Michael Field," 199.

91. Joseph Bristow traces Michael Field's hopes for, specifically, dramatic renown and a "place [...] among a rising generation of playwrights whose daring dramas were transforming the London stage" in his chapter on *Attila, My Attila!* in *Michael Field: Decadent Moderns*.
92. Pater, *Renaissance*, 190.
93. Smith, *The Theory of Moral Sentiments*, 77.
94. Forman-Barzilai, *Adam Smith and the Circles of Sympathy*, 63.
95. Thain, *Michael Field*, 67.
96. Field, *Tragic Mary*, v.
97. Pater, *Greek Studies*, 56–7.
98. Weliver, "Music, Crowd Control and the Female Performer," 60.
99. Field, *The Tragic Mary*, v.
100. Eastham, "Bacchic Transference," 492.
101. Ibid., 494.
102. Vadillo, "Another Renaissance," 119. See, also, Taft, "*The Tragic Mary*," 266 and Robertson, "From Martyr to Vampire," 321–39.
103. Field, *The Tragic Mary*, 68.
104. Ibid.
105. Ibid., 72.
106. Martin, "'Imperfectly Civilized,'" 351 and Cohen, "Whittier, Ballad Reading, and the Culture of Nineteenth-Century Poetry," 5.
107. Stone, "A Cinderella Among the Muses," 234.
108. Field, *The Tragic Mary*, 198.
109. Smith, *The Theory of Moral Sentiments*, 88.
110. Field, *The Tragic Mary*, 73.
111. Ibid.
112. I use the term "readers" to indicate that, despite Michael Field's desires, *The Tragic Mary* was never staged. During their life time, only one of their dramas was publicly performed: *A Question of Memory* (performed by The Independent Theatre Society in 1893).
113. Pater, "The School of Giorgione," 106.
114. Field, *The Tragic Mary*, 73–4.
115. Hughes, *Cambridge Introduction*, 7.
116. Rudy, *Electric Meters*, 9.
117. Field, "She was a royal lady born," ll. 13–16.
118. Harrington, "Michael Field and the Detachable Lyric," 225.
119. Field, *The Tragic Mary*, 95.
120. Ibid., 94, ll. 1–4.
121. See Maxwell, *Scents and Sensibility*.
122. Field, *The Tragic Mary*, 94, l. 9.
123. Martin, "Imperfectly Civilized," 345.
124. Field, *The Tragic Mary*, 100–1.
125. Alexiou, *The Ritual Lament*, 136.
126. Field, "I could wish to be dead," ll. 1–5.
127. *The Tragic Mary* is not the only verse drama in which Michael Field engages with the keen. Their play *Deirdre* (1903; 1918) also enacts an Irish keen.

128. Field, "I could wish to be dead," ll. 12–15.
129. Ibid., l. 12.
130. Johnson, *The Tragic Mary*, 123–4.
131. My thanks to Ellen Crowell for pointing out that while Michael Field experiments with this lyric innovation, W.B. Yeats perfects it in "The Wild Swans at Coole" with the tension between ballad form and lyric, private utterance.

6 Towards Empathy

1. Qtd. in Maxwell and Pulham, *Vernon Lee*, 4–5. Vernon Lee's commonplace book and envelope containing the rose can be found in the Vernon Lee Collection at Colby College. The collection holds correspondence, manuscripts, photographs, and personal documents and artifacts.
2. For a description of the white rose among the sheaf of letters, see Mannocchi's "Vernon Lee and Kit Anstruther-Thomson," 129–48. See, also, the introduction to Maxwell and Pullham's *Vernon Lee*.
3. Qtd. in Mannocchi, "Vernon Lee and Kit Anstruther-Thomson," 132.
4. Lee and Anstruther-Thomson, "Beauty and Ugliness," 544–68; 669–88. Subsequently, the essay was published in the collected edition: *'Beauty and Ugliness' and Other Studies in Psychological Aesthetics* (1912).
5. The 1912 revision and failed collaboration reveal a shift in Lee's understanding of empathy: Lee revises her considerations of empathy to read it as, primarily, a psychological process, as discussed in the final section of this chapter.
6. See Harrington, *Second Person Singular*.
7. See Townley, "Rewriting Paterian Sympathy," 861–72.
8. See, also, Mahoney, "Ethics and Empathy in the Literary Criticism of Vernon Lee," 193–210.
9. See Greiner, "1909: The Introduction of the Word 'Empathy' into English."
10. Morgan, *The Outward Mind*, 220.
11. See Kaplan, *Sacred Tears* and Burdett, "Is Empathy the End of Sentimentality?," 259–74.
12. Burdett, "Is Empathy the End of Sentimentality?," 259–60.
13. Arata, "Realism," 178.
14. "The Strange Death of Moral England" forms the title of Stefan Collini's epilogue to *Liberalism & Sociology* (1983).
15. Collini, *Liberalism & Sociology*, 251–2.
16. Burdett, "Is Empathy the End of Sentimentality?," 260.
17. Martin, *Modernism and the Rhythms of Sympathy*, 9.
18. Lee was the first English novelist to use the term: her first reference to the word is her diary entry for February 20, 1904, quoted in *Beauty and Ugliness* (1912) (Martin, *Modernism and the Rhythms of Sympathy*, 30).
19. Burdett, "Is Empathy the End of Sentimentality?," 261.
20. Bristow, "Vernon Lee," 119.

21. See, also, Morgan's *The Outward Mind* for a thorough and accessible overview of Lee's engagement with aestheticism and what he terms "object-oriented empathy."
22. Bunting, "Feelings of Vivid Fellowship," 204.
23. Qtd. in Mannocchi, "Vernon Lee and Kit Anstruther-Thomson."
24. Morgan reads Anstruther-Thomson's language in her essays and her usage of the first-person-plural pronoun as an attempt at inclusivity: the body as a collective possession and "the figure of a collective corporeality [that] recalls William Morris's emphasis on the ways in which art objects create communities by speaking to the shared bodily existence of those who make and sense it" (229–30).
25. See Gagnier, *Individualism, Decadence and Globalization*, and my previous chapter on Michael Field's engagement with similar concerns at the end of the century.
26. Qtd. in Mannocchi, "Vernon Lee and Kit Anstruther-Thomson."
27. Denisoff, "Queer Ecology," 152.
28. Lee and Anstruther-Thomson, "Beauty and Ugliness," 545. Quotations from "Beauty and Ugliness" in this portion of the chapter are from the essay's two-part publication in the *Contemporary Review*.
29. Lee and Anstruther-Thomson, *Art and Man*, 49.
30. Lee and Anstruther-Thomson, "Beauty and Ugliness," 686.
31. Ibid., 687.
32. Bunting, "Feelings of Vivid Fellowship," 207.
33. Morgan, *The Outward Mind*, 227.
34. Ehnenn, *Women's Literary Collaboration*, 66.
35. Lee, *The Beautiful*, 57.
36. Lee and Anstruther-Thomson, "Beauty and Ugliness," 546.
37. Lee, "Introduction," 34.
38. Qtd. in Bunting, "Feelings of Vivid Fellowship," 206.
39. Ibid.
40. Lee and Anstruther-Thomson, "Beauty and Ugliness," 159.
41. While Lee and Anstruther-Thomson's collaboration and romantic attachment ended after the 1897 publication of "Beauty and Ugliness," their friendship endured until Kit's death in 1921 (Mannocchi, "Vernon Lee and Kit Anstruther-Thomson," 129).
42. Bunting, "Feelings of Vivid Fellowship," 213.
43. See Evangelista, *British Aestheticism and Ancient Greece*; Maxwell and Pulham, *Vernon Lee*; Leighton, "Ghosts, Aestheticism and 'Vernon Lee'," 1–14; and Colby, *Vernon Lee*.
44. Vadillo describes Robinson's family salon and others in "New Woman Poets and the Culture of the *Salon* at the *Fin-de-Siècle*," 22–34.
45. Townley, "Vernon Lee and Elitism," 862.
46. Harrington, *Second Person Singular*, 80.
47. Harrington provides a succinct overview of the contemporary discussions surrounding aestheticism. See also Fletcher, "Some Aspects of Aestheticism,"

Notes to pages 191–201

and Maltz, *Beauty for the People. British Aestheticism and the Urban Working Classes, 1870–1900.*
48. Townley, "Vernon Lee and Elitism," 862.
49. Qtd. in Harrington, 81.
50. Harrington, *Second Person Singular*, 81.
51. Lee, *Selected Letters*.
52. Townley, "Vernon Lee and Elitism," 524. For a sampling of such scholarship, see Maltz, *Beauty for the People*; Morgan, *The Outward Mind*; Denisoff, "The Forest Beyond the Frame; and Zorn, *Vernon Lee: Aesthetics, History, and the Victorian Female Intellectual*.
53. Lee, *Selected Letters*.
54. I am thinking here of the final lines of Pater's famed "Conclusion": "For art comes to you proposing frankly to give nothing but the highest quality to your moments as they pass, and simply for those moments' sake."
55. Morgan, *The Outward Mind*, 226.
56. The reference could recall "Ruskinism: The Would-Be Study of a Conscience," in which Lee criticizes Ruskin's view on the moral value of art: "though art has no moral meaning, it has a moral value; art is happiness, and to bestow happiness is to create good." It could also refer to "A Dialogue on Poetic Morality," which contains the same argument and is dedicated to Robinson. See note in Vernon, *Selected Letters of Vernon Lee, 1856–1935*, vol. I.
57. Harrington, *Second Person Singular*, 79.
58. Ibid.
59. Lee, *Belcaro*, 1.
60. Ibid., 1–2.
61. Ibid., 5.
62. Pater, *The Renaissance*, ix.
63. As Townley identifies, Pater's disinterestedness or detachment yields self-absorption, while Lee's aesthetics is based on "interaction and intersubjectivity" (863).
64. Lee, *Belcaro*, 7.
65. Ibid., 8.
66. Robinson, "In Casa Paget," 936.
67. Harrington, *Second Person Singular*, 88.
68. Lee, *Belcaro*, 249–50.
69. Mahoney, "Ethics and Empathy," 199.
70. Lee, *Belcaro*, 273–4.
71. Evangelista, *British Aestheticism*, 63–4.
72. Maxwell and Pulham, *Vernon Lee*, 9.
73. Agnew, "Vernon Lee," 134.
74. Maltz, "Engaging 'Delicate Brains'," 213.
75. Ibid.
76. Lee and Anstruther-Thomson, "Beauty and Ugliness," 156–7. References to "Beauty and Ugliness" in this portion of the chapter will come from the 1912 collected volume.

77. Ibid., 160–1, original emphasis.
78. Ibid., 164.
79. Ibid., 174–5, original emphasis.
80. Ibid., 235.
81. Townley, "Vernon Lee and Elitism," 868.
82. Lee and Anstruther-Thomson, *Beauty and Ugliness*, 27–8.
83. Qtd. in Maltz, "Engaging 'Delicate Brains'," 223.
84. Townley, "Vernon Lee and Elitism," 869.
85. Lee and Anstruther-Thomson, *Beauty and Ugliness*, 153–4.
86. Greiner, *Sympathetic Realism*, 158.
87. Ibid., 159.
88. Lee and Anstruther-Thomson, *Beauty and Ugliness*, 20.
89. Mahoney, "Ethics and Empathy," 196.
90. Qtd. in Bunting, "Feelings of Vivid Fellowship," 215.

Conclusion

1. See Spuybroek, *The Sympathy of Things*, 108.
2. Qtd. in Spuybroek, *The Sympathy of Things*, 119.
3. Ibid., 119.
4. Ibid., 120.
5. Ibid., 121.
6. Gagnier, *Individualism, Decadence and Globalization*, 14.
7. Ibid.
8. Ibid., 16.
9. Qtd. in Spuybroek, *The Sympathy of Things*, 132.
10. Ibid.
11. Qtd. in Spuybroek, *The Sympathy of Things*, 133.
12. See Benjamin Morgan's intriguing chapter on empathy and Vernon Lee in *The Outward Mind* (2017).

Bibliography

Ablow, Rachel. *The Marriage of Minds: Reading Sympathy in the Victorian Marriage Plot*. Stanford University Press, 2007.
Alexiou, Margaret. "Antiphonal Structure and Antithetical Thought." *The Ritual Lament in Greek Tradition*. Edited by Dimitrios Yatromanolakis and Panagiotis Roilo. Rowman & Littlefield, 2002, pp. 131–60.
Alfano, Veronica and Andrew M. Stauffer. *Virtual Victorians: Networks, Connections, Technologies*. Palgrave Macmillan, 2015.
Anderson, Amanda. *Bleak Liberalism*. University of Chicago Press, 2016.
Anstruther-Thomson, Clementina. *Art and Man: Essays and Fragments*. Bodley Head, 1924.
Arata, Stephen. "Realism." *The Cambridge Companion to the Fin de Siècle*. Edited by Gail Marshall. Cambridge University Press, 2007, pp. 169–78.
Arseneau, Mary. "Pilgrimage and Postponement: Christina Rossetti's 'The Prince's Progress'." *Victorian Poetry*, vol. 32, no. 3/4, 1994, pp. 279–98.
Attridge, Derek. *Moving Words: Forms of English Poetry*. Oxford University Press, 2013.
Barrett Browning, Elizabeth. *Aurora Leigh*. Oxford University Press, 2008.
Barton, Anna. *Nineteenth-Century Poetry and Liberal Thought: Forms of Freedom*. Palgrave Macmillan, 2017.
Bednarz, James P. "The Collaborator as Thief: Ralegh's (Re)Vision of 'The Faerie Queene'." *English Literary History*, vol. 63, no. 2, 1996, pp. 279–307.
Bennett, Betty T. "Finding Mary Shelley in Her Letters." *Romantic Revisions*. Edited by Robert Brinkley and Keith Hanley. Cambridge University Press, 1998. Reprint in *Critical Essays on Mary Wollstonecraft Shelley*. Edited by Mary Lowe-Evans. Simon and Schuster, 1998, pp. 118–32.
  Mary Wollstonecraft Shelley: An Introduction. Johns Hopkins University Press, 1998.
Bickle, Sharon. *The Fowl and the Pussycat: Love Letters of Michael Field, 1876–1909*. University of Virginia Press, 2008.
Blain, Virginia. "'Michael Field, the Two-Headed Nightingale': Lesbian Text as Palimpsest." *Women's History Review*, vol. 52, no. 2, 1996, pp. 239–57.
Blair, Kirstie. *Victorian Poetry and the Culture of the Heart*. Clarendon, 2006.
Bristow, Joseph. "Reforming Victorian Poetry: Poetics after 1832." *The Cambridge Companion to Victorian Poetry*. Edited by Joseph Bristow. Cambridge University Press, 2000, pp. 1–24.

"Vernon Lee's Art of Feeling." *Tulsa Studies in Women's Literature*, vol. 25, no. 1, 2006, pp. 117–39.
Britton, Jeanne M. "Novelistic Sympathy in Mary Shelley's *Frankenstein*." *Studies in Romanticism*, vol. 48, no. 1, 2009, pp. 3–22.
Brooker, Jewel Spears. "Common Ground and Collaboration in T.S. Eliot." *The Centennial Review*, vol. 25, no. 3, 1981, pp. 225–38.
Bunting, Kirsty. "'Feelings of Vivid Fellowship': Vernon Lee and Clementina Anstruther-Thomson's Quest for Collaborative 'Aesthetic Sociability'." *Forum for Modern Language Studies*, vol. 52, no. 2, 2016, pp. 203–17.
Burdett, Carolyn. "Is Empathy the End of Sentimentality?" *Journal of Victorian Culture*, vol. 16, no. 2, 2011, pp. 259–74.
Butler, Marilyn. "Shelley and the Question of Joint Authorship." *Evaluating Shelley*. Edited by Timothy Clark and Jerrold E. Hogle. Edinburgh University Press, 1996, pp. 42–7.
Byrne, Joseph. "Blake, Joseph Johnson, and *The Gates of Paradise*." *The Wordsworth Circle*, vol. 44, no. 2/3, 2013, pp. 131–6.
Cameron, Kenneth Neill, ed. *The Carl H. Pforzheimer Library: Shelley and His Circle, 1773–1822*. Vol. II, Harvard University Press, 1961.
The Carl H. Pforzheimer Library: Shelley and His Circle, 1773–1822. Vol. III, Harvard University Press, 1970.
Carlson, Julie A. *England's First Family of Writers: Mary Wollstonecraft, William Godwin, Mary Shelley*. Johns Hopkins University Press, 2007.
Chandler, James. *An Archaeology of Sympathy: The Sentimental Mode in Literature and Cinema*. University of Chicago Press, 2013.
"The Languages of Sentiment." *Textual Practice*, vol. 22, no. 1, 2008, pp. 21–39.
Chapman, Alison. *The Afterlife of Christina Rossetti*. St. Martin's Press, 2000.
Clark, Peter. *Liberals and Social Democrats*. Cambridge University Press, 1978.
Clarke, Michael. *The Concise Oxford Dictionary of Art Terms – Pre-Raphaelite Brotherhood*. Oxford University Press, 2010.
Cohen, Michael. "Whittier, Ballad Reading, and the Culture of Nineteenth-Century Poetry." *Arizona Quarterly: A Journal of American Literature, Culture, and Theory*, vol. 64, no. 3, 2008, pp. 1–29.
Colby, Vineta. *Vernon Lee: A Literary Biography*. University of Virginia Press, 2003.
Colebrook, Frank. *William Morris: Master Printer*. Edited by William Peterson. Yellow Barn Press, 1989, p. 34.
Collini, Stefan. *Liberalism and Sociology*. Cambridge University Press, 1983.
Compton-Rickett, Arthur. *William Morris: A Study in Personality*. Dutton & Co., 1913. https://archive.org/details/williammorrisstuoocomprich.
Corbett, Mary Jean. "Reading Mary Shelley's Journals: Romantic Subjectivity and Feminist Criticism." *The Other Mary Shelley: Beyond Frankenstein*. Edited by Audrey A. Fisch, Anne K. Mellor, and Esther H. Schor. Oxford University Press, 1993, pp. 73–87.
Cox, Jeffrey N. and William Galperin. "Joseph Johnson." *Wordsworth Circle*, vol. 40, no. 2/3, 2009, pp. 93–5.

Crane, Walter. "Introduction." *The Easter Art Annual for 1898: The Work of Walter Crane with Notes by the Artist.* Edited by Walter Crane. Extra issue of *Art Journal*, 1898, pp. 1–32.

Crawford, Alan, ed. *By Hammer and Hand: The Arts and Crafts Movement in Birmingham.* Birmingham Museum and Art Gallery, 1984.

Crowell, Ellen. "Matthew Potolsky, *The Decadent Republic of Letters: Taste, Politics, and Cosmopolitan Community from Baudelaire to Beardsley.*" *Modern Philology*, vol. 113, no. 4, 2016, pp. 275–7.

Culler, Jonathan. *Theory of the Lyric.* Harvard University Press, 2015.

Darwall, Stephen. "Empathy, Sympathy, Care." *Philosophical Studies*, vol. 89, no. 2, 1998, pp. 261–82.

——— "Sympathetic Liberalism: Recent Work on Adam Smith." *Philosophy and Public Affairs*, vol. 28, no. 2, 1999, pp. 139–64.

Denisoff, Dennis. "The Queer Ecology of Vernon Lee's Transient Affections." *Feminist Modernist Studies*, vol. 3, no. 2, 2020, 148–61.

DeSpain, Jessica. "A Book Arts Pilgrimage: Arts and Crafts Socialism and the Kelmscott Chaucer." *Journal of William Morris Studies*, vol. 15, no. 4, 2004, pp. 74–90.

Donoghue, Emma. *We Are Michael Field.* Absolute Press, 1998.

Dowling, Linda. *The Vulgarization of Art: The Victorians and Aesthetic Democracy.* University of Virginia Press, 1996.

Draucker, Shannon. "Hearing, Sensing, Feeling Sound: On Music and Physiology in Victorian England, 1857–1894." Edited by Dino Franco Felluga. *BRANCH: Britain, Representation and Nineteenth-Century History.* Extension of *Romanticism and Victorianism on the Net*, 2018. www.branchcollective.org/?ps_articles=shannon-draucker-hearing-sensing-feeling-sound-on-music-and-physiology-in-victorian-england-1857-1894.

Duclaux, Madame (Mary Robinson). "In Casa Paget." *Country Life*, vol. 28, 1907, pp. 935–7.

Duncan, Ian, ed. Introduction. *The Private Memoirs and Confessions of a Justified Sinner.* James Hogg. Oxford University Press, 2010, pp ix–xxxiv.

Eastham, Andrew. "Bacchic Transference and Ecstatic Faith: Michael Field's *Callirrhoë* and the Origins of Drama." *Women's Studies*, vol. 40, no. 4, 2011, pp. 491–512.

Ede, Lisa and Andrea Lunsford. *Singular Texts/Plural Authors: Perspectives on Collaborative Writing.* SIU Press, 1990.

Ehnenn, Jill R. "'Our Brains Struck Fire Each from Each': Disidentification, Difference, and Desire in the Collaborative Aesthetics of Michael Field." Economies of Desire at the Victorian Fin de Siecle: Libidinal Lives. Edited by Jane Ford, Kim Edwards Keates, and Patricia Pulham. Routledge, 2015. pp. 180–203.

——— *Women's Literary Collaboration, Queerness, and Late-Victorian Culture.* Ashgate, 2008.

Evangelista, Stefano. *British Aestheticism and Ancient Greece.* Palgrave Macmillan, 2009.

Feldman, Paula R. and Diana Scott-Kilvert. *The Journals of Mary Shelley, 1814–1844*. 2 vols. Clarendon, 1987.
Ferris, Ina. *Book-Men, Book Clubs, and the Romantic Literary Sphere*. Palgrave Macmillan, 2015.
Field, Michael. *Binary Star: Leaves from the Journal and Letters of Michael Field, 1846–1914*. Edited by Ivor C. Treby. De Blackland Press, 2006.
—— "The Online Diaries of Michael Field." Accessed via the Michael Field Diary Archive, *Victorian Lives and Letters Consortium*, Center for Digital Humanities, University of South Carolina, current as of November 2021. http://tundra.csd.sc.edu/vllc/field.
—— *The Tragic Mary*. George Bell and Sons, 1890.
—— *Underneath the Bough: A Book of Verses*. Thomas B. Mosher, 1898.
"Fine Art Gossip." *Athenaeum*, no. 3391. October 22, 1892. Compiled in *The Athenaeum Journal of Literature, Science, the Fine Arts, Music, and the Drama: July to December 1892*. John C. Francis, 1892, pp. 559–60.
Fleischacker, Samuel. *A Third Concept of Liberty*. Princeton University Press, 1999.
Fletcher, Ian, "Some Aspects of Aestheticism." *Twilight of the Dawn: Studies in English Literature in Transition*. Edited by O. M. Brack, Jr. University of Arizona Press, 1987, pp. 1–33.
Flint, Christopher. *Family Fictions: Narrative and Domestic Relations in Britain, 1688–1798*. Stanford University Press, 1998.
Forman-Barzilai, Fonna. *Adam Smith and the Circles of Sympathy: Cosmopolitanism and Moral Theory*. Cambridge University Press, 2010.
Frazer, Michael L. *The Enlightenment of Sympathy: Justice and the Moral Sentiments in the Eighteenth Century and Today*. Oxford University Press, 2012.
Fulford, Tim. *Romantic Poetry and the Literary Coteries*. Palgrave Macmillan, 2015.
Gagnier, Regenia. *Individualism, Decadence and Globalization: On the Relationship of Part to Whole, 1859–1920*. Palgrave Macmillan, 2010.
Gaull, Marilyn. "Joseph Johnson: Webmaster." *Wordsworth Circle*, vol. 40, no. 2/3, 2009, pp. 107–10.
Glasier, J. Bruce. *William Morris and the Early Days of the Socialist Movement*. Longman, 1921.
Godwin, William. *Political Justice. The Political and Philosophical Writings of William Godwin*. Edited by Mark Philip. Vol. 4. Pickering & Chatto, 1993.
Goldberg, Gail Lynn. "Dante Gabriel Rossetti's 'Revising Hand': His Illustrations for Christina Rossetti's Poems." *Victorian Poetry*, vol. 20, no. 3/4, 1982, pp. 145–59.
Goodlad, Lauren M.E. "Beyond the Panopticon: The Critical Challenge of a Liberal Society." *Victorian Literature and the Victorian State: Character and Governance in a Liberal Society*. Johns Hopkins University Press, 2003, pp. 1–31.
Green, T.H. *Prolegomena to Ethics*. Edited by A.C. Bradley. Clarendon, 1883. https://archive.org/details/prolegomenatoeoogreeuoft
Greengarten, I.M. *Thomas Hill Green and the Development of Liberal-Democratic Thought*. University of Toronto Press, 1981.

Greiner, Rae. "1909: The Introduction of the Word 'Empathy' into English." *BRANCH: Britain, Representation and Nineteenth-Century History*. Edited by Dino Franco Felluga. Extension of *Romanticism and Victorianism on the Net*. www.branchcollective.org/?ps_articles=rae-greiner-1909-the-introduction-of-the-word-empathy-into-english.
  Sympathetic Realism in Nineteenth-Century British Fiction. Johns Hopkins University Press, 2012.
Griswold, Jr., Charles L. "Imagination: Morals, Science, and Arts." *The Cambridge Companion to Adam Smith*. Edited by Knud Haakonssen. Cambridge University Press, 2006, pp. 22–56.
Haakonssen, Knud. "Introduction." *The Theory of Moral Sentiments*. Edited by Knud Haakonssen. Cambridge University Press, 2002, pp. vii–xxiv.
Hadley, Elaine. *Living Liberalism: Practical Citizenship in Mid-Victorian Britain*. University of Chicago Press, 2010.
Harrington, Emily. "Michael Field and the Detachable Lyric." *Victorian Studies*, vol. 50, no. 2, 2008, pp. 221–32.
  Second Person Singular: Late Victorian Women Poets and the Bonds of Verse. University of Virginia Press, 2014.
Hall, Jason David and Alex Murray, eds. *Decadent Poetics: Literature and Form at the British Fin de Siècle*. Palgrave Macmillan, 2013.
Hanley, Ryan Patrick. "The Eighteenth-Century Context of Sympathy from Spinoza to Kant." *Sympathy: A History*. Edited by Eric Schliesser. Oxford University Press, 2015.
Hatch, James C., "Disruptive Affects: Shame, Disgust, and Sympathy in Frankenstein," *European Romantic Review*, vol. 19, no. 1, 2008, pp. 33–49.
Hays, Daisy. *Young Romantics: The Tangled Loves of English Poetry's Greatest Generation*. Farrar, Straus and Giroux, 2010.
Helsinger, Elizabeth K. *Poetry and the Pre-Raphaelite Arts: Dante Gabriel Rossetti & William Morris*. Yale University Press, 2008.
Hewitt, Martin. "Diary, Autobiography and the Practice of Life History." *Life Writing and Victorian Culture*. Edited by David Armigoni. Ashgate, 2006, pp. 21–40.
Hill, George Birbeck, ed. *Letters of Dante Gabriel Rossetti to William Allingham, 1854–1870*. T. Fisher Unwin, 1897. https://archive.org/details/lettersofdantega00rossrich.
Hines, Thomas. *Collaborative Form: Studies in the Relations of the Arts*. Kent State, 1991.
Hughes, Linda. *Cambridge Introduction to Victorian Poetry*. Cambridge University Press, 2010.
  "A Club of Their Own: The 'Literary Ladies,' New Women Writers, and Fin-de-Siècle Authorship." *Victorian Literature and Culture*, vol. 35, no. 1, 2007, pp. 233–60.
Hurley, Michael D. *Faith in Poetry: Verse Style as a Mode of Religious Belief*. Bloomsbury, 2017.
Inge, M. Thomas. "Collaboration and Concepts of Authorship." *Publications of the Modern Language Association of America*, vol. 116, no. 3, 2001, pp. 623–30.

Jaffe, Audrey. *Scenes of Sympathy: Identity and Representation in Victorian Fiction.* Cornell University Press, 2000.

Jamison, Anne. *Poetics en Passant: Redefining the Relationship Between Victorian and Modern Poetry.* Palgrave Macmillan, 2009.

Jensen, Robert. *Marketing Modernism in Fin-de-siècle Europe.* Princeton University Press, 1997.

Jervis, John. *Sympathetic Sentiments: Affect, Emotion and Spectacle in the Modern World.* Bloomsbury, 2015.

Johnson, Lionel. "*The Tragic Mary.* By Michael Field (Bell)." *The Academy,* no. 954, 1890, pp. 123–4. https://books.google.com/books?id=8RwcAQAAMAAJ&lpg=PA121&dq=august%201890%20the%20academy%20AND%20tragic%20mary&pg=PA124#v=onepage&q&f=true.

Kaplan, Fred. *Sacred Tears: Sentimentality in Victorian Literature.* Princeton University Press, 1987.

Keen, Suzanne. *Empathy and the Novel.* Oxford University Press, 2007.

Kelvin, Norman, ed. *The Collected Letters of William Morris, 1889–1892.* Vol. III. Princeton University Press, 1996.

The Collected Letters of William Morris, 1893–1896. Vol. IV. Princeton University Press, 1996.

"News from Nowhere and The Spoils of Poynton: Interiors and Exteriors." *William Morris: Centenary Essays.* Edited by Peter Faulkner and Peter Preston. Exeter University Press, 1999, pp. 107–21.

Kent, David A., ed. *The Achievement of Christina Rossetti.* Cornell University Press, 1987.

Koestenbaum, Wayne. *Double Talk: The Erotics of Male Literary Collaboration.* Routledge, 1989.

Kooistra, Lorraine Janzen. *Christina Rossetti and Illustration.* Ohio University Press, 2002.

Poetry, Pictures, and Popular Publishing: The Illustrated Gift Book and Victorian Visual Culture, 1855–1875. Ohio University Press, 2011.

Krawczyk, Scott. *Romantic Literary Families.* Palgrave Macmillan, 2009.

Kuchich, Greg. *Keats, Shelley, and Romantic Spenserianism.* Penn State, 2010.

Laird, Holly. *Women Coauthors.* University of Illinois Press, 2000.

Latour, Bruno. *Reassembling the Social: An Introduction to Actor-Network Theory.* Oxford University Press, 2005.

Lee, Vernon. *Belcaro: Being Essays on Sundry Aesthetical Questions.* T. Fisher Unwin, 1897.

Introduction. *Art and Man: Essays and Fragments,* Edited by C. Ansthruther-Thomson. Bodley Head, 1924, pp. 3–6.

Selected Letters of Vernon Lee, 1856–1935, vol. 1, 1865–1884. Edited by Amanda Gagel. Routledge, 2017, p. 706.

Lee, Vernon and Clementina Anstruther-Thomson. "Beauty and Ugliness." *Contemporary Review,* vols. 27 and 28, October and November 1897, pp. 544–68, 669–88.

'Beauty and Ugliness' and Other Studies in Psychological Aesthetics. John Lane, 1912.

Leighton, Angela. "Ghosts, Aestheticism and 'Vernon Lee'. *Victorian Literature and Culture*, vol. 28, no. 1, 2000, pp. 1–14.
Leps, Marie-Christine. *Apprehending the Criminal: The Production of Deviance in Nineteenth-Century Discourse*. Duke University Press, 1992.
London, Bette. *Writing Double: Women's Literary Partnerships*. Cornell University Press, 1999.
Lonsdale, Maragret. *Sister Dora*. Cambridge University Press, 1880.
MacCarthy, Fiona. *William Morris: A Life for Our Time*. Alfred Knopf, 1995.
Mackail, John William and John William. *The Life of William Morris*, 2 vols. Longmans, 1899.
Mahoney, Kristin. "Ethics and Empathy in the Literary Criticism of Vernon Lee." *Nineteenth-Century Prose*, vol. 43, no. 1/2, 2016, pp. 193–210.
Malfait, Olivia. "'Against the World': Michael Field, Female Marriage, and the Aura of Amateurism." *English Studies*, vol. 96, no. 2, 2015, pp. 157–72.
Maltz, Diana. *Beauty for the People: British Aestheticism and the Urban Working Classes, 1870–1900*. Palgrave Macmillan, 2005.
   "Engaging 'Delicate Brains': From Working-Class Enculturation to Upper-Class Lesbian Liberation in Vernon Lee and Kit Anstruther-Thomson's Psychological Aesthetics." *Women and British Aestheticism*. Edited by Talia Schaffer and Kathy Alexis Psomiades. University of Virginia Press, 1999, pp. 211–29.
Mandler, Peter. "Review: Elaine Hadley's *Living Liberalism*." *American Historical Review*, vol. 116, no. 3, 2011, pp. 871–2.
Mannocchi, Phyllis F. "Vernon Lee and Kit Anstruther-Thomson: A Study of Love and Collaboration Between Romantic Friends." *Women's Studies*, vol. 12, 1986, pp. 129–48.
Marcus, Laura. *Auto/Biographical Discourses: Criticism, Theory, Practice*. Manchester University Press, 1994.
Marsh, Jan. *Christina Rossetti: A Literary Biography*. Faber & Faber, 2012.
Marshall, David. "Adam Smith and the Theatricality of Moral Sentiments." *Critical Inquiry*, vol. 10, no. 5, 1984, pp. 592–613.
   The Figure of Theatre: Shaftesbury, Defoe, Adam Smith, and George Eliot. Columbia University Press, 1986.
   The Surprising Effects of Sympathy: Marivaux, Diderot, Rousseau, and Mary Shelley. University of Chicago Press, 1988.
Martin, Kirsty. *Modernism and the Rhythms of Sympathy: Vernon Lee, Virginia Woolf, D.H. Lawrence*. Oxford University Press, 2013.
Martin, Meredith "'Imperfectly Civilized': Ballads, Nations, and Histories of Form." *English Literary History*, vol. 82, no. 2, 2015, pp. 345–63.
Masten, Jeffrey. *Textual Intercourse: Collaboration, Authorship, and Sexualities in Renaissance Drama*. Cambridge University Press, 1997.
Maxwell, Catherine. *Scents and Sensibility: Perfume in Victorian Literary Culture*. Oxford University Press, 2017.
Maxwell, Catherine and Patricia Pulham, eds. *Vernon Lee: Decadence, Ethics, Aesthetics*. Palgrave Macmillan, 2006.
McGann, Jerome. *Black Riders: The Visible Language of Modernism*. Princeton University Press, 1993.

Dante Gabriel Rossetti and the Game That Must Be Lost. Yale University Press, 2000.

The Textual Condition. Princeton University Press, 1991.

Mellor, Anne. *Mary Shelley: Her Life, Her Fiction, Her Monsters.* Methuen, 1988.

Miller, Elizabeth Carolyn. *Slow Print: Literary Radicalism and Late Victorian Print Culture.* Stanford University Press, 2013.

"Sustainable Socialism: William Morris on Waste." *The Journal of Modern Craft*, vol. 4, no. 1, 2011, pp. 7–26.

Montes, Leonidas. "Das Adam Smith Problem: Its Origins, the Stage of the Current Debate, and One Implication for Our Understanding of Sympathy," *Journal of the History of Economic Thought*, vol. 35, 2003, pp. 63–90.

Moore, T. and D.C. Sturge, eds. *Works and Days: From the Journal of Michael Field.* John Murray, 1933.

Morgan, Benjamin. *The Outward Mind: Materalist Aesthetics in Victorian Science and Literature.* Chicago University Press, 2017.

Morris, William. "Art and Socialism (1884)." *The Collected Works of William Morris: Signs of Change; Lectures on Socialism.* Vol. 23. Edited by May Morris. Longmans, 1915, pp. 192–214.

"Art, Craft, and Life. A Chat with Mr. William Morris." *The Daily Chronicle.* October 9, 1893.

"How I Became a Socialist." *Justice*: 1894. Rpt. in *News from Nowhere and Other Writings.* Edited by Clive Wilmer. Penguin, 2004, pp. 378–83.

The Ideal Book: Essays and Lectures on the Arts of the Book. Edited by William S. Peterson. University of California Press, 1982.

"The Lesser Arts." *Hopes and Fears for Art.* London: 1882. Rpt. in *News from Nowhere and Other Writings.* Edited by Clive Wilmer. Penguin, 2004, pp. 233–54.

"The Lesser Arts of Life." *Architecture, Industry & Wealth: Collected Papers by William Morris.* Longmans, 1902, pp. 37–79.

News from Nowhere and Other Writings. Edited by Clive Wilmer. Penguin, 2004.

A Note by William Morris on His Aims in Founding the Kelmscott Press. Edited by Sydney Cockerell. Kelmscott Press, 1898.

"Some Thoughts on the Ornamented Manuscripts of the Middle Ages (c.1892)." *William Morris Archive.* http://morrisarchive.lib.uiowa.edu/items/show/1015.

The Unpublished Lectures. Edited by Eugene D. LeMire. Wayne State University Press, 1969.

"The Woodcuts of Gothic Books." *Journal of the Society of Arts*, vol. 40, 1892, pp. 246–57.

Morrison, Lucy. "Conduct (Un)Becoming to Ladies of Literature: How-to Guides for Romantic Women Writers." *Studies in Philology*, vol. 99, no. 2, 2002, pp. 202–28.

Murray, E.B. "Shelley's Contribution to Mary's *Frankenstein*." *Keats-Shelley Memorial Bulletin*, vol. 29, 1978, pp. 50–68.

Newlyn, Lucy. "Pantisocracy." *The Cambridge Companion to Coleridge*. Cambridge University Press, 2002.

Nieli, Russell. "Spheres of Intimacy and the Adam Smith Problem." *Journal of the History of Ideas*, vol. 48, 1986, pp. 611–24.

Noble, Marianne. *Rethinking Sympathy and Human Contact in Nineteenth-Century American Literature: Hawthorne, Douglass, Stowe, Dickinson*. Cambridge University Press, 2019.

Orr, Jennifer. *Literary Networks and Dissenting Print Culture in Romantic-Period Ireland*. Palgrave Macmillan, 2015.

Parker, Sarah and Ana Parejo Vadillo, eds. *Michael Field: Decadent Moderns*. Ohio University Press, 2019, pp. v + 289.

Pater, Walter. *Greek Studies: A Series of Essays*. Macmillan, 1910.

The Renaissance: Studies in Art and Poetry: The 1893 Text. Edited by Donald L. Hill. University of California Press, 1980, p. 532.

"Style." *Appreciations: With an Essay on Style*. Macmillan, 1889, pp. 1–36.

Pater, William. "The School of Giorgione." *The Renaissance: Studies in Art and Poetry: The 1893 Text*. Edited by Donald L. Hill. University of California Press, 1980.

Peterson, William S. *The Kelmscott Press: A History of William Morris's Typographical Adventure*. University of California Press, 1991.

Pevsner, Nikolaus. *Pioneers of Modern Design: From William Morris to Walter Gropius*. Yale University Press, 2005.

Pinch, Adela. *Thinking About Other People in Nineteenth-Century British Writing*. Cambridge University Press, 2010.

Poovey, Mary. *The Proper Lady and the Woman Writer: Ideology as Style in the Works of Mary Wollstonecraft, Mary Shelley, and Jane Austen*. University of Chicago Press, 1984.

Potolsky, Matthew. *The Decadent Republic of Letters: Taste, Politics, and Cosmopolitan Community from Baudelaire to Beardsley*. University of Pennsylvania Press, 2013.

Prins, Yopie and Virginia Jackson, eds. *The Lyric Theory Reader*. Johns Hopkins University Press, 2014.

"Lyrical Studies." *Victorian Literature and Culture*, vol. 27, no. 2, 1999, pp. 521–30.

Pujol, Angel. *Political Fraternity: Democracy Beyond Freedom and Equality*. Routledge, 2019.

Ricketts, Charles. "Michael Field." *Charles Ricketts, Everything for Art: Selected Writings*. Edited by Nicholas Frankel. The Rivendale Press, 2014.

Rieger, James. *Introduction to Frankenstein; or, the Modern Prometheus (The 1818 Text)*, 1974. Rpt. University of Chicago Press, 1982, pp. xi–xxxvii.

Robertson, Ritchie. "From Martyr to Vampire: The Figure of Mary Stuart in Drama from Vondel to Swinburne." *Who Is This Schiller Now?: Essays on His Reception and Significance*. Edited by Jeffrey L. High, Nicholas Martin, and Norbert Oeller. Camden House, 2011, pp. 321–39.

Robinson, Charles E. "Collaboration and Ventriloquism in Mary Shelley's Frankenstein." *La Questione Romantica*, vol. 1, no. 1, 2009, pp. 29–39.

The Frankenstein Notebooks: A Facsimile Editions: Manuscripts of the Younger Romantics. Vol. 9. Garland Publishing, 1996.

"Texts in Search of an Editor: Reflections on The Frankenstein Notebooks and on Editorial Authority." *Textual Studies and the Common Reader: Essays on Editing Novels and Novelists*. Edited by Alexander Pettit. University of Georgia Press, 2000, pp. 91–100.

Robinson, Duncan. *William Morris, Edward Burne-Jones and the Kelmscott Chaucer*. Gordon Fraser, 1982.

Robinson, Agnes Mary F. "In Casa Paget." Country Life (November 28, 1907): 935–7.

Ross, Robert. *Aubrey Beardsley*. John Lane, 1909. https://archive.org/details/aubreybeardsley00rossuoft.

Rossetti, Christina. *Goblin Market, the Prince's Progress, and Other Poems*. Macmillan, 1875. https://archive.org/details/goblinmarketpri01rossgoog.

The Letters of Christina Rossetti: A Digital Edition. Edited by Antony H. Harrison. University of Virginia Press, 2006. http://rotunda.upress.virginia.edu/crossetti/default.xqy.

The Poetical Works of Christina Georgina Rossetti with Memoir and Notes. Edited by William Michael Rossetti. Macmillan, 1904.

Rossetti, Dante Gabriel. *Collected Poetry and Prose*. Edited by Jerome McGann. Yale University Press, 2003.

Complete Writings and Pictures of Dante Gabriel Rossetti: A Hypermedia Archive. Edited by Jerome McGann. IATH and NINES Consortium, 2008. www.rossettiarchive.org.

The Correspondence of Dante Gabriel Rossetti. vol. 4. Edited by William E. Fredeman. Cambridge University Press, 2004.

Rossetti, William Michael, ed. *The Family Letters of Christina Georgina Rossetti*. Scribner, 1908. https://archive.org/details/familylettersofcoorossrich.

Rossetti Papers, 1862–1870. Sands & Co., 1903. https://archive.org/details/rossettipapers00rossuoft.

Ruskin: Rossetti: PreRaphaelitism, Papers 1854 to 1862. George Allen, 1899. https://archive.org/stream/ruskinrossettipr00rossrich#page/n9/mode/2up.

Rowland, Christopher. *Blake and the Bible*. Yale University Press, 2010.

Rudy, Jason R. *Electric Meters: Victorian Physiological Poetics*. Ohio University Press, 2009.

Saville, Julia F. "The Poetic Imaging of Michael Field." *The Fin-de-Siècle Poem: English Literary Culture and the 1890s*. Edited by Joseph Bristow. Ohio University Press, 2005, pp. 178–206.

Sawtell, Margaret. *Christina Rossetti: Her Life and Religion*. A.R. Mowbray, 1955.

Schaffer, Talia and Kathy Psomiades, eds. *Women and British Aestheticism*. University of Virginia Press, 2000.

Shelley, Mary. *Frankenstein*. Edited by Charles E. Robinson. Vintage, 2009a.

Frankenstein. Edited by Maurice Hindle. Penguin, 2003.

"Introduction to the 1831 Edition." *Frankenstein*. Edited by Charles E. Robinson. Vintage, 2009b, pp. 437–43.

The Letters of Mary Wollstonecraft Shelley. 3 vols. Edited by Betty T. Bennett. Johns Hopkins University Press, 1980–1988.
Shelley, Percy Bysshe. *The Letters of Percy Bysshe Shelley*. Vol. 1. Edited by Roger Ingpen. Pitman & Sons, 1909.
The Poetical Works of Percy Bysshe Shelley. Vol. 1. Edited by Mary Wollstonecraft Shelley. Moxon, 1839. https://archive.org/details/poeticalworksper11shelgoog.
Skoblow, Jeffrey. "Beyond Reading: Kelmscott and the Modern." *The Victorian Illustrated Book*. Edited by Richard Maxwell. University of Virginia Press, 2002, pp. 239–58.
Slinn, E. Warwick. "Experimental Form in Victorian Poetry." *The Cambridge Companion to Victorian Poetry*. Edited by Joseph Bristow. Cambridge University Press, 2000, pp. 46–66.
Sly, Ronald. *A Little Job for William Morris: A Memoir of Robert Catterson-Smith*. Jones and Sons, 2015.
Smith, Adam. *The Theory of Moral Sentiments*. Edited by Knud Haakonssen. Cambridge University Press, 2002, pp. 1–2.
Smith, Johanna M. "Hideous Progenies": Texts of Frankenstein. *Texts and Textuality: Textual Instability, Theory, and Interpretation*. Edited by Philip Cohen. Garland, 1997, pp. 121–40.
Smulders, Sharon. *Christina Rossetti Revisited*. Twain, 1996.
Somerville, E.Œ. and Martin Ross. "Two of a Trade." *Irish Writing*, vol. 1, 1946, pp. 79–85.
Sparling, Henry Halliday. *The Kelmscott Press and William Morris Master-Craftsman*. Macmillan, 1924. https://archive.org/details/kelmscottpress-wioospar.
Spinoza, Baruch. *Ethics*. Trans. C.H.R. Parkinson. Oxford University Press, 2000.
Spuybroek, Lars. *The Sympathy of Things*. 2nd ed. Bloomsbury, 2016.
Stetz, Margaret and Cheryl A. Wilson, eds. *Michael Field and Their World*. The Rivendale Press, 2007.
Stillinger, Jack. *Multiple Authorship and the Myth of Solitary Genius*. Oxford University Press, 1991.
Stocking, Marion Kingston, ed. *The Journals of Claire Clairmont*. Harvard University Press, 1968.
Stone, Marjorie. "A Cinderella Among the Muses." *Victorian Literature and Culture*, vol. 21, 1993, pp. 233–68.
Stone, Marjorie and Judith Thompson, eds. *Literary Couplings: Writing Couples, Collaborators, and the Construction of Authorship*. University of Wisconsin Press, 2006.
Sturgeon, Mary. *Michael Field*. G.G. Harrap, 1922.
Sugden, Robert. "Beyond Sympathy and Empathy: Adam Smith's Concept of Fellow-Feeling." *Economics and Philosophy*, vol. 18, no. 1, 2002, pp. 63–87.
Sunstein, Emily W. *Mary Shelley: Romance and Reality*. Johns Hopkins University Press, 1991.
Suriano, Gregory R. *The British Pre-Raphaelite Illustrators*. Oak Knoll, 2005.

Symons, Arthur. "The Decadent Movement in Literature." *Harper's Monthly Magazine* 1893, pp. 858–67.

Taft, Vicki. "*The Tragic Mary*: A Case Study in Michael Field's Understanding of Sexual Politics." *Nineteenth-Century Contexts*, vol. 23, no. 2, 2001, pp. 265–95.

Taussig, Gurion. *Coleridge and the Idea of Friendship, 1789–1804*. University of Delaware Press, 2002.

Thain, Marion. *'Michael Field': Poetry, Aestheticism and the Fin de Siècle*. Cambridge University Press, 2007.

ed. *The Lyric Poem: Formations and Transformation*. Cambridge University Press, 2013.

Thain, Marion and Ana Parejo Vadillo, eds. *Michael Field, The Poet: Published and Manuscript Materials*. Broadview, 2009.

"The Birmingham Municipal School of Art. With Many Illustrations of Its Students' Work—I." *Studio*, vol. 2, 1894, pp. 90–9.

Thomas, David Wayne. "Replicating Agency: Dante Gabriel Rossetti and Victorian Manchester." *Cultivating Victorians: Liberal Culture and the Aesthetic*. University of Pennsylvania Press, 2004, pp. 125–55.

Thomas, Kate. "Walter Pater and Michael Field: The Correspondence, with Other Unpublished Manuscript Materials." *Pater Newsletter*, Spring 2014, pp. 27–85.

"'What Time We Kiss': Michael Field's Queer Temporalities." *GLQ: A Journal of Lesbian and Gay Studies*, vol. 13, no. 2–3, 2007, pp. 353–67.

Townley, Sarah. "Rewriting Paterian Sympathy: Vernon Lee and Elitist Empathy," *Literature Compass*, vol. 9, no 11, 2012, pp. 861–72.

"Vernon Lee and Elitism: Redefining British Aestheticism." *English Literature in Transition Journal*, vol. 54, no. 4, 2011, pp. 523–38.

Tyler, Colin. "Thomas Hill Green." *The Stanford Encyclopedia of Philosophy*, Edited by Edward N.Zalta. Stanford University, Summer 2011. https://plato.stanford.edu/archives/sum2011/entries/green/.

Vadillo, Ana Parejo. "Aestheticism and Decoration: At Home with Michael Field." *Cahiers Victoriens & Edouardiens*, vol. 74, 2011, pp. 17–36.

"Another Renaissance: The Decadent Poetic Drama of A.C. Swinburne and Michael Field." *Decadent Poetics: Literature and Form at the British Fin de Siècle*. Edited by Jason David Hall and Alex Murray. Palgrave Macmillan, 2013, p. 119.

"New Woman Poets and the Culture of the *Salon* at the *Fin-de-Siècle*." *Women: A Cultural Review*, vol. 10, no. 1, 1999, pp. 22–34.

Vallance, Aymer. "The Revival of Tapestry-Weaving: An Interview with Mr. William Morris." *The International Studio*, vol. 3, 1894, p. 101.

"Sir Edward Burne-Jones's Designs for Painted Glass." *The International Studio*, vol. 42, 1910, pp. 91–103.

Vaninskaya, Anna. *William Morris and the Idea of Community: Romance, History, and Propaganda, 1880–1914*. Edinburgh University Press, 2010.

Weinstein, Jack Russell. *Adam Smith's Pluralism: Rationality, Education, and the Moral Sentiments*. Yale University Press, 2013.

"Sympathy, Difference, and Education: Social Unity in the Work of Adam Smith." *Economics and Philosophy*, vol. 22, no. 1, 2006, pp. 79–111.
Weliver, Phyllis. "Introduction." *The Figure of Music in Nineteenth-Century British Poetry*. Edited by Phyllis Weliver. Ashgate, 2005; paperback publication Routledge, 2016, pp. 1–24.
   Mary Gladstone and the Victorian Salon: Music, Literature, Liberalism. Cambridge University Press, 2017.
   "Music, Crowd Control and the Female Performer in Trilby." *The Idea of Music in Victorian Fiction* Edited by Sophie Fuller and Nicky Losseff. Ashgate, 2013, pp. 57–80.
Whelan, Timothy. *Other British Voices: Women, Poetry, and Religion, 1766–1840*. Palgrave Macmillan, 2015.
Wilson, Ross. *Shelley and the Apprehension of Life*. Cambridge University Press, 2013.
Winckles, Andrew O., Angela Rehbein, eds. *Women's Literary Networks and Romanticism: "A Tribe of Authoresses."* Liverpool University Press, 2017.
Witcher, Heather Bozant. "'with me': The Sympathetic Collaboration of Mary Godwin and Percy Bysshe Shelley." *Forum for Modern Language Studies*, vol. 52, no. 2, 2016, pp. 144–59.
Witcher, Heather Bozant and Amy Kahrmann Huseby, eds. *Defining Pre-Raphaelite Poetics*. Palgrave Macmillan, 2020.
"The Work of Walter Crane." *Art Journal*, Easter Annual, 1898 p. 10.
York, Lorraine. *Rethinking Women's Collaborative Writing: Power, Difference, Property*. University of Toronto Press, 2002.
Zorn, Christa. *Vernon Lee: Aesthetics, History, and the Victorian Female Intellectual*. Ohio University Press, 2003.

Index

Abinger Collection, 51
Ablow, Rachel, 22
acoustical research, 23
Adam Smith's Pluralism (Weinstein), 18, 25
Adonais (Shelley), 31
aesthetic democracy, 105–6, 141
aesthetic press, 11, 97, 108, 111
aesthetic press movement, 8. *See also* Kelmscott Press
aestheticism, 7
   Lee & Robinson collaboration and, 191–4
   Lee and Anstruther-Thomson's exploration of, 183
   "missionary aestheticism", 183, 191
   Paterian, 183, 191–3, 197
   political position, 191
aesthetics
   Anglo-American, 24
   association with moral feeling, 183
   Benjamin Morgan's materialist reading, 8
   in Vernon Lee's work, 182, 191
   Lee & Anstruther-Thomson collaboration and, 187, 202
   Lee & Robinson collaboration and, 183, 192, 194–200
   moral themes and, 64, 183
   of Theodor Lipps, 23
   physiological vs mechanical, 23
   relationship between feeling and, 204
Agamben, Giorgio, 26
age of reason, 15
Agnew, Lois, 200
Alastor (Shelley), 47–8, 50
Allen, Grant, 188
Allingham, William, 78, 91
Anderson, Amanda, 26, 27, 100
"Angel of the House, The" (Patmore), 170
Anstruther-Thomson, Clementina "Kit", 8, 12, 24. *See also* Lee & Anstruther-Thomson collaboration
   Art and Man, 187, 189

"Beauty and Ugliness" (1897), 182, 185–90
Beauty and Ugliness (1912), 24, 182, 189, 201–4
   "Old Lombard and Venetian Villas", 189
   relationship with Vernon Lee, 181–2
Arata, Stephen, 184
Aristotle, 170
Arseneau, Mary, 68, 71
art
   Christina Rossetti's interest, 65
   collaboration of literature and, 97, 109
   communal experience, 24, 76, 109, 112, 200
   Crane's conception, 136
   democratic understanding, 117, 146
   Lee & Anstruther-Thomson collaboration and, 187–9, 204
   Lee & Robinson collaboration and, 193, 196, 201
   liberalism and, 25, 28, 105
   Modernism and, 184
   morality and, 110
   Morris's conception, 96, 98, 99–100, 109–11, 112, 116, 130, 132, 139–42
   Pater's understanding, 157, 191
   poetry and in the Rossetti collaboration, 66–8, 76, 79
   poetry's connection to reform and, 29
   relief from the vulgarization of society, 11
   sympathetic collaboration and, 9
   Whistler's conception, 90
Art and Man (Anstruther-Thomson), 187, 189
Arthurian legend, Morris's fascination with, 107
Arts and Crafts Exhibition, New Gallery, 112
Arts and Crafts movement, 100, 112, 131
Ashbee, Charles Robert, 117
assimilation, as form of collaboration, 3
Associationist psychology, 23, 185, 201, 205
Athenaeum, The (journal), 117, 155
Atkinson, Charles, 45
Aubrey Beardsley (Ross), 130

250

Index

Aurora Leigh (Barrett Browning), 29, 73–5
authorship, impact of collaboration on perceptions of, 6
automatic writing, 1, 6
Avalon (Burne-Jones), 107

Bain, Alexander, 21, 23, 202
Balliol College, 86
Bancroft Collection, 87
Barrett Browning, Elizabeth, 29, 74, 75, 171
Barthes, Roland, 4
Barton, Anna, 26
Beardsley, Aubrey, 130
"Beauty and Ugliness" (Lee & Anstruther-Thomson - 1897), 182, 185–90
Beauty and Ugliness (Lee & Anstruther-Thomson - 1912), 24, 182, 189, 201–4
Bednarz, James P., 3
Belcaro (Lee), 183, 194–7, 198–200
Bentley, D.M.R., 85
Berenson, Bernard, 165, 188
Bergson, Henri, 109, 207
Besant, Walter, 150
Bickle, Sharon, 157
Birmingham School of Art, 120, 131
Blair, Kirstie, 175
Blake, William, 78
Bleak Liberalism (Anderson), 26
Blind, Mathilde, 191
Blunt, W.S., 114
book production, Morris's conception of, 109–10. *See also* Kelmscott Press
books, as collaborative acts, 67
Boos, Florence, 98
Bowden, William H., 95
Bradley, Katharine, 7. *See also* Field, Michael; Michael Field collaboration
  cancer diagnosis, 144
  letter to Robert Browning, 151
  nicknames, 156–7, 161
Bristow, Joseph, 28, 202
British Idealist school of philosophy, 86
Britton, Jeanne M., 56
Brooker, Jewel Spears, 3
Browning, Robert, 147, 149, 151, 165
Bunting, Kirsty, 188–9
Burdett, Carolyn, 184–5
Burne-Jones, Edward, 11, 86
  collaboration with Catterson-Smith, 121–8
  friendship with William Morris, 106, 130–1
  illustrations for *The Well at the World's End*, 134
  interest in Arthurian legend, 107

  role in producing the Kelmscott *Chaucer*, 98, 117–120
Butler, Marilyn, 33
Byron, Lord, 31, 50, 69

Callirhoë (Field), 150
Cameron, Julia Margaret, 83
Cameron, Kenneth Neill, 34
Carlyle, Thomas, 100, 105
Carpenter, William, 23
Catterson-Smith, Robert, 11, 120
  collaboration with Burne-Jones, 121–8
  role in producing the Kelmscott *Chaucer*, 98, 117–28
Caxton, William, 107, 114
Chartist poetry, 29
Chaucer, Works of (Kelmscott Press), 107, 114
  Catterson-Smith's and Burne-Jones's collaboration, 120–8
  ideal book status, 132
  producing the Kelmscott *Chaucer*, 117–20
  success of the venture, 122
  sympathetic translation in practice, 129–31
Childe Harold (Byron), 50
Christina Rossetti: A Literary Biography (Marsh), 68
Christina Rossetti and Illustration (Kooistra), 65
Clairmont, Jane "Claire", 34, 46–7, 50
Clark, Peter, 26
Cockerell, Sydney, 121
Colebrook, Frank, 95, 112, 113
Coleridge, Samuel Taylor, 33
"Collaborating with History" (Ehnenn), 170
collaboration, 12. *See also* sympathetic collaboration
  defining/redefining, 3–9
  feminist research, 6–7
  late eighteenth- and nineteenth century importance, 32–4, 206, 209
  Latourian approach, 4
  material aspects, 12
  sympathy and, 14, 18
  three-pronged approach, 8
collaborative process
  aesthetic press as embodiment of, 11
  as means of identifying with the other, 2
  gendered perspective, 150
  model framework, 2
  role of conversation, 4, 24
Collini, Stefan, 11, 101
Collins, Wilkie, 160
Come & See (Christina Rossetti), 74
Commonweal, 135–6, 137
communal relations, 11

Index

community building, sympathy and, 18–20
conduct books, 21
Cooper & Bradley collaboration. *See* Field, Michael; Michael Field collaboration
Cooper, Edith, 8. *See also* Michael Field collaboration
   cancer diagnosis, 144
   death, 144
   nicknames, 156–7
Corbett, Mary Jean, 37, 40
Cornforth, Fanny, 93
Costelloe, Mary, 165
Crane, Walter, 131, 135–8
Creative Mind: An Introduction to Metaphysics (Bergson), 207
Crowned Hippolytus, The (Robinson), 192
Crump, Rebecca, 68

Daily Chronicle, 120–1, 131
Dalziel Brothers, 78
Darmesteter, James, 181
Darwall, Stephen, 17, 25
Darwin, Charles, 21, 207
"Death of the Author" (Barthes), 4
Decadence, 9, 12, 14, 145, 200
Defence of Guenevere, The (Morris), 107, 115
Defining Pre-Raphaelite Poetics (Witcher/Huseby), 90
Denisoff, Dennis, 187
Descent of Man, The (Darwin), 21
Dial, The (Shannon & Ricketts), 131
"Dialogue on Poetic Morality, A" (Lee), 195, 198
Digby, Kenelm, 107
Dixon, Richard Watson, 106
Double Talk: The Erotics of Male Literary Collaboration (Koestenbaum), 6
Dowling, Linda, 97, 105–6, 110, 138–9, 141, 191
Dream of John Ball, A (Morris), 117, 120
Du Maurier, George, 115, 169
Dyce, William, 107

Easter Even (Christina Rossetti), 74
Ede, Lisa, 3–5
Ehnenn, Jill R., 1–2, 150, 170, 188
Einfühlung, Lipps' hypothesis, 23, 108, 185, 202–4, 208
Electric Meters (Rudy), 175
Eliot, George, 7
Ellis, Havelock, 151, 156
empathy
   concept of, 22, 23, 183
   impersonality of, 209
   interweaving of sympathy and, 206
   introduction into the English language, 12
   isolating effects of, 200–5

   Lee's and Anstruther-Thomson's usage of, 185
   sympathy vs, 183–5
   Theodor Lipps' conception of, 23, 108, 185, 202–4, 208
Enlightenment of Sympathy, The (Frazer), 15
Ethics (Spinoza), 151–2
Evangelista, Stefano, 200
evolution, Darwin's theory of, 207
Excursion (Wordsworth), 47

Family Fictions (Flint), 33
Faulkner, Charles, 106
feelings, regulation of, 21
fellow-feeling
   individual and communal viewpoints and, 11, 67
   Michael Field and, 149
   Morris and, 110, 112, 113–14
   nineteenth-century collaboration enabled by, 206
   other-orientation, 15
   Pre-Raphaelites and, 78
   production and, 114
   Rossetti collaboration and, 11
   Shelley collaboration and, 43
   Smithean sympathy and, 15, 184
   undermined by ugliness, 56
female collaboration
   challenge to traditional perspectives on authorship, 6
   feminist research, 6–7
feminist perspectives, 5–7, 39, 51, 75, 148, 154, 170, 193
feminist recovery scholarship, Michael Field's work and, 159
Field, Michael, 8, 11, 22. *See also* Michael Field collaboration
   nicknames, 156
   relationships with women, 165
   Vernon Lee and, 149, 160, 165
Fleischacker, Samuel, 102
Flint, Christopher, 33
Flower of Wrath, A (Field), 162
Forman-Barzilai, Fonna, 20, 166
Foucault, Michel, 4, 26, 136
Found (D.G. Rossetti), 64
Frankenstein (Wollstonecraft Shelley), 9–10, 50–62
   differing versions, 51–2
   Draft Notebooks, 53–4, 61
   P.B. Shelley's role in the development of, 52
   scholarly debate over the authorship of, 52
   sympathy and, 17
Frankenstein Notebooks, The (Robinson), 35, 52, 56
Fraternity, 28, 33, 34, 45, 59, 135, 136, 198

Frazer, Michael, 15, 25, 104
free love, 45–7
friendship
  influence of moral philosophy, 45
  Kelmscott Press and Morris's friendships, 106, 131
  Shelley collaboration and, 44–6, 49
Fulford, William, 106

Gagnier, Regenia, 161, 208
Gaskin, Arthur, 131, 134
Gaull, Marilyn, 33
Geneva, Lake, 50
Gere, Charles March, 11, 98, 117
  collaboration with Morris, 131–8
Germ, The (journal), 77
Gesamtkunstwerk, 90
Gilbert, Sandra, 6
"Girl, A" (Field), 153–4, 155–6, 157, 159, 166
Gladstone, Mary, 28
Gladstone, William Ewart, 101
Goblin Market (Christina Rossetti), 11, 66, 76–7, 79, 80–3, 84
  D.G. Rossetti's Iillustrations for, 78–80, 83–4
  influence on D.G. Rossetti's poetic and artistic work, 87–8, 90–3
  lyrical mode, 14, 88
  moral and social component, 84–7, 89
  reading as social mirror, 80, 84, 89
  Skeltonic meter, 84
Goblin Market, and Other Poems (Christina Rossetti), 66, 68
Godwin, William, 33, 34, 44, 51
Goldberg, Gail Lynn, 83
Golden Age of illustration, 66
Golden Legend, The (Caxton), 114, 119
Goodlad, Lauren M.E., 136
Gray, John, 144, 157, 162, 164, 165–6
Green, Thomas Hill, 86
Greiner, Rae, 2, 7, 21–2, 204
Griswold, Charles L., Jr., 17, 19
Groose, Karl, 188
Gubar, Susan, 6
Guest, William, 135, 138

Haakonssen, Knud, 102
habitual sympathy, concept of, 104, 106, 111
Hadley, Elaine, 26, 100
Hake, Thomas Gordon, 91
Hamlet and Ophelia (D.G. Rossetti), 164
Hanley, Ryan Patrick, 18
Harrington, Emily, 182, 191, 195, 198
Hatch, James C., 56
Hate (Wollstonecraft Godwin), 57
Hauntings (Lee), 191
Hays, Daisy, 53

Hegel, G.W.F., 13, 87
Heimann, Amelia, 65, 85
Helmholtz, Hermann von, 23
Helsinger, Elizabeth, 90
Hewitt, Martin, 158
Highgate Penitentiary, Christina Rossetti's voluntary work, 11, 85, 86, 89
Hines, Thomas, 3–4
His Aims in Founding the Kelmscott Press (Morris), 96, 108, 109
History of a Six Weeks' Tour (Wollstonecraft Shelley), 50
Hobhouse, L. T., 11
Hogg, Thomas Jefferson, 34, 39, 45
Holman Hunt, William, 64
Holyrood Palace, 149, 164, 165, 166, 167, 169, 176
Hookham, Thomas, 34
Hooper, William Harcourt, 115–17, 118, 119, 132
Houghton, Arthur Boyd, 78
Housman, Laurence, 78
Huet, Marie-Helene, 52
Hughes, Linda K., 150, 174
Hume, David, 15, 19
Hunt, Leigh, 31, 47
Huseby, Amy Kahrman, 90

ideal book
  Morris's conception, 96, 111, 114
  sympathetic translation in, 109–14
"Ideal Book, The" (Morris), 132
Idylls (Tennyson), 69
Illustrated London News, 115
illustrated poetry
  Christina Rossetti's production of, 65
  commodification during the 1860s, 67
  D.G. Rossetti's Illustrations for *Goblin Market, and Other Poems*, 78–80, 83–4
imagination, sympathy and, 16, 18–20
imaginative transportation, 15
  Christina Rossetti's experience, 88
  community formation and, 18–19, 29
  Gere and Morris's collaborative process and, 138
  in Shelley's writing, 42
  Michael Field collaboration and, 149, 169, 173
  Rossetti collaboration and, 93
  Smithean sympathy and, 102
  witnessing another's situation through, 16, 84, 157, 167
impartial spectator, 13, 14
  concept of, 18–20, 98, 103
  liberalism and, 28
  moral aspect, 104
  Morris's theory and, 106, 139, 140–2

impartial spectator (cont.)
  Rossetti collaboration and, 80
  society's self-regulation and, 106
"In Casa Paget" (Robinson), 197–8
Inge, M. Thomas, 3
"Is Empathy the End of Sentimentality?"
  (Burdett), 184

Jackson, Virginia, 13, 75
Jaffe, Audrey, 55
James, William, 109, 185, 188
Jamison, Anne, 84
"Jenny" (D.G. Rossetti), 87–8
Jervis, John, 18
Johnson Circle, 33–4
Johnson, Joseph, 33
Jowett, Benjamin, 86
justice, 25, 44
Justice (journal), 99

Kelmscott Manor, 134–5, 137
Kelmscott Press, 8, 11, 67, 77
  business and employment model, 99
  Catterson-Smith & Burne-Jones
    collaboration, 121–8
  founding, 95–7
  impartial spectatorship and liberal
    community, 102–6
  Morris and Gere's collaboration for *News
    from Nowhere*, 131–8
  Morris and William Harcourt Hooper, 115–17
  Morris's reasons for founding, 96, 108, 109,
    112, 113
  pleasure in the "lesser arts" and, 138–43
  producing the Kelmscott *Chaucer*, 117–20
  production process, 114–17
  Smithean sympathy and, 101, 102–6
  social experimentation and, 106–9
  sympathetic translation
    in practice, 129–31
    in the ideal book, 109–14
  "typographical adventure" account, 96,
    106–9
  view of as a liberal project, 97, 100–1
  "Wayzegoose", 142
  the William Morris paradox and, 98–101
Kelvin, Norman, 134–5
Koestenbaum, Wayne, 6
Kooistra, Lorraine Janzen, 65, 67–8, 73, 111
Krawczyk, Scott, 44
Künstlerroman, 74–5

La psychologie des foules (Le Bon), 169
Lady Lilith (D.G. Rossetti), 91–3
"Lady of Shalott, The" (Tennyson), 107

Laird, Holly, 6, 156
Lake Geneva, 50
Laon and Cyntha (Shelley), 48–9
Latour, Bruno, 4
Laurus Nobilis (Lee), 205
Le Bon, Gustave, 169
Lee & Anstruther-Thomson collaboration, 183
  "Beauty and Ugliness" (1897), 182, 185–90
  Beauty and Ugliness (1912), 24, 182, 189, 201–4
  embodied approach to art and beauty,
    187–9
  empathy, isolating effects of, 200–5
  exploration of aestheticism, 183
  failed sympathetic collaboration, 182–3, 190
  gallery experiments, 185, 188, 190, 202
  inclusion of separate names in *Contemporary
    Review*, 185
  inequitable standards, 189
  personal relationship, 181–2
  sympathy vs empathy, 183–5
Lee & Robinson collaboration
  aestheticism and, 191–4
  Belcaro, 194–7, 198–200
  companionate nature, 200
Lee, Vernon, 8, 12, 22, 23, 149–50
  "Beauty and Ugliness" (1897), 182, 190
  Beauty and Ugliness (1912), 24, 182, 189, 201–4
  Belcaro, 183, 194–7, 198–200
  comparison with Michael Field, 205
  "Dialogue on Poetic Morality", 195, 198
  Einfühlung and, 202–4, 208
  Hauntings, 191
  introduction to *Art and Man*, 189
  Laurus Nobilis, 205
  Lee & Robinson correspondence and
    dialogues, 183, 190, 192–4
  letter to Anstruther-Thomson, 181
  Michael Field's description, 160, 165
  Miss Brown, 197, 201
  "Old Lombard and Venetian Villas", 189
  publications in *Contemporary Review*, 185
  relationship with Anstruther-Thomson,
    181–2
  relationship with Robinson, A. Mary F.,
    191–4
  Ruskin's influence, 185
Lee-Hamilton, Eugene, 197
"Lesser Arts, The" (Morris), 139
Lethaby, William Richard, 129
"Letterpress Printing and Illustration"
  (Walker), 97
Levy, Amy, 191
Lewes, George Henry, 7, 23, 188
Leyland, Frederick, 93
liberal community development, 12

Index

liberalism, 11, 26–8
  Amanda Anderson's argument, 26–7
  art and, 25, 28, 105
  collaboration and, 2, 24–8
  concept of, 26
  Hadley's conception of "lived liberalism", 100
  poetry and, 28–30
  practical socialism and, 97
  shift away from sympathy and, 184
  Victorian, 2, 9
  William Morris's socialism and, 100–1, 138–42
Liberty, Equality, Fraternity, 33, 45
Lilith, Talmudic legend, 92
Lipps, Theodor, 23, 188, 202–4, 208
Literary Couplings (Stone & Thompson), 3, 7
literary production, inherently social nature, 9
lived collaboration, 96
lived community, 62, 93, 101, 109, 138–9
Locke, John, 25
London Labour and the London Poor (Mayhew), 208
London riots of 1887 (Bloody Sunday), 58
London, Bette, 6, 150
Lonsdale, Margaret, 85
Love-Lyrics & Songs of Protest, The (Blunt), 114
"Lovers" (Field), 144
Lucy, Charles, 65
Lunsford, Andrea, 3, 5
Lyell, Charles, 208
Lyric Poem and Aestheticism, The (Thain), 13
lyric, defined, 13

MacCarthy, Fiona, 107
Mackail, J.W., 139
Madox Brown, Ford, 65, 91
Mahoney, Kristin, 199
"Maids of Elfen-Mere" (D. G. Rossetti), 78, 91
Maltz, Diana, 201, 202, 203
Mantius, Aldus, 97
Marcus, Laura, 160
Marriage of Minds, The (Ablow), 22
Marsh, Jan, 68, 85
Martin, Kirsty, 184
Martin, Meredith, 171
Martin, Violet Florence, 1
Mary Gladstone and the Victorian Salon (Weliver), 27
Mary Stuart, Queen of Scots, 167, 169–71, 172–3, 175–6, 179
Masten, Jeffrey, 6
Mathilda (Wollestonecraft Shelley), 53
Maxwell, Catherine, 200
Mayhew, Henry, 208

McGann, Jerome J., 5, 67, 85, 91, 110
medievalism
  Kelmscott Press as return to, 107
  Morris's fascination and veneration of, 101, 106–8
mediumship, 6
Memoir (W.M. Rossetti), 89
Mémoires pour servir à l'histoire du Jacobinisme (Baurruel), 42
Mental and Moral Science (Bain), 21
mental physiology, 23
Meredith, George, 165
Michael Field collaboration
  "A Girl", 153–4, 155–6, 157–8, 159, 166
  Callirhöe, 150
  choice of pseudonym, 148, 150
  death of Whym Chow and, 160–3
  diaries, 158–63
  distinct voices, 167
  drama and balladry, 158–76
  feminist recovery scholarship and, 159
  Flower of Wrath, 162
  Holyrood Palace tour, 164–8
  horticultural "habit of work", 157
  influence of Decadent Aestheticism, 165, 166
  life-writing, textured approach to, 158–63
  "Lovers", 144
  Mystic Trees, 144
  poetry, 149–58
  references to eminent male thinkers, 165
  resurgence of scholarship on, 148
  rhythm and transgression, 176–80
  Sight and Song, 167
  Spinozan vs Smithean sympathy and, 151–2
  Stephania, 156
  sympathetic mirroring model, 148–9, 157, 166–7
  Tragic Mary, 149–80
  Underneath the Bough, 153, 155
  unity and separateness, 149–58
  Wattlefold, 144
  Works and Days, 144, 156
Michael Field: Decadent Moderns (Parker & Vadillo), 148, 165
Middle Ages, book production in, 110
Mill, John Stuart, 12, 25
Millais, John, 115
Miller, Elizabeth Carolyn, 98, 113, 135, 136–7
Mind (philosophical journal), 21
Mind's Monitor, The (Atkinson), 45
Miss Brown (Lee), 137, 201
"missionary aestheticism", 183, 191
Modernism, 7, 9, 12, 145–6, 183–4, 201, 206
Monstrous Imagination (Huet), 52
Moore, Thomas Sturge, 159

moral community
  Christina Rossetti's sense of, 84
  concept of, 17
  Kelmscott Press and, 96, 97
  networks of affinity and, 22
  Potolsky's view of the decadent community and, 146
  relational vs religious understanding, 18
  Rossetti collaboration and, 66, 72
  Shelley collaboration and, 34, 61
  sympathy and, 17, 24, 60, 84, 102
moral judgment, 20, 101–3
moral philosophy, 2
Morgan, Benjamin, 8, 23, 183
Morris & Company, 106
Morris, Jane, 83, 106
Morris, May, 142
Morris, William, 8, 11, 67, 77, 86, 95, 191. *See also Chaucer, Works of* (Kelmscott Press)
  aestheticism of illuminated manuscripts, 109–12
  Beardsley and, 130
  collaborations with Rossetti, 107
  Commonweal, 135–6
  death, 95, 96
  Defence of Guenevere, 107, 115
  Dream of John Ball, 117, 120
  friendship with Burne-Jones, 106, 130–1
  habitual sympathy, 104, 106, 111
  His Aims in Founding the Kelmscott Press, 96, 108, 109
  "Ideal Book", 132
  "Lesser Arts", 139
  News from Nowhere, 98, 107, 131–8
  Poems by the Way, 114
  reaction to London riots of 1887 (Bloody Sunday), 98
  relationship with his printers, 142
  Ruskin's influence on, 96, 97, 100, 109
  socialism
    conversion to, 98–101
    definition of, 99, 100
    liberalism and, 100–1, 138–42
    practical, 11, 97, 100, 139
  "Some Thoughts on the Ornamented Manuscripts of the Middle Ages", 110
  Story of the Glittering Plain, 96, 131
  sympathetic translation and, 109–14
  tapestry making, collaborative process, 112–13
  Well at the World's End, 114, 134
  "What Socialists Want", 105
  "Woodcuts of Gothic Books", 111
Morrison, Lucy, 21
Morte D'Arthur (Malory), 107, 130
"Morte D'Arthur" (Tennyson), 107
Moxon Tennyson, 91

Multiple Authorship and the Myth of Solitary Genius (Stillinger), 5
Murray, Charles Fairfax, 119
Murray, E. B., 53, 55
Music Master, The (Allingham), 91
Mystic Trees (Field), 144

"Nature of the Gothic" (Ruskin), 110
networks of affinity, 22
New Arcadia, The, 194
Newcomen, Teresa, 86
News from Nowhere (Morris), 98, 107
  animating principle, 138
  Morris and Gere's collaboration, 131–8
"*News from Nowhere* and *Spoils of Poynton*: Interiors and Exteriors" (Kelvin), 134–5
North London School of Drawing and Modeling, 65

"Of Queen's Gardens" (Ruskin), 170
"Of the Turnerian Picturesque" (Ruskin), 108
"Old Lombard and Venetian Villas" (Lee & Anstruther-Thomson), 189
On Liberty (Mill), 25
On the Origin of Species (Darwin), 207
Outward Mind, The (Morgan), 8
Oxford Brotherhood, 101, 106
Oxford's Bodleian Library, 51

Paget, Violet, 149, 181. *See also* Lee, Vernon
Parker, Sarah, 148, 165
Pater, Walter, 105, 157, 165, 168, 173, 185, 191
  Paterian aestheticism, 183, 191–3, 197
  "School of Giorgione", 173
  Studies in the History of the Renaissance, 191
Patmore, Coventry, 170
Pattison, Dorothy Wyndlow, 85
Peacock, Thomas Love, 34, 47
Peterson, William S., 95–6, 113–14, 118, 119, 131
Pevsner, Nikolaus, 100
Pinch, Adela, 23
Poems (D.G. Rossetti), 87, 91
Poems by the Way (Morris), 114
Poems, A New Edition (D.G. Rossetti), 87
Poetical Works of Christina Georgina Rossetti (W. M. Rossetti), 75
Poetics en Passant (Jamison), 84
poetry
  Chartist, 29
  Christina Rossetti's, 65, 77, 88
  community and, 24
  liberalism and, 28–30
  Michael Field's work, 148, 149–58, 159
  Mill on, 13
  nostalgic projection in, 171

Percy Bysshe Shelley's view of, 10
reformative qualities, 29, 47 49
Rossetti siblings' work, 66–8, 75, 76, 79–84
Shelley collaboration and, 50, 54
Poetry and the Pre-Raphaelite Arts (Helsinger), 90
Polidori, William, 50
Political Fraternity (Pujol), 33
Political Justice (Godwin), 44
Poovey, Mary, 52
Postlethwaite, John, 86
post-structuralism, 4, 6
Potolsky, Matthew, 145–6
practical socialism, 11, 97, 100, 139
Pre-Raphaelite Brotherhood, 64, 69, 71, 77, 83
  Christina Rossetti and, 77–9
Pre-Raphaelitism, 7, 10–11, 111, 112
Prince's Progress, and Other Poems, The (Christina Rossetti), 66
Prince's Progress, D.G. Rossetti's tournament suggestion, 69–70
Principles of Geology (Lyell), 208
Prins, Yopie, 13, 75
Proserpine (D.G. Rossetti), 90
psychological aesthetics, Vernon Lee's collaborative work, 183, 191, 201–4
Pujol, Angel, 33
Pulham, Patricia, 200
Punch, 115

Quaritch, Bernard, 119–20
queer ecology, 187
queer reframings of literary histories, 5
queer theory, Michael Field and, 147, 148

Reassembling the Social (Latour), 4
Red House, 99, 107
"Reforming Victorian Poetry" (Bristow), 28
Rethinking Women's Collaborative Writing (York), 6
Revolt of Islam, The (Shelley), 48
Ricketts, Charles, 145, 156, 161, 165
Rieger, James, 51
Robinson, A. Mary F., 8, 12, 182–3 *See also* Lee & Robinson collaboration
  Crowned Hippolytus, 193
  "In Casa Paget", 197–8
  Lee & Robinson correspondence and dialogues, 183, 190, 192–4
  relationship with Vernon Lee, 191–4
Robinson, Charles, 35 52, 55–6
Romantic period, importance of circles and networks, 33
Romanticism, 7, 183
  "lived liberalism" and, 100

lyric and, 13
"Rose of Venetia" (Ruskin), 166
Ross, Martin, 1
Ross, Robert, 130
Rossetti collaboration
  Christina attempts to retain creative control, 73
  Christina's revisions of her brother's works, 76–7
  disagreements between the siblings, 68–71
  fellow-feeling and, 67
  Goblin Market, 77–9
  influence on D.G. Rossetti's poetic and artistic work, 86–93
  "Jenny" and *Goblin Market*, 87–9
  Prince's Progress, 67–76
  sympathy and social concern in Christina's 'inner consciousness', 84–9
  union of illustration and verse, 79–84
  William Blake's influence, 78
Rossetti Papers (W. M. Rossetti), 72
Rossetti, Christina, 7, 10–11, 14. *See also Goblin Market* (Christina Rossetti)
  artistic abilities, 64–5
  Come & See, 74
  comparison to Elizabeth Barrett Browning, 74–5
  dream, 64
  Easter Even, 74
  Goblin Market, and Other Poems, 66, 68
  illustrated poetry, 65
  letters to D.G. Rossetti, 68–74
  Pre-Raphaelite Brotherhood and, 77–9
  Prince's Progress, and Other Poems, 66
  rhetorical strategy, 70–1
  Sing-Song, 66
  Speaking Likenesses, 66
  usage of "with me", 72–3
  voluntary work at Highgate Penitentiary, 11, 85, 86, 89
  writing process, 75–6
Rossetti, Dante Gabriel, 7, 10–11
  death, 106
  framing technique, 79, 91
  illustrations, 78–80, 83–4
  Jane Morris's affair with, 106
  "Jenny" and *Goblin Market*, 87–9
  Kelmscott Press and, 142
  Lady Lilith, 91–3
  letters to Christina, 68–74
  letters to "Fanny" Cornforth, 77
  on Christina's artistic potential, 64
  Oxford Union murals, 86
  Poems, 87, 91
  privileged status, 64
  reliance on communal aspect of writing, 71

Rossetti, Dante Gabriel (cont.)
  "Sonnets for Pictures", 91
  tournament suggestion for *Prince's Progress*, 69–70
  use of photography, 83
  vision of equal partnership between illustrator and poet, 78
  Whistler's influence, 91
Rossetti, Frances Mary Lavinia, 69
Rossetti, Maria, 80
Rossetti, William Michael, 68, 71–2, 75, 89
Rousseau, Jean-Jacques, 23
Royal Academy School of Arts, 65
Rudy, Jason R., 175
Ruskin, John, 77, 105, 110, 166, 170, 191
  influence on Vernon Lee, 185
  influence on William Morris, 96, 97, 100, 109
  "missionary aestheticism", 183
  "Nature of the Gothic", 110
  "Of Queen's Gardens", 170
  "Of the Turnerian Picturesque", 108
  "Rose of Venetia", 166
  Stones of Venice, 97

San Graal, Burne-Jones's lifetime obsession with, 107
Saville, Julia F., 165
Sawtell, Margaret, 85
Scapegoat, The (Holman Hunt), 64
"School of Giorgione, The" (Pater), 173
Scott, Walter, 107
Scottish Enlightenment, 19, 21, 22–3, 109
sentimentality, Victorian, 184–5, 201
Shannon, Charles, 130–1, 156, 161, 165
Shelley and His Circle (Cameron), 34
Shelley and the Apprehension of Life (Wilson), 10
Shelley collaboration
  characteristics of writing style, 35
  comparison with other nineteenth century collaborations, 22
  discussion of Wordsworth, 47
  evidence of in *Frankenstein*, 50–6
  Frankenstein manuscript as shared space, 53
  free love and ideal sympathetic communities, 44–50
  importance of conversation, 43
  liberal community of intellectuals, 47
  pet names, 53
  purchase of "Shelley and Mary's Journal Book", 36
  shared journal, 32, 34–44
    alternating pattern of entries, 40
    as private world, 37
    comparison and assimilation of writing styles, 40–3
    entries (arrival at Lucerne - both), 40
    entries (arrival at Noé - Shelley), 41
    entries (arrival in Paris - Shelley), 38
    entries (establishment of a social group – Shelley), 34
    entries (evidence of joint writing process – both), 35
    entries (feelings of Mary's bodily presence – Shelley), 34–5, 49
    events excluded from, 37
    evidence of encouragement of one another's literary endeavors, 43–4
    intent behind and function, 37
    omissions, 37
    uniqueness, 37
    use of dashes, 37, 39, 41, 46
  sympathetic narratives in the construction of *Frankenstein*, 50–63
  travels and shared life-writing, 34–44
Shelley, Charles, 36–7
Shelley, Elizabeth, 34
Shelley, Harriet, 36–7, 38–40
Shelley, Hellen, 34
Shelley, Mary, 7, 9, 17, 22. *See also Frankenstein* (Wollstonecraft Shelley)
  children, 31
  collaborative process of *Frankenstein*, 52
  Hate, 57
  History of a Six Weeks' Tour, 50
  Laon and Cynthia, 48–9
  relationship with Thomas Hogg, 45–7
  shared journal, 31
    book lists, 47
    "Journal of Sorrow", 63
Shelley, Percy Bysshe, 7, 9–10, 22, 29
  assimilation of Mary's narrative tone and form, 32
  commitment to radical reform, 45
  death and burial, 31
  feelings for Mary, 39
  pet name for Mary, 53
  social group formation plans, 34
Shelley, William, 47
Siddall, Elizabeth "Lizzie", 87, 106
Sidonia the Sorceress (Meinhold), 130
Sight and Song (Field), 167
Sing-Song (Christina Rossetti), 66
Singular Texts/Plural Authors (Ede & Lunsford), 3
"Sir Galahad" (Tennyson), 107
"Sir Launcelot and Queen Guinevere" (Tennyson), 107
Sister Dora (Lonsdale), 85
Skeltonic form, 84
Skoblow, Jeffrey, 110
Slinn, E. Warwick, 29
Slow Print (Miller), 135

Index

Smith, Adam, 8–9, 15. *See also* sympathy
  Theory of Moral Sentiments, 15, 20, 21, 38, 166, 184
  understanding liberalism through the sympathetic lens of, 100
  viewing moral judgment and social unity through the lens of, 101–2
Smith, Johanna M., 51–2
Smith, Sarah Phelps, 92
Smyth, Ethel, 202–3
social experimentation, Kelmscott Press and, 106–9
social mirror, 14, 17
  community and, 101–2, 103, 141, 152, 157
  friendship and, 45
  reading *Goblin Market* as, 80, 84, 89
  Shelley collaboration and, 55, 60
social order
  as product of the sympathetic process, 18
  Smith's moral philosophy, 21
  Smith's primary concern, 20
social processes, books as compilation of, 67
social reform, book production and, 97
social unity, 101–2
socialism, 11
  Morris's conversion to, 98–101
  Morris's definition of, 99, 100
  Morris's vision of a future society and, 113
  practical, 11, 97, 100, 139
Socialist League, Morris's activism, 105–6
socialist revolution, 136
Society for the Preservation of Ancient Buildings, 106
"Solidarity of Labour" (Crane), 135
"Some Thoughts on the Ornamented Manuscripts of the Middle Ages" (Morris), 110
Somerville, Edith Œnone, collaboration with Martin Ross, 1
"Sonnets for Pictures" (D.G. Rossetti), 91
Sparling, Henry Halliday, 129, 142
Speaking Likenesses (Christina Rossetti), 66
Spencer, Herbert, 23
Spenserian stanza, Shelley's use of, 48–9
Spinoza, Baruch, 149, 151
Spuybroek, Lars, 108–9, 207
St. Bride Foundation Institute, London, 95
Stephania (Field), 156
Stephen, Leslie, 22
Stillinger, Jack, 3, 5–6
Stone, Marjorie, 3, 7, 171
Stones of Venice, The (Ruskin), 97
Story of the Glittering Plain, The (Morris), 96, 131

Studies in the History of the Renaissance (Pater), 191
Swinburne, Algernon, 77
Switzerland, 50
Symonds, John Addington, 191, 192, 195
Symons, Arthur, 145, 165
sympathetic collaboration
  concept of, 2–3, 7–9, 12, 206–9
  facilitation of social reform through, 105
  framework for establishment of a moral and liberal community, 8–9, 18
  illumination of sympathy's liberal processes, 15, 18
  reliance upon separateness, 157
  Smithean liberalism and, 24–6, 28
  social reform and, 113
  understanding the other-oriented aspect of sympathy and, 15
sympathetic concord
  concept of, 16, 17
  Kelmscott Press and, 96, 101, 112
  Michael Field collaboration and, 148–9, 180
  of type and ornament in Morris's work, 132
  purpose, 84
  Rossetti collaboration and, 79, 83, 86, 88, 91
  Shelley collaboration and, 10, 11, 24, 37, 43, 55, 60
  Vernon Lee and, 182
sympathetic mirroring
  concept of, 166
  Michael Field's enactment, 148–9, 157, 166–7
Sympathetic Realism (Greiner), 7
Sympathetic Sentiments (Jervis), 18
sympathetic translation
  Catterson-Smith's description of the collaborative process in terms of, 121
  in practice, 129–31
  in the ideal book, 109–14
  Morris's belief in, 115, 117
sympathy
  Bergson's understanding, 207
  cognitive associations, 183
  community building and, 18–20
  comparison of Smithean and Bergsonian sympathy, 207
  defined, 15–17, 22
  evolution across the nineteenth century, 20–4
  French notion of, 23
  friendship and, 45
  German tradition, 23
  goal of, 18
  habitual sympathy, 104, 106, 111
  imagination and, 16, 18–20
  impartial judgment and, 19

sympathy (cont.)
  impartial spectator and, 18–20, 103–4
  invocation of in *Frankenstein*, 57–8
  Kelmscott Press and, 106
  linear nature, 19–20
  materialist understanding, 22
  moral community and, 17, 24, 60, 84, 102
  post-Smithean branches of study, 23
  relegation to the private sphere, 22
  Shelley's journal entries, 38–9
  Smithean, 15–20
  social intimacy of, 209
  Spinozan vs Smithean, 151
  Spinoza's conception of, 154
  Spuybroek's summary, 207
  vs empathy, 183–5, 204

Taussig, Gurion, 45
Tenniel, John, 115
Tennyson, Alfred Lord, 69–70, 71, 107, 166, 180
Textual Condition, The (McGann), 5
Textual Intercourse (Masten), 6
Thain, Marion, 13, 158, 160, 161, 167
Theory of Moral Sentiments, The (Smith), 15, 20, 21, 38, 166, 184
Thomas, Kate, 147
Thompson, Judith, 3, 7
Time and Free Will (Bergson), 207
Titchener, Edward Bradford, 183
tournament, D.G. Rossetti's suggestion for *Prince's Progress*, 69–70
Townley, Sarah, 183, 191
Trades Guild of Learning, 139
Tragic Mary, The (Field), 149–80
  drama and balladry, 168–76
  Holyrood Palace research, 164–8
  rhythm and transgression, 176–80
Trelawney, Edward, 31
triangulated gaze, of Lee and Anstruther-Thomson, 188
Trilby (Du Maurier), 169

Underneath the Bough (Field), 153, 155

Vadillo, Ana Parejo, 148
Vallance, Aymer, 119
Vaninskaya, Anna, 99, 100
Veblen, Thorstein, 99
Victorian liberalism, 2. *See also* liberalism
  collaboration's rootedness in, 2
Victorian poetry, 28–30, 66–8, 76, 79
Victorian Poetry and Culture of the Heart (Blair), 175
Vischer, Robert, 203

Wagner, Richard, 90
Walker, Emery, 96, 97, 115, 122
Walsall hospital, 85
Wattlefold (Field), 144
"Wayzegoose", 142
Wealth of Nations, The (Smith), 21
Webb, Beatrice, 158
Webster, Augusta, 191
Weinstein, Jack Russell, 18, 20, 25, 26, 102, 104
Weliver, Phyllis, 26, 27–8, 86, 101, 169
Well at the World's End, The (Morris), 114, 134
"What is an Author?" (Foucault), 4
"What is Poetry?" (Mill), 13
"What Socialists Want" (Morris), 105
Whistler, James McNeill, 90
Wilde, Oscar, 105, 165, 191
Wilding, Alexa, 93
William Morris and the Idea of Community (Vaninskaya), 99
Wilson, Ross, 10
Witcher, Heather Bozant, 90
Wollstonecraft Godwin, Mary, comparison with Christina Rossetti, 72
Wollstonecraft Shelley, Mary, 31. *See* Shelley, Mary
  journal entries, 31
Wollstonecraft, Mary, 33, 34
Woman in White, The (Collins), 160
Women Coauthors (Laird), 6
Women's Literary Collaboration, Queerness, and Late-Victorian Culture (Ehnenn), 1–2, 6
"Woodcuts of Gothic Books, The" (Morris), 111
Wordsworth, William, 47
Works and Days (Field), 144, 156
  blurred private/public boundaries, 168
  clean nature, 161
  entries (Edinburgh and Holyrood), 167–8
  entries (Whym Chow), 160, 161–3
  interpretive framework, 160
  Moore's editorial preface, 159
  narrative dialogism, 149
  sympathetic mirroring in, 148, 157
  writing style, 161–3
Works of Geoffrey Chaucer, The (Kelmscott Press). *See* Chaucer, *Works of* (Kelmscott Press)
World War I, 184
Writing Double: Women's Literary Partnerships (London), 6

York, Lorraine, 6

CAMBRIDGE STUDIES IN NINETEENTH-CENTURY
LITERATURE AND CULTURE

General Editors
Kate Flint, *University of Southern California*
Clare Pettitt, *King's College London*

Titles published

1. The Sickroom in Victorian Fiction: The Art of Being Ill
MIRIAM BAILIN, *Washington University*

2. Muscular Christianity: Embodying the Victorian Age
edited by DONALD E. HALL, *California State University, Northridge*

3. Victorian Masculinities:
Manhood and Masculine Poetics in Early Victorian Literature and Art
HERBERT SUSSMAN, *Northeastern University, Boston*

4. Byron and the Victorians
ANDREW ELFENBEIN, *University of Minnesota*

5. Literature in the Marketplace:
Nineteenth-Century British Publishing and the Circulation of Books
edited by JOHN O. JORDAN, *University of California, Santa Cruz*
and ROBERT L. PATTEN, *Rice University, Houston*

6. Victorian Photography, Painting and Poetry
LINDSAY SMITH, *University of Sussex*

7. Charlotte Brontë and Victorian Psychology
SALLY SHUTTLEWORTH, *University of Sheffield*

8. The Gothic Body: Sexuality, Materialism and Degeneration at
the *Fin de Siècle*
KELLY HURLEY, *University of Colorado at Boulder*

9. Rereading Walter Pater
WILLIAM F. SHUTER, *Eastern Michigan University*

10. Remaking Queen Victoria
edited by MARGARET HOMANS, *Yale University*
and ADRIENNE MUNICH, *State University of New York, Stony Brook*

11. Disease, Desire, and the Body in Victorian Women's Popular Novels
PAMELA K. GILBERT, *University of Florida*

12. Realism, Representation, and the Arts in Nineteenth-Century Literature
ALISON BYERLY, *Middlebury College, Vermont*

13. Literary Culture and the Pacific
   VANESSA SMITH, *University of Sydney*

14. Professional Domesticity in the Victorian Novel
   Women, Work and Home
   MONICA F. COHEN

15. Victorian Renovations of the Novel:
   Narrative Annexes and the Boundaries of Representation
   SUZANNE KEEN, *Washington and Lee University, Virginia*

16. Actresses on the Victorian Stage:
   Feminine Performance and the Galatea Myth
   GAIL MARSHALL, *University of Leeds*

17. Death and the Mother from Dickens to Freud:
   Victorian Fiction and the Anxiety of Origin
   CAROLYN DEVER, *Vanderbilt University, Tennessee*

18. Ancestry and Narrative in Nineteenth-Century British Literature:
   Blood Relations from Edgeworth to Hardy
   SOPHIE GILMARTIN, *Royal Holloway, University of London*

19. Dickens, Novel Reading, and the Victorian Popular Theatre
   DEBORAH VLOCK

20. After Dickens: Reading, Adaptation and Performance
   JOHN GLAVIN, *Georgetown University, Washington D C*

21. Victorian Women Writers and the Woman Question
   edited by NICOLA DIANE THOMPSON, *Kingston University, London*

22. Rhythm and Will in Victorian Poetry
   MATTHEW CAMPBELL, *University of Sheffield*

23. Gender, Race, and the Writing of Empire:
   Public Discourse and the Boer War
   PAULA M. KREBS, *Wheaton College, Massachusetts*

24. Ruskin's God
   MICHAEL WHEELER, *University of Southampton*

25. Dickens and the Daughter of the House
   HILARY M. SCHOR, *University of Southern California*

26. Detective Fiction and the Rise of Forensic Science
   RONALD R. THOMAS, *Trinity College, Hartford, Connecticut*

27. Testimony and Advocacy in Victorian Law, Literature, and Theology
   JAN-MELISSA SCHRAMM, *Trinity Hall, Cambridge*

28. Victorian Writing about Risk:
Imagining a Safe England in a Dangerous World
ELAINE FREEDGOOD, *University of Pennsylvania*

29. Physiognomy and the Meaning of Expression
in Nineteenth-Century Culture
LUCY HARTLEY, *University of Southampton*

30. The Victorian Parlour: A Cultural Study
THAD LOGAN, *Rice University, Houston*

31. Aestheticism and Sexual Parody 1840–1940
DENNIS DENISOFF, *Ryerson University, Toronto*

32. Literature, Technology and Magical Thinking, 1880–1920
PAMELA THURSCHWELL, *University College London*

33. Fairies in Nineteenth-Century Art and Literature
NICOLA BOWN, *Birkbeck, University of London*

34. George Eliot and the British Empire
NANCY HENRY, *The State University of New York,
Binghamton*

35. Women's Poetry and Religion in Victorian England:
Jewish Identity and Christian Culture
CYNTHIA SCHEINBERG, *Mills College, California*

36. Victorian Literature and the Anorexic Body
ANNA KRUGOVOY SILVER, *Mercer University, Georgia*

37. Eavesdropping in the Novel from Austen to Proust
ANN GAYLIN, *Yale University*

38. Missionary Writing and Empire, 1800–1860
ANNA JOHNSTON, *University of Tasmania*

39. London and the Culture of Homosexuality, 1885–1914
MATT COOK, *Keele University*

40. Fiction, Famine, and the Rise of Economics in Victorian
Britain and Ireland
GORDON BIGELOW, *Rhodes College, Tennessee*

41. Gender and the Victorian Periodical
HILARY FRASER, *Birkbeck, University of London*
JUDITH JOHNSTON and STEPHANIE GREEN, *University of
Western Australia*

42. The Victorian Supernatural
edited by NICOLA BOWN, *Birkbeck College, London*
CAROLYN BURDETT, *London Metropolitan University*
and PAMELA THURSCHWELL, *University College London*

43. The Indian Mutiny and the British Imagination
GAUTAM CHAKRAVARTY, *University of Delhi*

44. The Revolution in Popular Literature: Print, Politics and the People
IAN HAYWOOD, *Roehampton University of Surrey*

45. Science in the Nineteenth-Century Periodical:
Reading the Magazine of Nature
GEOFFREY CANTOR, *University of Leeds*
GOWAN DAWSON, *University of Leicester*
GRAEME GOODAY, *University of Leeds*
RICHARD NOAKES, *University of Cambridge*
SALLY SHUTTLEWORTH, *University of Sheffield*
and JONATHAN R. TOPHAM, *University of Leeds*

46. Literature and Medicine in Nineteenth-Century Britain
from Mary Shelley to George Eliot
JANIS MCLARREN CALDWELL, *Wake Forest University*

47. The Child Writer from Austen to Woolf
edited by CHRISTINE ALEXANDER, *University of New South Wales*
and JULIET MCMASTER, *University of Alberta*

48. From Dickens to Dracula:
Gothic, Economics, and Victorian Fiction
GAIL TURLEY HOUSTON, *University of New Mexico*

49. Voice and the Victorian Storyteller
IVAN KREILKAMP, *University of Indiana*

50. Charles Darwin and Victorian Visual Culture
JONATHAN SMITH, *University of Michigan-Dearborn*

51. Catholicism, Sexual Deviance, and Victorian Gothic Culture
PATRICK R. O'MALLEY, *Georgetown University*

52. Epic and Empire in Nineteenth-Century Britain
SIMON DENTITH, *University of Gloucestershire*

53. Victorian Honeymoons: Journeys to the Conjugal
HELENA MICHIE, *Rice University*

54. The Jewess in Nineteenth-Century British Literary Culture
NADIA VALMAN, *University of Southampton*

55. Ireland, India and Nationalism in Nineteenth-Century Literature
JULIA WRIGHT, *Dalhousie University*

56. Dickens and the Popular Radical Imagination
SALLY LEDGER, *Birkbeck, University of London*

57. Darwin, Literature and Victorian Respectability
GOWAN DAWSON, *University of Leicester*

58. 'Michael Field':
Poetry, Aestheticism and the *Fin de Siècle*
MARION THAIN, *University of Birmingham*

59. Colonies, Cults and Evolution:
Literature, Science and Culture in Nineteenth-Century Writing
DAVID AMIGONI, *Keele University*

60. Realism, Photography and Nineteenth-Century Fiction
DANIEL A. NOVAK, *Lousiana State University*

61. Caribbean Culture and British Fiction in the Atlantic World, 1780–1870
TIM WATSON, *University of Miami*

62. The Poetry of Chartism: Aesthetics, Politics, History
MICHAEL SANDERS, *University of Manchester*

63. Literature and Dance in Nineteenth-Century Britain:
Jane Austen to the New Woman
CHERYL WILSON, *Indiana University*

64. Shakespeare and Victorian Women
GAIL MARSHALL, *Oxford Brookes University*

65. The Tragi-Comedy of Victorian Fatherhood
VALERIE SANDERS, *University of Hull*

66. Darwin and the Memory of the Human:
Evolution, Savages, and South America
CANNON SCHMITT, *University of Toronto*

67. From Sketch to Novel:
The Development of Victorian Fiction
AMANPAL GARCHA, *Ohio State University*

68. The Crimean War and the British Imagination
STEFANIE MARKOVITS, *Yale University*

69. Shock, Memory and the Unconscious in Victorian Fiction
JILL L. MATUS, *University of Toronto*

70. Sensation and Modernity in the 1860s
NICHOLAS DALY, *University College Dublin*

71. Ghost-Seers, Detectives, and Spiritualists:
Theories of Vision in Victorian Literature and Science
SRDJAN SMAJIĆ, *Furman University*

72. Satire in an Age of Realism
   AARON MATZ, *Scripps College, California*

73. Thinking About Other People in Nineteenth-Century British Writing
   ADELA PINCH, *University of Michigan*

74. Tuberculosis and the Victorian Literary Imagination
   KATHERINE BYRNE, *University of Ulster, Coleraine*

75. Urban Realism and the Cosmopolitan Imagination in the Nineteenth Century: Visible City, Invisible World
   TANYA AGATHOCLEOUS, *Hunter College, City University of New York*

76. Women, Literature, and the Domesticated Landscape: England's Disciples of Flora, 1780–1870
   JUDITH W. PAGE, *University of Florida*
   ELISE L. SMITH, *Millsaps College, Mississippi*

77. Time and the Moment in Victorian Literature and Society
   SUE ZEMKA, *University of Colorado*

78. Popular Fiction and Brain Science in the Late Nineteenth Century
   ANNE STILES, *Washington State University*

79. Picturing Reform in Victorian Britain
   JANICE CARLISLE, *Yale University*

80. Atonement and Self-Sacrifice in Nineteenth-Century Narrative
   JAN-MELISSA SCHRAMM, *University of Cambridge*

81. The Silver Fork Novel: Fashionable Fiction in the Age of Reform
   EDWARD COPELAND, *Pomona College, California*

82. Oscar Wilde and Ancient Greece
   IAIN ROSS, *Colchester Royal Grammar School*

83. The Poetry of Victorian Scientists: Style, Science and Nonsense
   DANIEL BROWN, *University of Southampton*

84. Moral Authority, Men of Science, and the Victorian Novel
   ANNE DEWITT, *Princeton Writing Program*

85. China and the Victorian Imagination: Empires Entwined
   ROSS G. FORMAN, *University of Warwick*

86. Dickens's Style
   edited by DANIEL TYLER, *University of Oxford*

87. The Formation of the Victorian Literary Profession
   RICHARD SALMON, *University of Leeds*

88. Before George Eliot: Marian Evans and the Periodical Press
   FIONNUALA DILLANE, *University College Dublin*

89. The Victorian Novel and the Space of Art: Fictional Form on Display
    DEHN GILMORE, *California Institute of Technology*

90. George Eliot and Money: Economics, Ethics and Literature
    DERMOT COLEMAN, *Independent Scholar*

91. Masculinity and the New Imperialism: Rewriting Manhood in British Popular Literature, 1870–1914
    BRADLEY DEANE, *University of Minnesota*

92. Evolution and Victorian Culture
    edited by BERNARD LIGHTMAN, *York University, Toronto*
    and BENNETT ZON, *University of Durham*

93. Victorian Literature, Energy, and the Ecological Imagination
    ALLEN MACDUFFIE, *University of Texas, Austin*

94. Popular Literature, Authorship and the Occult in Late Victorian Britain
    ANDREW MCCANN, *Dartmouth College, New Hampshire*

95. Women Writing Art History in the Nineteenth Century: Looking Like a Woman
    HILARY FRASER BIRKBECK, *University of London*

96. Relics of Death in Victorian Literature and Culture
    DEBORAH LUTZ, *Long Island University, C. W. Post Campus*

97. The Demographic Imagination and the Nineteenth-Century City: Paris, London, New York
    NICHOLAS DALY, *University College Dublin*

98. Dickens and the Business of Death
    CLAIRE WOOD, *University of York*

99. Translation as Transformation in Victorian Poetry
    ANNMARIE DRURY, *Queens College, City University of New York*

100. The Bigamy Plot: Sensation and Convention in the Victorian Novel
    MAIA MCALEAVEY, *Boston College, Massachusetts*

101. English Fiction and the Evolution of Language, 1850–1914
    WILL ABBERLEY, *University of Oxford*

102. The Racial Hand in the Victorian Imagination
    AVIVA BRIEFEL, *Bowdoin College, Maine*

103. Evolution and Imagination in Victorian Children's Literature
    JESSICA STRALEY, *University of Utah*

104. Writing Arctic Disaster: Authorship and Exploration
    ADRIANA CRACIUN, *University of California, Riverside*

105. Science, Fiction, and the *Fin-de-Siècle* Periodical Press
   WILL TATTERSDILL, *University of Birmingham*

106. Democratising Beauty in Nineteenth-Century Britain: Art and the Politics of Public Life
   LUCY HARTLEY, *University of Michigan*

107. Everyday Words and the Character of Prose in Nineteenth-Century Britain
   JONATHAN FARINA, *Seton Hall University, New Jersey*

108. Gerard Manley Hopkins and the Poetry of Religious Experience
   MARTIN DUBOIS, *Newcastle University*

109. Blindness and Writing: From Wordsworth to Gissing
   HEATHER TILLEY, *Birkbeck College, University of London*

110. An Underground History of Early Victorian Fiction: Chartism, Radical Print Culture, and the Social Problem Novel
   GREGORY VARGO, *New York University*

111. Automatism and Creative Acts in the Age of New Psychology
   LINDA M. AUSTIN, *Oklahoma State University*

112. Idleness and Aesthetic Consciousness, 1815–1900
   RICHARD ADELMAN, *University of Sussex*

113. Poetry, Media, and the Material Body: Autopoetics in Nineteenth-Century Britain
   ASHLEY MILLER, *Albion College, Michigan*

114. Malaria and Victorian Fictions of Empire
   JESSICA HOWELL, *Texas A&M University*

115. The Brontës and the Idea of the Human: Science, Ethics, and the Victorian Imagination
   edited by ALEXANDRA LEWIS, *University of Aberdeen*

116. The Political Lives of Victorian Animals: Liberal Creatures in Literature and Culture
   ANNA FEUERSTEIN, *University of Hawai'i-Manoa*

117. The Divine in the Commonplace: Recent Natural Histories and the Novel in Britain
   AMY KING, *St John's University, New York*

118. Plagiarizing the Victorian Novel: Imitation, Parody, Aftertext
   ADAM ABRAHAM, *Virginia Commonwealth University*

119. Literature, Print Culture, and Media Technologies, 1880–1900: Many Inventions
   RICHARD MENKE, *University of Georgia*

120. Aging, Duration, and the English Novel: Growing Old from
Dickens to Woolf
JACOB JEWUSIAK, *Newcastle University*

121. Autobiography, Sensation, and the Commodification of
Identity in Victorian Narrative: Life upon the Exchange
SEAN GRASS, *Rochester Institute of Technology*

122. Settler Colonialism in Victorian Literature: Economics and
Political Identity in the Networks of Empire
PHILLIP STEER, *Massey University, Auckland*

123. Mimicry and Display in Victorian Literary Culture: Nature,
Science and the Nineteenth-Century Imagination
WILL ABBERLEY, *University of Sussex*

124. Victorian Women and Wayward Reading: Crises of Identification
MARISA PALACIOS KNOX, *University of Texas Rio Grande Valley*

125. The Victorian Cult of Shakespeare: Bardology in
the Nineteenth Century
CHARLES LAPORTE, *University of Washington*

126. Children's Literature and the Rise of 'Mind Cure': Positive Thinking and
Pseudo-Science at the Fin de Siècle
ANNE STILES, *Saint Louis University, Missouri*

127. Virtual Play and the Victorian Novel: The Ethics and Aesthetics of
Fictional Experience
TIMOTHY GAO, *Nanyang Technological University*

128. Colonial Law in India and the Victorian Imagination
LEILA NETI, *Occidental College, Los Angeles*

129. Convalescence in the Nineteenth-Century Novel: The Afterlife of
Victorian Illness
HOSANNA KRIENKE, *University of Wyoming*

130. Stylistic Virtue and Victorian Fiction: Form, Ethics and the Novel
MATTHEW SUSSMAN, *The University of Sydney*

131. Scottish Women's Writing in the Long Nineteenth Century: The Romance
of Everyday Life
JULIET SHIELDS, *University of Washington*

132. Reimagining Dinosaurs in Late Victorian and Edwardian Literature: How
the 'Terrible Lizard' Became a Transatlantic Cultural Icon
RICHARD FALLON, *The University of Birmingham*

133. Decadent Ecology in British Literature and Art, 1860–1910: Decay, Desire,
and the Pagan Revival
DENNIS DENISOFF, *University of Tulsa*

134. Vagrancy in the Victorian Age: Representing the Wandering Poor in Nineteenth-Century Literature and Culture
    ALISTAIR ROBINSON, *New College of the Humanities*
135. Collaborative Writing in the Long Nineteenth Century: Sympathetic Partnerships and Artistic Creation
    HEATHER BOZANT WITCHER, *Auburn University at Montgomery*

For EU product safety concerns, contact us at Calle de José Abascal, 56–1°, 28003 Madrid, Spain or eugpsr@cambridge.org.

www.ingramcontent.com/pod-product-compliance
Lightning Source LLC
LaVergne TN
LVHW020342260326
834688LV00045B/1489